Contents

For my dear late wife, Aileen, and my wonderful family.

Acknowledgements

I would first like to thank all the people in my memoirs class at the University of the Third Age, for their input and ongoing friendship.

Editor's Note

My grandfather has been blessed with a very lucky life. As you will read, he has had many brushes with death, and many great escapes. Good things have always come to him, and sometimes it seems like the stars aligned over his head; I tend to think of Mr. Magoo (since I have only known him since the age of 72) and my mother frequently refers to him as human Teflon. My grandfather has had an incredibly exciting life, an incredibly lucky life and an incredibly interesting life. More has happened to him than I think many of us can hope for in any of our lives, and none of it seems to be the direct result of anything my grandfather has ever elected to do. He is by no means a thrill seeker, an adventurer or an adrenaline junkie.

What this does mean, however, is that he has got a lot of stories to tell. And, for the best part of my life, he has sat there on our sofa, gently telling us as many stories from his life as he can remember. Too many, in fact. Too many for any of us to keep track of, and certainly too many to fit into a single book. He has made coats for royalty, spent an evening with Ingrid Bergman and traversed Europe as a teenager.

How he has managed to live into his nineties through everything that has happened I can only attribute to his outlook on life. If there is anything my grandfather has taught me, it is that the life of temperament is one that leads to happiness. I am a firm believer in the Aristotelian notion that the modest character is the one who is, in totality, happy, rather than the ups and downs of many lives' extremes, and I believe that the strongest example of the virtuous soul is someone like my grandfather. I have never seen him arrogant in his successes, and I have seen him deal with adversity with stoicism. He has never become envious, never been irked by a challenge and the wellbeing of his family bears always in his determining. In Aristotle's own words: "He does not expose himself needlessly to danger […] but he is willing, in great crises, to give even in his life […] He is of a disposition to do men service, though he is ashamed to have a service done to him. […] He is open in his dislikes and preferences; he talks and acts frankly […] He never feels malice, and always forgets and passes over injuries […] It is no concern of his that he should be praised, or that others should be blamed. He does not speak evil of others […] he is not prone to vehemence, for he thinks nothing very important […] He bears the accidents of life with dignity and grace, making the best of his circumstances, like a skilful general who marshals his limited forces with all the strategy of war." My grandfather would tell you himself that he has had a happy life, and has lead a good life because of it.

Perhaps, then, it is not luck, or fate, that gave my grandfather the experiences he has had. Perhaps the Gods had nothing to do with him escaping the Nazis, marrying my grandmother and growing old in a house full of people that love him. Perhaps good things come to good people. Or, perhaps, it is this fair-minded nature that has allowed him to have all these things which are, all in all, I think better than any one amazing or terrible thing. My grandfather is not the greatest man that ever lived, and he is by no means perfect, but it is undeniable that being the greatest may have not lead him to lead such a full and good life.

My grandfather started writing his life story after the death of my grandmother, as a way of coping with the loss, as a way of finding new friends and, I believe, because someone new was needed to share all those stories with. He represents a catalogue of tales, both good and tragic, not just from his life but those who he has lived alongside, and those stories need remembering. He has lived through what is arguably the most important period of history this world has seen, and his first-hand experiences living through it are something that are not just unique but irreplaceable.

This book only goes up to 1964, which is the year after my mother was born, purely because my grandfather's life – all 93 (and counting) years of it – has been so expansive and so interesting it simply cannot be entirely contained within one book. Please, bear with it; my grandfather was born in Poland

and, as you will read, did not have a traditional education, so the writing is, in parts, a bit clunky. But what matters is the reason he started this book: to tell the story of his life.

Aleks Phillips
Editor and proud Grandson

Introduction

Let me introduce myself: I, Henryk Aleksander Griebel – known as Tim[1] – was born into a middle class, orthodox Jewish family on 14th September 1925, in Nowy Sacz near Krakow, Southern Poland.

Until 1919, when the state of Poland was created following the end of the First World War, that part of the country had been under the occupation of the Austro-Hungarian Empire. The town had a population of roughly eleven thousand, of which just under half were Jewish. The town was split by the River Dunayec. To the north of the river there was the Town Hall, businesses, shops and where the majority of the middle class population lived in apartments. South of the river was a mixture of small industrial factories and workshops.

Most of the ultra-orthodox Jewish community, known as Chasidics, lived alongside the farmers and farm workers, who worked in the rural areas around the town.

The original family name was Cantorthan Grübel, a traditional Germanic name that originated in Bavaria, which we had to change in 1932 as the Polish government put into law that all citizens with German names had to convert them to Polish.

My paternal grandfather was an orthodox Jew. He wore a black kaftan and a stramel[2]; this piece of apparel went back to between the 17th -18th centuries. I remember the kaftan he wore had two large outside pockets, in one pocket he used to keep cooked salted dried peas and in the other cooked dried broad beans. Whenever I saw him the first thing I did was to put my hands in his pockets and to help myself to some.

My grandfather was quite an important man within the Jewish community, being a kosher butcher and sausage maker. His knowledge of animals had to be as good as a veterinary

---

[1] I'll explain that one later.
[2] An orthodox Jewish hat with sable tails around it.

doctor, as he had to inspect the animals to be free of diseases before they were considered kosher. Born in 1878, my paternal grandmother also came from an orthodox background. I think the two were married in 1896, although I cannot be sure; I wasn't born and any records from that area and time seldom survive. By the time I was born, my grandmother had given birth to twenty-two children including six sets of twins, but only thirteen survived, nine brothers and four sisters. My father being the oldest and my youngest uncle was a year above me in school. They lived within the Jewish community south of the river and owned a big house on the main road with the shop in the front.[3]

1 - Photo of my father.

The house had six bedrooms with high ceilings, a very large kitchen with an enormous stove and a large built-in boiler, which was also used as the dining-room and lounge.

The reason I tell you the house had high ceilings is because, as the story goes, when the family grew too large for the house, half-floors were put in for extra sleeping space.

My grandparents' shop was not all that large and always smelt of freshly butchered meat. I grew up with the smell, so the smell of raw meat and blood never really bothered me. There

---

[3] There is a non-kosher butcher shop on this site to this day.

were sides of beef or lamb hanging from the ceiling, salami, garlic sausage, viennas and kabanos. There were big rolls of dried gut skins that were used for sausage making. Like any good business, nothing was left to waste; I remember piles of dried skins from the butchered animals waiting to go to the tanners' to be made into hides for leather. We had a massive cellar that stored the ice needed to keep the meat chilled.

The side of the building was let out to a man who rented out bicycles by the hour and so there were always a dozen-or-so leaning against the house. So many bikes being around was why I was taught to ride at a young age. It was a very thriving concern, as it was the only other way of getting around, unless you had a horse and cart. That said, there was the railway, but that did not cover the local villages. There were a few taxies (I think they were old even before World War I), but they were an expensive and only used in an emergency by the more affluent people.

The town itself was in a valley surrounded by the Tatra Mountains. For four or five months of the year the roads were impassable, first through mud, then snow drifts and ice. It was practically impossible to travel except on skis or by horse-drawn sledges. I recall the sledges had a little bench in the back where sometimes they used to strap larges pieces of luggage. As young boys we used to wait for them to pass us and jump on the back and sit on the bench to take us up the street. The drivers knew we were there and we knew that they knew, so they used to try flipping their whips backwards. It was all done in good; we all knew each other. Occasionally, there were one or two who were not very nice, but we learnt to avoid them.

My grandmother became known as the 'fixer'. One of her specialities was to help ultra-orthodox boys avoid military service. At that time there was no time limit on the length you served. When a boy was conscripted into the army, many families used to say Kaddish – a prayer for the dead – as in the army he could not observe the Jewish rituals and eat kosher food, so the new conscript was considered dead within the community. They were as fanatical as some of the radical communities we read about today. The more enlightened Jewish community took a different view.

There were different ways to be exempted from military service. The most common were if you were crippled; blinded in the right eye, you had your right trigger finger missing or the big toe damaged or missing such that you could not march. The people who performed these mutilations were known by many names – maimer, crippler etc. My grandmother knew the right people to approach to arrange their services for a small commission. This, I must add, was not exclusive to the Jewish community either in Poland or Russia. I observed the same thing happening in the Middle-East and when serving during World War II. I was stationed in Egypt, where I met an Egyptian army officer who told me they had got wise to this practice and they had a company of men with missing trigger fingers and one company of men blinded in the right eye, who were taught to shoot left handed.

2 - A picture of the market square in Nowy Sacz, Poland.

---

[4] Known in German as 'Lemberg', as it was in the Austro-Hungarian Empire and now it is part of Russia.

My maternal grandparents were totally different to paternal ones. The family name was Diestenfeld and my grandmother's maiden name was Kholer. The family originated from Lwow[4]. The family moved to Nowy Sacz during 1906/1907. They were not very orthodox and were more enlightened when it came to the ways of the modern world.

My maternal grandmother was born in 1872 and died 1916 and came from a fairly prosperous and well-educated family.

Unlike my grandfather, who was born 1869/70 and of whom I do not know much, as no one would speak about him. All I know is that he held many low paid jobs and was a notorious womaniser. He went off and left the family and as far as I know died during the holocaust. They had eight children, seven sons and one daughter (my mother), but in total only six survived. I can remember all their names as most of them played some part in my life.

The oldest, Albert, born 1890, became a Communist and escaped from Poland in 1920 and went as an illegal immigrant to the USA, where he was in hiding from the authorities for fifty years. Even when we had legal papers for him, I never met him and he died in 1974.

John, born 1892 and who moved to Vienna to study law, eventually became a commercial judge to the Austrian Government in 1936 and is recorded in the Austrian Government Yearly Book. He was also managing director of Petrol Block, which was the cartel for the oil industry in the Balkans, and a correspondent for Reuters. He was a great linguist, having to travel a great deal, and was known to speak twenty languages including Chinese and Japanese. He held Diplomatic credentials until Hitler invaded Austria during 1938 and the entire family escaped, leaving everything behind.

One thing that aided such a meteoric career was that during the First World War he was an officer in the Austrian army and was captured by the Russians. Speaking fluent Russian, he escaped and was awarded one of the highest decorations and promoted to a senior rank. After the war he married into a wealthy family and had one daughter, Susie, born in 1920.

3 - My mother Jozefa standing in between my Uncles John and Zygmunt. Both are wearing their Austrian uniform from their service in WWI. My mother was known for her very long, blonde hair.

When they escaped in 1938, they came to London where he intended to go into business with my uncle Joe (Joseph) but decided that this was not for him and he and his family left for the USA, where he had contacts in the Petroleum Industry and was offered a job. This did not go well and he and his wife had to find alternative employment. Uncle John died in 1943 from throat cancer and unfortunately none of the family could attend his funeral as it was wartime. I never knew when his wife died. Cousin Susie died in the 1990's.

My Aunt Erna, John's wife, whom I only met four times, made quite a success and became a nurse and then a matron in a hospital. I only know that cousin Susie married a taxi driver who she divorced later on in her life.

Uncle Chaim was born in 1895. I do not know much about him, except he was a dentist and had served in the Austrian army during the First World War as an officer as he had been university educated. He was killed in 1915 on the Eastern Front by a sabre cut not far from where the family lived.

I was told many times by my mother that when her mother had heard of his death, she had had a nightmare of him lying on the battlefield, bleeding to death.

She persuaded Uncle John, who by this time was a senior officer, to take her to the battlefield to recover his body. He managed to arrange this and she found him just as she had seen in the dream, in a pool of blood which was still moist; he had died just hours before they had arrived. He was brought home and buried in the local Jewish cemetery.

Uncle Herman, born in 1895, I again do not have too much knowledge of. He served in the army in the First World War where he became shell-shocked and was placed in a mental institution. I believe he died in the Holocaust.

Uncle Izydor was born in 1898. He was one of the two brothers who never went to university. He served in the army and I learnt from my parents who hid him that he deserted during the latter part of the Great War. Eventually he was captured and jailed but was spared further punishment by the influence of his serving brothers, also having lost a brother in the service of his country.

He was a very practical man, who wrote in beautiful copperplate style. Both he and my father went to the same school and were good friends since they were young boys until his death in 1973. He had several jobs as a book keeper until, in the early 1930's, he started working for a margarine firm called 'Amade'. Employed as a salesman, he was allocated a small lorry with a driver to service and deliver margarine in quite a large area. He stayed with this firm until the outbreak for the Second World War. He was married to Aunt Giza and they had a daughter named Dora, two years younger than myself. We all lived in apartments within the same building.

When War broke out, he decided that the he, his wife and daughter should move eastwards to Lwow, where his other brother was going, being close to the Russian border. They did manage to reach Lwow but there split up for safety reasons, however Aunt Giza and Dora were arrested by the Gestapo and both died in 1942 during the Holocaust.

4 - Dora Diestenfeld, last pictured in 1936. This is the only surviving photo we have of her, and the only way of remembering her.

Uncle Izydor survived and managed to cross into Russia where he was interned till after the war. He worked as a book keeper for the camp administration until 1947 and eventually came to England in 1948 with help from other members of the family[5], but died in London in 1973.

Uncle Zygmunt, born in 1900, studied at Krakow, the second oldest university in Europe. He received his BA in Economics and went into banking eventually became manager and director and then a partner. He married Aunt Zofie in 1927 they had a daughter named Dana born in 1928 and a son Gustav born in 1938.

---

[5] Details of this come later on in the story.

Aunt Zofie was very beautiful and though I only met her three times she was extremely kind to me when I stayed in her apartment in Krakow, situated by the river Vistula before leaving for England. Her family were very wealthy and owned a large share of Suchards Chocolate Factory in Switzerland. At their wedding Uncle Zygmunt was made a non-executive director of the company.

He was not a very popular man, as he could be very mean and secretive. His G-d was making money, but I suppose that can be expected from a banker. I must add that he was always very kind to me when I was a young lad.

When war broke out he also decided to move his family to Lwow because of the family connection. My mother told me that he managed to transfer a large sum of hard currency to his friend who was a banker in Switzerland and also managed to take money in different currencies with him.

They managed to reach Lwow and for the sake of security also thought it best to split up. Dana was placed with a Polish farming family and Zofie and Gustav with another. Uncle Zygmunt was hidden in a tiny room in a Ladies' Tailoring establishment. Unfortunately, Aunt Zofie with her son were caught and it is unknown if they were betrayed to the Gestapo. They perished in 1942.[6]

My mother Jozefa (also known as Pepie), was born in 1901, and had a fairly hard life, being the only girl with seven brothers. She completed elementary school, but her further education had to be cut short when she turned twelve, though she did manage to teach herself to speak five languages. Her youngest brother was born (Uncle Joe) in 1912. It had been a difficult birth, which left her mother in poor health. Thus she had to take on responsibilities for running the house and especially for looking after her young brother. She did have a very tough time during the First World

---

[6] We know this from the records at Yad Vashem (The Jewish Holocaust Memorial where records are kept) and from other family members.

War and if it had not been for her elder brothers, sending food and money I do not think she and Uncle Joe would have survived.

Her mother died after a long illness in 1916 and thus she became the surrogate mother to Uncle Joe until her marriage to my father in 1924.

She was most beautiful and had very blond long hair, which she grew till it reached the ground and she used to coil it around her head, which was very fashionable in Austria. Another favourite pastime was to crochet and she made many lovely things. Though right-handed, she always used the crochet needle in her left hand. Surprisingly, she never could knit.

Her mother taught her to cook in which she excelled so much that years later, when my friend were invited for Saturday lunches, they would always ask when they would next be invited and suggested she open a restaurant. Like her family, she did have a very modern outlook on life and was interested in anything new and modern; like her brothers, she had an interest in Zionism. Mum died from brain haemorrhage two weeks before Passover in 1976.

Uncle Joe, born 1912, had the most influence in shaping my life, there being a rather large gap in age between him and his brothers, whom by the time he was born most were away from home. As I mentioned he became very attached to my mother and this strong bond lasted till his death in 1967.

When, at the age of twelve, in 1924, his sister and my father married, it was decided by the family that my mother could no longer be responsible for him as she would like to start her own family. A decision was made that Uncle John in Vienna should look after him.

There was one problem: Uncle John's wife, Aunt Erna, refused to have him in the house. So, the family thought that he should be placed in an orphanage similar to that of Dr. Bernardo's Home. As he was nearly thirteen, Uncle John arranged an apprenticeship, in one of the best fur firms (Horowitz), in Vienna. Fur workers were the best paid craftsmen of all the different trades and apprenticeships were at a premium.

He was a great sportsman and joined several sports clubs. He became a weightlifter, wrestler and played football in goal for a local Viennese club.

In those days fur workers were taught to specialise in different furs to become an expert. His specialisation was foxes. During the 1920/1930's there were very few good furriers in England and most wealthy people travelled to France or Carlsbad, but mainly to Vienna, to buy fur garments.

Harrods, who had the largest fur department and workshop in England, used to send their buyers to Austria after the season to buy what furs were left with their patterns. They used to display the coats in their windows and if a customer wanted a garment it would be copied from the original.

Fox furs were very popular in England and the Calman Links Company was the foremost firm here in England and headhunted Uncle Joe. He was not happy working for them and decided to open his own business.

The firm was named Vienna Fur Models and premises were taken at 1, Dover Street, London W1. I believe Uncle John and Uncle Zygmunt supplied most of the money as an investment but had nothing to do with the running of the company. The firm became very popular within British high society and wealthy refugees. This was mainly because Uncle John spent his life moving in diplomatic circles and Uncle Zygmunt in banking circles.

Uncle Joe brought with him to England one fur cutter named Steiner and an elegant machinist and finisher who was his girlfriend and later his fiancée. Her name was Sofia. I never knew her original name, only that she came from Czechoslovakia.

At that time to have a limited company in England you had to have one English subject as a director on your letter heading. In order to have an English director Sofia agreed to a marriage of convenience with Mr Day, who I think worked as a bookkeeper. Of course, he was given some money for this with a promise of more when they divorced. He was given a token one share and made a director. Sofia became a British subject automatically on her marriage. They never lived together and divorced after two years and all the time I knew her I called her Mrs Day.

5 - Portrait of Uncle Joe, to whom I and my family owe our lives.

My father was born in 1898 as Hirsh Simon Gruebel. He being the oldest son, he was automatically selected after finishing his primary school to join Yeshiva[7]. Within orthodox families it was regarded as a great catch for a Jewish girl to marry – although it was a quite some expense to the father-in-law in the marriage contract. Included in the dowry was how much the father of the bride had to contribute for the boy's upkeep until finishing his studies, especially if he wanted to become a Rabbi.

My father studied for five years, but when he started to study the Kabbalah, he found it was unsettling, with all the mystic teaching, and he decided to leave. Having learnt a considerable amount at yeshiva he was, until his death in 1997 at the age of 89 years, able to discuss and argue the finer points of the Torah and Talmud, with the rabbis, which was one of his great joys.

After he left yeshiva, which at the time it was a great disappointment to his family, he worked in his father's butchery

---

[7] The Jewish School for boys where they study the Bible, Talmud and Religious Law for seven years.

as a stock buyer, where it was discovered that he had the knack for that part of the business and could make good deals. He worked there until just before his marriage to my mother in 1924.

He had known my mother for several years through her brother Izydor, who was his closest friend. My mother could not marry until her younger brother was old enough to go to Vienna, so there was no choice but to wait.

Their marriage, like any, was not without problem though. Mother's family were not considered orthodox Jews because of their very modern outlook and their relaxed attitude to traditional Jewish rules: they wanted my mother to shave her head and wear a wig, which was the custom of orthodox women on their marriage. Mother flatly refused and his family urged him to cancel the wedding. Being very much in love, he refused his family their request.

As it happened in most such circumstances, his family decided to totally ignore them except for some brothers and sisters and they were never invited for the Jewish high holydays or family functions, excepting when one of his brother got married. My father was very close to his brother and insisted in coming to the wedding. I remember as a small child the wedding, which was held outdoors with music and dancing very late into the night.

My life started, as I mentioned at the start of the book on the 14th September, 1925 in Nowy Sacz and I whilst my name was Henryk Alexander, my Hebrew name was Chaim Sender. It must have been a very lucky date as I know now that on at least four occasions I should have died. I have been told by my parents that mine was a very difficult birth and my mother had to be hospitalised. The food there was so awful that she made my father smuggle food in, her favourite being salted herring which she said helped her to survive.

Mother owned a grocery shop which my father bought in her name, which was a blessing years later. She found it hard to run the shop and look after me as well as the home, and she hired a nanny called Zosia who stayed with us for several years and when my sister was born five years later, she looked after her also.

At fourteen months I still was not walking and it was decided that there was something wrong with my legs. Many doctors suggested different forms of treatment, including local peasant treatments and prayer. At that time in Poland medicine was still practically in the 19th century and in some cases very primitive. All I knew most of my treatments were painful.

When I was 2 ½ years old feeling came to my legs and everyone thought it was a miracle. A very good local doctor told my parents that in his opinion it was probably a pinched nerve in my spine. Soon I was able to walk and run, so to celebrate my father bought me a tricycle, which I used to buzz around everywhere. There was no stopping me!

I was coming to an age when I should have soon been going to some sort of kindergarten but at that time there was no such thing. Most children before school age were looked after by Jewish teachers' wives in small groups to supplement their income.

Father heard of a Scheme for educating Jewish children in Modern Hebrew. This was instigated by a Baron Hirsch in Germany, who was a very wealthy philanthropist, believed in Palestine and the Zionist Movement. He invested in Palestine, buying land for the immigrants to start kibbutzim. He also offered Jewish communities' money to start Hebrew schools by putting up half the money if the community found the other half. The idea was the children would be taught Modern Hebrew so when they grew up and wanted to go to Palestine, they would be well prepared.

Nine other families with children of the same age were persuaded to join the scheme by my father. When the school opened it was in one room with one teacher and ten children.

In the autumn if 1928 I started kindergarten. For us children it was a place of fun. We were taught to sing in Hebrew songs from the kibbutzim, learn both the Hebrew and Polish alphabets and count using our fingers in both languages. Our lovely teacher must have been in her early twenties and I believe her name was Hana and us mischievous kids adored her for all her patience. I stayed there till the age of five by which time there were about seventeen children enlisted.

We lived within a short walking distance of a convent, magnificent church, synagogue and an ancient castle occupied by a titled family who owned the estate. The town was situated on the River Dunayec, which is a tributary of the main Polish river, the Vistula.

Nowy Sacz was the administrative town for that part of Galicia in the Tatra Mountains. Our address was Rynek 3 (No. 3, Market). The house overlooked a big ancient 15th century market with a large Town Hall and County Court, all in French architectural style. The apartment we lived in was on the first floor and Uncle Izydor lived on the ground floor. The block had fourteen flats. My father owned three quarters of this block and a dentist owned the other quarter. It was three-sided block and within the courtyard there was a long building, divided into two. At one end there was a cabinet maker and at the other a coffin maker, which could be quite confusing! You could drive a horse and coach from the market through this courtyard through into the nest street. This was only done when wood was delivered to the workshops.

By 1929, father, being involved in property and investments, had made a substantial amount of money and decided we should move to a larger apartment as my mother was expecting another baby and also Zosia the nanny would be living with us. He found a place on Jan Sobiesky Road (Ulica Jan Sobiesky), which was very convenient for my mother as her shop was at the other end of the street and also it was easier to get me to school. There was a small park close by where we often played. I remember the park having two large statues, one of Copernicus and one of Sienkewicz, who wrote 'Que Vadis'.

This apartment was a lovely place with large rooms and an indoor toilet, which was a real luxury in those days, there was a small room which had a bath tub in it and served as a bathroom and the kitchen had a big stove and sink. One thing we did have was an enormous aspidistra plant.

Not far away was a horse and cattle market and also close to my mother's shop was another market selling poultry, fish, fruit and vegetables, which was important for the shop.

My sister, Rozia was born in 1930. Everything was ready but before the birth the apartment was rearranged. I used to share a room with my parents and Zosia, of course, had her own room. After Rozia was born, mother being very protective put her cot in their bedroom and I had to sleep in Zosia's room. She had quite a large bed. This was not unusual in Poland and the arrangement worked very well.

That autumn term when I started school, Zosia would push the pram with my sister in it and make me hold onto the handle at the side as we walked along. On the way home when I was collected we used to stop at my mother's shop to have tea with her.

Zosia was a staunch Catholic and so on the way to the shop we always passed a small church where she stopped for confession and prayer. She made me swear not to tell my parents as they would be furious with her for taking me into a church but I really did not care about stopping at the church; by the age of seven I could recite the prayers by heart in Latin.

Shortly after Rozia's birth Uncle Joe, came for a visit from Vienna. He had just finished his apprenticeship and wanted a holiday before starting a job as a fully-qualified furrier. He wanted to meet his sister and the children and he made a great fuss over me. Uncle Joe brought lots of gifts for all of us, but especially for me as I was the only boy in the family. I was so excited when he presented me with a pair of skis, a red leather jacket and a pair of ear muffs.

There was a slight problem with the skis. In those days you used to measure the skis; if you could touch the tip of them, they would be the right size for you. Mine were about six inches too long but I did manage to ski with them, though they were a bit heavy for me. When I turned eight years old, they became the right size.

The red leather jacket had a zip, which was just coming into fashion and not many people knew how they worked. My Mum pulled the zip up rather sharply and caught my throat. Needless to say, I screamed in pain and there was blood everywhere. Eventually the jacket was unzipped and a long shallow cut was seen near my throat. Since then I have always been rather hesitant of wearing anything zipped near my throat.

Being winter, I wanted to show off the skis to my friend but had to wait for the boots and trousers to be made to go with them. I already had ice skates as well as my friends, so we enjoyed the winter sports. When all the gear was ready, I could hardly wait to start. Zosia took me to the park where I tried to ski, falling over an awful lot, but eventually I got the hang of it.

Uncle Joe was great fun and at the time he was training for a weightlifting competition. I watched in amazement how he ate pounds of butter and dozens of raw eggs to put on weight. He used to suck the eggs and taught me the technique.

Sometimes he would lie down on the settee and stretch his arm out and asked me to sit on his hand and lift me up and down as a weight and then he would turnover and repeat the weight lifting exercise with his other arm. Also amongst his equipment were spring stretchers. He used four springs and after he finished he dismantled three and left one for me to play with. I could not pull apart the spring more than two inches apart and I swore that when I was older I would pull the four springs just like my uncle.

When I was nearly six years old I started once again to have pains in my right leg. Everybody thought it was the old problem returning and my parents were terrified that I may not be able to walk again. Several doctors came to check me and for some reason one the doctors prescribed that I should eat ham, I suppose because it was a very lean meat. My father had to get dispensation from the rabbi first.

I was made to stay in bed until luckily another doctor diagnosed, that I had a big blind abscess growing in my groin. From then on he started the painful process of trying to draw it out. I had to have hot poultices made from boiled wheat and wrapped around the groin day and night, which actually made it bigger till came to a head. Remember, there were no anaesthetics at that time. When the time came to lance the abscess, the doctor brought with him two men to hold me down, when performing this operation. The lance must have been very sharp. While screaming my head off, I looked down and it was all over. An enormous lump of puss popped out, which gave me great relief from the pain. The pain returned when the doctor put a wick into the hole to drain the wound, which had to be done twice a day.

I recovered very quickly and soon was back at school. This was the year I met my first girlfriend. She joined the school in the spring, a very pretty blond girl with lovely long wavy hair. She sat next to me and we became friends during the lunch break. Her name was Duska Birnbaum, (one of the few names I remember). Both our families knew each other; her father was one of the largest egg wholesalers. We were inseparable until I changed schools and then came to England.

Towards the end of 1932, things started going wrong financially for my father. He owned some property in Germany and with the Nazis getting more and more powerful, he tried to sell this property. Everyone was trying to sell at that time but he was unable to sell his. In 1933, when Hitler became chancellor of Germany, laws were passed which deprived my father of his property. I never found oud out what exactly happened but it had a large effect on his income. He could no longer afford our large apartment and we could not move to our old flat as it was let on lease to a tenant.

The school needed bigger premises so my father exchanged our apartment for their premises and the school was able to expand. After a further few months Dad's finances deteriorated and reliance was on my mother's shop, but that was only seasonal income.

We moved again and this time into the storage room at the back of the shop. Sadly Zosia had to leave and after school I had to help out in the shop. One of my jobs was helping to make ice cream. When the ice cream container was filled with milk, cream, eggs, sugar and vanilla, it was placed in a wooden tub with ice packed round it. There was a geared handle on top, which I had to turn for a very long time till the ice cream was made.

Ice blocks were delivered everyday as there was no refrigeration. I liked making ice cream as when I finished I was always given a large bowl of ice cream with strawberries.

There were other perks working in the shop, as there were many travelling salesmen advertising their wares: jams, custard, jellies, chocolate, sweets and biscuits. They used my mother's shop a lot, being opposite a large market. Usually after they finished for the day and there were a lot of samples to eat.

1933 was an eventful year in which it was the first time I had a brush with death. My sister had turned three years old and she was to start kindergarten. As we no longer had our nanny, my parents decided I should take her on my way to school as the kindergarten and the school were attached. This was fine for a couple of months. However, one day we were walking along as usual and, crossing a small turning, a drunken Pole with horses and a large cart came tearing around the corner, out of control, heading straight for us. I just managed to push my sister aside but I was knocked down under the horses. The driver managed to stop just in time, preventing the steel wheels going over me. I still occasionally have nightmares of my lying under the horses with their hooves missing me by a fraction of an inch.

People came running and pulled me away, thinking I was badly hurt but all I had was a large graze on my leg where a hoof caught me. As it was only a short distance from the school my sister and I were taken there, where a teacher poured a lot of iodine, which was even more painful, then a large dressing. We were then cleaned up and taken home to explain to my parents what had happened. Mother insisted that I was checked over by the family doctor who confirmed all was well I was sent back to school the following day.

Helping in the shop, I soon learnt a lot about the business dealings with the local farmers. Most of the nearby farms reared cattle, sheep and goats. The summer grazing land was high in the mountains and the peasants were called 'Gurals'. They wore thick felt embroidery adorned trousers, shirts and waistcoats. Footwear was a type of moccasin boots. This outfit is still worn in Southern Poland to this day. In springtime, when the snow had melted, they took their flocks up the mountains for grazing and there they stayed all summer. The weather in the mountains was quite cool, especially at night so they wore long waistcoats made of sheepskins with the fur on the inside for added warmth and fur outside to keep out the rain.

Every spring they came to the shop to buy their supplies: flour, sugar, salt, dried fruit, coffee, tea, needles, cottons, ribbons etc. This was all done on credit. Late in the summer when they sold their livestock, they came to pay off their debts in cash, goods i.e. skins, smoked cheeses, sour cream and local fruit. There was a lot of bargaining and I soon learnt to bargain with the peasants' sons, which usually came accompanying them.

The boys who were old enough to go with the flocks used to carve whistles and flutes and many other beautiful things that we used to sell in the shop. These they would barter for chocolate, sweets, coloured ribbons and other things for their girlfriends.

The cheeses were fantastic; they were made from goats' milk and smoked over their fires, which made them very hard like parmesan. Pictures were carved on them and people used to hang them up in their kitchens as decorations. It was not possible to cut them. You had either to shave slivers or grate the cheese. It was particularly delicious on toasted bread with butter.[8]

Some other things happened that year. At long last I was given permission to go to the park by myself and play with my friends. These were happy times; we played many games and would also listen to the music played on the bandstand. In the

---

[8] In 2004 when in Poland I managed to buy some but it wasn't the same. It was softer in texture, certainly not the same.

autumn we would look for conkers, carrying thick branches which we threw up into the trees to dislodge the conkers always checking that there were no old pieces of wood that may be dangerous. One day, unfortunately, I did not see a big piece of wood, which came crashing down and knocked me out. I soon recovered with a swollen lump to the right on my forehead and which can still be faintly seen to this day.

It was also the year that the school formed a Jewish Cub/Scout Movement called in Hebrew Habonim. We loved it and were given uniforms and caps. As most of the activities were in summer (summers were very long and hot), we wore white t-shirts, blue shorts and a school-type peak cap in blue and white. We used to go on short marches to a wood just outside the town where we ate our sandwiches and drank cold drinks, learn a few scout things and, in the evening, the scoutmasters lit a bonfire and we'd sit around singing songs from Palestine and telling stories on how kibbutzim were formed and how the Sabras lived and worked.

Now that I was eight years old, my father decided I should go to Cheder.[9] Of course there was a problem. Since my kindergarten I had been taught modern Hebrew but anything religious had to be said using the ancient Hebrew language; it was the same difference between modern English and Chaucer's English. There were no Liberal Synagogues then and if there were they would not be recognised by the orthodox.

There is a tremendous difference between the two in pronunciation and chanting. When I tried to read passages from the Torah it was very noticeable and the rabbi was furious with me. He would shout while pinching my cheek and pulling my ear.

At school I had a similar problem when I read the text. I started slipping into the old style Hebrew and I was often be told off but never punished. At home I tried telling father my problem, but to no avail. He just insisted that I had to learn for my Bar Mitzvah[10] as the rabbi wanted and that we were orthodox Jews.

---

[9] A school usually ran by a retired rabbi to prepare boys to be able to read and understand the Torah for their Bar Mitzvah.

This was the first time my education was messed with. The downside of all this teaching was that I had to start going to synagogue every Saturday in order to practice. Certainly, I did not like it and most times tried to get out of going but, again, there was no choice. The only good thing was that my grandparents lived just across the road from the synagogue and after the service I would visit then and see some of my aunts and was given sweets and biscuits.

The worst time for me was the Day of Atonement (Yom Kippur). The synagogue had a congregation of between 1000-1200 men and women. The men prayed downstairs and the women were upstairs. The window was very small and set high up in the wall. Needless to say it meant there was little ventilation.

The preparation for the Day of Atonement was that you washed or bathed thoroughly the evening before it started and changed into yours best clothes. Before starting the fast we sat down to the meal, which was similar to that for a Friday night except the prayers were slightly different. The time for starting the fast was dictated by the rabbi and strictly adhered to. And all arrived on time for the start of the service. Kol Nidre, which is at the beginning, was sung by the Cantor, which is the most sad and moving. Indeed, I think, the most beautiful pieces music ever written.

The next morning my father would be at the synagogue by eight o'clock, though some very pious men would pray all night. My instructions were to be there by 10 o'clock, at the time when the rabbi would be doing the first reading from the Torah. As young boys, we were allowed to leave the service several times during the day, but had to be back for what was considered the important prayers. The service lasted till nightfall and then we went home to break the fast.

If you can imagine, all these people in a stuffy environment not having been able to brush their teeth (as water

---

[10] A Bar Mitzvah is a sort of a ceremony for a boy on his thirteenth birthday when he is considered to be a man in the Jewish faith.

was not permitted during the twenty-five hours of the fast) the smell became unbearable. Some people fainted because of it. Us boys were always given small bottles of spirit of ammonia, slightly diluted, encase we or anyone else felt faint. Being under thirteen years old we were not required to fast but competed among ourselves on how long we would last before eating or having a glass of water.

The breaking of the fast was always wonderful, which always started with a prayer for wine, then bread with honey. My mother always prepared chicken soup, meat with vegetables, potato pancakes, finally finishing with puddings and sweets.

Towards the end of the year my father's financial position improved considerably and my parents started to make preparations to move back to their old apartment in the centre of the town. We moved just before the end of the year and, of course, the aspidistra came too.

It was like we had never been away.

1934

1934 was an eventful year. One thing that delighted me was that my favourite Uncle Izydor, my mother's brother and father's oldest friend moved into the apartment below us with his wife Giza and daughter Dora. She was three years younger than me, and used to play with my sister Rozia and myself.

Uncle Izydor was working for a margarine firm, as mentioned earlier, and during my holidays often took me on his rounds. His customers often spoiled me with sweets, soft drinks and ice cream. None of my friends had a motorized vehicle and always were curious as to how it was to ride in one.

Uncle Izydor was a handyman and good at carving using his penknife. One of the few present he gave me was a penknife of my own and he taught me to carve wood. Acquiring wood was no problem as there was a carpenter's workshop in the courtyard. I became skilled and made mainly swords and daggers but also designed and made match-firing guns. I showed my efforts to my school teacher who immediately asked me to make some swords and daggers for school plays, especially for the festivals of Hanukah and Purim.

Uncle Izydor at that time acquired a crystal set radio. Radios were in their infancy in Poland and not many people had one. Though you were supposed to have a licence, which cost very little, no one bothered. The set had to have a very long aerial and my job was to climb to the attic where it was fixed all the way round and drop the end down through the attic window to my Uncle, as one never left the aerial longer than one had to for fear you would be reported to the authorities as uncle had no licence.

Mother was very excited at receiving a letter from Uncle Joe in Vienna who had finished his apprenticeship in the fur trade where he was employed by an important firm Horowitz, who were shortly moving to London and he would be going with them.

As I said before when he went to London he was headhunted by Calman Links and Mr Taylor, whom I met many years later, told me that he suggested to me Uncle Joe should join the firm once he was established in England and later I learnt that they were the royal furriers. In those days it was every Jewish family's hope in Eastern Europe to have permission to come to England or the United States. It was very difficult as there were very small quotas and the only other way was if a firm wanted a specialist in a particular craft. Joe also wrote that once he was settled he would write from England and tell her all about his life there.

That spring I received from my father the only ever hiding from him. I used to walk to Cheder, which was situated halfway between our home and the River Dunayec; often after classes I used to go to the river with friends to look for fresh mussel shells or go the park to play. I always told mother where I would be but this time forgot.

Spring that year was early and there was warm rain for about six days. The town itself was on high ground by the river, which cut a ravine through one side of Nowy Sacz which it flowed through, but it often flooded on the outskirts, which was on much lower ground. On that day there was an emergency warning issued as the snow from the mountains melted at a faster rate than usual and serious flooding was expected. As it was the first sunny day of spring my friends and I decided we would go and play by the river. We noticed that the river level was slightly higher but knew not of the flood warnings and took no notice and continued playing as usual.

We used to go home late in the afternoons and when we did leave we noticed that the banks of the river were flooding. Still, we took no notice; it was not an unusual occurrence. We played on our way home and used to get in just before dark.

As I walked in through the door, my parents were shouting at me as to where I had been. Having no idea what the fuss was about and before I could find out my father took me by the scruff of my neck, bent me over and whacked me with his belt. Still, I did not realise till years later that it must have been a reaction of his fear for me as a father, not anger, because he never hit me thereafter.

The flood was one of the worst in history of the town. The water rose between ten and fifteen metres. By the morning huge parts of the lower town – as far as one could see – was flooded. There was no fresh drinking water and the only water available was outside the castle in the well. The Local Authorities had small tankers made of wood like barrels, which were fixed on carts to supply the outlying parts of the town with water. People living in the centre had to queue at the well with all sorts of containers to get their water.

We had one high bridge, where we went to see how high the water had risen.

There were terrible sights. I saw wooden houses with people clinging to the roof floating by with no chance of being rescued as the current was very strong. There were several dead bodies. The worst was a screaming baby in a cot floating by that could not be saved.

The main flood lasted for about two weeks, but it did not dry up until late in the summer.

One funny incident happened that year. My sister Rozia and I had sort love/hate relation. While playing she annoyed me about something and in retaliation I dipped my teaspoon in some hot tea and touched her on her bare shoulder. She screamed in pain and while I was running away from her she kicked me in the crotch. It was so powerful it laid me out for two days.

That year in autumn Mum and Dad told me that I would be leaving my Hebrew school and go to the local Council school to prepare me for exams for entry to the Gymnasium at the age of twelve. I was heartbroken as I would be leaving all my pals, teachers and my girlfriend Duska.

One consolation was that the new school was just opposite my Grandparents' house and my youngest Uncle was in the same school a year above me. In Poland at that time school used to start at half eight in the morning and finish at one o'clock. The arrangement was that I would eat my lunch at my grandparents' before going home.

My grandfather, being a Kosher butcher, was a producer of salami, salt beef and viennas and so my lunch usually consisted of either salt beef or viennas with sauerkraut, pickles and black bread with butter, which I love to this day. When Granddad was making sausages he often let me help him. He used proper skins made either from cow or sheep intestine which were dried and rolled into large balls. He owned an enormous mincer with a large nozzle in which he ground up the meat and spices. My job was to thread the gut skin onto the nozzle and hold in place, which he would then proceed to fill with the mixture of meat and spices in a long length. He would then give me a little measuring stick to measure the length of the sausage where he would twist and tie with string later to be cut into individual sausages. The string of sausages was then placed in a large boiler. My aunties and uncles, when they were around, used to make a big fuss of me. My aunties always gave me cheesecake or any other cake to take home with me, and, of course, I was never short of sausages!

My schooling was messed with again. The curriculum in my new school was a bit different from my Hebrew school and I was a bit behind other boys in Polish, History and Geography classes, which did not endear me to my teachers. I received very little bullying as a new student, as the boys at the gymnasium knew I had my big uncle in a higher class and most of them knew my family.

In those days, if you left a job which you had permission to work in England for, you lost your permit to work and you had to return to your country of origin. If you could start a business with an English director, however, you were allowed to stay, and this is what Joe intended to do. In his letter, Uncle Joe mentioned that as soon as he was established he would write again and possibly come to visit. The name of his firm was "Vienna Fur Models" and it was based at No.1, Dover St. London W.1.

Since Hitler had come to power in Germany, anti-Semitism in Europe was accelerating exponentially, especially in South Poland among the Catholic peasants. One of the worst things I experienced that year was the result of this surge of anti-Semitism, wherein the change in political mood had allowed racist thoughts to bubble up into violence. When returning home from school one day, I saw a large crowd chasing a man. I could not see whom it was that they were chasing and, as I was curious as to what was happening, I ran with them. The crowd chased the man past the Town Hall to the Convent garden where they started beating him. At the time I could not see exactly what was happening as I was only a small boy and the crowd was quite large. Suddenly police whistles were heard and the crowd dispersed. Then I could finally see: a Jewish man in his Kaftan and Stramel, beaten to death, lying in a pool of blood. I ran to the end of the garden where I was terribly sick and scared; I had never seen a dead body before.

When I arrived home Mum asked me what was wrong as I looked so ill; I told her what had happened and straight away she made me promise to her that I would avoid all crowds and gatherings from then on. This experience left a lasting impression on me as to how ignorant people could be and how easy it was for people to direct their anger towards innocent Jews.

Towards the summer Dad's finances started to diminish as it was becoming difficult to do business, as like the Germans the Poles started to boycott Jewish firms. On many walls posters appeared with copies of Nazi cartoons depicting the Jews, and more Hassidic boys were bullied and beaten up. Life became fearful and hard on a daily basis. One had to be very careful where you walked.

1935

That year one of the funniest things happened to me, although it did not seem funny at the time. Our apartment had parquet floors and every week the maid had to polish them with wax on big brushes which she wore on her feet, similar to in the painting 'Floor Polishers' by Russell Flint. We used to use large tins of wax which Dad bought whenever it was necessary from the paint and wax factory near my school. On this one occasion, Dad decided that, as I was nearby, I should collect the wax.

I went to the factory with a note from Dad and they gave me the tin of wax. The journey home was about a kilometre. Summers in Poland were hot (35-38°c) and of course the wax melted. I was trying to get home quickly, and in doing so I tripped and fell down, grazing my knees. The tin burst open and I was smothered in wax from head to toe. When I arrived home Mum looked at me in horror, thinking I had been attacked by the Poles. When I explained what had happened she was so relieved that all she said was "Take off your clothes and tell the maid to heat some water for a bath." When Dad came home all he said was that I should pick up another tin of wax the following day and not to try not to do something as stupid as trying to run all the way home.

One other thing comes to mind from that year. My father's oldest sister married a man from Czechoslovakia. It was an arranged marriage, which was usual in the Orthodox Community and orthodox Jewish girls would never go out without a chaperone with a man on a date; it just wasn't done. As far as I know he came from a well-to-do family and had his own business. It was going to be a big Hassidic wedding and both families looked forward to the big occasion. The wedding was to be a few weeks before Rosh Hashanah, the Jewish new year.

First, the wedding service was held at Grandfather's synagogue just across the road from his house and after the service they crossed back again where their long tables were stacked with all sorts of wine, spirits and juices. Most of the Hassidic community was invited as grandfather was an important man in the community being a Kosher butcher.

It was the only time since their marriage that Mum and Dad were invited to a family gathering since the row over Mum shaving her head. Everyone wore their best clothes and I had a suit made especially for the   occasion. There was a fantastic Klezmer band (Jewish travelling musicians) and men danced with men, women with women and husbands danced with their wives holding handkerchiefs between them. There were Hassidic dancers doing the Kozatzki (Russian style dances) with wine bottles balanced on their forehead, and there were singers both male and female singing both Hebrew and Hassidic songs. There were also some Christian neighbours who knew and did business with the family who had come along. The wedding went on most of the night and the celebration continued the next day for relatives from far and wide who could not make it for the day of the wedding, as they travelled mostly on horseback or horse and cart.

At the wedding I made myself ill by eating too much and had a terrible headache from pinching glasses of wine when no one was looking. When my Grandmother saw how I was she put me straight to bed. The happy couple left the following day and, unfortunately, I never saw them again as the whole family perished in the holocaust.

During the summer on Sundays when the weather was hot we always went to a little beach on the river Dunayec. Although it wasn't the best river to swim as it had a very strong current and extremely cold the water coming from the high Tatra mountains where there was always snow, we enjoyed ourselves there. Our group consisted Mum, Dad, Rozia, Uncle Izydor, Aunty Giza, Cousin Dora and myself. We usually used to paddle in the river.

One particular Sunday we were in our usual place when Dad decided to take a dip. We were all either playing or sunbathing when we heard a shout from Dad. We all turned around and saw that Dad had fallen into the strong current and was being swept down the river. None of us could swim but Uncle Izydor, seeing what was happening, started running along the river bank and managed to grab Dad's hand and pull him on to the bank of the river. By that time several other men helped my uncle to lay Dad, who was partly unconscious having swallowed a lot of water, on the grass verge. After they pumped his chest he coughed and spluttered out the water and soon he was back to his old self. It was only later on that it dawned on me how easily I could have lost my Dad and Uncle that day.

1936

1936 started very badly for my Dad financially. Several of his investments were losing money and his income had diminished considerably; most of the income came from Mum's shop, which was no longer being used by the Germans and Poles. Although, we as kids didn't notice it as Mum and Dad made sure we had everything we needed in clothes and food, certain luxuries had started to go missing.

After Easter we had a letter from Uncle Joe in England informing us that he was coming to visit us on his way to see his brother John in Vienna. We all waited with anticipation for his arrival, not only us but many of his old friends in Poland, some of whom had relations in England and wished to hear news of them.

He arrived in July and brought presents for everyone; I received a pencil box with a complete set of protractors, with a small ruler which I did not quite understand as it was marked in inches. Growing up in Europe, I had only been taught the metric system and knew nothing about the Imperial one.

Mum and Dad had a long discussion with Joe about Dad's financial situation and how it was being so affected by the increase in anti-Semitism in Poland. He was fearful for my mother his sister and he wished to do something about it. He asked me whether I would like to come and live in England. My answer was a big 'yes'.

I later learned from Mum and Dad that uncle Joe went to Vienna to see uncle John – who was part of Austrian government – if he could use his influence to acquire a visa for the family to go to England.

Mum and Dad explained to me that we would be going to England in stages, as there was a quota for foreign nationals: first Dad to establish himself helping Uncle Joe in his business, then me to go to an English school to learn the English way of life and to become an assimilated English boy, and then Mum and Rozia. We all waited with anticipation the rest of the year for when the visas would come.

1937

In the beginning of the year we heard from Uncle John that progress was being made in acquiring Dad's visa and that he would be going to England by the end of May. My visa was taking longer as they were also looking for a school that would be suitable for me. When I did, I would have to travel via Uncle Zygmunt in Krakow and then to Uncle John in Vienna. There was great excitement at the prospect of a move to England and Mum, as usual, started to prepare outfits for me to take on my journey.

During his visit from England, Uncle Joe brought lots of fashion books and magazines for Mum, including some men's fashions and told her what sort of weather I could expect in England, summers being hot and humid. Mum decided that I should have a suit made in white linen and for colder weather as well as four pairs of trousers and a jacket.

In May the day came when Dad was going to leave for England. We all looked on the map to see what journey he was taking and worked out the mileage. First he would have to travel through Germany, then Holland where he would catch a boat to Harwich. From Harwich he would travel on to London where he would meet Uncle Joe. To a young boy it looked a huge distance, never thinking I would be travelling a greater distance when I would go. When the day came for Dad to leave us we all saw him off at the railway station with hugs and kisses. We felt both sad and excited hoping that soon we could be all together again.

Just after Dad left news arrived that my visa was being processed and that once I was in Krakow with Uncle Zygmunt my passport would be issued with a visa to Czechoslovakia and Austria for me to be able to go to Uncle John who would arrange my visa to England.

My great journey towards a new life started June 18th 1937. Mum, Rozia and myself drove to the railway station in an open horse-drawn carriage. As we were riding most of my friends, family and acquaintances who knew I was leaving for England waved all along the route. Mum and Rozia, with tears in their eyes, hugged me and kissed me before seeing me settled on the train to Krakow. I was just 11 ½ years of age. The journey to Krakow was only one hour and Uncle Zygmunt met me at the station to take me to his home. Uncle Zygmunt lived in the large Jewish quarter called Kazimiesh just short distance from the castle. The quarter dates to the 12th century when King Kazimiesh invited the Jews and gave them land to settle and start trading, commerce and banking in order that Poland became affluent. Uncle Zygmunt had a large apartment on the bank of river Vistula, which is the main river in Poland flowing from the Tatra mountains all the way through Poland to the Baltic sea.

Uncle Zygmunt and auntie Zosia were very kind to me and straight away Zosia offered me some food with cream cakes and tea afterwards. I had my own room and Zosia made a great fuss over me. I spent five happy days with them until my passport and visas for Czechoslovakia and Austria were settled.

During those five days Uncle Zygmunt took me sightseeing around Krakow. We saw Wawel Castle, museums, we rowed on the river and Zygmunt bought me a lot of ice-cream;

they were happy times. When it was time for me to depart for the next part of my journey he produced a small leather suitcase – about eighteen inches by twelve by four – full of different chocolate bars made by Suchard. He explained to me that it was for my journey to England and it had to last me until I arrived there. He also gave me a little leather bag with different currencies wrapped separately for my journey. I had Czech krone, Austrian schillings, Swiss francs and French francs. They were mostly silver and the total value was about £10 English, which was a lot of money in those days. He told me to be careful how I spend it as it was to be my emergency fund.

He explained to me that I would be going to Vienna and at each border I would have to show my passport twice – once leaving the country and once entering the next country. When I arrived in Vienna I would be met by my Uncle John, whom I had not seen since I was four. Just in case he didn't recognise me, he had a picture of what I looked like to recognise me by.

6 - The photo from my first passport

The day came when we had to say our goodbyes to Uncle Zygmunt, Auntie Zosia, Cousin Dana and baby Gustav. I did not realise at the time that this would be the last time that I would ever see Auntie Zosia and Cousin Gustav as they both would perish in the holocaust.

The journey to Vienna lasted 4 –4 ½ hours, at a distance of about 320 Km (200 miles); it was the longest journey I ever made. I arrived at the railway station in Vienna just after lunch. I could not see my Uncle John as there were several hundred people on the platform so I stayed by the carriage where I got off, hoping that my Uncle would find me. When the crowd cleared I saw a man standing at the exit of the platform, I started walking towards him hoping that it was my Uncle. I recognised him right away; it was he who had difficulty recognising me. He was looking for a small boy and the only picture he had of me was taken when I was six. He gave me a big hug and took my suitcase and we mounted a horse-drawn carriage to go to his apartment. On the way he asked me about Mum and Rozia, if they were well and also about Uncle Zygmunt and his family and how I spent my time in Krakow. I told him they were all well and described to him all the places that Uncle Zygmunt had showed me. I also told him how kind Auntie Zosia and Dana had been to me.

Uncle John's apartment was in an exclusive part of Vienna where most Embassy and Diplomatic staff lived. It was a very large apartment and beautifully furnished. I had never met my auntie Erna or their daughter Susie before this point and their reception was quite cool. I think they were so assimilated to the Austrian society, especially since Uncle John was part of the Austrian government as a senior commercial judge, their thinking was that anyone coming from Poland or eastern Europe was a peasant and the lowest of the low, even if they were family.

The maid made some food for all of us, some cakes and biscuits, but I had some odd looks from my Aunt when I sat down in one of the easy chairs, not knowing why. As soon as I got up she walked to the chair, dusted and puffed up the cushions. I thought it was very strange.

After tea Uncle John led me to his study where we discussed what I was going to do while waiting for my visa to England, which would take about four weeks. He explained that I would not be staying in his apartment but with another cousin on

Auntie Erna's side of the family, who had a son my age who would be my companion whilst I was staying in Vienna. He also mentioned that he would be allowing me 10 Austrian Shillings a day pocket money to spend going about the town. 10 shillings was a lot of money for a boy of my age and I was lucky to have it.

Auntie Erna did not know what a favour she did for me by not letting me stay with her. I soon settled in my Cousin's apartment. Every day, when we finished breakfast, my cousin – who was only two months older than me –would leave the apartment with me and travel to the Prater, a permanent amusement park in Vienna. It has a large Ferris wheel and many sideshows and theatres. It also had a motor racing track on which children could race small cars with real petrol engines; it was our favourite. They used to say that you could never see all the shows as they changed so frequently. We had a wonderful time and both of us had sufficient money to see many of the attractions. We usually had our lunch and tea there before going back home. That was one of the best times that I had had in my life as I had never been to an amusement park before.

I visited my Uncle several times in his office and that was an experience all on its own. At the entrance he had a policeman on duty, and then when you entered his main office there were four secretaries, of which one took me to another office where there was another lady who was his private secretary, who took me to another door, knocked and entered, where my Uncle was seated behind a large desk. He kissed and hugged me and asked me how I was getting on, he then opened a large drawer full of foreign used postage stamps and told me to help myself to as many as I wanted for my collection. He also gave me my pocket money for the following week. On the last visit to his office he informed me that my visas to travel to England would be ready by the 22nd July 1937 and shortly after that date I would be travelling to Paris, about 1200km (or about 760 miles) away. Uncle also suggested that on the Sunday before I depart he would like me to spend it with him on the river Danube, although I would still be sleeping at my cousins. After we did that, he then took me on a tour of Vienna. He pointed out some impressive buildings and then guided me around the old Palace where they held Strauss concerts and at Christmas.

On the Sunday, which was a beautiful day, Uncle picked me up from my cousin's house in his horse-drawn carriage and we drove to his beach house on the river. Vienna was a much bigger town that the one I had come from, with much larger houses and a lot more traffic, and it all made me feel very important that I was riding through all of it with my uncle, who was a very important person in Vienna. It was also very pleasant. There were several other houses nearby, all about the same size. The summer house was more of a hut, and had just one room and was built in wood; it was very small and came with a million mosquitos. Inside, there was a settee, table, chairs and some lounge chairs, a cooker and the usual cups and saucers.

We were greeted by a lady of ample proportions who was already there to serve us some coffee and cakes before promptly disappearing.[11] In front of each beach house on the Danube there was small bonfire. I could not understand on a hot day the purpose of having one. My uncle explained that they were there to make smoke to keep the mosquitoes at bay. I thought this was a bit late as I had already been bitten half a dozen times.

I have heard a lot about the blue Danube, but all saw was a river that was filthy brown in colour. We had lunch and tea; by that time I was bitten at least a dozen times more and looked as if I had chickenpox, except the spots were larger – I could not stop scratching and I had big red blotches all over me. On the way back to my cousin's apartment we stopped at a chemist and Uncle John bought some ointment for my bites and a box of plasters, explaining to me how I was to use them. In Poland, we seldom used plasters and if anyone had a cut a cloth bandage was used, so it was a great novelty for me to use them.

On the way to my cousin's, Uncle John informed me that this was my last day in Vienna as my visa had arrived and I would be leaving the following day in the late afternoon, arriving

---

[11] A few years later, I discovered that she had been my Uncle's mistress.

in Paris at lunchtime to be met by my Uncle Joe. He also told me that we would have lunch together where he would explain everything to me about my journey. When morning came, I was all excited for, at last, I was leaving for the remaining part of my journey to England.

By the time Uncle John came to pick me up I had everything packed and waiting. We all said our goodbyes, promising to keep in touch, but unfortunately we never did; all of them perished in the holocaust. Uncle took my suitcase and I carried my little case, still ¾ -full of chocolates that Uncle Zygmunt had given me. We went to a restaurant where he explained how I would be travelling. We would be leaving the restaurant to arrive at the main railway station at 3.30 p.m. to board the train leaving for Paris at 4 o'clock. I would be travelling 2nd class on the Orient Express through Switzerland, then across France all the way to Paris.

Uncle gave me my passport and explained that I would have to show it twice at each border, which I already knew having travelled to Austria. He also gave me some money to spend on the journey to buy food and drink on the train. When we finished our lunch we drove to the station where the train was waiting. My face was still covered with plasters from the mosquito bites and I looked as if I had been in some sort of an accident. Uncle explained to the other passengers that there was nothing wrong with me and that the plasters were covering my mosquito bites. Uncle then put my suitcases on the luggage rack and conversed with some of the passengers if they would be so kind as to keep an eye on me until I arrived in Paris. We said our goodbyes and mentioned that I would be seeing him in London the following year.

The train departed and I was on my way, on a long journey to a new life. I have never been on a train that long; it had dining and sleeping cars and carriages that had individual compartments with corridors where the attendants were able to wheel their trolleys along with food, chocolates, different drinks, cigarettes and tobacco. There were five other passengers in my compartment, two couples and a single man who spend most of the time reading books and magazines. When we journeyed into Switzerland, the scenery was breath-taking: although I came from the Tatra mountains, this was something else entirely. The mountains were much higher and were covered in ice and snow. I was taught in school about the Alps but I had never realised how beautiful they were.

I bought some food and drink from the attendant and, when I had finished my meal, I opened my little case and offered chocolate to everyone in my compartment. They asked me how come I had so much chocolate, so I explained that my Uncle in Poland was a director at Suchards and gave me this case for my journey.

When night fell I was too excited to sleep, watching the lights of villages and towns that we passed all the way to Berne, which was the last stop before the French border. In the morning and after Customs checks we were at last on the way to Paris. When the train arrived in Paris, we all descended from it. I thanked my fellow travellers for helping me on my journey and I started looking for my Uncle Joe. There were many people on the platform but no Uncle. I waited by the train and suddenly a lady and a gentleman approached me and asked me what my name was. I told them and they informed me that Uncle Joe was unable to come and so he had sent them to fetch me. They introduced themselves to me as Mrs Sofia Day and Mr Paul Steiner and they both worked for my Uncle. They both spoke German and Czech and we were able to have some sort of conversation. They told me that we had to catch the boat train at 3.30 p.m., but they had a problem: Uncle Joe had miscalculated how much my ticket would cost and did not give them enough money for my fare, so they asked me if I had any money. Should I not have had enough they would have had to contact one of my Uncle's friends in Paris to advance the money. I told them that I had both Swiss and French francs. We counted out how much I had and it was enough to make up the balance. After we acquired my ticket we had a quick lunch and changed stations for the boat train, so I saw very little of Paris. We boarded the boat train to Calais and arrived there at 4.30 p.m. to catch the 5.30 boat to Folkestone.

I had never seen a seaport or the sea before or a seagoing boat, so everything about Calais was very exciting for me. The weather was warm and I felt quite comfortable in my white linen suit. Mrs Day asked me if I had a jumper or a coat for she worried that I would be cold once we were on the open sea. She then explained that once we were on the boat I should stay inside to keep warm. Of course, I never stayed inside as the boat and everything on it was new to me and I wanted to see it all. I went on deck – the wind was very cold and chilled me to the bone. I soon went back inside the boat where Mrs Day gave me a hot drink and told me that we would be docking soon.

We docked just after seven o'clock in the evening, the date was the 26th July 1937. We went through Customs and, just as we passed the barrier, there was my Father and Uncle waiting for me. They hugged me and kissed me, making a big fuss. We then all crossed over to the railway platform where the train for London was waiting. We all boarded the train and as soon as we were in the carriage, Dad opened his attaché case and produced a small bunch of bananas and an orange. I had not seen a banana or an orange for nearly a year as they were a huge luxury in Poland at the time and we seldom ate them, so it was a great treat for me. I peeled one of the bananas and started eating it but I was so tired from not sleeping the night before that I fell asleep. I had to be awakened when we reached Victoria Station. I was very disappointed that this happened as I never saw the English countryside on my first day. We arrived in the late evening and, as we left the train through the barrier, we walked to another entrance where I had my first experience of travelling on the London Underground.

I did not know about the underground and wondered why we were walking down the stairs. My Dad explained to me that under London there was a wide network of trains going to hundreds of different stations, and as then London was the largest city in the world, it was necessary for people to travel quickly. The journey was very quick and short and before long we arrived at Oxford Circus. There waited another surprise: *escalators*. I had never seen them before. I thought how marvellous it was to be able to go up the stairs without having to climb them. When we came out of the station there was another surprise for me, the London Bus. Uncle explained that this was another way of travelling in London. I thought the buses were wonderful – I had never seen anything like them. They were beautiful, having two decks and a lovely red colour. Dad asked me if I was thirsty. I hadn't had a drink since lunch in Paris, so of course I said yes.

As we were walking, I marvelled at all the adverts lit up in neon lights. The day had turned to evening, but after short walk we arrived at a Fortes milk bar in Upper Regent Street, next to the News cinema. As we sat down on the tall stools, I admired the stainless steel counter and all its accessories. Uncle ordered, telling that he had asked for a special treat for me.

The man behind the counter, who wore a uniform and a forage cap, took a stainless steel container went to a machine that squirted milk into it. Then, he got a scoop of chocolate ice cream and some other ingredients. He clipped the container to another machine which made terrible noise, and then he poured the contents into a tall glass put two straws and placed it in front of me. I took a big suck and I thought it was the most wonderful drink I ever had.

That was my first introduction to a milkshake. When we finished our drinks we boarded for my first ride on a bus to Chalk Farm where Dad and Uncle had digs in Fellows Road. When we got in they put me into bed, where I went to sleep immediately.

My first day in London started out a bit dramatically. I woke up around nine o'clock and tried looking for my Dad and my Uncle, neither of whom were around. I thought maybe they had gone for breakfast. I looked at the table and I noticed that there was a note under the milk bottle, four silver half-crowns, a map of London and a Polish/English dictionary. There was also bread and butter and the remainder of my bananas from the train. The note stated that Dad and Uncle had to go to work and they had left me to sleep as I looked very tired from my journey. The note also stated that the two circles on the map, one showed where I was and the other showed my destination. I was to wash and dress and, after I had eaten my breakfast, I was to ask the landlady to point me in the right direction to my destination. At the bottom of the note was the family firm's address: Vienna Fur Models, 1 Dover Street, W.1. At about 10.30 a.m. I left the house after being instructed by the landlady using the dictionary and sign language, as she neither spoke German or Polish it was very difficult for me to understand which direction to take. I took my dictionary and money with me but I must have misunderstood the landlady as I later discovered that I was walking in the wrong direction; I was walking towards Camden Town instead of Swiss Cottage. When I had walked for about 15 minutes I saw a Policeman. I knew he was Policeman as I had a picture of one in a book that Uncle gave me about England. I approached him with my dictionary and my map and gave me an odd look as I was still wearing my white suit. After a few minutes he understood what I needed to know.

He showed me on the map where I was and which way I should be going. He gave me directions back to Chalk Farm and where I should turn left for Swiss Cottage. When I arrived at Swiss Cottage, I had to ask directions again which became more difficult. In those days if you asked anyone for directions, they didn't tell you the name of the street where you were to turn but instead the name of the pub that was on the corner. Eventually I managed to reach St John's Wood and then Baker Street. Being lunch time I watched with wonder the hustle and bustle and the amount of people in the street. As it was only a month since the coronation of King George VI, in every shop window were displays of the new King and Queen. Every building seemed to have a flag pole with a Union Jack hanging from it. The other displays in the windows were wonderful and I stood enraptured by them, eventually I managed to reach Oxford Street, the Marble Arch end. I again had to ask directions and a very kind gentleman pointed out on my map where I had to turn right for Bond Street. I started walking down Oxford Street there were soldiers everywhere in their different uniforms that had taken part in the coronation march. Most of them look like they were from the British dominions and colonies. It was at that moment that I thought how mighty and vast Great Britain was – up until that point I had only seen in my life two black men and here I was seeing so many in their pristine uniforms.

As I walked along it was like a fairy land, especially the shops with the little model trains and buses travelling in circles on rails. When I reached Selfridges I thought it was the most amazing store of them all. The windows on the ground floor and the ledges on the first floor had pride of place representing all the Dominions and Colonies with their own coat of arms. I was mesmerised by all the toys in the window displays; coming from a small town, seeing all of it was unimaginable to me.

I spent quite a lot of time looking at them and at all the other stores. I did not have anything to eat or drink as I had no idea the value of my English money or what anything would cost, so I didn't dare to go to the shop to buy anything. Also, I didn't know where the public toilets were or how I would find them.

Eventually I arrived at Bond Street where again I had to ask directions. Fortunately, I found another policeman who walked me a short distance and showed me on my map where I was and where I had to turn right for Grafton St. and left into Dover St. He also pointed out on the map that I would have to walk all the way down Dover St. to number 1. I arrived at the firm around 4 o'clock, where father was outside waiting impatiently for me. The first thing that he asked me was where I had been, I told him I had walked from the digs and the difficulties I had getting here. He then said that they had left me enough money for a bus or a taxi, so I told him that they should have explained to me what number bus I should take and how much it would cost as I knew nothing of English currency, and as for taxis I had no idea how to call one. Only then did he begin to realise what problems they had put me through and how little knowledge I had of London.

Dad to took me into the firm's building and again I discovered something new – the Lift. It was one of those old-fashioned ones with the doors made of steel rods which folded like a concertina when opening and shutting. We were whisked up to the second floor where it stopped and, having liked the ride, I asked Dad if we could go a few times up and down.

He right away told me that the lift was not a toy to play with and it was mainly used to transport customers and goods and I must not ever play with it. When we came out of the lift we faced a door with the firm's name on it. We entered a large room with a sofa, easy chairs, glass table, an ashtray on a stand and a large desk with a chair. All the furniture was in chrome tubular steel and the furnishings covered in royal blue leather. At the desk sat a very beautiful girl whom my Uncle Joe was talking to, but as soon as he saw me, he gave me a big hug and introduced me to the girl. Her name was Molly Molineux and he explained that she was a showroom model. He also had to explain to me what a model was, as I always understood that a model was a dress or a toy, never a woman.

Uncle then asked me if I had eaten and I told him that I hadn't, but that I would like a glass of water. After I had my drink he told Dad that he would be taking me for a meal and going shopping to buy me some new garments, then showing some of the places around the district. When we descended in the lift to the ground floor to go out, you are supposed to turn the light off, which we didn't. The gates were shut and uncle told me to turn the light off, so I put my arm through the grill to reach the switch. Uncle noticed what I had done grabbed my arm just as somebody above pressed the button for the lift to ascend. If he had not pulled my arm, a second later I would have lost it. Afterwards, it hit me how injured I would have been and how careful I had to be with all the new things I was experiencing. We left the building and crossed the road where there was a small J. Lyons tea room.

It was there that, for the first time, I was introduced to fish and chips with tomato sauce to compliment. In south Poland, most of the fish that was eaten were river fish, as we were a long way from the sea, and they were usually made into fish balls or were jellied. I thought the food was delicious and from then until I spoke better English, nearly every time I went out to eat I had fish and chips. After we finished eating we went to Oxford Street where Uncle took me to a big store – I think it was John Lewis –

and told me that he was going to buy me some new clothes to make me look more like an English schoolboy than somebody that just come from colonies or South America. He bought me shorts, jacket – all in a grey colour – and an elasticised belt with a snake fastener. They had no shoes in wide fittings so I had to wear my boots. When I changed in to my new outfit and looked in the mirror my transformation was complete.

When we returned from lunch in the late afternoon and entered the showroom, the whole floor was covered in Ocelot skins. Dad informed Uncle that the auction house had delivered the skins after they had been expected and it was too late to put them into safe cold storage. The firm did not have enough insurance to cover any loss should it be burgled, so after a long discussion between Dad and Uncle they decided that we would have to spend the night at the firm to guard the skins.

I didn't know at that time that much about the fur trade, so Dad explained to me that Uncle had gone to a fur auction and bought all the top lots of Ocelot skins, which had to be marked before going to the dressers .When they came back they would be matched up with one another into similar-looking furs, which would then be put into bundles to go on to make jackets and coats. The firm would keep the best furs and the rest would be sent back to the auction house to be sold on.

In the office I was given tea and biscuit, paper and pencils, and a picture book to look at. The office accountant was a Mr. McKenzie, who told me he was a Scot, but I could not understand him and Uncle had to explain to me where he came from. Later, when I could speak more English we became friends and he was always very kind to me. When the staff departed home Dad ordered from Joe Lyons the usual: fish and chips, and for pudding apple pie and custard, which was another thing that was new for me as I had never had custard before. I found it delicious. For drink I also had something new: my first Coca Cola, which I enjoyed.

After the meal, Dad made a bed for me to sleep on and gave me a book to look at while he and Uncle went into the office to do some work. I don't know when I went to sleep but when I woke up Uncle was opening all the windows to let out all the smell from the raw skins and spraying some scent to make the air smell sweeter. As soon as the staff started work, Uncle took myself and Dad for breakfast. This time we walked a short distance along Piccadilly towards the circus where, on the right side there was another, much bigger Joe Lyons and I was introduced to an English breakfast.

Uncle kept on encouraging me to eat a lot of tomato sauce, saying it was good for me and kept on shaking the bottle over the plate until it was awash with the stuff. After breakfast we all walked to the Jermyn Street barbers where Dad and Uncle had a shave before we all went to a Turkish bath nearby. Turkish baths were no new thing to me as they were similar to a Mikva[12].

Having been refreshed with breakfast and bath Dad had to go back to the firm. Uncle decided to give me a sightseeing tour around the West End. We walked to Piccadilly Circus, then Regent Street where I was captivated by the fantastic shops and neon signs. I was also introduced to the Aladdin's Cave that was Hamley's. Uncle bought me several toys, mainly small wind-up racing cars. After the excitement of Hamley's we walked to Oxford Circus, turned left into Oxford Street where he introduced me to another marvellous shop called Woolworth. It took my breath away; the size of the store and the wonderful things it sold, especially toys. I managed to persuade Uncle to buy me a toy revolver with caps, belt and holster and some toy soldiers, drawing books and coloured pencils.

We then walked back to the firm and when we arrived it was lunchtime. Dad took me for lunch for the usual fish and chips. I did not realise at the time that Dad not being able to speak much English didn't know to order anything else. The rest of the afternoon I spent in the office with my picture book and my new toys until it was time to go home to our digs, thus finishing my first full day in England.

---

[12] A Jewish ritual bath. Couples usually bathe together in it before marriage so they can start their lives together afresh.

Before going to bed, Dad and Uncle decided to discuss with me what I was to do for the next few days and what arrangement had been made about my school. I was told I would be travelling to the business by myself, this time they had written instructions about how to get there and what transport to take. I would have an allowance of a Half Crown a day to cover my fares, food and refreshments that I should need during the day.

By this time I roughly understood what was the cost of my daily requirements was and the different values of the currency. Next, we discussed my school; Uncle explained that I had been accepted to a school called Manor House. I was told that it was a Prep school, but I did not know what a Prep school was. The nearest description I was given was that it prepared you for entering university. Manor House was both a day school and a boarding school. Again, what a boarding school was had to be explained to me. I would be attending as a day school boy and it was impossible for Dad and Uncle to look after me as they had a business to run, so I would be living with an English family called the Joneses, who had a boy the same age as me. I found out that Mr. Jones was a civil servant – a manager of a labour exchange near Waterloo Station – and was a friend of my Uncle. I was also informed that we were going to meet the family that Sunday. They lived in Nightingale Lane, Wandsworth Common and my school was in Clapham Common, North Side and that meant I would have to take a short bus ride in the morning and evening. I soon got used to travelling to different places around London by myself, but my favourite pastime was either to visit Hamley's or Woolworth's to spend my spare cash on toys.

Another one of my favourite things to do in the day was to wonder around St James' park, which was just across from our firm. I would walk through the park to Buckingham Palace and watch the changing of the guard, then walk back to listen to the band playing on the bandstand. When Sunday came I was looking forward to the meeting with apprehension. We were invited to tea at four o'clock and it was a long journey from Chalk Farm.

We eventually arrived at the house, which was an old Victorian detached house that stood three stories high with stained-glass windows in the front door. We were greeted by Mr. Jones, who was tall, smartly dressed man, took us in to the lounge where we were introduced to the family. The boy's name was Ray; we sort of looked at each other but we could not converse as neither of us could speak the other's language (however, now we do, to this day we still keep in touch). We sat down and we were served with cakes and biscuit. Dad and Uncle were in deep conversation with the Joneses; I supposed that they were discussing what the necessities would be for my school and what sort of payment they would require for looking after me. The arrangement, when it was finalised, was that I would be coming to stay with them the following Friday. We said our goodbyes and, on the way back to London, Uncle suggested that we break from our journey home and have diner at Lyon's Corner House at Marble Arch. When we arrived there, the place was very big and very impressive; the waitresses wore uniforms and on the stage there was a pianist playing and a female violinist accompanying him. The meal was marvellous, especially the ice-cream at the end of it.

The next few days flew by, but on Thursday Uncle told me that the Joneses had had second thoughts about having me stay with them and withdrew the offer of having me, as Mrs. Jones decided that it would be too much for her to look after a boy who had no knowledge of English. The good news was that Mr. Jones suggested his deputy, a Mr. Abbott, who was married and had a daughter two years younger than me would be able to look after me during my school holidays and I would be a boarder in school.

It was arranged to meet him the following Friday to discuss arrangements. Mr. Abbott came to the firm and straightaway I liked him. He was the same age as my father, spoke some German through being in the army during the occupation after the First World War. We agreed that all of us would go down to Ewell in Surrey where he lived. The journey from Waterloo was quite short and Mr. Abbott met us at the station and we had a short walk to his house. I did not know at the time that this was real English suburbia. The house was situated

in a cul-de-sac of fourteen houses, all of which were slightly
different to one another, but all had been built in early thirties.
They were beautifully kept with the lawn in front cut and
manicured. We entered the house and met his wife and daughter.
When we introduced ourselves he said that if I was going to live
with them I will have to call him Uncle Charlie and his wife
Auntie Sofie which I did for the rest of their lives. Their
daughter's name was Jean and we still keep in touch. Auntie
Sofie prepared tea for us in their wonderful garden – it was my
first introduction to an English suburban tea. What surprised me
were the sandwiches, which were filled with meat paste,
cucumber and cream cheese; they were so thin I could eat them
three at a time. Whilst they were eating Auntie Sofie took me
upstairs and showed me the room where I would sleep, the
cupboard where I could put all my clothed and the bathroom
where to put my washing paraphernalia, during which, although
we could not converse, we managed with sign language. My
Uncle, father and Uncle Charlie was decided that I would be
joining the family the following Saturday. I would receive pocket
money of one shilling a week, which was twice as much as the
boys in my school were receiving.

On Saturday, Uncle Charlie arrived at our digs to pick me up,
Uncle Joe hailed a taxi we all drove to Waterloo Station. We said
our goodbyes, Dad told me that he and Uncle would come to see
me in couple weeks' time, and then it was time to part ways.
	The journey to Ewell was only seventeen minutes and
when we arrived we walked to his house carrying my luggage.
When we arrived, Auntie took me straight away to my room,
emptied my suitcase on my bed and, as it was nearly tea, we
decided to sort everything afterwards. Uncle Charlie explained
that Saturday they have what is called a high tea so that Auntie
Sofie did not have to cook an evening meal. I did not quite
understand what he meant so I sat down at the table which was
laid out with the food that we were going to eat. There were ham
slices, lumps of cheese, bread and butter and a large bowl of
lettuce with cut tomatoes, cucumber and spring onions. Uncle

Charlie dished out the ham and we all helped ourselves to everything else. Everyone around me was helping themselves to a bottle of white stuff and pouring it on the salad, but I had no idea what it was. I was told that it was called salad cream; in Poland, we only ever used French dressing. I had a little taste and found it delicious. After we had our first course, Auntie produced a trifle, home baked fruitcake, raspberry sponge and fruit for pudding. When we had finished our meal, Auntie and I went up to my room to sort out my things and to hang up my clothes in the wardrobe. She threw out my white linen suit and made Uncle Charlie explain to me that the suit was totally unsuitable for England and the plus fours were only worn by men playing golf or older men. In the country, boys of my age wore grey shorts and jacket with long socks below the knees and I was told that we would be going shopping during the week for extra clothing. Later I discovered she made use of my white suit by making a costume out of it.

When everything was put away, we went down to spend the evening in the lounge. There was a large bookcase with set of pictorial encyclopaedia which I was told were for my use. I was told to look at books at any time, which would help me with my English. In the lounge there was also a large table and chairs, which I found out later were made by Uncle Charlie in his spare time as wood working was his hobby, and he had a workshop in his garage instead of a car. There was also a large wireless on a small table next to the open fireplace (which was also new for me) as at home we had tiled fire stoves to heat the rooms and in winter to dry our clothes on. There were photo pictures on the walls and a beautiful white Indian carpet.

When we were all in the lounge, Uncle Charlie presented me with a toy racing car and said I could play with it on the table. That was when I made one of my biggest mistakes. Uncle Charlie and Auntie Sofie were listening to one of the shows on the radio and I was playing with my car on the table, on which I thought Auntie had left a cushion and as I was playing I kept moving it and I pushed it off the table. I had not realised that it was a tea cosy on top of a teapot. I had never seen a tea cosy before – I had not seen a lot of things in England before, as you can probably tell by now. As it hit the floor there was a big crash of broken china and the white Indian carpet was covered with tea and tea leaves. I was totally aghast at what I had done, but Auntie Sofie came over to me put her arms around me held me, stopping me worrying. She then went in to the kitchen, brought a small pale off water with some cleaning liquid in it and sponged the tea stain in the carpet. I tried to help her, but she would not let me. She worked on the stain for some time and eventually managed to get the stain out.

Before going to bed, he asked me if I could ride a bike. I told him although I had never possessed one, I had ridden one many times. He explained to me – which took some time as neither one of us spoke that much German – that Auntie Sofie and Jean went shopping to the village every day and once or twice a week to neighbouring small towns Sutton, Cheam, and Epsom. He then mentioned that Auntie had an old bike that I could have for my own use which he would show me in the morning. I was all excited and thanked them several times for this wonderful gift.

Soon after, Jean and I were sent to bed. It was strangely quiet, not being used to the silence of the country after the noise of London. Next morning, after breakfast, auntie took me to the garage and showed it to me, it was her old lady's model with a basket in front on the handle bars, and the brakes were the old fashion rod type. I thought it was the most beautiful present I ever had. At long last I had my own bike. Auntie told me that we were going shopping to the village and that we would be going on our bikes. Wherever we went, Auntie Sofie used to stop to speak to people she knew and always introduced me to them; most of them were very curious and usually asked about Poland. I had a lot of difficulty explaining as my knowledge of English was still very limited and I think most of them did not know where Poland was. We also used to stop at several houses where there were elderly widows living. Auntie always asked them if they needed any shopping from the village which we used to drop off for them on the way back.

From that time on I went everywhere on my bike. Nonesuch Park, which was just at the top of the road, used to be my favourite place to go to play, before they cut of a big section off to build a bypass to Epsom. One of the things I got hooked on whilst living there was comics. One my favourites was a pink one in colour in broadsheet size which was all pictures and I could make out the stories by looking at them. I also started picking up some words of which I made a list of to ask Uncle Charlie what they meant; slowly I started learning to speak English.

The Abbotts were friendly with a family living next door by the name of Boudy. The husband was a director of Stanley Gibbons, famous for trading in coin and stamp collections. They were very kind to me; the husband, who also spoke some German, asked me a lot of questions about Poland. Later, when I could converse a bit better in English he started showing me his stamp albums. He had a large collection of English stamps. Once, when I was asked over for tea he asked me if I ever collected stamps, I told him that I had a small collection of Polish stamps and a large mixed bag of world stamps which my Uncle John gave me in Vienna. He then took a large box from one of his cupboards in the lounge which was full of English stamps from the Victorian, Edwardian and George V eras. He then started sorting them and, as a surprise, he picked up a stamp album which he gave to me, as well as a bag full of English stamps that he had sorted out before and one of his firms catalogue. He told me that that all this was for me to start an English stamp collection of my own. I thanked him for this marvellous gift and every time I came to Ewell for my holidays he always added to my collection. Unfortunately, the collection I had was lost in the Blitz on London during the war.

There was another family that were friends of Abbotts; their name was Mr. and Mrs. Perry. They were considered to be wealthy – the husband was a director of Imperial Chemical Industries (I.C.I.) and they lived in a bigger house with a monkey tree in the front garden. They also had a 14 horse-power Austin and, as a treat on weekends, he used to take all us or a run to his golf club. I realised years later that it was the R.A.C. club at

Epsom where I would go once a year for lunch with my old school friends.

The days flew by and about fortnight after I was at the Abbotts', Auntie informed me that she had received a list from my school detailing all the things I would require as a boarder, and that we would be going to London to shop at the shop Swan & Edgar, which had an arrangement with my school to supply school uniforms and sport gear. She also told me that we would be lunching with Dad and Uncle Joe.

When the day came, Auntie, Jean and I boarded the train to Waterloo and then a bus from the station to St. James' Park station, which was close to the firm. When Uncle saw me he was surprised how much I had advanced with my English and took us all for lunch to Joe Lyons. After lunch we left Dad and Uncle as they had to return back to the firm and we walked to the store which was on the corner of Regent Street and Piccadilly Circus. When we entered the store to me it looked enormous with the amount of goods it stocked. We went in to the boy's department, where I was to be fitted with a grey flannel suit.

I tried on several suits and we came across a problem: the trousers fitted me perfectly, but the jackets were about two inches too small. As the suits came as a two-piece set there was a long discussion between Auntie and the manager whether to buy a larger suit and alter the trousers. Eventually Auntie decided that I would keep the trousers and we would take the jacket from another suit. I had no more trouble with rest of my clothing until it came to trying on my new shoes. Before the war it seemed that in England very few firms made shoes in broad-fitting sizes and, unfortunately, I have a very broad foot. Having always had handmade boots and shoes in Poland, that problem had never arisen before this point. We went to the Men's department to see if any of their shoes would fit me but to no avail, so we went to the main shoe department to see if they could do something for me. I tried several pairs of shoes and eventually the only shoes that would fit me were brogues so I became the only boy in school who did not have plain shoes. We than went to the sport department where I was fitted out with white flannel trouser white shirts, pullover and blazer with school colours around the edges, school cap and ties, cricket bat with gloves and pads. Then we had to choose my football gear, shorts, shirts, socks, in school colours boots and shin pads, then a wooden racket and balls to play a game on a three-sided concrete court called Rackets, and finally shorts, vest, boxing gloves and plimsolls. I knew nothing about these games except football which I had played in Poland. There were so many parcels that Auntie arranged the whole lot to be delivered to Uncle Joe's firm so Dad and he would bring them down to Ewell.

7 - Me in my new school outfit.

After we left the store and walked along Oxford Street. Auntie did some more shopping for herself and then we returned back to Ewell in time to cook supper for Uncle Charlie. As the weeks went by, I gradually began to speak and understand more and more English. Uncle Charlie bought me a kit to build a model airplane in which I became very interested and spend a lot of time building it.

As the time was getting near for me to join my school, I was becoming more excited as well as a little apprehensive. The day I would join my school was in September, a few days after my birthday. Auntie explained that she would be going with me and, as a boarder, we would be travelling a day before the school started, to meet the Headmaster, matron and other staff, even the boiler man whose job would be to polish my shoes and boots. When the great day came, all my clothes were packed into a large trunk. I also took with me a small case that was my tuck box which Auntie stuffed with jams, marmalade, Marmite, biscuits and small cakes, of which she told me that they were extras to eat at tea time. After all the packing was finished we all went to the station, Uncle helping with the luggage, we said our goodbyes and Auntie and I were off. When we arrived at Waterloo station, Auntie got hold of a porter to take my luggage to the taxi rank and arrange a taxi to take us to my school. When we arrived we drove through large gates with the school name above them. The drive led us to a large building with very prestigious entrance through which we entered. We rung one of those old fashioned pull bells and a maid opened the door asking us whom we required. Auntie informed her that I was a new boy joining the school and that the Headmaster was expecting us.

The maid called the porter to take my luggage and asked us to wait while she went to tell the Headmaster of our arrivals. I looked around in the hall where we were waiting, which was filled with First World War memorabilia; there were rifles, different models of steel helmets, uniforms and many pictures of old pupils who were in army uniforms. When the maid came back she escorted us to the Headmaster's private study. When we entered there were already two gentlemen who wore long black gowns and a funny sort of hat. Later I had to be explained that all school masters that had a university degree were entitled to wear academic attire – it was called cap and gown. The elderly gentleman introduced himself Dr. Maxwell – he was the headmaster – and the other gentleman was Mr. Blackwell who was to be my housemaster. Mr. Blackwell spoke German thankfully. The Headmaster explained to us that the school was divided into four houses and that my house would be Wilberforce house. While Auntie was discussing with the Head details about fees, pocket money, holidays and half term, Mr. Blackwell took me on a tour of the school. He showed me a huge, long room, explaining as he did to me that this was where the assembly and morning prayers were held every morning. He then pointed out along the wall, which looked like massive doors that reached right up to the ceiling and explained that they were partitions which divided the room into four smaller sections, which became the 3rd, 4th, 5th and 6th year classes. I would be in the 3rd year class which meant I would drop a year; he explained that because my English was so limited, it would be impossible for me to do the 4th year curriculum.

He then took me up stairs to the first floor and showed me another large room which he explained was the common room for both for junior and senior boys, which was used by pupils during their leisure time to read books and comics and play games. It was also used for choir practice and amateur plays. Then we walked to the second floor where he introduced me to the matron, who was a very kind and helpful lady. He explained that she was responsible for looking after the boys' health and needs other than schooling; she was a qualified nurse and should I be ill there was a small infirmary for which she was responsible. Before leaving me with the matron, Mr. Blackwell informed me that besides being my housemaster he would be my history teacher. The matron took me to the fourth floor to continue the tour of the rest of the building. There were seven dormitories on the floor. She opened one of the doors to a large room which had eight beds, beside each of which there was a small wardrobe with draws underneath, a wash stand with basin and a jug on top. She pointed to one of the beds and said that that bed was to be mine, speaking slowly so that I could understand. She told me what clothes to put in the wardrobe and those that I did not need every day, which was mainly sport gear, should be kept in the trunk. She then proceeded to explain that a maid would come every morning and evening to fill our jugs with hot water to wash with morning and evening. There was also a bathroom and a rotor in which order we could use it. We then went back with my tuck box to the floor below where there was a whole wall of small lockers; she pointed out to one of lockers, gave me a key and told me to put all my goodies inside and anything else that I wanted secure like stamps album, camera and comics.

The matron then took me back to the Headmaster's study where there was another master, who I discovered was a junior sport master. He proceeded to take me around the grounds to the racket courts and pointed out all the places in the grounds that were out of bounds, such as Headmaster's garden. When we returned back to the study once more, Auntie was waiting for me having finished her business with the Headmaster. Preparing to leave, she asked me if I was happy with what I had seen of the school to which I replied that yes, I had. She also informed me that Dad and Uncle Joe arranged for me to stay with her and Uncle Charlie for the Christmas holidays, as Dad would be away in Paris and when the time would come, arrangements would be made for me to travel back to Ewell. A taxi was arranged to take her back to Waterloo Station and I waited with her until it arrived.

After Auntie left, the sport master took me to show me the dining room, which was another very large room with a dozen long tables and chairs. He explained that this was for boarders only and the table at the top was for the Headmaster and teaching staff. There were to be four meals a day, except Sunday when dinner would be served at lunchtime and, since it was coming to lunchtime we would be having it together as most of the boarders wouldn't be arriving until that afternoon. The lunch consisted of soup, a sandwich, fruit and a glass of milk. It was a bit of a boring meal, but it was sufficient to sustain us. While we were eating he told me the times that the meals were served: breakfast 8a.m., lunch 12.45p.m., tea 4p.m. and supper at 6.30p.m. Classes started at 9a.m. until 12.30p.m. and again at 2p.m. until 3.30p.m., and after tea at 4.30p.m. We had to do our homework for one hour a night before our free recreation time, after which we had our supper.

Juniors went to bed at 7.30p.m., third years at 8.30p.m. and seniors at 10p.m. He then handed me over to the matron who told me to go to the dormitory to amuse myself reading my comics while waiting for new roommates. I was a bit apprehensive about meeting the new boys as I wasn't quite sure how we would get on, what with me being Jewish and not being able to speak much English. The first boy to arrive was called Arthur Figgins. We introduced ourselves and during our discussion I found out that he lived in Cricklewood with his family (which was not far from where my family was living in London at the time), and that his father was a civil servant who spent most of his time abroad. He was the same age and height as me and we took to each other right away; he collected stamps so right away we had something in common. Soon after arrived four junior boys between 7- and 9-years-old, whose fathers were also Civil Servants in India and Ceylon, then two more boys arrived who were friends of Arthur. He introduced me to each of them; one was named Charlie Leys, the other Monty Montenbaum. Both Charlie and Monty's parents were divorced and so they lived with their mothers during their holidays in London. I soon lost my apprehension as we all seemed to get on so well together.

As it was nearly teatime we went to our lockers to get our cakes and jams and proceeded to the dining room where I discovered that the tables were allocated according to different houses. We decided that we would all sit together in the future. The tea at school consisted four slices of bread and butter with two slices spread with meat or fish paste the other two with thinly spread jam, and a small piece of fruit cake was also provided. Of course, our own goodies were swapped around among ourselves. During teatime Monty pointed at the ceiling in the dining room where there were hundreds and hundreds small pieces of rolled up paper stuck to the ceiling, Monty explained to me that one of the traditions in school was that every new boy took a small piece of paper wrote his name, address and date of joining the school rolled it up tight then you chewed the end it until it was pulpy and when it was it was nice and moist you threw it up to the ceiling where it stuck. The trick was to do it without being seen by a master. I made one right away and managed to stick it up without being caught. Then he pointed out to an enormous grandfather clock which stood at the far end of the room, explaining that the clock had a door at the back and every new boy made a small flag on a pin with his name and date and stuck it inside. Arthur, Charlie and he would help me so that I would not be caught. The other tradition to become 'one of the boys' was, during summer, when the strawberries had ripened in the Headmaster's garden, to acquire one of them without being caught nabbing them. Monty said that he and the boys would help me with that task too.

After tea, matron called the four of us and, as we were the oldest in the dormitory, we were told that we would have to look after the youngsters in the morning, making sure that they wash, clean their teeth, dress and comb their hair with whatever dressing they had. She also informed those of us who were new to leave our shoes outside the dormitory door to be cleaned and polished and that they would be there for collection in the morning, then we were left to go to the common room to swap stamps, read comics or whatever other activity we were interested in. Charlie had a model fighter plane kit which he was building so we discussed which was the best way to build it as I had already build one which I left in Ewell.

At 6.30p.m. we went down to dinner which started with the Headmaster saying grace. The meal was edible but not great, we started with so-called onion soup which was more like boiled onions in bouillon, which made me dislike boiled onion to this day, meat pie with mash, cabbage and carrots and for pudding we had tapioca which no one liked but me. After dinner the time was our own, we went to play in the school grounds, I asked Arthur how do you play rackets on the rackets court, and he explained the game to me with difficulty so he suggested that the following evening if it wasn't raining we would bring our bats and balls and we would play a game. I thought it was very kind of him but he said not at all as he was third form racket captain and he wanted to see how I would adapt to the game. Soon it was our bedtime. When we entered the dormitory our jugs with hot water were waiting for us and by each bed there was a saucer with a glass of milk and a biscuit. We quickly washed and changed in to our pyjamas and dressing gown, matron came to check whether we had done a good job getting the younger boys to bed, and then the lights went out at 9p.m. We were told we could play games as long we were quite or read our books and comics. We all had torches, so if one of us had a good book or comic we carried on reading under the blankets. So ended my first day in school.

The next day after breakfast we went to the assembly hall where there were tables with many books on them. There was also a large notice board with the curriculum for the autumn term for each class. We all were given our notebooks, then we were directed to one of the tables relating to our classed where we were issued with whole lot of books that we would be using during our school year. We were also issued with exercise books and stationáry, although most of us had fountain pens. Mine was a Swan, which had to be filled with an eye dropper. We were then allocated our desks. They were the type that the seat and the desk were one unit and had a white ceramic inkwell in the right hand corner. I had a quick look at my books which were maths, geography, history, English grammar and another English book which I discovered later was English literature. Also, there were language books; I recognised one as French grammar but the other one I did not recognise until one of my friends told me that it was Latin grammar. We were then told that there would be no prep in the evening on the first day but we would be required to gather in the common room so that we could be evaluated for what sport and leisure activities we would do during the term, then the partitions were drawn across the room our classes started.

The first class was mathematics taken by a Mr. Austin. It suited me fine as I realised that I was a bit more advanced than what I was being taught. English grammar was very difficult as I hardly could understand what the teacher was saying; I also found difficulty with understanding history but it was very interesting as the history book had many pictures which helped me understand what the lecture was about. Geography was easy as I was always interested in maps, hoping to visit some of the countries when I was older. However, most of the geography lessons there were about Britain and the British Empire. I did not realised how vast the dominions and the colonies were. The real difficulty came when it came to us having French and Latin lessons.

Although languages were taught in Polish schools, they did not start doing so until students were twelve years old, and the teachers at Manor House tried to teach me grammar in these languages when I could hardly understand the English they were referencing, so rather than learning English and then French and Latin, I was left to learn parrot-fashion the words and the grammar without understanding of what it was I was learning. I felt very isolated and alone until I got a better grasp on the language.

My friends also told me that each class had a detention book. I wasn't quite sure what they meant, so they explained that if someone misbehaved in the class – such as talking during the lessons or flicking blotting paper – your name was entered in the book and after prep you lost your play time. Instead, in that time you were made to write a specific number of lines for half or the whole hour, depending on how badly behaved you had been. In severe case, like smoking, spitting, arguing with the teacher and especially being caught stealing the Headmaster's strawberries, you could get the cane. The Headmaster had the privilege of administrating this punishment. My friends and I were not bad, but we were mischievous. We managed in my first term to acquire more detention time that it was possible to do in a term. I was lucky not having to do lines for my punishment for the masters who were in charge of detention thought that my time would be spend better learning as much English pronunciation as possible, so they gave me Shakespeare plays like Twelfth Night to read and learn. By the end of the term I could remember passages from the plays but, again, understood very little of what they meant. Myself and my friends also discussed our teachers – which were tolerant and which were strict. One of the masters that every boy hated was a Mr. Rees who also had a son in fourth form. I was told by my friends to totally ignore and never to speak to him. I asked why and I was told that he was a 'Sneak' and had been put in 'Coventry'.

I did not know what 'Sneak' was so they explained to me that he told tales about the boys to his father and some of them were punished. Among the boys, 'Sneaking' was considered the worst thing you could do and putting someone in 'Coventry' meant that you were totally ignored and no one would have anything to do with you.

I had one nasty incident that day. After tea I was the first one for assembly in the common room to read my new comic before my friends came. I found myself a comfortable easy chair at the top end of the room. As I was reading a senior boy came up to me and started shouting at me and speaking very fast in English and finishing saying do you understand. Of course, I didn't understand so I said "no". He then grabbed me and pushed me on to the floor. Just then another senior boy, who must have come in as I was being shouted at, grabbed hold of him, shaking him hard and telling him off in very loud voice. The other boy was trying to explain what he had said to me and what my reply was, and the other boy shouted at him again telling him that of course I didn't understand what he was saying, as I did not speak English and should anything like this happen again he would be up before the Headmaster. The other boy left red-faced and the other introduced himself to me and told me that he was the Head Prefect, he also explained to me that although this was the common room, it was divided into two parts, the dividing line being the partition rails in the floor. The top end was for the seniors and the other end was for the juniors. I told him that I was sorry but no one had told me the rules, he then told me that I shouldn't have any more trouble as he would be keeping an eye on me. I thanked him for his kindness and he left. I found out later that the aggressive boy was the son of the Italian ambassador at the time; he left at the end of the term.

When we eventually assembled in the common room, we were asked by different sports captains what games one could and would like to play. I put my name down for football and rugby. The cricket captain asked me why I didn't put my name down to play cricket, so I told him I knew nothing about the game and never played it. He suggested that either the following Wednesday or Saturday – which were our half days when we would play sports on either Clapham Common or Spencer Fields – he would try me out in the cricket nets. The outcome was that I was chosen for all three second eleven teams, but I was useless in athletics, I suppose because of the problems I had with my legs when I was a child. Then it was the turn of the music teacher, he asked me if I could sing. I told him that in Poland I had sung in a choir, and so straight away he tested my voice, which had already broken. After the test he told me that my voice had a quite good tenor sound and that I would be a useful addition to the choir so he would like me to join. I didn't realise at the time that it was a church choir. Next came the drama teacher, but I told him I had no interest in acting as I had tried it and was no good at it. I also joined a photographic group which came to be one of my hobbies in school.

The school had an O.T.C. unit (Officers Training Corps), but you couldn't join until you were sixteen. But they also had a junior O.T.C., which was similar to the army cadets. I was told I could join although I wasn't British, as many nations at the time sent their young men to train at Sandhurst, then return home to re-join their own units.

My friends, who already were members, persuaded me to join, telling me what great fun it was to be a member. The following week, when the junior O.T.C. squad was formed, I became a member of it. We were allocated uniforms similar to the army cadets in khaki with a forage cap. Our racket court became part of our rifle range; we had to lay down sandbags before pinning our targets on them and firing our rifles. We didn't use full bore army rifles but BSA Martini action 22. calibre. We were taught map reading, field craft and marching drills. We were supposed to go for two weeks to an army camp for training at the end of our spring term, but something went wrong and we never went. Later on, all this training became very useful when I was called up for the army.

One of the subjects I had to do was scripture. I was okay at the subject when studying the Old Testament, but I knew nothing of the New Testament. Singing lessons were mainly learning hymns and our school song, which at the time I didn't understand until later, but I sang them parrot fashion.

One of the sports I hated was boxing. To box you have to pump yourself up mentally to dislike the boy you were going up against enough that you wanted to hit him. I could never do that successfully and I was usually beaten. After a few weeks I asked my sportsmaster if he would take me out of the boxing team so I could do something different. He suggested Indian clubs exercises which I enjoyed very much.

A few weeks into term, my friends told me that we were going to have a "midnight feast". I didn't know what it meant so they described how that, from time to time, they saved their pocket money and then on the Saturday, when we were not playing games, they would go to the Clapham Common shopping centre called The Plough to buy goodies.

When Saturday came, we went down to The Plough and bought jellies, tinned fruit, sardines, rolls, biscuits, ginger beer and, if we could afford it, some corned beef. We had to smuggle all these goodies back into school without being caught, for the feast to start after midnight. I asked one of my friends how we were going to make the jellies and I was told that when the maid brought our hot water to wash, we would save one off the jugs to melt our jellies.

The shopping was a great success. When we went, there was a grocery store which had an automatic machine where you could insert 3d. or. 6d. coins and it dispensed different tins of food. I thought it was a marvellous machine as I had never seen one before. The feast was a great success, except for the jellies which never set so we had to have liquid jelly with our tinned fruit. Our difficulty arose when it came to the disposal of our tins and cardboard wrappers. There was an eight foot wall around the grounds which divided our school from a girls' school on the other side. To get rid of all of our refuse, we threw the rubbish over the wall and, of course, the girls threw it back again. There must have been a lot of harsh correspondence between the two headmasters and we were all questioned about it and we were always pillars of innocence and the matter used to be settled quite amicably. On other Saturdays when we went shopping, we used to go to Clapham Junction where there was a much bigger shopping area like Woolworths where we used to buy our toys, which was a most enjoyable way to spend our afternoon. About the fourth Saturday after I joined the school something remarkable happen to me when we went shopping at Clapham Common.

When we arrived, there was a huge crowed waving Union Jacks and a massive police presence. We asked one of the policemen what was happening and he informed us that King George VI and Queen Elizabeth were coming to open some civic building. We decided to stay and see them. The police sorted out the crowd and made sure that all the young children were in front. Suddenly a convoy of Daimler limousines arrived and stopped in front of us. When all the people had dismounted and started walking with their couriers and security escorts, I recognised the King from his pictures, shaking hands with local councillors on the way to the building.

People were cheering and waving their flags and I thought how marvellous it was. There I was, a Jewish boy from a little town in Poland, seeing the English monarch amongst his people without a military presence and only minimal security. I was bit disappointed seeing the King wearing a bowler hat and a dark suit and the Queen wearing a hat with flowers after seeing their coronation photos when I had walked down Oxford Street; I thought it was a bit tame, but the whole experience was very exciting. Then I never would have thought that years later my wife and I would have the honour of being invited by their daughter Queen Elizabeth II to a reception at Buckingham Palace.

One of the things that we were taught at school was sewing. We had to learn to mend socks, sew on buttons and make a flannel glove to wash with. Later on, all these things became very useful to me in the army, in my bachelor days and later on in my work.

During my first term I began to fall into a routine, but there were several amusing things that happen that term just before the half term. I was called to the Headmaster's study, not knowing what to think, wondering if I had done something wrong, but when I entered standing there was Molly, my uncle's showroom model, who rushed towards me and gave me a big hug. The Headmaster suggested we have some tea and then left us together. She was as beautiful as ever. She gave me a half crown and told me all the news about Dad and Uncle. She then told me the reason for her visit was on behalf of the family to see how I had been progressing in speaking English and was surprised at how far I had come in such a short space of time. The other reason for her visit was to make arrangements for my half term. She explained that I would not be able to come up to London during the half term as it was a very busy time for Dad and Uncle with the firm. Instead she would be picking me up to take me in her car to auntie Sofie in Ewell. We chatted for a while but she had to return back to the firm. I walked her back to her car, which was an open two-seater M.G., we said our goodbyes and she left. When I walked back to the school building I found myself very popular not only with my friends but also with some of the senior boys; not only did I know a beautiful model but one with an M.G., which was every boys' dream car at the time. The seniors especially asked me if she would be coming again and if they could be introduced to her. I told them that I would see what I could do.

Shortly after I returned from my half term, Dad came to visit me in school. We had the usual tea with the Headmaster and then he left us alone to talk. We both started to try out on each other our English, to see which of us had improved the most; it seemed I had advanced much more than he. He then told me all the news; how the firm was doing and that he had started evening classes to improve his English. One of the things he had to do for his lessons was to read Dickens novels. He always had his attaché case with him, like most men on the continent, and he had it with him today. Half way through the conversation he opened it, reaching in and took out a small roasted shoulder of lamb and told me to start eating it. I started laughing, asking him why he had brought this food. He told me that he had read in a Dickens novel how badly the boys in boarding schools were feed and never had enough food. I then had to explain to him that those were Victorian stories and things were very much different now; the school gave me plenty of food to eat.

Then he started telling me that he had a letter from Mum and Rozia informing him that they were having a tough time back in Poland, being short of money. He told me he was working on some schemes to be able to send them some money and goods. One such scheme was that, although Uncle couldn't pay him wages as he didn't have a work permit and could only give him money for food, fares and rent, Uncle could give him a concession to all the fur off-cuts and Mink and Sable tails that could be sold to give him some income. He would staple ten Sable tails between two pieces of cardboard and send them as a letter to Mum, who could then sell them on to Hasidic Jews, who used them to make their hats. (I think at that time the going rate per tail was 20 Zloty, about £1, which was great help to her.) Another one off his schemes involved him getting my uncle Joe to guarantee a bank loan for £500 for three months. Before the war the bank rate for loans was 1.75%. He then paid his loan into a building society account which paid 2.5%. Every three months, he would pay back the money to the bank and then do the same thing all over again. Even though it wasn't much profit, it gave him some extra cash. He then told me that he had to go Paris as, although I had an indefinite student visa to stay in England, he was on a visitor's visa, which had to be renewed abroad every six months. One of Uncle's friends in Paris was to arrange for the renewal so he could come back to England. In the two years before the war he had to travel to France, Belgium, Germany and Holland for his visa. The last one expired 19th September, 1939, eighteen days after the outbreak of war.

Talking to the Headmaster, Dad discovered that I was learning the New Testament in my scripture class which made him a bit upset. He asked the Head for me to stop having lessons about Christianity. The outcome was that, although I stayed in the class, I was given a pictorial encyclopaedia to read the English words, but I still managed to hear the lessons. Towards the end of term we had to do exams; I asked the teacher if I could do the paper as well as I didn't want to be the odd one out. The teacher didn't object and let me do it (but more on that in a bit).

8 - Myself and Dad in the school photo taken in 1937.

In the October of my first term I got to know about Guy Fawkes, as I knew nothing about him. We heard the whole story about him in our history lesson about how he tried to kill the king and destroy the parliament and since his death we celebrate the occasion. Charlie told me that lots of the boys had some of their own fireworks but each form had a kitty of money with which they bought fireworks in bulk for all of us. We all had to put 2d a week in the kitty. By the time it came to Bonfire Night, we were able to buy a surprising amount of fireworks. When the celebrations came we had an enormous bonfire and setting off our fireworks which was tremendous fun.

About a month before the end of the term, Monty suggested that I start collecting small bits of chalk that were left by the teachers when they were using the big blackboards. I asked him why and he explained that at the end of the term when the whole school is assembled in the great hall, the Headmaster and the house masters gave speeches, distributed certificates and sport prizes for our exams and sport achievements. We also received our school reports from our house masters to give to our parents. Before the assembly there were always chalk fights which consisted of filling small paper bags with ground up chalk and throwing them at the boys from different classes. We also had water pistols filled with water and chalk mixture to squirt at them and they did the same to us.

One source where there was a good supply of ground chalk was from the teachers' chalk sharpeners. There was always a big rush for who would acquire the contents of the chalk sharpeners. When the term ended we all assembled in the great hall and the chalk fights started. It was all in good fun but as soon the Headmaster and the rest of the teachers arrived the fights stopped. The Head and the rest of the teachers walked in wearing their gowns in a thick white haze and a very wet floor and to the top of the hall where there was a long table and chairs for them to sit. The Head never mentioned our fighting, just ignored it as if it had never occurred. We then all had to stand up and sing our school song and then the speeches started, which were not too long and after the speeches came the prize giving. I was surprised and pleased that I came 2nd in scripture and my prize was a copy of the New Testament, which I gave to auntie Sofie and Uncle Charlie. After all the ceremonies finished we went up to our house masters to receive our school reports in a sealed envelope, which we were not allowed to open.

The next morning, after breakfast, we all said our goodbyes, wishing each other a happy Christmas and a healthy new year, hoping to all see each other next term.

Molly arrived in her car at 10a.m. I was waiting for her with my luggage which was loaded into the back of her car and we drove down to the Abbotts' in Ewell. So ended my first autumn term in school in December 1937. After Molly dropped me off at the Abbotts', Auntie Sofie was delighted with my progress that I made in speaking English and that at last I would be able to converse with her properly. She told me all the news about Uncle, Jean and the neighbours. She also told me what plans she had made for us during my holidays. As Christmas was only three weeks away we would be going shopping several times to buy gifts to give to each other. I asked her why as I knew very little about Christmas celebrations, coming from an orthodox Jewish family. In Poland, Christmas was mainly a religious festive occasion and an excuse to get drunk and insult the Jews. She than started telling me that in England, although it is a religious holiday, it is also a big festive occasion where people give each other presents which are placed under the Christmas tree and opened on Christmas morning after breakfast. After that, preparation start for a large dinner which usually consists of roasted turkey, stuffing, Cranberry sauce, sausages, gravy and a lot of vegetables, after that comes the traditional Christmas pudding with thick cream on top, the following day we go visiting family, friends and neighbours. She also told me that in two weeks' time we would be going to London to see Dad, who had just come back from France, and Uncle Joe, with whom we would be having lunch and doing a bit more shopping. In our spare time while waiting to go to London, Jean and I started making Christmas decorations for the Christmas tree and the dining room. Eventually, when the day came to travel to London we were all excited with anticipation and when we arrived we were not disappointed.

From the train station we went straight to the firm. There were lots of hugs and kisses, and then we began to swap all the news. Dad had received another letter from Mum and the update was not good; the anti-Semitism in Poland was growing worse and the conditions were getting very bad. Dad and Uncle were trying their hardest to see if there was a way to bring Mum and Rozia over to England as soon as possible. After he had told us this, Uncle suggested that we leave all our things in the office with Molly and go to admire all the windows in Oxford Street and Regent Street, then return so that all of us could have some lunch together. We left the firm and, as we walked down

Burlington Street, the shop decorations grew bigger and better. As we approached Regent Street, the decorations were out of this world, especially those in Hamley's – in their windows were the Meccano sets made up into cranes, cars, trains and steam engines all moving. Walking towards Oxford Circus, we passed Liberty which had another fantastic windows display, then we turned left in to Oxford Street.

Walking towards Marble Arch the decorations seemed to get even larger and more extravagant, especially John Lewis and Debenhams, until we until we came to Selfridges which was in a class of its own. Crowds of people were pressed up at the windows, each of which had motifs of different fairy tales with figures and animals all moving; it was very difficult to get near, but we managed to get to the front. We followed the crowd all the way around the different displays, which were absolutely magical and very beautiful. After we had seen enough we went in to find the Grotto where there was a Father Christmas, who had hundreds of toys. We didn't buy any as time was getting short; Auntie had a quick look around the ladies department and then it was time to go back for lunch. To me, Christmas was much more festive in England, and came with an emphasis on gift giving, toys and merriment, whereas back in Poland I had viewed it as a purely religious holiday.

Uncle took us to a nearby restaurant and after we finished our meal we all went shopping. Uncle bought several presents for Auntie Sofie and Jean, whiskey and cigars for Uncle Charlie. He also bought some for me which he gave to Auntie Sofie without me seeing so she could give them to me on Christmas day. After we finished our shopping, we returned to the firm where, in his office, were many turkeys all parcelled for the staff. He picked a large one out and gave it to Auntie to take back to Ewell. Dad had come back from France only a week before, so we managed to have a good chat about how I was getting on in school. He was also surprised at how much I had shot up in height. He told as this was the busiest time in the fur trade it would not be possible for him to see me until just before I would be going back to school.

Soon, it was time for us to return to Ewell. Dad and Uncle went with us to Waterloo Station with all our parcels, where we arranged to meet Uncle Charlie and we all returned together to Ewell. The next few days went quickly by. Jean and I did a bit more shopping, buying some gifts for Auntie and Uncle. The preparation and excitement about the day started weeks in advance and only fed the anticipation. Everyone was looking forward to Christmas and there was a sense of collective merriment, with each family trying to create the best Christmas. When Christmas Eve arrived we were all excited; there was a fairly large Christmas tree in the lounge all decorated with small lights and chocolate figures. I was told that our presents would be under it on Christmas day and we would be able to open them after breakfast.

The next morning we all awoke with eagerness, we washed and dressed quickly, went down to breakfast and, after we finished eating, we were told to go to the lounge but not to open our presents until the whole family was all together there.

It was all thrilling when we started opening our presents and we were all pleasantly surprised at the things that we were given. I had a Meccano starter set wind-up toy car and plane, a pencil box with loads of coloured pencils, lots of comics and a packet of stamps from our neighbour next door. When we finished unwrapping all our presents, Auntie departed back to the kitchen and, although the turkey had been cooking for some time, she still had a lot of other things to prepare for our dinner. I was looking forward to eating turkey as I had never tasted it before. In Poland most people ate chicken, duck or goose; turkey, as far as I remember, was not the first choice in poultry. Jean and I played with our toys until dinner while Uncle helped Auntie to prepare the table in the dining room. There were crackers by each place setting, which at that time I did not know what they were for. The dinner started with soup then Auntie brought the roast turkey on a carving board and placed it before Uncle, then she returned to the kitchen for the potatoes and the rest of the vegetables. Uncle started carving, asking each of us whether we wanted leg or breast or both, before putting the meat on each plate which was then passed to each off us after which we helped ourselves to the potatoes and other vegetables. We then pulled our crackers which, inside, had a small toy, a joke and, most importantly, a paper hat which we put on our heads before we started to eat. When we finished eating the turkey and the table had been cleared, Auntie went back to the kitchen and brought back a large Christmas pudding which she placed in front Uncle, who in turn poured Brandy on top of it and set it alight. It was all new to me and I thought how wonderful it all was.

After the flames died down, Uncle served us a portion of pudding and we helped ourselves to some thick cream from a big bowl and a sprinkle of icing sugar on top. After the meal, Auntie and Uncle left Jean and I to play while they went into the kitchen to wash up and tidy the dining room. We were all so full that all we wanted to do was to relax. Sometime later, Auntie told us that we would not be having tea but a high tea towards the evening. About six o'clock Auntie went into the kitchen and produced ham and turkey sandwiches, pickles chutney, salad, mince pies and Christmas cake with thick marzipan and icing on top with fruit trifle and tea to follow. Of course, all this was new to me as I had never taken part in Christmas celebrations.

For next few days I thought that the turkey had somehow grown in size and seemed never ending; there was no refrigeration so we had turkey for every meal: cold, casseroled, sandwiches and salad with turkey pie. Thank God when the New Year came we were finished with the turkey.

So that's how the year 1937 ended for me.

1938

The New Year started with preparations for me returning to school. Auntie Jean and I went shopping to the local Co-op to buy some new shirts and underwear as I had grown out of my old ones. As a surprise, Auntie told me to try on some grey long trousers which fitted, me so she bought me two pairs matching my school jacket, explaining that she had received a letter from the Headmaster that in the coming term all boys in my year would be able to wear them.

The rest of my holidays were spent indoors as the weather was expectedly cold and damp. We could not go out to the park, so to pass the time we either read or played with our toys and soon it was time for me to go back to school. When I returned, I was delighted to see that all my friends had also returned. We all looked smart and grown-up in our long trousers. We started swapping stories about what we had done over the break and what presents we had received and then we did the usual swapping of comics, stamps and cigarette cards.

Spring term was usually boring, the weather being mostly bad and that mean we could not play many outdoor sports on the common, but we did managed to practice on the Rackets court.

There was an announcement on the notice board that from the beginning of this term, once a month, we would be having a social evening with the girl's school adjacent to us, to learn etiquette, how to dance and how to behave like gentleman. There were the usual comments from some of the boys like 'Yuck' and that dancing was only for sissies, but most of us looked forward to the social.

Those of us who had sisters were alright, but when you mentioned to the other boys girls you got a response of blushing and shyness. The first social was quite a success and most of us enjoyed it. We were taught how to ask a girl to dance and how to hold her and, although we were all a bit bashful and self-conscious, when it came to dancing I felt a bit embarrassed, feeling that I had two left feet. I think that feeling went both ways, as I noticed that the girls were also very bashful and blushed a lot.

The socials nearly came to an abrupt end at one point. Some of us were having a midnight feast and, to get rid of the rubbish and tins, they threw them over the girl's school wall, which the girls found and threw them back again. Unfortunately, our Headmaster was going by when they fell on the path in front of him. Right away there were letters between the two Heads and accusations of who was at fault. The outcome was that all the pupils that attended the social came before the Head, who told us that should any of us ever behave in this ungentlemanly manner again the socials would be cancelled and any boy caught throwing rubbish would be expelled from the school for the remainder of the term. After that we never had any trouble and had to find some other way getting rid of our rubbish. Just before half term, Charlie asked me if I would like to spend it with him and his mother and that his mother would get in touch with Auntie to see if it was all right with Dad and make all the arrangements. I thought it was a marvellous idea, as Charlie lived in Camden Road, not far from where Dad and Uncle Joe lived and it would give me an opportunity to see them. When the time came, Charlie and I travelled on the northern line to Camden Town where we were met by his mother who was most welcoming.

Charlie's mother was accompanied by a gentleman whom I discovered later was her new man since her divorce and that one of her reasons inviting me was so that Charlie had a companion to go to different places with and she would have more time with her man. The whole arrangement worked out very well, every morning she gave us money, but we had to tell her where we were going. We went to Madam Tussauds, the cinema, but our most popular place was the news cinema at Marble Arch, which showed loads of cartoons and also had one of the first televisions sets – the type where you looked at a mirror that reflected the picture from the television tube. I managed to take Charlie to the firm and introduce him to Dad and Uncle Joe, but otherwise we were on our own. We had a wonderful time wondering around the West End, but like all things it all came to an end and soon we had to return to school.

The time seemed to pass slowly. At the beginning of March we heard that the Germans had occupied Austria. For the family it was a worrying time as Uncle John, who was still a member of the Austrian government, couldn't be contacted. I didn't understand all that was happening, but I knew it wasn't good. There was nothing in the papers about the anti-Semitism in Europe, as they were more interested in what was going on in

Spain as it was closer to home. They seemed to know very little and didn't believe what they did hear. To the Brits, it was all happening 'over there', so my family in England only heard about what was happening through letters. Even people in Poland didn't believe what was happening. But back in England, it wasn't about the holocaust as everyone was worrying about a war between England and Germany. There was even a propaganda poster in my school comparing how many tanks, planes, ships etc. we had versus the Germans.

As the term was finishing, Dad wrote that although I was going to the Abbotts' I would be coming first to him, as we had been invited by his cousins, the Ratners, for Seder[13], who lived in Stanford Hill and had a son Victor who was about four years younger than me and a daughter a year younger. The husband was a jeweller and a cousin to the jewellers of the same name. Between 1970-80, Victor became quite a famous doctor in Hollywood and many of the film stars became his patients. He was the personal doctor to Elizabeth Taylor and often had to fly to her home in Hollywood. He made headlines in the nineties when he died in suspicious circumstances at his home in the south of France and there was a big court case against his wife and lover.

Before Passover, I travelled to London to be with Dad and Uncle. This was to be my first Passover in England. Before going to the Ratners and partaking in the festivities, Dad and Uncle made sure I was presentable, to make good impression. When we arrived, Dad's cousin Sadie made a big fuss over me, introducing me to some more distant cousins and then told me to go and play with Miriam and Victor while the men went to the synagogue for prayer before the meal. When they all returned from the synagogue we sat down to start the Seder, which seemed to go on for ever. I stayed up for a while for the prayers after the meal, which could have gone on for another two hours, but Victor and I not having done our Bar Mitzvah were allowed to go and lay down. I was half asleep when the meal finished.

---

[13] The meal that traditionally takes place on the first night(s) of Passover.

We thanked the Ratners for the invitation to the Seder, said our goodbyes and went back to our digs where I immediately fell straight asleep. Although orthodox Jews observe two nights of Seders, Dad allowed me to go back to Ewell for the remainder of my holiday. At long last I was allowed to travel by myself to Ewell. Auntie met me at the station to help me with my case and, as usual, made a big fuss over me, telling me how I looked, spoke and behaved like a proper English boy. We had tea and Auntie made my favourite raspberry and cream sponge for me. When Uncle Charlie came home he was also surprised at my progress, saying that now we would be able to have proper discussions.

Through our talks I discovered that Uncle Charlie had served for four years in the army during the First World War, as a gunner on the western front in all the main battles. He would never talked about the battles themselves. He then spent another year in Germany with the occupying force; this was where he learned to speak some German. His present job was as Deputy Director at the labour exchange near Waterloo Station. From then on, it became much easier to discuss many other subjects. His hobby was woodworking and he loved working in oak and made several pieces of furniture in the Tudor style, including a big table that went in the dining room, on which I had played on the first day with my toy car and broke the infamous tea pot. At that time, he was working on a large model of a Galleon called the Golden Hind and asked if I would help. He taught me to safely use a chisel, saw, plane and drill. We worked on the Galleon every holiday, but we never finished it as the war meant we went our separate ways. However, we always kept in touch until he died, aged 97. I still converse with Jean once or twice a year.

The summer term was my favourite as there was so much to do and, as my English was improving, I was finding my studies much easier to do. I remained in second eleven football rugby and cricket teams. There were still football and rugby matches to play before the cricket season started. Just before the rugby season finished, I had an unfortunate accident: while being tackled by a boy from the other team he kicked my knee and dislocated my kneecap. I was taken back to school where the Matron put a cold pack on it and called the doctor, who inspected and prodded my knee. In the end he put an elasticised bandage on it and told me that I had to rest my leg for the next few days and not to put any pressure on it.

I didn't know how good the doctor was but my knee was never right again, as it gave way when dancing one time and plague me with pain all my life. My late wife Aileen, who was an extremely good dancer, was always very suspicious of my excuses not to dance because of the pain in my knee. The injury put a stop to all my sport activities, which made me very sad and I had to spend my spare time reading books. Dad wrote that he and Uncle Joe had received a letter from Uncle John, saying he and his family had escaped from Austria via Hungary and then Romania, where he would obtain a visa for all off them to come to England. Dad was also worried about his sister, who lived in Czechoslovakia, as he had lost contact with her and her family. He never heard from them again; they all lost their lives in the holocaust.

In school, suddenly, on our notice board appeared large maps of Europe and pictures how our forces compared with the Germans. Of course, we had a much larger army with the commonwealth and colonial troops, larger navy with bigger guns and a far more superior air force, with Spitfires and Hurricanes. The word 'Hun' came more and more into conversation and our training in the O.T.C. junior section became more intense; we spent more time on the rifle range and did much more map reading. There was much talk about the war and how when we were older we and had been called up which part off the service we would like to join.

When half term came, I went down to Ewell for a few days. Auntie Sofie had some good and some bad news for me. The good news was that, when my summer holidays started, we would be going again for a week to the seaside to a place called Herne Bay on the South coast. I was terribly excited as had heard a lot about seaside holidays from my friends and how much they had enjoyed them. The only sea I had seen at that point was on the boat crossing the channel when coming to England, so it would be another great experience for me.

The bad news was that I would be changing my school again. Auntie told me she had a letter from the Headmaster that he was very sorry that the school was closing as it was being sold. It had come into some difficult circumstances and he had communicated with the Headmaster of Highfield School near Wandsworth Common, which I knew well having played football against their team, for me to transfer there. The school was about half the size of my present school and so he could only accept some of us. The school had no facilities for boarders but arrangements could be made to board a certain amount of us with teachers who lived locally in larger houses. He also suggested that Mr. Blackwell, whose house was only fifty yards away from the school, was willing to have me. Auntie told me that she would be discussing all these things with Dad and Uncle Joe.

The other news was that I would be thirteen in September and when we came back from our holidays, I would be farmed out to an orthodox Jewish family in Croydon who had a boy the same age as me to study the Torah for my Bar Mitzvah. This was a big blow to me as I had hoped with all the uprooting, I would escape all the rigmarole of having to do a Bar Mitzvah, but I suppose it could not be helped and I knew I had to make the best of it. When I and my friends returned to school from our half term, we all had the feeling of sadness at the prospect of changing our school as we had all made some good friends and enjoyed our school. We could not envisage what the change would be like.

For me it wasn't so bad, but for my friends, as they had been pupils at Manor House since they were seven, it was devastating. For me, it would be the third change in two and half years, but for me what was bad, for the first time in two and half years I had stable life and had made some great friends. The good news was that when everything was sorted out both Charlie and Arthur would be joining me at Highfield and be boarders with me at Mr. Blackwell also. Unfortunately, Monty's mother, who was divorced and married again, was moving to Devon and he would be going to a school there.

During the term those of us who were going to Highfield were taken there to see what the school and classes were like. The curriculum was similar to our own and we would be able to use most of our books there. There were fewer classes and they only had boys up to age sixteen instead of eighteen, but the sadness stayed with us having to leave our school and lose all our other friends we had made.

Towards the end of the term there was the usual swapping of addresses and promises to keep in touch and write, but of course most of these things never happened. As the term was coming to an end I was getting more and more excited towards my holiday at the seaside. We were to have an end of term school party with speeches by all the masters; the party was terrific, the speeches were very sad but also very funny, the Head told us many recollections of the past and about former pupils at what they got up to. We finished our party with three cheers for the Head and the school song with tears in our eyes.

After the party we had our last dinner with all the popular dishes and the deserts that we liked especially; jellies, trifles and sponge cakes. Some of the boys ate too much and were sick but recovered by the morning to be ready to go home. So finished my year in this marvellous school.

In the morning, Molly came and took me with my luggage to auntie Sofie in Ewell and after she left Auntie told me what discussions she had had with Dad and Uncle Joe of the plans for our holidays. We would be going to Herne Bay at the end of the week without Uncle Charlie, as he could not get away from his job. We would be staying in a boarding house facing the sea only a few yards from the beach and after the holidays Dad would be coming to Ewell to pick me up to take me to Croydon to the family that I would be staying with to study for my Bar Mitzvah.

There was a great excitement when the day came for us to go to Herne Bay. We packed our cases with summer clothes, swimming trunks, towels and shorts, buckets and spades. We then caught the train to London where we changed trains. When we were nearing Herne Bay, I saw a great expanse of water and the beach. When we arrived we took a taxi to the boarding house where we unpacked in our rooms. I was very impatient to go to the beach, but Auntie insisted that we have lunch first. At last, after lunch, we went down to the beach with our swimming costumes, towels, beach balls and, of course, buckets and spades. Once we arrived on the beach, Jean and I changed quickly under our towels into our bathing suits and rushed jumping into the sea, not realising how cold the water would be. But I soon overcame the shock I found it very pleasant.

There were many boys and girls swimming in the sea and those that couldn't were jumping off the break water posts trying to swim. I thought it was a brilliant idea as I didn't swim and I thought I would try it. As I was climbing on the break water Auntie came up and asked me what I intended to do. I explained to her that I wanted to learn to swim by jumping off the brake water. She then explained to me how dangerous the sea can be and that she would walk with me along the brake water to see the depth of the water and find out how far I could go out. I started to jump into the sea, really enjoying it and in two days, with the help of some of the boys, I was able to do the breast stroke. It wasn't great, but could be improved with practice. I have never been a good swimmer and I swim very slowly, but I can swim thanks to that holiday.

There was another family staying in the boarding house with two daughters, one was about seven the other, Mary, about my age with whom I got on very well. At that time there was a Disney film called Snow White showing at the cinema and we and the other family decided to go to see it. When we sat in the cinema, I somehow found myself sitting next to Mary. We both enjoyed the film and just before it finished, while the lights were still off, she held my hand and pressed a piece of paper in it to which I quickly put in my pocket. When we arrived back at our accommodation I opened the note which I never forgot: "Mary, 105 Tufnell Park Rd.", and underneath: "if you ever come to London if you can please call." I did manage to see her once and have tea with her parents. While there I explained to her that, being a boarder in school I had very little opportunity to come to this part of London, but I would try and visit again. I unfortunately never had the chance and we lost contact.

The holiday seemed to pass very quickly and soon it was time to go back to Ewell. Uncle Charlie met us at the station and we told him what a super holiday we had had. Then he told me that Dad had phoned and would be picking me up on Sunday to take me to Croydon. When Dad arrived that Sunday, he chatted to Abbotts for a while, giving them the date when I would be returning to stay with them before going back to school. We said our goodbyes and caught the train to London where we then caught a bus all the way to Croydon. On the way he asked me all about my holidays and if I had enjoyed it; I told him all about me learning to swim and how great the water was.

9 - On my first summer holiday in England.

I was a bit hesitant about learning orthodox Hebrew again, as it had been nearly two years since I had even looked at a prayer book. I was also worried about what sort of people I would be staying with. When we arrived at their house, which was a detached four-bedroom house with a large garden in a very pleasant road, the family greeted us with their son Maurice. We introduced ourselves and were invited in to have tea with them. While having tea, Dad discussed with them in Yiddish, which he found much easier to converse in than in English. He asked them who the Rabbi would be who would be teaching me my portion of the Torah, the fees for the service and the date and address of the synagogue where the service would be held at and, of course, the cost of staying with them. When all the details were sorted, Dad said his goodbyes I walked him to the bus stop. I promised him that I would let him know how I was progressing. When I arrived back at the house the lady of the house[14] made me very welcome and was surprised that I spoke such good English. She took me upstairs, showed me my room which looked very comfortable. In it there was a pile of books and comics on a side table beside the bed; she told me that Dad had informed her that I read a lot. She also told me what time we all had our meals and what time I had to be ready in the morning to go and meet the rabbi for my first lesson.

The next morning, when I sat down for breakfast Maurice gave me a funny look and asked me where my Kippur[15] was. Apparently, they were worn all the time by orthodox Jews, whereas I had only known to wear them when I was in synagogue or performing a ritual such as a Seder. I looked and I noticed that he and his father were wearing one; I apologised for the indiscretion and I told them that I only had my school cap with me. They quickly found one for me and told me to use it until I had acquired one of my own. The breakfast started with a small prayer and one after we had eaten; this ritual was done at every meal and, of course, everything we ate was strictly Kosher. I hadn't mixed with any orthodox Jews for the past two years and it wasn't until this moment that I realised just how anglicised I had become.

After breakfast, Maurice and I walked to the rabbi for our lessons. He was a kindly man with a white beard and long side locks and a large black hat on his head. He already knew Maurice but, not knowing me, he wanted the whole history of my Hebrew education. I told him all about myself and my family and the

---

[14] I forget the names of the family members.
[15] Yiddish term for a Yarmulke, or Jewish skull cap.

difficulty I had reading orthodox script. He then asked me if I had brought my Tefillin[16], then I realised that laying Tefillin every morning would be a part of the course.

I told him that I didn't have any, so he told me not to worry as he had a spare set for practice and he was sure that Dad would buy me a set before my Bar Mitzvah, then he asked us to sit down and he brought two books to test how well we could read the Hebrew. Maurice had no trouble and read quite well, but when it came to me I had great difficulty, not only struggling with the correct orthodox pronunciation, but I didn't realised how much I had forgot in the last twenty months of not reading Hebrew, having instead to concentrate on other languages in school. Learning to read a portion of the Torah is difficult at the best of times as it has to be chanted, but the writing had the vowel sounds indicated under the letters in different shapes of dots and it had the chant notes above the letters. However, to make things even harder, the vowel markings and the chant notes are not in the Torah scroll, so you had to learn them by heart for the real thing.

After I had finished reading my piece the Rabbi looked at me and said: "I will have my work cut out to teach you and we only have five weeks to do it in. You will not only study with me but you would take the books with you and read them every evening for an hour with Maurice to help you." The lessons would be Sunday to Thursday, from 9.30-11a.m. and 2-3.30p.m., which meant that, including reading with Maurice, I would be having 20 hours tuition a week, not counting the time in the morning with Maurice teaching me to lay Tefillin. The Rabbi was a kindly man but a very hard taskmaster.

My free time, when I had any, I spent in the garden playing with Maurice and with all the help from him and the Rabbi my reading improved swiftly over the following weeks.

---

[16] Two small boxes containing scrolls of parchment inscribed with verses from the Torah, with leather bindings to wrap around parts of the body. One is worn on the forehead and one on the left arm with the bindings wound around your arm in a certain way. They are a part of the orthodox prayer ritual.

Shortly before the great day came, Dad phoned to tell me that he and Uncle would be coming together to Croydon to support me during the Bar Mitzvah service. They would come to the house so that we could all go to the synagogue together and after the service we would return back to Central London for a celebratory meal. Then, I would be staying the night with them before going back to Ewell to prepare for starting in my new school. When the Saturday came to go to Synagogue, all my clothes were spick and span, wearing my new Kippur and carrying my new prayer shawl and book in my special bag. The only thing that was missing were Dad and Uncle. We all waited for them as long as we could, but we had to leave for the synagogue to be there before the service started. I was very worried as to why Dad and Uncle hadn't turned up, only adding to the anxiety of reading the Torah in front of a congregation. Maurice and I were the only ones to have our Bar Mitzvah that day.

The first row in front of the Bimah[17] was reserved for the families; I kept looking for Dad and Uncle but they still had not arrived. The service started and, when it came to the part where it was time to read the Torah, Maurice and I were called up to the Bimah by our Hebrew names to read our portion. As Dad was still absent, Maurice's father stepped up with me in his place to accompany me to read my portion of the Torah. When the service finished there was no sign of Dad or Uncle so I accompanied Maurice and his family back to his house.

There was a big party laid on for Maurice and all his relations came with present for him. I was invited to join the party for high tea. I remember Maurice received five Fountain pens and several gold watches and when he got up to thank everyone he started by saying "today I became a fountain pen". I wasn't envious as I already had a gold fountain pen and a watch and all the family I had at that time was Dad and Uncle. When tea was nearly over Dad arrived by himself; he was very upset and

---

[17] The raised platform at the front of the sanctuary of a synagogue where there is a table on which the Torah is read.

apologetic. He thanked the family for looking after me and Maurice's father for taking his place and standing with me when I read my portion of the Torah. He then explained that he and Uncle were all ready to come but they had a call from the Police that the firm's alarm had gone off and Uncle had to rush back to the West End to attend to it. Dad had waited for him to come back, but when he could not wait for him any longer he took a bus to Croydon and, after little while, he discovered that he was on the wrong bus which made him even later.

He was invited to have some tea while arranging where the payments for all the services that had I received were to be sent as, being the Sabbath, payments could not be made as it constituted work in the eyes of the Jewish law. Shortly after tea we said our goodbyes, thanked the family for looking after me and Maurice for all the help he had given me. We travelled back to Central London, where Uncle was waiting for us. He told Dad that the alarm went off because of an electrical fault, which had been fixed. He had also booked a table at a restaurant for our dinner. We had a short rest and afterwards we went for our meal. During the meal Dad and Uncle gave me some money to buy myself a present. So finished my momentous day, relieved from all my learning and worries and that I had done everything correctly; now I was officially a man with the trauma of a Bar Mitzvah ceremony behind me.

The following day, Dad and I went for a walk in Regent's Park and dad told me he had received another letter from Mum. It said that although things were getting very difficult in Poland for Jews, she was managing and both her and Rozia were in good health. We had a snack for lunch and then we went back to his digs to pick up my cases to travel back to Ewell. When I arrived at the Abbotts', they were delighted to see me and asked me all about my Bar Mitzvah and how the whole performance went. I told them how hard I had worked to prepare but that it was all worth it and everything went relatively smoothly, despite Dad and Uncle missing it.

Auntie suggested we have some tea and discuss my new school. She told me that she had gone through my clothes in my absence and the only new thing that I would require for the start of school would be a new blazer with a school badge and a Latin motto (which when translated was "Work Pleases Me"). There was no requirement to have one in any specific colour but I did need a new cap and tie which I would acquire in school. She then produced a set of large Indian clubs and told me that they were on the list from the school of things I would require for doing exercises and in no doubt I would have instruction how to use them. I looked at the clubs and I wondered if we would be fighting with them. She then suggested that I better start sorting all the stuff that I would be taking to my new school, which was starting the following Monday. We would be going there on Sunday, to Mr. Blackwell's to settle in, after meeting Dad and Uncle in London.

The week went by very quickly and I spent a lot of time sorting out my possessions. On Sunday, after breakfast, we went on our journey to London where Dad and Uncle met us. We dumped my luggage at the firm and we all went for lunch. During lunch, Uncle told us that the best way to get to the school was to catch the 19 bus at Green Park tube station, which was just opposite the firm, which would take us to Trinity Road in Wandsworth Common, just outside the school. After lunch, we walked back to the firm, collected my luggage and we all went to the bus stop. Having visited the school before when playing football against them, I knew exactly where to get off on the bus. Auntie had Mr. Blackwell's address, which wasn't difficult to find as it was just at the bottom of the road where the school was situated. We rang the bell and the Blackwells greeted us. They told me to leave my luggage in the hall and invited us to have some tea.

After tea, Mrs. Blackwell took us upstairs so we could inspect my room. It was a large room which I would be sharing with Arthur, Charlie and another boy, a year older than us named Edward from another school, who would not be arriving until supper time. There was an adjacent room which would be housing younger boys age 8-9 and we, the older boys, would have to keep our eyes on them. She then showed me all the other facilities that were upstairs. Then we went down where there was a very large room which was to be our common room and an enormous garden at the back with a door in the bottom fence which opened straight onto the common. Soon Auntie had to leave as she had a long journey home. I walked to the bus stop for her journey back to Green Park.

I went back to the house and was told to unpack while waiting impatiently for Arthur and Charlie to arrive. They both came just before supper with the new boy Edward. We all started talking, catching up with the news of what we did over our holidays. They all asked me how I got on with my Bar Mitzvah. Edward, the new boy, seemed to be our type and would fit nicely into our group. We all sat down to our supper and, while eating, Mr. Blackwell told us all about our new school. He then asked us if we had our Indian clubs as they were quite important as they would be part of our morning exercise. We would be getting up at half seven in the morning to wash, dress, have our breakfast and be at school for assembly and prayers by nine o'clock. After assembly we would assemble on the lawn for twenty minutes to exercise with our clubs. Those of us who never had used them before would be taught. The exercise would not very difficult and we should be able to pick up the routine very quickly. One thing the school didn't have was an O.T.C which was a big disappointment to me as I enjoyed shooting on the range and the map reading. The Headmaster's name was Dr. Law.

After dinner, we all went to our common room where we deposited all our comics and books that we had collected during our holidays for all of us to use. We got to know Edward a bit better and discussed our new hobbies, as well as if we had any stamps or cigarette cards to swap. After a while, Mr. Blackwell brought us some cocoa and biscuits before going to bed at nine o'clock, with lights out at ten. We all thought everything was satisfactory at Blackwell's and we all went very happily to bed.

The next morning, at breakfast, we were very eager to go to our new school and find out what the teachers and lessons were like. We were a few minutes early for the assembly and one of the boys told us that only third and fourth year pupils had to do the club exercises on the lawn. Before the assembly, which was held in the main hall, our names were called out to make sure we were all there. We then sung and said our prayer ('Our Father who art in heaven'). When the assembly finished, we were told by one of the teachers to change into shorts and singlets and join the other boys with our clubs on the lawn. When we arrived there was a man putting up a folding table and placing on it a portable Gramophone with a stack of records. I discovered later that he was our Sport master. There were about forty to forty-five boys. The sport master asked the boys that used the clubs before to step aside and reminded them to form three lines with spaces between them. While the other boys were practicing, he explained to us the principle and ways to use the clubs. The clubs were made from wood shaped like a bulbous Crème De Menthe bottle with a lip along the narrow neck to stop them slipping out of your fingers. They weighed between 1-3lbs, you held one in each hand and swing them around your head and back again to complete a circle. You do the exercise to music that is played on the gramophone. The music played were waltzes which had fast and slow rhythms. We had to practice at first very slowly as there was always a danger of hitting oneself on back of the head before you got the hang of it. There were many combinations of the exercises which we were to learn later. I managed to master the swinging of them quickly and enjoyed the exercises very much.

After we finished our exercises we changed back into our uniforms and went to our different classrooms where we met the rest of the boys in our class. Most boys were day borders and lived locally. There was quite a difference between this school and my last one and although the lessons were similar, the discipline was much more relaxed and there was much more horsing around. Those of us who were boarders had lunch at school and the others usually either had a packed lunch or went home and were back in school for two o'clock. One of the boys that we made friends with was the son of the Governor of Wandsworth prison and sometimes took the four of us there for tea. Once there we were taken on a tour and shown around the cells. One of the things we were shown was the death cell where they kept prisoners before they were hanged. It was a smallish room, with a small barred window, consisting of a bed, wash basin and a big bucket. There was also a table where the prisoner and the prison guard had their meals. All this was very interesting but a bit scary.

At this school we had much more freedom than in Manor House. Although we had to do our homework, often after tea, if it was still light, we were allowed to play on the lawn or go through the garden gate onto the common.

Most of the teachers were very kind and my favourite was a maths teacher, Mr. Austin, who was always very interesting. Several weeks after I joined the school I was made a junior prefect. All it meant was that I had to keep some sort of discipline during our breaks in the playground and look out for any bullying.

I and my friends settled down to our school routine, but Edward was always came up with some sort of scheme. None of us have ever smoked and one day he suggested that we ought to try it. As we were adventurous we agreed. He, being the oldest, and looked older than any of us, would buy the cigarettes and matches, and we would give him 3 pence each to purchase the cigarettes. We knew if we were caught the punishment would be the cane and I would lose my position as a prefect. On Saturday, when we went shopping in Clapham Junction, Edward went in to the tobacconist and bought the cigarettes and matches. I didn't know that he bought the strongest ones on the market called Passing Cloud. That night after supper we went to bed and when the lights were out we switched our torches on and quietly opened all the windows in our bedroom. Edward opened the box of cigarettes, passed them around and we lit up. After a few puffs we all felt dizzy and sick. We stopped smoking and laid down on our beds to recover. Arthur was the only one that had to rush out to the toilet to be sick. In the morning I asked Edward if all cigarettes had the same effect; his reply was he didn't know but it was the brand that his father smoked. I didn't smoke again until I was sixteen.

In Clapham Junction there was a variety theatre to which we often wished we could go to and see the shows but couldn't afford. Edward came up with a scheme that someone told him of how we could all get in. He would buy a ticket in the 'Gods' while we waited at the emergency exit at the back of the theatre for ten minutes after he had gone in. While there he would go to the toilet which was next to the back stairs, run down to the emergency exit open it to let us in, we would all go into the toilet and slip into the theatre one at a time where he was sitting.

The scheme worked quite well for a while until one of us was nearly caught. We decided that enough was enough and we stopped doing it. In those days most boys dreamt of owning a motorbike; there was a large second-hand motorbike garage at Clapham Junction and whenever we were there we used to gawk at the motorbikes, the prices ranged from £1 and 10 shillings to £25. After a while, Edward suggested that after Christmas, when we all had some money given to us, when we got back to school we should go and see if we had enough money to buy a motorbike and although we could not ride one on the road Edward suggested that if we all spoke to Mr. Blackwell we could use the large back garden to learn to ride. At first Mr. Blackwell was not keen on the idea but we told him it would be very educational for us to learn mechanics working on the bike and, as we didn't have a lot of money to buy a working machine, we would have to buy one that we would have to take to pieces and restore from a manual before it would be serviceable. After our plea he became quite enthusiastic and suggested we use his shed for our parts and tools. Receiving the O.K. from Mr. Blackwell we decided to spend as little as possible of our pocket money and start saving for our project.

As the term was coming to an end, we started to prepare for our Christmas holidays. I would be going to Ewell, but during that time I would also be going to London before the festivities to spend a week with Dad and Uncle and, if it was possible, they would come for Christmas dinner at the Abbotts'. When it was time to depart we all gave the Blackwell's small gifts that we had bought for them, we wished each other compliments of the season and, hoping to see each other next term, left for our homes.

It was so good to see the Abbotts again and I really felt that this was my home, being able to converse with them properly and understand the humour on the radio so that we could laugh together was a wonderful experience. Auntie told me of the arrangements that have been made for us to go to London. I forgot how much I missed riding the bike with Auntie and visiting friends in the village.

But, soon it was time for me to go to London. When I arrived the whole place looked like an Aladdin's cave, there was such gaiety and energy. Not since coronation had I seen shops so decorated with all the goodies. Everyone seemed to be looking forwards to the festivities. I made my way to the firm where Dad and Uncle, as usual, made a big fuss over me and wanted to know all about my new school and my accommodation. It was decided that we would go out for lunch but first I had to say 'hello' to the staff in the workroom. It was so nice to see them all again and to be able to understand them and converse without losing half of what they were saying. There were some new faces in the workroom, refugees from Vienna and old friends of my Uncle, who had worked with him when he lived there.

When we returned from lunch, dad told me that he had received word that conditions in Poland had worsened. He and Uncle feared for mum and Rozia; they had no faith in Mr. Chamberlain's piece of paper and were trying to secure visas for them to join us in the UK. Uncle Joe knew a lot of influential people and Uncle John in America still had a lot of friends in the diplomatic service and they were both trying to acquire the necessary document. During the week, dad and Uncle had very little time for me except in the evening, as it was their busiest time of the year for business. They gave me lots of pocket money to go and amuse myself with. I didn't spend it all and saved a portion of the money towards the motorbike.

On Saturday, the firm closed at one o'clock and we all went for a lunch near Regent's Park, after which we went for a walk in the park. While walking, Uncle told me that he that he had a special treat for me. The following morning, after breakfast, he would be taking me to Petticoat Lane market in the East End of London.

That morning, we took the tube to Aldgate East where the market was situated. The place was amazing. In Poland I grew up with markets but this one was astounding. There were hundreds of stalls selling anything you could think to buy. Most of the stallholders were ether Cockney or Jewish; the Jewish stallholders spoke between themselves in Yiddish instead of English, and the Cockney had a language of their own. I still recollect watching a man who sold crockery with fascination as he loaded a very large tray up with a complete dinner service and proceeded to auction it down from a half-crown to sixpence and, if no one bought it, he would drop and smash the whole lot on the ground beside him where there already was a big pile of broken china.

Being near Christmas time, the fronts of the butcher's shops were decked out with turkeys, ducks, chickens and many other varieties of fowl, as well as large joints of ham and pork. As a keen meat eater, this was pure decadence. In the market there were many stalls selling spirits, cigars, chocolates, fancy lighters, toys etc. Uncle bought a whole box of Ronson pencils, about fifty, with some lighters, a few cases of wine, quite a few bottles of spirits, boxes of cigars and packs of cigarettes . We then went to the butchers where he bought quite a few turkeys; I was very pleased. Uncle seemed to know many of the traders and they knew him. All these goods were to be delivered to his firm two days before Christmas; the butcher that sold the turkeys had a cold storage where the birds would be kept until delivery.

When we returned and met Dad, I told him with excitement what a wonderful day I had had. The next day, I was going back to Ewell when Uncle Joe asked me to come to the firm before I went. As I didn't have much luggage, he was sending with me a parcel for the Abbotts. I would have to wait until the goods arrived, and the office would parcel up everything for me so that I would be able to manage them comfortably.

While waiting, I went into the workroom to wish the staff compliments of the season. There was a lovely atmosphere of joviality, with paper chains and decorations hanging on the walls. Eventually, the goods arrived and somebody in the office parcelled up the ones I had to take with me. As I was leaving, Uncle Joe gave me some extra pocket money to spend as he couldn't come to the station to see me off, as he had several customers coming to collect their garments for Christmas and he had to attend to them personally. Dad helped me with the parcels to Waterloo station and told me that Uncle Charlie would meet me in Ewell. He also mentioned that if possible he and Uncle would try to come down on Boxing Day to have dinner with us, but if it was not possible they would definitely see me before I went back to school.

Christmas came with all the excitement of decorating the rooms and placing the presents under the Christmas tree. There were more presents for me than I expected, which were from dad and Uncle Joe who, unbeknownst to me, had put them with the parcels that I had brought down from London. On Christmas morning, when we opened our presents I had a few more toys, comics and books that I never expected but I was delighted to have. Jean and I played with our toys until dinner time, which was similar to the previous one, and as usual we all ate too much.

Unfortunately Dad and Uncle couldn't come down on Boxing Day because of work, but they did come down the following weekend to see us and to say goodbye to me before going back to school which was at the beginning of the New Year.

1939

The spring term started and all my boarding friends were back. We exchanged the usual news, but what was most on our minds was if we had saved enough money to buy our motorbike. We agreed that as this was going to be a communal project, we would all contribute the same amount of our savings in to the kitty. The first Saturday that we were able to go to Clapham Junction we made a bee line to the motorbike garage. The owner recognised us from our previous visits and knew what we had in our mind to buy. He knew that we didn't have much money, so he suggested that he had an old bike that at present wasn't working. It needed striping and some parts would have to be replaced like the brake linings, gaskets and some other small bits and pieces. Otherwise the bike was in sound condition and rust free. The bike was large and, if I remember correctly, had a 750cc engine. We asked the price, the owner said that he was willing to sell it with all spare parts and a manual for 35/- (1-75). There was no guarantee, but should there be a major fault he would replace the part for free. We told him we would be back after we had discussed the project amongst ourselves. We had enough money in the kitty plus extra for emergencies and we thought that it was a fair deal, so we went back and told the garage owner that he had deal.

After we paid for the motorbike, Edward signed the necessary documents as he was the oldest. We decided that as we couldn't afford to have the bike delivered we would have to push it back to Wandsworth. The garage owner also supplied us with a large wooden box with all the parts and tools that he promised. We strapped it securely on the seat of the bike and started back to our residence. Although there were four of us it was extremely difficult as the bike was very heavy and had no brakes, so going down the hill we had to put the bike in gear to stop it running away from us. We had to stop many times to get our breath back and the passers-by gave us the usual banter like "Are you going to the scrap yard? Then you're going the wrong way," and more uncomplimentary remarks. Eventually after several hours we arrived at the back of the garden and pushed the bike through the gate to our shed. Mr. Blackwell came out to have a look and thought that we had taken on more that we were capable of. He looked at the manual, wished us luck and informed us that his wife had prepared the tea and was waiting for us. We were all extremely excited about our project and while we were having our tea we couldn't stop discussing what part of the bike we were going to start on first. It was decided that the engine, brakes and all the mowing parts would have to be stripped and the rest of it including the frame would be cleaned with a wire brush and paraffin, checked for rust and then slightly oiled to stop it rusting.

For the next few weeks most of our spare time and conversation was spent discussing or working on the bike. Although we had a manual and Mr. Blackwell gave us some help, we still had to make many journeys to the garage for help, explanation and to collect a few spare parts like bolts and washers. A lot of our spare time was spent trying to understand the manual and how everything went together.

The work progressed slowly but as the time went by it became easier as our knowledge improved. Some eight weeks later we were ready to try starting the bike for its first trial. We acquired some fuel in a can and poured it into the tank, we gave the honour of starting the bike to Edward who kick-started and nothing happened which was great disappointment. We check the bike to see if we were missing any parts but everything seemed to be in the right place, then someone suggested we needed the fuel tap to be opened; we looked and found the fuel tap shut. The tap was opened quickly and Edward gave a few kick starts and the bike came alive with enormous roar that blasted our ears, everyone was shouting to turn off the engine. When the silence descended, we discovered that the silencer had no baffle plates; it was the only part that we never checked. Quickly we asked permission of Mr. Blackwell if we could go to the garage to acquire a new one which he readily gave as he was as keen as us to see the bike working. The owner of the garage was very kind and he replaced the silencer free of charge.

When we returned there was great excitement as we fitted the new silencer. Edward again kick-started the bike and when the engine began to run it had a beautiful purring noise. As Edward was the only one who had ridden a motorbike before, having practiced on the one that his father owned, went on it around the garden. Everything was working which gave us a great feeling of success. We then took turns in trying to ride the bike and we realised that it wasn't quite the same as riding a pushbike and it would take a little while before we had the experience to ride it properly. Although I managed to ride it and fell of it many times, I never rode a motorbike on a public road until I was serving in the Army in Egypt.

When the term finished, as usual, I was to spend my holidays with the Abbotts and then with Dad and Uncle before going back to school. This time when I arrived to see Dad there was great excitement. At long last we heard from mum that she would be receiving a six-month visa for her and Rozia to come to England and would be arriving at the end of June, landing at Harwich. There was also news that Uncle Zygmunt would also be coming on business in the middle of August so we would be having a big family gathering. I went back to school very excited and told all my friends of the great news and they were all happy for me, knowing how much I had missed them.

There was more and more talk about the war. The Headmaster, who had served in the First World War, gave a talk how we would beat the Hun. I was asked questions about Poland and was asked to give small lecture and answer questions about Poland, the country and what the people were like.

The term fell in to the usual routine of studying and in my spare time trying to ride the bike. I fell off many times, acquiring minor cuts and bruises, but improving each time.

During the half term, when I was in Ewell auntie Sofie informed me that as soon the term finished we would be going to Bognor Regis for our summer holidays and then to London to spend some time with mum and Rozia, but that would be arranged after we came back from our holiday. What sort of accommodation would be available for me, as Dad still had to go abroad every six month to renew his visa and didn't have a permanent address in the country, was still yet to be worked out, and Mum would be using Uncle's address for the authorities as she would be staying at his place for time being, which was very small.

Dad received a letter from Mum with the date and time of her and Rozia's arrival at Harwich. Towards the end of June, Uncle phoned the school to ask for permission for me to travel to the firm from which we would all be travelling to Harwich to meet them.

When the day arrived, just before boarding the train we bought Bananas and Oranges for Rozia which were a great luxury in Poland and with great excitement we boarded the train. When we arrived at Harwich we were about an hour early. Luckily it was a sunny day so while waiting we spent our time watching other boats arriving.

At last the boat arrived and we waited for it to dock. As they disembarked we waited at the custom barrier and as they walked through we all rushed towards them kissing and hugging. Mum didn't look like she had changed much since I saw her last, but Rozia had shot up in height quite a lot. We acquired a porter to take their luggage to the train and then we settled down in our seats. We couldn't stop asking questions of each other. I gave Rozia the oranges and bananas of which she straight away ate some (she always maintained that I ate most of the bananas on the journey). Mum could not believe how much I had grown and told me that I was speaking Polish like an Englishman. When we eventually arrived in London, Dad arranged where I would be staying with them for the rest of week before going back to school. I was informed that Auntie Sofie had arranged for Rozia to go to Bourne Hall School in Ewell as a boarder and we would be spending part of our summer holidays together. During the week I took Mum and Rozia around the West End and showed them the stores and the places I discovered and it had the same effect of excitement on them as it had had on me a couple years ago.

One of the places Mum enjoyed was Berwick Market, which was quite easy to reach from the firm and so it was easy for her to go shopping. Mum discovered that she could buy very fresh fish and chickens there, as well as a few other things that she required. I had to accompany Mum and Rozia on their shopping trips to translate, but mum soon discovered that some of the stall holders were Jewish and spoke Yiddish and so soon was able to make many of the purchases herself.

I had a long conversation with Mum about the rest of the family and about her journey to England, which was totally different to mine. She and Rozia had had to travel through

Germany and Holland, so before commencing their journey, both luckily being blonde, Mum had to convince Rozia that while travelling she mustn't mention anything Jewish and that she was just a Polish girl. Mum herself spoke perfect German. Soon after crossing the Polish border into Germany, they picked up passengers, one of which being an S.S. officer travelling to the Dutch border. He started a conversation with Mum and, as she replied in perfect German, he took them to be of German descent. Mum had to be very careful that Rozia didn't say the wrong thing, but luckily he didn't speak Polish. For the rest of the journey they never had any trouble with other officials on the train, as they saw the S.S. officer conversing with Mother. She was ever so relieved when he departed just before the Dutch border.

I returned to school and, when the term finished I went down to Abbott's as we would be going to Bognor at the end of the week. This resort was totally different to Herne Bay, having beautiful sandy beaches instead of stones. The downside was that they had a very noisy fairground which played "South of the Border" over and over again night and day driving us crazy.

When we came back from our holidays Dad phoned that Uncle Zygmunt would be arriving in England the second week in August, and that he and Uncle Joe wanted me come to London to look after Zygmunt, Mum and Rozia. When I arrived at the firm Uncle Zygmunt was already there. He couldn't believe how much I had changed and how well I could converse in English with everyone. Although he spoke some English, he had had difficulty getting around and shopping, which was what I was going to be helping him with.

Uncle Charlie was invited to meet him in the evening after work and have a meal with us. During our meal Uncle Charlie invited Uncle Zygmunt to come back with me when I returned to Ewell to spend a few days with the family. He enjoyed his stay with the Abbotts and, before leaving to go back to London, he invited Uncle Charlie to go back with him to Poland for a week's holiday to stay with *his* family. Uncle Charlie discussed the idea with Auntie Sofia, and told Zygmunt that he would like very much to accept his offer. After that things moved very quickly; Uncle Charlie obtained his passport, visa and was leaving with uncle Zygmunt on the 22nd August to be back on the 30th August.

The news on the radio was getting very depressing and spoke more about the Germans wanting to take the Polish corridor and threatening to march into Poland. We were very worried about Uncle Charlie going and about the rest of the family still living there, but Uncle Charlie kept on saying that all that talk was scaremongering, France and Britain having a non-aggression pact with Poland meaning Germany wouldn't dare to attack and it would be perfectly safe for him to go on his holiday.

The week that they went to Poland, the situation with Germany deteriorated and all the countries in Europe started to mobilise. We became very worried about him and our family. It was a great relief when he returned on the morning of 31st August, but we were still very fearful for our family. Uncle Charlie told us all about his holiday and what a wonderful time he had with Auntie Zosia and Uncle Zygmunt, who took him to many places in the country including Zakopany, a wonderful holiday resort in the Tatra mountains.

On Friday, 1st September the Germans marched in to Poland and on the radio there was talk about the French and British ultimatum to the Germans, to stop the war by 11a.m. Sunday 3rd September. On that day, after breakfast, in anticipation, we turned on the radio to hear the news. At 11 o'clock, during our morning break, the Prime Minister Mr. Chamberlain made a statement that there had been no reply from Germany; United Kingdom and Germany were at war. Shortly after the announcement the air raid siren sounded. We all rushed to get our gas masks and sit down under the stairs. However, soon after the all clear sounded and it seemed that it had been a false alarm, the Observer Corps having mistaken a civilian plane landing at Croydon airport for a German one.

A few days later Auntie Sofie received a letter from my school informing her that, because of the war, it would be closing as pupils had begun to be evacuated, many parents already having made arrangements for their children to go to other schools in the country away from London.

Mr. Lowe, the headmaster, made the suggestion that there were two senior masters at the school who had houses with a sizeable amount of accommodation and were preparing to start a small school of about fifteen pupils to teach them privately, one of them being Mr. Austin. I liked Mr. Austin, who had taught me in both of my schools, and I told Auntie that I would like to be taught by him. Auntie told me that she would have to look at all the different possibilities and then we would have to go to London to see the family and discuss the whole matter of my schooling to decide what would be the best for me.

When we met the family I told them that Mr. Austin was a very good teacher and his wife had also been a teacher and, as several of my friends had arranged to go already, and I didn't want to have another change of school, I should go too. The family agreed and so Auntie began making all the arrangements. I would be staying with her family until the new term started, but going to Mr. Austin's a day early to settle in. The Austins lived in Stoke Goldington, a small village seven miles from Northampton, the house situated on the main road with the Green bus stop only few yards away which made it very convenient.

On the day of my departure, Auntie and I travelled to London and then to Victoria Green line bus depot where she made sure that I catch the correct bus. We said our goodbyes and I was off again for a new change in my life.

The journey was very pleasant and we drove through some wonderful and peaceful countryside; no one would have thought that we were at war. Eventually, I arrived and Mr. Austin was waiting for me to help with my luggage into the house. There he introduced me to his wife, young son and a very lovely daughter Ann Maurine – known as "Bubbles" – who was two years older than me. We all shook hands and Bubbles squeezed my hand very hard; I realised then that we would be friends. Mr. Austin informed me that Charlie and Arthur would be joining me the following day with several other boys from my previous school. Altogether the would there would be fifteen of us, seven about my age with me being the oldest the other eight being younger, between seven and eight years old. I would be the only prefect, having been one before and it would be my job to keep order in the dorms. There were to be two classes, with Mr. Austin taking the class with the older boys while Mrs. Austin with Bubbles helping taking the youngsters. Our curriculum would be English, Maths, Geography, History and one language, either French or German. The house, which in the past had been part of a large farm, was covered with a thatched roof and had now at its base a grocer shop and a post office; the only one in the village. There were six bedrooms on two floors. Mr. Austin helped me with my luggage upstairs to the attic, to what was the largest bedroom in the house where there were three beds. One was a large double bed and two were singles. He explained the sleeping arrangements, that three of youngest boys would be sleeping in the double bed and Bubbles and I in the single ones. Our job would be to look after young boys who were often homesick and had a tendency to cry and be sick during the night.

There was quite a lot of land nearby. At the back of the house there was an orchard and a two-storey barn, of which the upper floor was to be used as our hobby and common room whilst the ground floor was to be used as a workshop and a storage room. Bordering the house were farms.

Bedtime for the younger boys was eight o'clock and one of mine and Bubble's jobs was to see to it that they washed and settled down into bed. The rest of the bedtimes were the same as at Mr. Blackwell's, except for mine which was not until ten thirty, as Bubbles and I had to check that everything was secure before going to bed.

Being September-time and the evenings being warm and still light, before I and Bubbles went to bed, we would often go for a walk in the fields and it wasn't long before we indulged in some quite intimate moments. We both knew what went where but she told me straight away that this was as far she was willing to go as, being a virgin, she was saving herself for the man she would marry.

I settled in to the new term, which became a lot of fun. The lessons with Mr. Austin were much easier as we were a much smaller class and he had more time to explain things to us. Several times we were asked by the farmers if we could help with the harvest, as most of the men were in the forces. We cut the wheat and stacked them into bundles, sometimes we hunted for rats and mice in the barns. Rationing started, so we hunted for jam jars to put each boy's rations of sugar and preservatives to good use making blackberry and blackcurrant jam, which we picked and were in abundance. There was only a small allowance of sugar per person from the Ministry of Food – at that time there were several basic food rations, but we were all fed sufficiently – so the sugar we needed for the jam was collected by taking a spoonful of sugar from each of our jars; it took several weeks to get enough.

Mr. Austin started to take us out, weather permitting, during the evenings for long walks, usually about five miles, to teach us some field crafts. Nearby there were large woods through which we often walked and he used to show us the different type of mushrooms, both edible and poisonous. I still don't know which is which. There were some wild cherry trees from which we picked the fruit and, although they were very sour, once they were cooked with apples and a bit of sugar they were delicious. He also taught us to listen to the cries of stoats when they hunted rabbits. Once we heard one and we quickly ran to the sound. We shooed the stoat away and put the dead rabbit in one of the small sacks we always carried with us. The rabbits were a welcome addition to our meat rations and were made into wonderful pies and stews which we all enjoyed. Mr. Austin managed to obtain permission from the Lord of the manor to fish on his stretch of the river Ouse for trout. As there were no fishing parties for the duration of the war, they made a brilliant addition to our diet.

1939/40

In the autumn the weather changed and became very cold and then it started snowing just before the start of my Christmas holiday. As usual, I spent my holiday with the Abbotts and then with my family in London before going back to school. When I left London by coach to go back to school the condition on the roads became more and more difficult. Although in many places the roads were cleared with snow ploughs, some were still snowed up and I wondered how we would manage to reach our destination. Eventually the coach reached Stoke Goldington, the journey taking nearly an hour longer.

The conditions didn't improve for several days. Most of the vehicles had snow chains on their wheels to help driving in the snow. Several snow ploughs were being used to clear the main roads, but the minor roads were practically impassable. The snow drifts were as high as the hedges and in some places higher than the telegraph poles. Some of the pupils arrived back a day late because of the weather condition. For us it was a lot fun to walk on top of the hedgerows, although there were some mishaps when some of us fell through the gaps and we had to dig them out.

A few weeks after the term started Mr. Austin called me into his study to tell me that he had a received a letter from Dad with some documents for me to sign stating that a permit had been acquired for me to be evacuated with other children to America. I told him straight away that I had no intention to go to America and to have another change in my life and anyhow I wanted to stay in England with my family. The outcome was that Mum and Uncle Joe came to Stoke Goldington to see me and to persuade me to sign the documents, but I wouldn't budge and they realised how strong I felt about the whole idea and they finally gave up. A few month later I felt that I was lucky as one of the ships that was taking children to America was torpedoed and sunk, with many of the children drowning. I always thought: I could have been on that ship.

A few days after the term started Bubbles told me that her mother wanted her to take driving lessons. The Austins owned a car which was used for collecting supplies for the shop and school and once she passed her test she would be able to share the chores with her mother.

There was a man in the village who owned a garage and who was a qualified driving instructor and it was decided that he would be her instructor. Those days it was much easier to pass a driving test; you only had about ten lessons before you were capable of passing your test. On the day of her last lesson, when Bubbles came back she was very unhappy and agitated. I asked her what was wrong and she wouldn't talk to me. After a while she told me what happened.

After her last lesson had finished the instructor suggested to her that they sit in the back of the car to do her oral test. Before she knew what was happening he pushed her down into the seat and tried to seduce her. She attempted to push him away but he was much too strong for her. I suggested to her that we should speak to her parents but she insisted not to as it would be her word against his and would cause a big scandal. Her biggest worry was that he might have made her pregnant. After that all intimacy between us stopped as she was terribly worried that her period wouldn't come.

One evening, a few weeks later, we went for one of our usual walks and when we reached the fields we started kissing and fumbling. Bubbles turned to me and said that she wanted us to make love. I asked her if she was quite sure and, if she was, we would have to take precautions as I had no intentions of making her pregnant. The nearest place that we could acquire contraceptives was Northampton and I suggested that I would pay for them, but there was no way I could get there without a lot of questions. Bubbles insisted that she would pay half of the cost of the contraceptives and there would be no problem of going to Northampton as she went there once a week with her mother to buy provisions.

We then decided that the best place and time for us to spend together would be, instead of going for our evening walk, to go to the common room in the barn where there was an enormous easy chair which would suit our purpose. I don't recollect who seduced who but it left me with a wonderful feeling and completely relaxed. As it was coming to the end of the term, we continued with our affair as many times we had the opportunity.

The term finished and this time I wasn't going to the Abbotts' as Mum and Dad wanted to see more of me and, as it was nearing Passover, we were going to have the first proper Seder as a family since we left Poland. Dad told me that this would be the last term with Austins as there wasn't much happening with the war (it was called 'the phoney war') and He and Uncle were trying to enter me to one of the local schools which were still opened for me to matriculate. After my holidays in London I went back to the Abbotts' for fourteen days before going back to school. My love affair with Bubbles continued as strong as ever and after few weeks decided that we would try and move one of our beds to a position in the bedroom where the floor boards didn't creek. After several tries we found a place and from then onwards we managed to sleep together occasionally when the young boys were asleep.

About half way through the term the Germans started their Blitzkrieg in France and the war news began getting worse. Eventually we heard the news that our forces were encircled at the French port Dunkirk and the navy was trying to evacuate them back to England.

As boys, we couldn't quite understand what was happening until convoy after convoy of Lorries started coming through the village on the way to Northampton. On board were troops with no equipment, who were partially dressed in uniforms and some only in a vest and pants still holding their rifles, looking absolutely worn out. The residents in village began making sandwiches and big pots of tea and handed them to us boys to pass on to them as they went through. This went on for three days and nights.

Soon after Dunkirk the L.D.V. (Land Defence Force, which later became the Home Guard) was formed and the government asked for volunteers and there were plenty. Myself and a few older boys wanted to join but we were too young. Mr. Austin joined and mentioned to the officer in charge that I had some training in the junior O.T.C. and I was quite capable of firing, stripping and assembling a rifle. A few weeks later, a consignment of Canadian rifles Cal. 300 arrived. (I think they were used in the First World War.) I was asked if I was prepared to clean them as they were covered in thick hard grease, which of course I accepted and was made an honouree member of the L.D.V. There were the usual rumours of spies landing in the fields and often the L.D.V. was called out to help searching for them, but they never found one.

A few weeks before the term finished, Dad informed me that just after I would be leaving to stay with the Abbotts, the firm will have moved from its present premises to No.8 Grafton St. London W1, next door to the Medici Gallery and only a short distance from where the firm was situated before. The new premises consisted of five floors, plus two floors of cellars below. The firm didn't require all the rooms, so Uncle converted the top floor to a small flat for Mum and Dad with a small room for me to stay in when I was in London.

The last few days of the term with Bubbles were both joyful and sad as I was leaving and I didn't know when I would be seeing her again. The last day came and it was time for me to pack my things to be ready in order to catch the bus. Bubbles persuaded her parents to let her help me to pack my belongings, of which I had quite a lot, which was wonderful for I discovered that, except for the shop staff, everyone was occupied with some other tasks and we had the house to ourselves. We packed all my things as quickly as we could, then undressed, hopped in to bed and made wonderful love hoping it wouldn't be for the last time. We made the usual promises that I would come up as soon it was possible, but meanwhile we would write to each other. The whole Austin family came to the bus stop to say goodbye and Mrs. Austin told me if ever should I wish to come up for a visit there always would be a bed available for me. Bubbles helped me on to the bus with my cases and we said goodbye with tears in our eyes.

On the journey to London I was feeling very sad. Of course I wanted to see the family, but I was getting fed up with changing school again as it would be the fifth in three years. When I arrived at Victoria station Dad was waiting for me. He acquired a taxi to take us to Grafton St. The flat was small and, being in the attic of the building, the ceiling was sloping. My room was the smallest but it was sufficient as I would be out most of the time wandering around London.

The fashion in fur coats at that time was to have big padded shoulders, so the firm had to have special pads made, which were very difficult to acquire. Uncle asked Mum if she would speak to the designer about showing her the required shape of the pads and if she was able to make them. If this was possible, he would have liked her to have the job. She could, and Mum began being employed by the firm making the shoulder pads. They were very time consuming but I think she liked doing them.

After several weeks being in London waiting to go to my new school, I was getting fed up doing nothing, so Uncle suggested that maybe I would like to help out in the workroom doing small jobs and running errands for the staff. Although I was under age and so couldn't be officially employed and paid, he said he would increase my pocket money. I jumped at the chance and thoroughly enjoyed the experience.

Towards the end of July, the family had a meeting about my future as the school that I was supposed to attend had closed down. They had a talk with me that as I was nearing my fifteenth birthday and I would eligible to start work at that age. Knowing that I wasn't very scholastic and it would take at least two school years for me to matriculate through, losing so much learning time in changing schools and as I would eventually be joining the firm anyway, it would be more practical that I started my apprenticeship on my birthday. The choice was mine to make and I was told to take my time to give my answer. I thought very carefully about the offer as it would affect the rest of my life. Also, this was the one of the reasons I originally came to England – to join Uncle in the firm – so I told my parents that my answer was yes and that I would join the firm.

At the beginning of August 1940, we had the first bombing of London. It didn't last very long and I thought at that time that it was merely a taste of things yet to come. Although there were many shelters in the West End, especially in the underground stations, we were allocated a place in the cellar of the Royal Institute, Albemarle St. W1., which was just across the road from the firm. It was a marvellous place with its own water supply from a well in the basement. At first, the bombings were very sparse, but on the 7th August the Germans started the Blitzkrieg on London, which became Battle of Britain.

The bombers came in waves day and night. They managed to severely bomb the docklands area and set them alight. They were burning for three days and nights and the sky was so bright from the fires that you were able to read a newspaper at night without a light. Despite all this, people carried on as if nothing had happened and got on with their days. I walked all the way from Hammersmith to St John's Wood during a raid one night, with buildings on fire around me and it didn't bother me. People adapted to the new routine: as the Germans started bombing only by night, people would work for the day, go home, collect their things and go to the shelter for the night.

Our shelter became like a club and a glamorous one at that; there were some local actresses, actors and quite a few French ladies of the night. As some of them were bombed out, Uncle used to offer them the spare room that we had at the firm until they found new accommodation. Later some of them became the firm's best customers. In the shelter we had raffles, auctions, all sorts, with all the proceeds given to the forces; charitable organisations. There were some actors who performed comic sketches and others who used to read poetry.

On the evening of September 7th, a week before my birthday, the blitz started. In the morning I had to go to the

Labour exchange on the corner of Berwick market and Poland St. to acquire my National Health card. On that day the air raid warning sounded so frequently that it made my journey to the Labour exchange practically impossible as many stores in Oxford St. were still burning. Eventually, after two hours, I arrived at the exchange and acquired the relevant documents and became a fully-fledged worker. My starting pay was 10/-(50p) a week and as an apprentice I had to do all the menial jobs like sweeping floors, which were covered with fluff, run errands for the cutters and machinists, learning to nail fur skins on to the boards and delivering parcels to the customers. On September 15th, the day after my birthday, when I started working, the R.A.F. broke the German air force and shot down a record number of German planes. At the time it was reported the total was 185 planes shot down but later corrected that the figure had been slightly exaggerated. I was able to watch the dogfights in the sky, which were amazing and the best birthday present I had. I also saw the plane that fell on Buckingham Palace.

The night of my birthday we had the worst bombing raid of the war. We were in the shelter and we were told early in the evening that the bombers were approaching London. Gradually the explosions were getting nearer and nearer and then one exploded that sounded like it was right overhead which scared us all.

In the morning we emerged from the shelter and, walking back to the firm, we found the streets covered in glass and rubble which made it very difficult to walk. When we eventually reached the firm we found out that a very large bomb had exploded at the back of the building, blowing all our doors and windows out. Most of the ceilings were also badly damaged, the front doors of our building were found half way down Dover St. Next door to our firm was No. 10, which was empty and only slightly damaged and was available to rent. Uncle quickly managed to acquire the lease and managed to find some of the workman that had worked for him before to make temporary repairs and, luckily, in a very short time we were able to move. It was business as usual and the firm stayed at that address until the lease ran out in 1982.

For the next few weeks the air raids continued and we had to keep on running to the shelters. The conditions sometimes became quite terrifying but also exciting, watching the dog fights in the sky. Gradually I began enjoying learning my trade, but about six weeks after I started working Uncle told me that as we had a lot of customers in the north of the country and that it was very difficult for them to come to London. He was going to open a branch in Leeds and he was sending Mr. Steiner – a master furrier – with his family as a manager, Mrs. Day – a machinist finisher – and he wanted me to go as apprentice and general helper. We would be leaving in two weeks' time. My pay would be increased to (£2) a week. He also rented a large house in the Harehills district of Leeds for us all to live in together; we would all be having our breakfast together but the rest of our meals we would have to provide for ourselves. Mum and Dad agreed to the idea of me going. I think they felt that I would be safer in Leeds than in London. I wasn't all that keen on the idea of moving again, but having done it so many times in the past I quite used to it.

When the time came for us to go I packed all my things and we all travelled by train to Leeds together. Our accommodation was a big four-bedroom detached house with a large garden in the back. There was a large kitchen, lounge and dining room and the bedrooms were also large and quite comfortable. Our showroom and workroom was situated in the centre of the town which meant we would have to travel to town together on the tram.

It was all very new to me having to cook for myself. For lunch I usually had a sandwich and fruit but for my evening meal I cooked soups, sausages and eggs when I could acquire them, beans on toast or spaghetti which were simple meals that didn't require a lot of cooking. It was becoming more and more difficult to buy food as more were being gradually rationed. I became friendly with the manager of the local grocery store, Lipton's, where I used to do all my shopping. He knew the position I was in and occasionally offered me a case of tinned spaghetti and extra cheese.

At the beginning, in a new town I was very lonely but I soon discovered that there was a Jewish boys' club which I joined. Most of the boys were local, but it was a mixed crowd as there were quite a few boys who had come from Europe on the Kindetransport who lived in a huge house in the Roundhay district of Leeds. Soon I was able to make friends with them and some of the local boys. One of them was a boy called Barry Stone, who came from a wealthy family that owned factory that made all sort of brushes, especially shaving brushes, who used to invite some of us to his house for tea. There was another boy, Tony, who was about my age and an apprentice at the Burton clothing factory and we took to each other straight away. He was earning about the same as me and was living on his own in a small rented room. He asked me if I would like to rent a large room with him that he knew was available and share the rent and our provisions which would be easier on our finances. I thought about the proposition and as the cost of living was going up, sharing our finances would be a good solution to make our money go further. I discussed the whole idea with Mr. Steiner and he agreed that it was a good idea.

We rented a large room on the ground floor in a not very fissionable part of Leeds district called 'Chapeltown' which was very similar to London's East End. There were two single beds with the usual wardrobe and everything that was required in a furnished room. There was also a gas cooker and a coal fireplace for which we had to buy coal, payment for the cooker was a Shilling meter. The house was occupied mainly by married women with children whose husbands were serving in the forces, except the front room on the ground floor next to us, which we later discovered was rented to two amateur prostitutes. We were to make acquaintance with them later through unusual circumstances. One early morning there was a large knock on our door and, when I opened it, both of our next door neighbours rushed in asking us to hide them. We asked them why and they explained that they had a couple Canadian soldiers as customers and after they had done their business the soldiers had left and the girls had gone to sleep, but soon after the soldiers returned wanting to spend the night with them. They were knocking on their window and banging on their door which made them scared and the only thing they thought of doing was to come to us to hide. Tony and I quickly dressed and by the time we arrived at the front door there were several woman residents shouting at the soldiers to go away or they would call the police. After more shouting they got the message and things quietened down and we managed to go back to sleep. The following evening, while having our meal, the two girls marched in with a bottle of Whiskey, a carton of cigarettes, some chocolate and several tins Corned beef and Spam as a thank you gift for the previous night. We didn't want to accept the gifts but they insisted and told us that they had received many goods from the Canadian soldiers they went out with.

They asked us if it would be all right if, in the case they had any more trouble, to hide in our room. We thought about and saw no reason to refuse so we gave them a spare key, as during the day, when we were at work, the room was kept locked. The girls were very grateful and often used to leave goodies in our room like spirits, chocolate, tins of meat and cigarettes.

One of the perks of working in Leeds was that I had to travel to London once a month to collect goods and materials for the workroom which gave me a weekend in London. One of the things I was asked to bring back was cigarettes of which there was a great shortage in Leeds. On my first trip I discovered that Mum had a small suitcase which was suitable for carrying the cigarettes back to Leeds. I knew a tobacconist in Burton St. from whom I used to buy cigarettes for the staff in our firm and I knew the manager. I explained to him my requirements and he was very sympathetic. Although he could supply me five cartons of two hundred cigarettes, only a small portion would be in popular brands. The rest would have to be in brands that were not very well known. I bought what he offered me and when I arrived back in Leeds Mrs. Day and Mr. Steiner were delighted with my purchase. From then on they used to reward me with a £1 every time on top of what I paid for the cigarettes in London.

There were many refugees that escaped from Europe to England and then to London and some of them were our cousins, second cousins and even third cousins of which we never knew existed. Most were professional people such as doctors, dentists, solicitors and teachers. They couldn't find work as they did not have English degrees.

In one incident that happened with the relations on one of my visits to London was when I arrived, Uncle Joe asked me if I would be willing to help out one of Mum and his cousins with some work, who was an unemployed doctor. Of course I agreed. He then asked me to go to the top floor bathroom where the doctor needed help. When I opened the door to the bathroom there was a very strong smell of alcohol. He introduced himself as Dr. David Koller. He then proceeded to explain to me what sort of help he needed from me. He was making a hair restorer to a formula he had acquired while escaping from Poland and as he couldn't get a job as a Doctor until he finished studying for his English qualification, he had several friends who had chemist shops and would be willing to stock his product to make some sort of living. The bath was filled about two thirds with surgical spirit he then proceeded to mix in some sort of chemicals which made the mixture go a purple colour. My job was to stir until the mixture was an even colour, then he gave me a big syringe with which I had to fill hundreds of small bottles and then put a fancy stopper in them. I was then told to wipe them dry and finish the whole process by sticking a printed label on them. I think I managed to do about two hundred but during that time, the room having very little ventilation, I had to keep rushing out of the room before the fumes overwhelmed me. Afterwards, when I saw Uncle Joe, I asked him that next time to hire somebody else to do the job in a bigger room with ventilation because of the fumes which would make anyone working there dizzy. I never heard any more about the lotion or whether it was a success.

Having our own place, myself and Tony were able to invite some of our friends from the club to have small parties, which were a lot of fun. Not having a lot of money to spend we had to budget very carefully and no matter how carefully we budgeted we used to run out of funds by Thursday night. All we could afford to eat for our supper from the fish and chip shop was either four slices of bread and dripping or a small portion of chips. For Friday breakfast we had bread and jam with tea and for lunch we usually had Marmite sandwiches and, as we didn't get paid until Saturday lunchtime, things used to get a little difficult. Some of the boys whom we knew in the club who were from the Kindertransport knew of our predicament suggested that we have our Friday night meal with them in their big house. We asked them how it would be possible and they told us not to worry as there always were forty to fifty boys continually changing their accommodation, so no one would notice another two boys. For us it was a life saver. About forty-five years later I met one of the boys in London who was a jeweller in Forbets Place of Carnaby St. Another boy, from the same group, who was a judge in Leeds I met on a cruise, but that's another story.

1941

In spring, when I was in London for Passover, I was informed by Uncle Joe that that come June I would be returning to work in London. Although I liked Leeds, I did miss London. When I returned to Leeds I told Tony of the firm's decision, and he said to me to not worry about our accommodation as he knew several other boys that lived in digs and he was sure that one of them would like to take my place.

In the beginning of June I returned to London to work for the firm, and my salary dropped back to £1 a week. While in Leeds I had acquired a taste for Western books and I always carried one in my overall pocket to read during my breaks, which became fortunate and simultaneously unfortunate for me; a few weeks after I started working I had a slight food poisoning which made me run frequently to the toilet. After several times having visited the toilet, Uncle observed that I had a book in my pocket came to a wrong conclusion that I had been going to the toilet to read my book. He started shouting at me and he wouldn't listen to my explanation and then he fired me. Dad came over and calmed the situation. He then took me away and phoned a firm that he knew just a short distance away in Conduit St. named Hewitt and Vincent who hired me straight away at 30/- (£1.50) a week, which improved my finances.

The new firm was not quite the same standard as my Uncles and by now I knew enough to hold down what my new job required. The factory foreman was a Mr. Lake who seemed to be worried about keeping his job and would not pass on any of his skills and teach me. Every time I went to his bench for instruction, he would turn his back on his work so that I couldn't see what he was doing, which didn't worry me as I managed to do all my jobs to the firm's satisfaction regardless.

Three months after joining the firm, and just before my sixteenth birthday, I received a letter from the labour exchange requesting me to report to be directed for war work when I reached my sixteenth birthday. Just before reporting to the labour exchange I managed to visit the Abbotts in Ewell and tell them all the latest news. Towards the end of my visit, when I was due to return to London, being just a day before my birthday, Uncle Charlie decided as a birthday treat to take me to his local pub for a drink.

When we entered the pub we found a table and Uncle Charlie told me to sit down while he bought our drinks. When he returned he placed in front of me a half pint of beer, a packet of cigarettes, one of his pipes and an ounce of tobacco. "Tomorrow you will legally be able to buy all these things for yourself, so I thought I'd buy your first. I can't teach you anything about women; *that* you would have to find out for yourself," he said. I returned to London and the following day and reported for war work at the exchange. From there I was sent to an engineering firm just a short distance from where we were living at that time; our address was 92 Langford Court, St. John's Wood and the firm was just around the corner in Loudon Rd. It was as a big house with a large garage which was turned into a factory workshop making small metal components.

My first job there was operating a guillotine, which chopped thin strips from a narrow large roll of thin steel sheeting, which later were hardened to make springs for different firearms. It was quite a frightening experience as there was no safety guard and so quite good possibility you could lose your finger if you didn't take care. Shortly after that I was assigned to a small press to punch out fibre washers, which was a terribly boring job. These jobs were paid by the piece and those days if you finished the task and were waiting for the next one you didn't receive any pay during the waiting period. I wasn't all that happy working for this firm and just before the end of the year I asked the Labour Exchange to direct me to another firm.

1942

In the New Year the Labour Exchange secured me a job with another engineering firm in Cumberland Mews, near Marble Arch. The firm occupied all the garages and all the upstairs rooms of the mews. The firm was totally different to the previous one and the management was very supportive of us. On the first day, Mr. Williams, who was one of the directors of the firm and the factory manager, asked me what I knew of Capstan Lathe machines. I told him very little but I had used a lathe machine in school. He then proceeded to tell me that at present he didn't have a machine ready for me but he did have three very old capstan lathes which were all in pieces and he was restoring them. As he had many other duties in the firm he would like me to assist him in the restoration project, to which I readily accepted. He then explained to me that that the beds of the lathes were pitted with rust and would have to be completely scraped by hand and made accurately flat to fit the other parts, which were also rusty and would have to be scraped and cleaned before we would be able to put the machine together.

The job took ten weeks to complete and when the machines were working I felt a great sense of pride and joy of what I had accomplished. Mr. Williams called me into his office and told me how pleased he was with my progress. He then told me that the Government had evacuated a large part of the women's population in Gibraltar and we would be receiving twenty five of them for training in the factory. The firm would be organising a drilling section for them to train using big pillar drills, and he was promoting me to a Charge Hand to be in charge of them. He then informed me that along with the promotion I would be receiving a pay increase to compensate me for not working on piece work.

I told him I had no knowledge of drill work but he said not to worry as I would be working at with him for at least a month to set up the drill section and by then I would have all the knowledge that I would require to run it. So, at sixteen and a half, I became what must be the youngest Charge Hand in a war work factory.

When I joined the firm there was another boy my age who had joined a few days earlier. His name was Alfred 'Freddie' Popper, who came to England about the same time as me from Czechoslovakia was only a month older and who had had a similar education to mine and we struck up a friendship practically straight away. We started going out together to different places of interest, having similar tastes. One of the places we used to frequent was the Speakers' Corner in Hyde Park, which usually was a lot of fun as we enjoyed listening to different arguments being heartily debated. One Saturday, while we were listening to a speaker being heckled, I noticed a very attractive girl nearby who was having a heated argument with the speaker about Jewish and Christian religions. After the argument was over I managed to talk to her and found out that her name was Joy she was half Jewish. I invited her to have tea with Freddie and myself at Lyons Corner House to continue our discussion. After we had had our tea and we were leaving I asked her if she would be willing to go out on a date with me to the pictures the following Saturday, to which she agreed.

That Saturday we met at the cinema and decided what picture to see. After we had seen the film we decided to have a meal and while we were eating she told me she wasn't very keen on my name, Henry, and that I looked more like a Timothy. She said that in future she would call me 'Tim'. I thought about it and I quite liked the name. We went out together for a few month until she and her family moved to the north of England and the relationship between us gradually diminished, but by then everyone I knew was calling me Tim and the name stuck with me for the rest of my life.

Freddie and I joined North West London Jewish boys' club, which had a company of Army Cadets using the premises for training. We decided to join the Cadets to train for army certificate A, knowing that sooner or later we would be called up into the army and the certificate would enable us to apply for officers commission. We soon made some good friends, one of whom was Reggie Gold[18], who was my platoon sergeant. Another was David (I forget his last name), who was later to be killed at Arnhem. For me the training was easy as I already acquired that knowledge in my first school in the Junior O.T.C. There was a great rivalry between Reggie and myself, for he was very keen to join the army and be commissioned. Six months later, when we sat for the first part of our examination for certificate A, I came first and he came third. He was a bit upset by the results but a few weeks later when we sat for the second part of the exam, which was much harder, he came first and I third. Freddie didn't do very well and soon lost interest in the cadets.

One day Freddie told me that he heard about a new club that was being formed for boys of all nations at No. 30 Pont St., South Kensington called the International Youth. He said that we ought to go and see if it was suitable for us to join. £5,000 for the club to be set up had been provided by Lady Bonham Carter and Sir Stafford Cripps. The idea was that, as there were so many boys from different nationalities living in London at the time, we would mix and learn from each other our different cultures. We decided that at the first opportunity we would go and see what the club was like.

---

[18] More about Reggie later.

When we arrived at the club we were met by one of the committee members who showed us around the premises and took us to an office where he introduced us to the other members of the committee. During our discussions we discovered that most of the members were our age, with some being slightly older. We decided to join and one of the members of the organising committee asked us if we would be willing to sit on some of the committees as one of their problems was that they were very short of members that spoke English as well as other languages and it would be most helpful if we would join some of them. We agreed and we found ourselves on the entertainment, dance, and lecture committees. I also agreed to be on the dance committee and one of my jobs was to sell tickets to the dance on Saturday night at 2/6 (12/ ½ p). Although I was a poor dancer through my old knee injury, the tickets stand was an extremely good place to meet girls and whilst at International Youth I was never short of girlfriends.

As members of the lecture committee we had to arrange lectures by different speakers. In my time there we had lectures from the likes of George Bernard Shaw, Professor Job, J. B. Priestley, Lady Bonham Carter, Aldous Huxley and Sir Stafford Cripps, most of whom I remember as I met several times.[19] Often we had to arrange talks by high-ranking Russian officers on exchange visits to England, Members of Parliament and officials from the Russian friendship organisations. On the sport Committee we mainly had to organise table tennis tournaments with other clubs in which I enjoyed playing and competing. It was a lovely club and we went there as often as we could.

Back in the firm, having been in charge of the drill section for about two months, I began to make some improvements and designed several tools to improve production for which I was paid a handsome bonus.

---

[19] There were many more well-known speakers and guests, most of whom I remember being Russian Army generals visiting the embassy in London, but over time I have forgotten most of them.

One evening, before the end of the shift, Mr. Williams came to the workshop to have a discussion with me about my work. He told me that everyone was very happy with my work, but that was not the reason that he had come to see me. The firm was thinking of starting a night shift – at first it would just be a small trial affair – but there was the problem of the firm not having enough management to spare for the night shift. He then asked if I would be willing to take the Monday, Wednesday and Friday night shift in addition to my day shift; he would take the other nights. In those days the employment rules were that you were paid for the first two hours of overtime at a rate of 1¼, then the next four hours at 1½, and if you worked after two o'clock in the morning you were paid at double time until the end of the shift. I worked out that my salary would be in the region of £12, which was a lot of money to me.

Mr. Williams also told me that he would arrange a camp bed for me in the office where I could lie down and if anyone had a problem in the factory they could come and wake me up. I thought about the offer and decided to take it. I worked the two shifts system for just under ten month until Mr. Williams left the firm. The firm employed a new manager who wasn't all that fond of me and I believe he wanted to employ one of his friends or relations to replace me. By then I was so tired I would have had to stop working two shifts for health reasons anyway, being so tired and worn out working such long hours, so Freddie and I asked to be released from the firm to find employment in another firm in Great Portland Street.

Just before we left the firm we decided that working such long hours and our commitments to International Youth we didn't have the time for the army cadets.

We had a meeting with our commanding officer at the Cadets explaining our problem and he agreed that as long as we attended a company drill every six to eight weeks and we kept our uniforms clean and our boots polished, we could keep them.

The new factory was totally different to my old one. It had the latest state of the art "Herbert" Capstan Lathe with 32 speeds and could produce components accurate to 2,000th of an inch. In fact, everything was brand new with banks of neon lighting above the machines. There was a bigger work force and we were all supplied with fresh overalls twice a week. The factory mainly produced parts for fighter planes, landing gear parts for Rolls Royce aircraft engines, torpedo engine parts and gears for clockworks in S.O.S. boxes that were placed in lifeboats that could send a signal when a boat was sunk. The work was much more accurate to what I had been used to but I soon managed to do the job. I didn't earn as much money as I had in my last job, but the work was much more satisfying. The firm was run on a piece-time system by a Foreman and an elderly Charge Hand. They and several other worker who were members of the Engineering Union and that caused friction with the non-union members. The piece work was always timed by the Forman on the slowest worker and the system was such that the amount they produced in that time was the amount you had to produce for your basic pay per hour. Anything you produced over that amount you were paid extra for each piece.

Most of the staff were young married women or girls, men who had been rejected for the forces on medical grounds and older men who were too old to fight. A lot of the younger women and men liked to chat and have a smoke, taking time off from their machines, not caring very much for the war production, so long as they earned a bit more than the basic rate they were quite happy. For myself, Freddie and a few of the other workers, all we wanted was to get on with our jobs and earn as much as we could. We didn't smoke, chat or play around so we earned considerably more money than the others, which brought us in conflict with the union members. We soon discovered that when some of the good jobs were finished we were transferred to much more difficult ones, the Foreman thinking that they would take us longer to complete and so we wouldn't earn as much money, but it didn't work and we still managed to earn nearly as much as we had earned before.

After several weeks we were informed that the firm had a night shift and Freddie and I would have to do four weeks on and four weeks off, like some of the other members of our day shift.

We didn't mind as it increased our pay and that's when we had another conflict with the Foreman, one which became very serious. We were making parts for aircraft landing gears and we were left written instructions in the office every night that the day shift had made only so many components and we were not to make more than 10% more than they had made. This was ridiculous as the shift started at 8p.m. and finished at 7a.m. – a full eleven hours – as opposed to the day shift which was only eight hours. We used to finish our quota by 2a.m. and then either go to sleep, play cards or read a book. After a week of not being able to earn more money we took no notice of the instructions and carried on working the whole shift, making more components than the day shift. After a few days the Foreman appeared at the beginning of our night shift and told us all that we must obey his instructions that he left us. At the time we, the whole country, were fighting for our lives and he was trying to appease his union members. As there were quite a few of us who were fed up with the union, we told him that either he let us work the full shift or perhaps he would prefer it if we went with the story to the newspapers, how the union was trying to sabotage war production. After that we had very little trouble from him or the union.

The air raids were less frequent but still quite severe and some of us were roped in to doing fire watching both on the roof and on the ground. The system was such that, as soon the air raid siren sounded, we sent the work force to a large public shelter opposite the firm across the road. Although we had our own shelter in the firm's basement, most of the staff were apprehensive sheltering with about 35 tons of machinery above their head. There was a big block of flats in a side street near the firm that had many ladies of the night living there who didn't like using the public shelter. Having discovered that we had one in the firm's basement, and knowing some of us through chatting to us when we were doing our fire watching rounds, they approached us to ask if it would be possible for them to use our shelter during the raids. We discussed it with our Charge Hand and agreed to their request. It became very beneficial to us as they always brought us presents like American cigarettes, whiskey, chocolate and sometimes nylon stockings which were most welcome.

One of the problems in the factory were the women whose husbands were either in the forces abroad or prisoners of war and were lacking in male attention. During the raids some of them used to wait until everyone had left for the shelter and then rush to the basement where we were sheltering and plonk themselves on our laps, being very friendly and saying that they were scared. There was one that was very keen on me and it became embarrassing when I had to tell her that I never went out with married women and never dated women that I worked with.

As time went by Freddie and I managed to get a few days off to have a holiday break and we decided that we would go to Leeds to visit some of my old friends. As travelling in wartime was sometimes difficult, we decided that we would hitchhike wearing our cadet uniforms. Being in uniform, getting lifts was quite easy as most lorry drivers, seeing two men in uniform walking asking for a lift would stop and take us as far as they were going. Then, when we stopped at a roadside café, they would insist on buying us some food and drink and then they found some of their driver friends to take us further on our journey. Once we arrived in Leeds, I contacted Barry Stone who invited us right away to stay in his house. We managed to see a few more of my old friends, who invited us to several parties and we had a wonderful time before we had to return to London the same way as we came.

1943

Early in the spring of 1943, Freddie and I were becoming fed up with our jobs and decided that we would like to join the R.A.F. There was a recruiting office in Great Portland St. only a small distance from our factory, where we went to enquire what our options were. When we arrived the recruiting sergeant asked us how old we were; we were 17 ¾, which was at that time the minimum age for joining. He then told us we would have to take a medical test to see if we were fit enough for the service. Then we had to go to another office where there was an R.A.F. officer who took our details, like what sort of school we had attended, where we were working, what sort of job we were doing and if we had undergone any military training.

After we answered the questions he asked us what branch of the R.A.F. we would like to join. We both wanted to be fighter pilots, as I am sure any young boy wanted to be at the time. He informed us that this would not be possible as that branch had too many applicants and he gave us a book with a list of the other branches that were available. When we finished our interview he informed us that we would receive an official letter from the R.A.F. informing us whether we have been accepted or not.

On the way back to the firm I asked Freddie not to mention to his mother that we applied to join the R.A.F., knowing that she would tell my mother, but of course he did. When I arrived home in the evening both Mum and Dad had a go at me about why I had decided to join the R.A.F. I explained to them that I only enquired about joining and that soon I would be called up anyway, so I would like to join a service of my choice. As it happened, none of this mattered as we both received an official letter from the R.A.F. informing us that as we were in a reserved occupation doing essential war work, we would not be able to join up until the firm released us from our job, so for the time being we were stuck in our jobs.

1944

On June 6th, it was announced that the second front had started landing in Normandy with the Allied armies. On receiving the news there were great jubilations but also great fear for our friends, having already lost one at Arnhem and another at Dieppe. Freddie and I tried again to join the army, as we were very eager to volunteer to serve in Europe where we would have a better chance of acquiring information of our relations, almost all of which we hadn't heard from since the beginning of the war. Hearing all the horror stories of the atrocities against the Jews, we were very apprehensive of what we might find, but were rejected again.

On the Tuesday evening after the D-Day landings, there was a very thick London fog that had no visibility. I heard this funny engine noise high in the clouds unlike any other that I had heard before. It didn't sound like an aircraft engine or any other engine we had heard overhead in any of the air raids or Blitzes. It made a low, ominous rumbling noise, but no one could see what it was because of the fog. It was very frightening for a few seconds after the noise of the engine stopped there was a huge explosion. It wasn't until the following day that it was announced that this was Hitler's terror weapon, the V.1 rocket.

The following few weeks were terrible as they were coming over London very frequently and all you could do was, as soon you heard that terrible noise of the engine stopping, to duck into the nearest bomb shelter. As the British air defences improved there were fewer of them coming over, but there were still some terrible incidents. One lunchtime, when I was on day shift at the firm, a V.1. dropped not far away from the Middlesex Hospital, just round the corner from the firm. Air raid wardens were asking for volunteers to help to dig out the casualties. Several workers joined Freddie and myself to go to the bombed site.

When we arrived there it was a terrible sight of destruction and carnage. The building that had been hit was just a pile of rubble. There were people buried underneath, several people dead and many injured. The worst sight was that of those dead caught in the explosion with their body parts missing; legs, arms, one without their head. Some of us were sick from looking at this terrible sight but soon we started helping the wardens with removing the rubble but a few minutes later several policeman arrived, who began removing us from the site, telling us we were not trained to do rescue work and we could be endangering ourselves and the survivors. We were informed that an official rescue team was on its way and would be arriving in few minutes.

As we walked back to our firm we felt very sick and when we entered everyone was asking us what happened. We told them what destruction and carnage there was and that we didn't want to talk about it as we were sick and distressed from what we witnessed. It took Freddie and I a long time to get over the scene we witnessed.

A few months later my mother was caught in a blast from one of these bombs just outside Café De Paris in Regent St. and was knocked down unconscious, but thank God she was only slightly injured and recovered very quickly. In July, soon after the bombardment by the V.1., Hitler sent his ultimate terror weapon over London: the V.2., a rocket which came without any sound before exploding. Where the explosion happened the devastation was horrendous, with many houses flattened and many people killed. Usually, there were no survivors, so everyone was even more scared, but as was typical throughout the war, most people carried with their work.

As the Allied army advanced along the coast of Northern France, V.2 rockets became fewer and fewer as their range diminished and eventually they stopped altogether. Freddie and I in our spare time carried on with our cadets and our club work, but were frustrated with not being able to be in one of the services. At the beginning of November, we both had a letter from the war office that at long last the firm has released us from war work and we would be called up to the Army. The letter included a questionnaire about which army I would like to join. I had the choice of going into the British, Polish or the Jewish Brigade. I don't know why Freddie had only two options – British or Czech Army – but I sent my form back stating my choice was to be in the British army, as I now considered myself a British subject. Freddie chose the Czech army and received his call-up papers two weeks before me. His date was two weeks before Christmas and mine was the 2nd of January 1945, to report to Maidstone Barracks, Pioneer company.

Mum and Dad were very worried and I tried to cheer them up by telling them that maybe I would be able to be posted to Europe and find out what had happened to our family and that would take good care of myself. At the firm the staff arranged a small going away party for me. They also made a collection which came to £14 which I thought was very generous of them.

In the letter from the War Office there was a list of what to bring with me when reporting to my unit. It was just the bare essentials as all traces of civilian clothing I would have to take back home on my first pass. Mum and Dad came to see me off at the station and there were quite a lot of other boys with their parents and girlfriends. Eventually, when the train departed, I discovered that in my compartment there were Jewish boys from the continent who couldn't speak a lot of English and were all reporting to the same Pioneer Company as I was. I wasn't very happy joining the Pioneer Company as I wanted to be in the tank corps.

When we arrived at Maidstone there were many other boys from other parts of the country. We were met by several Sergeants who sorted us out in different Platoons and proceeded to march us to our billets and allocate our beds, bedding and little wardrobes to put our suitcases in and later on hang our uniforms. When everything was sorted out we were marched to the Quartermaster's store to be kitted out with our uniforms and everything that went with it: shirts, underwear, socks, boots, one pair of gaiters, one pair of braces, one web belt with brasses, two web ammunition pouches, one small pack and one large pack all with webbing belts, one block of Blanco to clean all the webbing, one Forage hat, two mess tins, one boot brush, one tin boot polish, a set of knife, fork and spoon, one tooth brush, one razor, one packet of razor blades, one shaving brush, one Housewife[20] to repair our uniform and a sweater.

The last thing we were issued were our dog tags with our name, number and religion pressed on. My army number was 13121185; you never forget your army number, it's with you all your life. After we collected all our gear we were marched back to our billets and ordered to change into our uniforms, pack all our civilian cloth into our suitcases to take home, then we were dismissed, told to have our lunch and report back at 2 o'clock to

---

[20] A canvas pouch containing sewing equipment.

our billet to be shown how we would have to layout and prepare our kit for morning inspection, especially how to polish our boots, clean our brasses and Blanco our belts and gaiters. We were then told that all other information, meal times, parades and should you be required to report to the company office, would be posted on the notice board outside the company office which we must read every morning.

Our barracks housed 32 men, or a platoon, consisting of one Sergeant, one Corporal, two Lance Corporals and 27 privates. Our platoon commander was a Lieutenant who slept in the officer's quarters. There were 3 platoons in a company plus a small H.Q. detachment making it a total of about 120 men usually commanded by a Captain or a Major. After inspection we were marched to the armoury where we were issued with our rifles and a bayonets and all the cleaning equipment which we had to sign for and then we were marched to the training hut where we were given instructions as to how to clean and strip a rifle for morning inspection. For me it was very easy as I had done this many times both in the junior O.T.C. and army Cadets. There were several other boys that had served in the Cadets and when some of the boys had seen how quickly we finished our task came over an asked us to help them as they couldn't understand the instructions as they didn't speak much English. It was lucky for them that some of us spoke several languages and we were able to help them.

One of the good things about being in the Pioneer Corps was that, because we were already in a Regiment, we were paid 6 pence a day extra as trained soldiers. The next day we were marched to the company office where we individually met our Company Commander. We were called individually by our name and number in alphabetical order and eventually it was my turn to be called in. The Commander was a young Lieutenant who asked me where I lived, what school I had gone to, what sort of work I had been doing and if I had any military training. I told him about my service in the Junior O.T.C. and Army Cadets where I passed my Certificate A which I had in my billet. He right away told me to fetch it and report back with it. It only took me a few minutes to retrieve it and report back. He looked at certificate and made a note on the report sheet that he was filling out and then asked me which service I would like to serve in. I told him the Tank Corps.

Eventually we were all processed and marched back to our billets, dismissed for our lunch and told to report on parade at 2 o'clock where we would start training for marching, saluting and rifle drill. Our training started with the usual dressing the ranks when marching, doing left and right turns, with the rifle doing slop arms, present arms and order arms. For some of us it was easy as we had some sort of training for others it was total chaos; rifles kept being dropped, people were marching out of step all to the annoyance of drill Sergeant and Corporals. There was a lot of shouting, swearing and other uncomplimentary words but after two hours some sort of order prevailed. Just before we were dismissed we were told that our real training would start in the morning. The following morning we fell out on to the parade ground where our training started, which was similar to what we had experienced the day before but much more intense until we could do the drill correctly and continued after lunch till we could do it reasonably well.

After we were dismissed the platoon sergeant told me and another boy to stay behind and then told us as we both served in the Army Cadets he was making us billet orderlies as we already knew the drill and, with the exception of sighting our rifles and range practice, we would be excused all other duties. Then He proceeded to tell us what our duties would be keeping the billet clean and polished including the metal waste basket which had to be polished mirror bright, making sure that the beds and the kit on top were properly lined up.

The billet had two rows of beds. Each morning we had to make sure our beds were lined up and distanced correctly. We had to unroll a cloth line with certain distances marked out on it, lay it on the floor stretched out taut for the beds to be lined up with it. Then it was carefully stretched across the beds where all the blankets had to be correctly folded with the big pack on top, all the webbing with brasses polished and the boots with their toecaps polished to a mirror shine with their soles upwards with the studs also polished, all lined up against the cloth line. Otherwise, after lunch, when the boys went for further training, we would have to check that nothing was out of line in case of a spot inspection.

The time went by very quickly as the posting to Maidstone for basic training was for a duration of six weeks and at the end of it we would be posted to our respective Regiments. I had a pleasant surprise meeting my old friend and sergeant from the Army Cadets Reggie Gold. He had just finished his training and was being posted to the local regiment the Queens Own for ten weeks to do his Corps training. We had a chat and a drink in the pub, catching each other up about where some of our friends were and agreed to keep in touch if possible as at present neither of us knew where we would wind up.

You didn't make many friends in the army during the six weeks of basic training for we all knew we would be splitting, being posted to other units, although I did make one friend and we did swap our home addresses so we could meet again when we were civilians. His name was Fritz Devries, he was born in Holland but educated in England and was slightly older than me. His family owned a huge farm in Kent growing large quantities of fruit and vegetables. He invited me several times to the farm to meet his parents and enjoy the meals his mother used to make. We lost touch when we were in the forces but when I was demobbed and home again there was a letter from him giving me all the news of his family and what had happen to him while he was away in the Army. The family bought much more land, sold their old house and bought a much bigger one in Carshalton Beaches. In the end I did accept his offer and went to stay with them. We swapped stories of our experiences in the army but it wasn't the same feeling as before. He was engaged to be married and talked mainly about his future wife and what they planned to do looking forward whilst all I wanted after nearly three years in the desert away from home was to have a lot fun and exciting times and have as many girlfriends as I could. When we said goodbye I think we both knew that this was the last goodbye and we would not meet again; our aspirations and lives had grown to be completely different since our time together in the army.

In the fourth week of our training we had to do a seven mile march. Everyone had to attend without exceptions. We had to wear our full battle kit including packs and rifle. This was to check our training and our state of health after which we were to have a medical check-up and reassessment as to what branch of army service you would be posted. The training was not that hard and as we marched we had a break every hour. In between we did some field craft by crawling on our stomachs then running up the hill with fixed bayonets on our rifles, shouting and then dropping again on our stomachs on a special range where we fired five rounds of ammunition at set up targets. After this we had a rest and then lunch before Lorries came to pick us up to take us back to our barracks for our medical check-up. I found the training quite easy but there were the usual grumbles from some others that the march was too hard and the field craft to long.

A few days later my name was posted on the notice board to report to my platoon commanding Officer. I wondered what I had done wrong which made me a bit anxious and when I eventually saw him he was quite friendly and we had a little chat of how I was enjoining being the army and then he told me that on my record sheet my progress had been very good, especially my shooting where I scored the highest marks in my platoon. Then he told me that the company C.O. had a look at my record and seeing that I had passed my Cert. A he would be recommending me to appear before the War Office Selection Board (W.O.S.B.) so they could decide whether I would be suitable candidate for Officers commission and that I should be hearing from them shortly. Then he mentioned that I had passed my medical and I was perfectly fit apart for the varicose veins in my legs; they had swollen from marching and he was downgrading me from A1 to A2. It would not make any difference to my application for commission but I would not be able serve in Tank or Infantry Regiment. Instead I would be posted to the Royal Army Service Corps.

Our six weeks training finished on the last Saturday and there was to be a passing out parade. All the companies of National Servicemen, the Pioneer Corps and the Jewish Brigade would be marching on the parade ground past a local General and our Colonel. The day before the parade we were inspected to make sure that our uniforms were properly pressed, webbing properly Blancoed and boots and brasses polished to a mirror finish. Our rifles were inspected that there was not a speck of dust left on them and we kept them wrapped up as much as possible. We were inspected several times by our corporals and sergeant before they were satisfied with our appearance. When Saturday came we all assembled in our own units. There was a band from the Royal West Kent Regiment; all in all there were about six hundred men on parade from different units. We were called to attention and the inspection started by the senior officers walking up and down the ranks looking at our smart turnout. When the inspection was over the officers returned to their raised stand we were ordered to stand at ease while the Colonel gave a short speech how pleased he was with our training and our turn out and wished us all well in whatever we chose to do in our army career. When he finished the Regimental Sergeant Major called the parade to attention, ordered left turn quick march and with the band in front playing the march pass we proceeded, we marched all around the parade ground pass, the saluting stand and as each unit passed the stand company commanders gave order eyes left while he saluted with his sword. When it was over we were dismissed.

The next day our postings appeared on the notice board and I discovered that I had been posted to a R.A.S.C. company stationed at Carlisle in the north of England. I would be issued with a 72 hour pass travel warrants and the time I had to report at the barracks in Carlisle.

When I arrived in London on my 72 Hour pass I went straight home to see Mum and Dad and to get rid of all my gear including my rifle. When I arrived they were so surprised to see me as I didn't tell them I was coming. They hugged me and thought that I looked very healthy but skinny and Mum straight away started to try to feed me, saying that the army was not feeding me enough. I told them that the food in the army was very good and our rations were far bigger and better than the ones they were getting at home. After we had some tea I left Mum and Dad to visit Uncle Joe at the firm and after a hug and a chat he insisted of giving me some money to enjoy myself while on my leave. I also visited my old engineering firm to see some of my old friends who insisted on taking me to the local pub for a few drinks. Time passed very quickly and the following day it was time for me to travel to Carlisle. It was a miserable journey as it rained most of the time through very bleak scenery. The only good thing was that when we stopped at some of the stations there were ladies from different organizations serving us cheese or corned beef sandwiches and big mugs of tea. There were quite a lot of soldiers on the train going to Carlisle to the same unit as myself. When we eventually arrived at our destination and descended from the train there were Sergeants waiting for us to direct us to Lorries which were waiting for us to board to take us to our units.

When we arrived at our destination we found ourselves in a huge army camp. It was one of the new camps build shortly before the war by Leslie Hore-Belisha MP, who was the War Minister at that time. It consisted of one very long barrack hut with three smaller one branching off on either side. The longer barrack had all the baths, showers, toilets and wash basins to do our ablutions with running hot and cold water. The smaller barracks that were protruding on each side each had 24 beds. We were allocated our quarters and then told the times of our meals, as well as where the mess hall and the canteen were situated. We were also informed of where and when we were to parade in the morning and where our company office and the notice board was situated. The time of our morning parade was to be 0900 hours. Next morning reveille being at 0700 hours.

After we had washed, shaved and had our breakfast we fell in onto the parade ground where the platoon commander gave us a welcoming speech after which he passed us on to our sergeant who explained to us what the course would consist of and what sort of training we were to have. Then he introduced us to our instructors who would be teaching us how to drive and how to perform vehicle maintenance. We were then marched to the vehicle car park where we were to be allocated a vehicle on which we would be training. When I saw the vehicle I was allocated I thought it was a joke. It was a three-ton Albion (they went out of business before the war). It must have been built during or just after the First World War. It was chain driven which meant it had a sort of big bicycle chain, about 7-8 inches wide, running on the outside of the vehicle, connecting the front and back wheels which drove it. It made a tremendous noise and to change gear it was a nightmare. The top speed was between 40-45 mph with the wind behind it. The instructor explained to me that before D Day the company was stripped of all their modern vehicles to be used for the landings on the French coast.

The next morning our training started in earnest. We were all eager to start as it was a big thing in those days to hold a driving licence. My instructor told me to sit in the driver's seat and then he sat beside me and proceeded to explain how to drive the lorry to me, as well as what information the gauges on the dashboard showed. He then showed me the procedure of double declutching to change gears. He quipped that if I could manage to drive this vehicle I would never have trouble driving anything ever again.

While we were stationery he made me practice changing gear and made sure that I understood all the gauges. He took a small book and read to me all the laws and regulations with regards to driving, such as sticking your hand out of the window and giving information to other drivers whether you are turning, and to recognise all the road signs related to driving. After all this had been gone through we were off. I had terrible time changing gears. I somehow couldn't synchronise my action of pushing the clutch in and then changing gear and we were both getting frustrated until suddenly I got the hang of it and I began to enjoy the ride. The roads were mainly clear except for military traffic and it was quite easy to avoid them. After two hours we returned back to camp car park where the instructor helped me to park my vehicle in line with other company vehicles.

In the afternoon we had our first lesson on how to maintain our vehicles and understand the workings of the engine, gears and transmission. One of the things you were taught is changing and repairing your tyre. Army lorry wheels are made in two halves in order to be able to change the tyre easily and quickly and the nuts on these bolts holding together the two halves are painted red; you must never undo these nuts until all the air is discharged from the tyre. The reason for this is that if the air pressure is left in the tyre it could blow off one half of the metal wheel could injure you badly. There had been several deaths reported through carelessness changing tyres.

In the next couple days the instructor showed me how to reverse safely, do a three-point turn and what gear to use going up and down the steep roads. After we finished each day he would fill my progress report sheet. On the final day of training he informed me that I would be taking my driving test the following day. I was a bit nervous as I thought that I hadn't had enough practice driving, but the instructor seemed confident that I was ready for my test.

When morning came and I started driving I was a bit tense. We were driving the usual route and we hadn't driven very far when the instructor suggested that, as we were not far from the hills on the Scottish side of the border, we should drive there to give me a bit more practice before my test. When we eventually arrived at the place where he would be testing me, I had to drive up a very steep hill and then down again, do a three point turn, do a turn in the middle of the road and then reverse into a very narrow turning. When I completed these tasks we drove a little further, where I had to show him my knowledge of hand signals. We then drove back to our camp. When we were in the car park where he questioned me on maintenance and care of the vehicle. After we had finished he told me that I had passed and the report would be forwarded onto my company commander.

The next day my name appeared on the company notice board to report to the Company office to see my commanding officer who notified me that the result of my test was good enough to be driver In Charge (I.C.) and I would be issued with a 3-ton Bedford lorry, as well as another driver to assist me, and I would be starting convoy training. This all made me very proud.

Convoy training lasted two weeks and consisted of keeping the vehicle at constant speed and correct spacing when driving. It could get quite boring but it was a necessary part of our training and taught me a great deal of discipline. During the time I was training I was called to see my company C.O. who notified me that there had been a communication from the War Office, saying that I had been selected for W.O.S.B. and I would be informed of the date I would be appearing before it. Meanwhile I had become what was called potential Cadet Officer. I was issued with a yellow lanyard to wear on my left shoulder and a yellow flash in my Forage Cap. The C.O. also asked me how I was getting on with my second driver. I told him I didn't know much about him but we were working well together. I then asked him if there was anything I should know about him. He informed me that I was the third driver that he had worked with and the previous two complained that he was difficult to work with. Tom (the other driver's name) had been injured in the head during the early part of the war and had lost a small part of his skull which was replaced with a stainless steel plate and this injury meant his speech was a bit slow. I told him I had no complaints as long he pulled his weight and did what was required of him.

When our convoy training finished we had to go on details, delivering goods and supplies all over the country. Some of us did two or three vehicle convoys, others made single vehicle deliveries. My detail was a single vehicle and I had to deliver several packing cases containing machinery from Liverpool to the London Silvertown district and then return back to Carlisle. We set of early in the morning in very miserable, wet weather but it was an easy journey as Tom, my second driver, came from Liverpool and knew the area where we had to pick up our load well. The load was loaded on the lorry quickly, enabling us to reach London just after lunch.

Neither Tom nor I knew where Silvertown was situated in London and that was when our trouble started. During the war, all the signposts and many street names were removed to confuse the Germans should they invade and every time we stopped to ask the way, me with a slight accent and Tom with his slow speech, who we were asking took us for an enemy and gave us the wrong directions. It took us three hours before we found our destination.

When we finished unloading I decided to call my Parents to surprise them since I was in London. Mum answered the phone and she was so delighted. Straight away she asked me if I would be able to stop and have a meal. I explained to her that there were two of us and asked her if she could put us up for the night. I knew that there were no beds available in the flat for us to sleep on so I told Mum we had our blankets and it would be no trouble to sleep on the floor as we were used to sleeping rough. Mum asked us to come over straight away and that there would be tea waiting for us. We would all have dinner when Dad came home from work.

Straight away I drove to St. John's Wood and parked outside the block of flats. Mum opened the door and greeted us and then asked me what I was doing in London. I said that I would explain everything when Dad, who was on the way home from work, arrived so that I wouldn't have to explain everything twice. When Dad arrived I explained to them both all about our journey and the trouble we had finding the place to deliver to. After dinner Mum asked me how long we would be staying replied that we could only stay the night and that we would have to leave early in the morning to report back to our camp in Carlisle. It was wonderful to have some of Mum's food for a change instead of army rations. In the morning, before saying our goodbyes, Tom and I gave Mum all our surplus rations that we had, such as tea, sugar, cheese, tins of beef and tins of fruit. The journey was an uneventful one and made it back to camp just before lunch.

Back at camp, our Company consisted of men from all parts of the country like the Brummies (from Birmingham), Geordies (from Newcastle) and Scousers (from Liverpool) who, when off duty relaxing in the N.A.F.F.I., usually sat together in their own groups and did not like others joining them. I was lucky being a foreigner as I was accepted generally and made several friends among the Brummies. Occasionally we were given 48 hour passes, which was not long enough time for me to go down to London. On one of these passes Bob, one of my Brummie friends, invited me to stay at his house in Birmingham for the weekend with his other two friends who lived nearby and would be coming with us, to which I readily agreed. We managed to get a lift and when we arrived at his parents' house they made me most welcome.

During the afternoon Bob asked me if I had ever been to a dog race or bet on dogs, as he and his other two mates were going dog racing and they would like me to join them. I agreed as I had never seen a dog race before. When we arrived at the track it was all very exciting, with so many people shouting, watching their chosen dogs run and encouraging them to run faster. Then, after the race was over, rushing to place their bets on to the next race. Bob asked me to give him £1. I asked him what was it for and he said we were going to make some money. We watched all the races and when it was time for us to leave Bob told us to wait for him as he had to settle something and when he returned he then handed each of us some money. He gave me £10 and he told me that was my share of my winnings from my £1. I discovered later that he and his friends were part of the Birmingham race gangs that used to fix races.

Back in the barracks, one funny thing that happened to me was when my name appeared in orders on the notice board. The office clerk had spelt my name wrong – instead Griebel he had put 'Grable'. Friends started calling me Betty because at the time there was a famous film star called Betty Grable and the name stuck with me through my army career.

When our six weeks training was up we received our new posting. The company was being posted to Gateshead, near

Newcastle upon Tyne, for further training on heavy goods and tank transporter vehicles. We were also due to be trained on amphibious vehicles (the Ducks), which were the most difficult of all as there was so much to learn about controls and the waterproofing, which had to be done each morning which was a most filthy job and usually left one covered in grease from head to toe. The tank transporters usually had three personnel as they were very difficult to manage going on the narrow roads and around the corners. When we travelled through some of the small villages they had to be guided by the two extra people; there were several incidents where a driver took the corner too sharply and several residents lost a corner of their cottages.

Most of our training consisted of convoy driving to the docks, picking up loads from the quayside and delivering them to the local units. We were all hoping that our company would soon join our army in European theatre of war.

When our training finished we had a lot of spare time, the local people were very kind to us. They made arrangements that we were provided one cinema and one theatre ticket every week for those who wished to go. Also, there was a list of addresses from local families who would welcome us for tea on Saturday or Sunday. I found the people living locally the friendliest I had ever met.

We were getting very bored doing nothing and we were all looking for something to occupy our time with. There was a Smith's Crisps factory near by which had been turned into a bakery and one of my Brummie friends found out that they were short of staff for the night shift and he asked if I would interested to go with him to see if they would employ us.

I approved of the idea and when we arrived at the factory office we were introduced to the Foreman who explained to us what the job would entail, which was loading trays filled with bread dough onto an oven conveyer belt. When they reached the other end of the oven they were baked and had to be loaded onto trolleys and wheeled to the waiting lorries. The shift started at 7p.m. and finished at 5a.m. with a one hour break for a meal. He then told us that the work was boring but the pay was good (18

Shillings (90p) per shift, which was equivalent to £30 in today's money). We agreed straight away to start that night and the shift passed very quickly. Everything was new to us and the staff, who were mainly women, were most helpful and friendly to us. The bakery also produced cakes and pies and in the morning, after we were paid, the night Foreman gave us a large sack full of misshapen loaves of bread, cakes and pies for us to take back to our camp and asked us if we would continue working the night shift. We explained to him that we were waiting for our posting but until then we would carry on working the shifts.

Going back to camp we had to pass the guard room and as we passed the guard Sgt. asked us where we had been as he was going to report us 'Absent without Leave' which was chargeable offence. We told him what we had been doing and we were quite willing to contribute some of our spoils to him and the Corporal and should we receive any more we would share with them again. The arrangement worked very well until our posting arrived and we were never reported or charged.

We only worked at the bakery for the next eighteen nights as soon enough our new posting arrived. The whole company was being posted to Burma and meanwhile we would be moving to Skegness while waiting for our embarkation leave.

Moving to Skegness was like having a holiday. We were billeted in empty private houses right on the seafront with all mod-cons. There were four of us to a room and all we had to do was report once a day for morning parade at 9a.m. and the rest of the day was our own. Our mess hall was situated in a Butlin's holiday camp which had been occupied by the R.A.F.

The war in Europe came to an end on May 13th, V.E. Day, which we celebrated with a dinner and couple bottles of beer each. There was a great sense of joy that we had beaten the Germans, but we knew that the war was not over as there was still fighting in the far East. Otherwise, it was just a case of waiting to go overseas. Two days after V.E. Day we were given two weeks embarkation leave with orders to report at the end of our leave to the camp in Dover near the docks to embark on a ship to the Far East.

I spent some of my leave seeing my friends from my old factory which was gradually being shut down for a lack of orders, since the war was drawing to a close. I also visited my other friends in my Uncle's firm and my friends at the International Youth Club. They were all very kind to me and always wanted to entertain me by taking me to a pub for a few drinks, but somehow I could not relax; all I wanted was to re-join my unit. Being in the army after a while set you apart from your civilian friends for their aspirations were different from yours.

After my leave was over and I travelled to our Dover camp. On arrival we were paraded and brought to attention, our C.O. explained to us all about our journey. The boat that we would be embarking on would only take us across the Channel to Calais where we would board a train which would take us right across France to Toulon; we would be the first party to travel on this new network called the Matlock Route right through to the south of France. Once we arrived in Toulon we would stay in a transit camp before boarding a larger ship and sail to Port Said in Egypt where we would disembark and wait again in a transit camp for a troop ship to take us to the Far East.

After this had all been explained to us, we had our pay parade and were paid in French Francs (200Fr to the £1) in bundles of small notes which made us feel quite rich. We were then dismissed to have our lunch and ordered to parade back at quay site at 1400 hours with all our kit to board the ship. It was small Channel boat and when we departed it wasn't very stable and a lot of us were sick including myself.

Once we had disembarked in Calais we boarded the train that was waiting for us. Our Platoon managed to secure the first carriage behind the engine. It was a long carriage with open compartments, seats back to back, luggage rack above them and a table between the facing seats. My Brummie friends succeeded in securing a block of six seats so that we could all travel together and as soon we had sorted out our gear we started to sort out our sleeping arrangements. We worked out that one of us could sleep on the roof rack, we could tie two blankets like hammocks between two roof racks, two could sleep on the seats and one on the floor. We drew lots for our places and everything was most satisfactory.

The train had to travel very slowly and in some places one could have walked faster. The devastation in some of the places that we passed was terrible, others looked as if they had never been touched by the war. Travelling across some of the railway bridges was a frightening experience as most of them were blown up during the war and had been repaired by army engineers. When you travelled across them and looked down out of the window all you saw was bare railway sleepers with just the rails across them with nothing underneath to hold them up. You could see several hundred feet down where the river ran.

After a while the journey became boring and in the army when you are with a group of bored soldiers you usually start playing cards. One of the popular gambling card games was called 'Brag' and as we had been paid at the beginning of our journey there was plenty of money to play with. The games started quite small but the winners from the small games joined the winners from the other small games from other carriages and the stakes became higher and higher. The games went on most of the time that we were on the train and on the last day some of the big winners decided to hold one last high-stakes game with me and my Brummie friends as we were the high winners in our carriage. As we still had about a half a day before disembarking in Toulon it gave us plenty of time for a game. After several hours the game had to stop, my friends and I found ourselves having won just over £1,400 with my share being £240, which became very useful to supplement my pay for a long time.

When we reached Toulon and disembarked there were trucks waiting to take us to our transit camp. The temperature was in the nineties and the whole place was a mad house. There were so many camps: British, Canadian, Poles, French, Jewish Brigade and refugees. The earth was so churned up that in some place there was about 12-15 inches of dust and when walking you sunk into it right over your boots. The condition in inside the tents that we were allocated was the same. Luckily we were told that we would only be staying there for three nights before boarding a small pre-war French luxury liner, the *Ville de Oran*, in which we would sail to Port Said. When we boarded the boat we thought we would have a pleasant journey but it was a little crowded and after we left the port it was beginning to be uncomfortable.

First we were told that we would be sleeping in three shifts, which meant that I would be sharing a bunk with two other men, each of us having the use of it for eight hours. We were then given a token with the number of our bunk and we drew lots in which order we would be sleeping. Then we were told that fresh water would only be available for two hours in the morning and evening for washing and drinking and with the temperature being into the nineties even at sea it was imperative to make sure that the water bottle was always filled. The worst were the meals; although breakfast was reasonable, lunch and dinner were disgusting. For lunch we had pilchards and chips with bread, fruit and tea, and at dinner we were again given pilchards with boiled potatoes and stewed vegetables and horrible French suet pudding with tasteless custard which was served every day on our journey.

The first day the weather was very pleasant but the following morning, as we were sailing through Messina Straight, the weather changed into a furious storm. The boat started pitching badly, most of us started feeling sick but the worst was to come. About one hour in to the storm the ship lost one of its two propellers and the boat started to corkscrewing which made the condition even worse. By then most of us were vomiting above and below the decks and the smell was nauseating and although the Captain reduced the speed we were travelling at it wasn't much help.

The journey through the straights lasted about six hours before we were in calmer water once again. The smell lingered and it was practically impossible to keep down any of the horrible food that was being served and my diet consisted mainly of bread and very sweet tea until we reached Alexandria where the ship had to have a new propeller fitted, whilst we were to wait on board until our transfer to our transit camp in Port Said.

The troops were in very mutinous mood with having had shortages of water and ghastly food and as soon the ship docked and the crew departed on shore leave they broke into the food store and distributed some of the food to our cooks to make us a decent meal, being the first one since we left Toulon. The next day there was some talk of all of us being put on a charge of mutiny but eventually the whole thing blew over and we never heard anything more about it.

The following morning after breakfast we paraded on the quayside with our full kit, our name and number being called out as we were assigned to our lorries to take us to the base depot at Port Said, to wait for the arrival of the troop ship to take us to the Far East. Our camp in Port Said was a part of a huge base in the desert. After leaving the lorries we were marched to the Q/M stores where we were issued with our summer uniforms of Kaki Drill and all our other bits and pieces necessary for a tropical climate and then marched to the armoury to deposit our rifles for safe keeping. After we finished with all the formalities we were marched to our tent billets and assigned to our tents. The tents were huge and could sleep up to ten men but we were allocated only six to a tent which allowed one quite a lot of space. For our beds we were issued with two sets of metal triangles about 10" high with a metal bar join them on which you rested three 6'6" long and 9" wide planks of wood on which you laid a canvas paillasse filled with straw and then your three blankets, one under and two on top. There was also a table and chairs. It was all a bit primitive but as we were not stopping there for long it was sufficient. After we sorted out our gear we paraded again to be given information as to where our company office and mess hall were situated. After that we were dismissed for the rest of the day.

After two days waiting for our ship we were ordered to parade and the Company Commander told us about the good news and the bad news of what was going to happen to our company. As the war in Europe had finished some of the troops that would have been shipped there would now be going to the Far East. The good news was that we would be staying in the

Middle East, the bad news was that the Company would be broken up and the men posted to other General Transport (G.T) companies to replace the men that were being demobbed. It was a great blow to us as we had formed some strong friendships during our training. We were also informed that while waiting to be posted there would be jobs to do around the base and every morning we would have to check the company notice board to see what jobs each of us had been allocated.

The next morning my name appeared on the notice board for me to report to the company's office where I was seen by a Platoon Commander who informed me that going through the records my name came up that I spoke some German and the camp police, who were in charge of the German prisoners of war who were repairing the camp roads, needed someone to converse with them. I explained to him that my knowledge of German was limited, but it seemed that it didn't really matter and I was being promoted to the rank of acting Lance Corporal, which I would retain as long I was in the Camp police. The rank was only such that I had the authority to order the prisoners about. I also had to do escort duties and be in charge of the prisoners who acted as guards in the back of our lorries, stopping the Egyptians stealing our loads when collecting or delivering goods to, at that time, one of the largest supply depots in the world in Tel El-Kabeer. I enjoyed working with the prisoners and most troops were friendly towards them as they were mostly from General Rommel's Africa corps. In their spare times they made some beautiful objects from the aluminium sheeting which they scrounged from crashed aircraft bodies, like cigarette cases, lighters, trinket boxes and picture frames, which they would swap with us in exchange for cigarettes and food. We were issued every week with a tin of 50 cigarettes and as I had always been a pipe smoker, I used to send four tins to my father most months, as we were allowed to send a package home every month. I always had some spare tins which I swapped with the prisoners for some of the things they made. To this day I still have some of the objects I got off them, one of which being this beautiful aluminium cigarette case which has a scene of pyramids and palm trees pierced into it, with a stain glass effect made by melting old toothbrushes down.

One morning, after about three weeks into the job I woke up not feeling particularly well and decided to join the sick parade in order to see the Medical Officer (M.O.) In the army, if you get sick you had to pack all your gear into your kitbag to deposit at the Q/M stores for safe keeping and all you took with you was your small pack with you, which you filled with Pyjamas, washing and shaving gear, towel, underwear and socks. I notified my Sgt. that I was reporting sick and marched off to the M.O. room which was some distance away. There was a large queue of other troops waiting to see the doctor and eventually it was my turn to see him. He took my temperature and checked my pulse, after which he said that I had a slight fever from too much sun. He prescribed a few aspirins, gave me a chit, excused me of duties and told me to go back to my tent, lay down drink a lot of water and should my condition not improve to come back to the Medical Inspection room (M.I.) during the evening sick parade. I went back to my tent and lay down, trying to have some sleep, but I was feeling more feverish and hot by the minute. I laid there until it was time for the evening sick parade. I started walking towards the M.I. room when everything went black. When I woke up I found myself in a comfortable bed with white sheets, which turned out to be in an army hospital. I was no longer feverish, but I felt terribly weak. A nurse came offered me a cold drink and informed me that I had had a bad bout of Malaria and had been unconscious for nearly four days.

One of the nurses seemed to be bit cool towards me and I couldn't make out why. I asked one of the other nurses what the reason was for it and she told me that when I was unconscious I had sworn at her. I thought that it was a bit silly as I wasn't conscious at that time, but I apologised to her and after that our relationship improved. I stayed in the hospital several more days before I was discharged. Before leaving the hospital I was told by the M.O. that every year I would have a recurrence of the disease which would come in the form of a fever and when that happens I would have to acquire medical tablets for it from the M.O. and to stay in bed for at least two days to get over it. I found out later when my Dad was seriously ill and needed blood transfusion the hospital couldn't use my blood because of having Malaria.

When I returned back to my unit, I was told that there was news of my new posting; I was being posted to 286 Company G.T based in Alexandria where I would have to report to in seven day's times. I would lose my rank of L/corporal and revert to Driver I.C. One of my new company vehicles returning from a detail would pick me up and take me to my new abode. On the appointed day, late in the afternoon, a 10-ton truck arrived. I put my gear in the back of the truck and we were away. On the journey the driver told me about the Company; it had two bases in Alexandria. The winter one was situated right on the seafront with proper barrack huts. The other was in a Palm Court, the accommodation being tents a, further inside the town. The journey took about four hours with several stops for refreshments on the way. When we arrived in camp it was pitch black. I reported at the company office but it seemed that no one knew anything about me. Eventually a Sgt arrived telling me that, as he had no orders about me and he couldn't assign me accommodation until everything was sorted out, he told me to pick up my kit and we walk to a huge tent which was the company's recreation tent where there was a billiard table and suggested that I sleep on it. I was so tired that I dumped everything, rolled out my blankets on the table and went to sleep.

The next morning I reported to my new Company Commander who told me that there had been a mix-up with my orders and that I hadn't been expected for another two days but as I was already here everything would be sorted out to accommodate my early arrival. He asked me if I had any experience on 10-ton trucks, and I informed him that in my records there would be a note that I qualified on heavy goods. The company consisted of 10-ton Mack trucks and 8-ton Studebaker articulated trucks, both American in make. Later they were changed to 10-ton Leylands. The company didn't have a spare vehicle for me so for the time being I was to be assigned to drive the Commanding Officer's 10hp Austin staff car. I didn't realised at the time that working for my Commanding Officer I would actually be his batman.

The job entailed getting up early in the morning, which wasn't hard as it was the summer and the reveille was at 5.30a.m. I had to shave, wash and dress smartly, then proceed to the cookhouse to get a container of hot water for him to shave and wash. As we were under canvas there were no such facilities in his tent. While he was making his ablutions, I had to go to the officers' mess and acquire some tea for him, before laying his uniform out for him, polish his leather belt and shoes. Although I received a small increase in pay, I hated the job. The Commanding Officer wasn't well liked and although his rank was supposedly Major, his actual rank was Lieutenant acting Captain temporary Major on short service commission. With so many men being moved about and demobbed, there were lots of cases of people being temporarily promoted several times. There were several Regular Army officers who were much more respected, especially my Platoon Commander, Captain Foulks. After few days, as I got used to the routine, I began to hate the job even more. The major was a womaniser, and I was made to drive him to the nearby hospital where there were many social functions. He had several girlfriends there and I had to drive him and his girlfriend-for-the-evening, who was nearly always drunk, to a small hotel a few miles away and wait for them outside while they had their fun and games. After they finished I had to drive him back to his quarters in our camp and the girl to hers in the hospital, which meant that some days I didn't arrive back at camp until well after 11p.m.

I hated the job so much that I asked to see my company commander to see if he could find a replacement for me and move me to a different job. He explained to me that until the next batch of drivers went home he didn't have an available vehicle to assign to me. Then I had a bit of luck. One of the drivers in my tent told me that there was a driver living in the adjacent tent who was a batman the C.O. before me. He had managed to get out of the job and as soon as I found out that, I went searching for him, before finding him in the canteen. I asked him how he had succeeded in being released from the job.

He explained to me that the Major had a thing about drivers, when driving and pulling away, doing so in second gear instead of the first, as he feared that the car would break down in the middle of nowhere. Also he couldn't stand cold tea in the morning. I thanked him for the information and from then on I started to bring the Major fairly cool tea in the morning, and I didn't do a very good job of cleaning his gear, which he kept on complaining about to me. Then I started driving in second gear when pulling away from the curb which made him very annoyed and often shouted from the back: "Driver Griebel, start in the first gear!" and I would say "Sorry, Sir." and do it over and over again. Two days later I was relieved of my duties as a batman and assigned a new job driving a water tanker with a sprinkler attached at the back, which I had to drive around the camp during summer as our camp was in a large Palm court with about 100 date palms. The soil being basically sand, our heavy vehicles churned the tracks up making the whole area very dusty. In order to keep the dust down my job was to drive around the tracks all day, sprinkling them with water in order to keep the dirt moist. It was a boring job but it had certain rewards. One of the things I had to do as part of my job was to supply the Dhobi Walla (laundry man), by the name of Abdullah, with water to do our company's laundry. In the army, when abroad, you had to pay for your laundry to be done and our Khaki Drill uniforms had to be starch and pressed. It didn't cost much but it still took a chunk out of your pay. The uniforms had to be handed in every morning and collected in the evening to wear the following day. By supplying Abdullah with water he wouldn't accept any payment from me for my laundry and, realising that I never abused him like some of the other soldiers by swearing at him, we developed a good relationship.

The other thing that happened was that at the back of the camp, behind the wire there was a village where the army acquired most of the labourers that worked in many of the camps. On the second day on my new job a girl appeared at the boundary

156

wire with a large container asking me if I would be so kind as to
fill it with water. I didn't know why she needed the water so I
asked Abdullah who told me that, although the camp has plenty
of fresh water, the village had none and the villagers had to
mainly use the water from the so called "sweet water canal", from
which they caught many diseases. Every time the girl came I
never saw her properly as she always wore an Egyptian peasant
dress, which hid the wearer very well. A few days there came to
the wire a girl in a European dress with a container to be filled
with water. She was very good looking and for a moment I didn't
realise that it was the same girl from the village. She explained to
me that although her family lived in the village, she only came
down sometimes to help her family with work, but she herself
lived in the centre of Alexandria where she worked in a night
club as a singer and dancer. After she collected the water she
would go back to her own place. Then she said that when she was
away her younger sister would be coming with a container for
water and asked me if I would fill it for her to which I readily
agreed. As we were chatting she asked me that, being so kind for
supplying her and the family with water, she would like to invite
me as her guest to the club where she worked. I said I would be
delighted and we made arrangements for the following Saturday
night when I was off duty. I then asked her if it would be all right
if I came in uniform as I had no civilian clothed and she told me
that the club she worked in was one of the few clubs that were in
bounds and many servicemen and women used it to be
entertained.

I was looking forwards to going to this club. When
Saturday came I waited for her at the camp gate with anticipation.
I had to tell the guard Sgt where I was going as things at that time
in Egypt were a bit doggy and dangerous. The orders at that time
were that if you were going into town you had to go in groups of
four or give the location of where you could be reached. She
came in a taxi dead on time and we drove to the club. I wanted to
pay for the taxi but she wouldn't allow it and told me that the taxi
driver had an arrangement with the club, who paid him a fixed
fee once a month to transport the staff. When we entered the club

I was introduced to the owner who I discovered was her uncle, who told me that he had heard about my kindness to her and her family. He then took me to a table right next to the dancefloor where several other civilians were sitting who worked for the British administration. He then asked me what I wished to drink, called a waiter over and gave him my order and told me should I wish to eat or have any more to drinks I should feel free to order anything I wished from the waiter. I didn't want anything to eat as I had already eaten in the camp but I did help myself to some olives, bits of cheese, nuts and wonderful little pastries that were on the table.

The show was quite good and entertaining. The girl had a good voice and was an excellent dancer and, when the show finished, she came to my table where we had a drink and a chat together. Before long it was time for me to leave back to my camp. I thanked her and her uncle for a most enjoyable evening and they insisted that I take one of their taxis back to my camp.

The job lasted only another couple of weeks. When my name appeared on the notice board, I reported to my platoon Commander, who informed me that the company had a detail to pick up ten new Bedford lorries from Tel El-Kabeer to be delivered to Haifa in Palestine, but there was no spare Sgt. to take command of the convoy, and having gone through company records and seen that I had passed my Cert. A, I would be in charge of the convoy and given the rank of Local Temporary Acting Sgt. for the duration of commanding the convoy. On the following Monday I and nine other drivers would be given rations and transportation to Tel-El-Kabeer to pick up the vehicles, check them thoroughly for any damages and that all the parts and tools were with them, then I was to sign for them and allocate them to my drivers. Then in the morning we were to proceed to travel to Haifa at 20-25mph to run in the engines. When arriving in Haifa I was to drive the vehicles to 5.B.O.D. (British Army Depot) and hand them over. As the whole journey should take four days, we were to stay until Friday when one of our company vehicles would pick us up for our return journey.

I was to hand over the water tanker and all the equipment to another driver and explain to him the job. When I told him what to do, I also let him know about supplying the girl with water when coming to the wire, whether he did or not I never found out. On Monday, after lunch, we were transported to Tel-El-Kabeer by the motor pool where I was met by a Sgt. who took us to our allocated tents. We were told to dump our gear and then we proceeded to the vehicle park where our ten Bedfords were. They were the latest design, having observation hatches in the roof and all the equipment waiting for us to be checked individually before I signed for them. It was a lengthy process which took about 5 hours, having to stop for tea a few times. When we finished the inspection the M.T. Sgt. told us that the vehicles had just been unloaded from a cargo ship and hadn't been run in yet so we would have to do it. He also gave me a route map with two places marked of units where I was to stage for the night in the Sinai desert.

The journey would take about 2-3 days. A Sgt. and two corporals with a breakdown vehicle would be joining me as they were being posted to Haifa at the same time. I dismissed the drivers for their supper and told them to be at the reveille for 5a.m. the following morning. I would arrange with the catering Sgt. to provide breakfast at 5.30a.m. for us to leave at 6.30a.m. I also suggested to them to have an early night as tomorrow we had a long day ahead of us.

10 - Men on the convoy to Palestine, 1945. I am pictured sitting in the centre.

I went to bed as soon as I could but at about 3a.m. someone came into my tent asking for Sgt. Griebel. As it was pitch black I called out: "what do you want?" A man came to my bed carrying a torch and I saw that he was the Lieutenant in an infantry regiment. He introduced himself and told me that there was an emergency in Palestine and he had received a change of orders for me which he would give me before we left in the morning and that he needed our pay books. I got up and went to collect the pay books with everyone grumbling for being woken up. In the morning I paraded my men for inspection and to receive their pay books back. The Lieutenant returned each man his Pay book, dismissed the parade and asked me to join him in his tent, which was also his temporary headquarters. He asked me to sit down and told me that he had to have all our Pay books for a reason, to see if there were any Jewish personnel on this trip. The only one was me and as there was currently trouble in Palestine I could be excused going, in case I had divided loyalties. I replied that first and foremost I was a British soldier and had applied for British citizenship; I chose to join the British army and I hoped to settle in England after my service in the army. I also told him that during W.W.I several of my uncles served in the Austrian army and for all I knew they possibly killed other Jews in the opposing armies, and should we be attacked I would do my duty like any other British soldier.

After my little speech he got up and shook my hand and gave me my new orders. Due to the unrest in Palestine my small convoy had become an operational convoy. I was to transport the Lieutenant and his company of infantry to Haifa. He would be in charge of the operation but my responsibility would be the vehicles. He then told me that his orders were to reach Haifa, which was about 250miles away, in 20 hours, staging only once at Raffa. I tried to explain to him that the vehicles hadn't been run in or tested and it would be unsafe to travel at high speeds not knowing how good the brakes were or how sound the engine cooling system was. He told me that it couldn't be helped as his orders were to get to Haifa at maximum speed and as soon the troops were redistributed and loaded on to the vehicles we would depart. He would be taking point and leading the convoy and the Sgt. Major and myself would take the rear to pick up any stragglers. We left at 7a.m. that morning. We drove on the military road build by the British army pass the Pyramids and then across the Suez Canal into the Sinai desert. The Sinai desert is very different from the Sahara and is mostly black rock with the sand laying on top, which shifts all the time and makes the road very slippery and dangerous. The road runs along the canal and after an hour of fast driving, when we were staging for our first morning brake, as predicted the brakes on the third vehicle in front of me failed and smashed into the vehicle in front of him badly damaging his radiator, so instead of a 20 minute brake it took 2 hours to repair his brakes and radiator. In the desert, every driver carries a pint enamel mug in his vehicle and usually 4 gallon old petrol tin with the top cut off which you can half fill with sand and part fill with petrol to make yourself a little stove to make tea or a hot meal and you usually share the stove with other drivers. When we started again the lieutenant decided to drive even faster to make up the time and when we were at our second brake stop the vehicle in front of me stopped dead with steam pouring out its engine.

I stopped my vehicle to see what the problem was and the driver informed me that his engine had completely cut out. I looked at his engine thermometer and saw that the needle was way past the safety mark and I knew that the engine had completely seized up. The breakdown vehicle with the engineer Sgt and two fitters arrived and after assessing the damage they informed me that there was nothing they could do and the vehicle would have to be towed on a tow bar all the way to Haifa and it would have to travel at a slower speed as there we troops on the back. About hour later we reached our next brake stop where we distributed the troops onto the remaining vehicles before we could set off again.

When we resumed our journey the Lieutenant still insisted on driving at high speed and we managed to make our next stop without any incidents but when we left after lunch for our next break I noticed that my steering was malfunctioning. I told the

Sgt. Major that I would have to slow down to about half the speed of the convoy as it wasn't safe to drive any faster. About half an hour later the Officer realised that I wasn't following the convoy and turned back to enquire why I wasn't keeping up with the convoy. I explained to him that my steering was not responding properly and showed him that I could turn my steering wheel half way round before there was any response. He told me that it could not be helped and ordered me to keep up with the convoy. I asked him if he would give me a written order as in my opinion the vehicle was not safe and if anything happened I would have proof that I had to obey orders. He told that he would write me out the order at the next stop for a break before continuing to Raffa. At the next break I asked the Lieutenant for my order, he told that he would give me the my order when we reach Raffa as he had no time as he had to make his report to H.Q in Haifa of our progress.

The sand in the Sinai desert shifts all the time and sometimes you get a sand dune covering the middle of the road. After the break, when we started again on the on our last leg of our journey to Raffa the convoy had to slowdown and go around a sand dune obstructing the middle of the road. When it came to my turn to go around my steering totally gave way and I hit the dune, turning the truck over. As I went over a small embankment the truck flipped over three more times with me in it. I still had the prescience to switch my ignition before I was knocked unconscious. I was pulled out through the observation hatch and the Sgt. Major managed to get out by himself the same way. Unfortunately, of the seventeen troops in the back, eleven had to be hospitalised for check-ups. The wounded were loaded on some of the trucks and taken to the Raffa hospital to be checked out. The rest of us stayed for the night and the following day proceeded with the remains of the convoy to Haifa to drop the troops off and deliver our trucks to our destination. I was just a passenger as I was in no condition to drive, but several others that were more seriously injured had to stay behind in the hospital. The only injury that I sustained was a cut on the back of my hand, though my hands were shaking from shock so much that I had difficulties using my knife and fork to cut up my meat when eating our evening meal.

The next day, after a short drive, we reached Haifa. The day we arrived was the day that a Jewish terrorist organisation blew up the storage oil tanks at the docks and you could see the black smoke covering the sky. We dropped off the troops at the infantry barracks and then drove the remaining trucks to 5 B.O.D. where I made my full report to the Commanding Officer of what had occurred on the journey.

The Major who was the Commanding Officer at the depot told me that there would have to be a court of inquiry and I would be informed at my company where and when it would be held. Meanwhile, the drivers and myself that were going back to Alexandria would be billeted at the depot until our transport arrived. Otherwise, the time was ours.

I had a reason for wanting to be in Haifa. In the last letter from Mum and Dad they wrote that if I got a chance to visit Haifa or Jerusalem, I should try to trace two of Mum's female cousins by the name Kholer that had settled in Palestine in between 1920-21. They were both professors and, as far as Mum knew, they were teaching in Jerusalem but their home was in Haifa. The family had lost contact with them. While in Haifa I decided to visit the offices of the Jewish Agency to see if I could acquire some information about my second cousins.

I managed to find out where their office was situated and, when I arrived and opened the door, there were two men about my age sitting there, who gave me a very hostile look. They asked me what I wanted; I forgot that at that time I was wearing a British uniform, which wasn't all that popular then. I explained to them that I was Jewish and my quest was to find my family. They then asked my name and to see my Pay Book and I jokingly asked them if they wanted me to drop my trousers also, but they didn't have much of a sense of humour and told me to come back at fifteen hundred hours to see if they had any news. Having spare time, I decided to wander around Haifa, stopping for Falafel and salad and a wonderful fresh orange juice. By then it was time for me to return to the Jewish Agency to see if they had any news. When I arrived there the atmosphere was totally different, very friendly and they offered me a cold orange juice.

I was then asked questions like how I was treated in the army what was the feeling in England was towards the Jews. Then they told me that they had managed to trace my cousins and, although they lived in Haifa, they were in Jerusalem for a teachers' conference where they would be staying for the next four days. One of the men in the office suggested that, as he was going to Jerusalem that evening, if I wished to I could accompany him and he would arrange transport for me to return to Haifa in the morning. I thanked him but I explained to him that at present there was a curfew and my party was travelling early in the morning back to my unit in Egypt, but if he would be so kind as to give me the cousins' address I would pass it on to my Mother and she would no doubt correspond with them. I thanked them for all their help and left.

My journey back to Egypt was uneventful. I reported to my platoon commander, returned my Sgt's stripes[21] (as I held only a temporary rank), and then gave him my report of what had happened on the journey to Haifa. He told me that he would help me to write up a full report for the court of inquiry but in the meanwhile he would be giving me three days' leave to get over the accident and, as there were no spare vehicles, he was assigning me temporally to work in the M.T. office until one was available.

About ten days later, towards the end of August, I was ordered to report to my Platoon Commander, who informed me that there was a convoy being assembled of 77 brand new 10-ton Leylands, which were to be delivered to Tripoli, Libya. At a distance of 1,700 miles, the company was collecting all the spare drivers from all the surrounding units and, as I had no vehicle, if I had recovered sufficiently from my accident, I was to join them. I told

---

[21] They were made out of brass with a pin on the back so that they could be pinned on one sleeve or removed at will.

him I was perfectly fit and I would like to join the convoy as I was sick to death doing office work.

The next day my orders were posted on the notice board to report to a Captain whose name eludes me but who was to be in command of the convoy. He was a regular army officer who had been stationed in the Middle East several years. When I reported to him he straight away told me that there was a shortage of sergeants, and having looked through my records he noticed that I was still waiting for my interview with the war office selection board for my commission and having been an acting Sgt. on a previous convoy he was appointing me again to the rank of temporary unpaid acting Sgt. For the duration of the convoy. He then gave me the brass Sgt. stripes to pin on my sleeve and proceeded to tell me what my duties would be.

There would be five other vehicles with the convoy: a jeep and a small staff car, a Hillman Minks plus three 3-ton Bedford lories, which would be our supply trucks. I would be issued with the Jeep. He would spend most of the time with me in the Jeep as we would be the point of the convoy. Also, we would have to check the convoy from time to time for a correct spacing between each vehicle, which should be between 60-65 feet. He would use the staff car only when the weather was bad. I would also have to check in with him every night and report that all the vehicles had arrived at the staging area without incident and would be available for travel the following day. I would have to make sure that I always had spare jerry cans of water and fuel to supply other vehicles should they need them. Should the weather be bad he would be at the point of the convoy in his staff car and I would have to do the spacing of the convoy on my own and then join behind him.

The journey started well enough, travelling from Tel- El-Kabeer to our company in Alexandria to pick up our Bedford supply lorries which were loaded with our food rations, fuel and most importantly a 500-gallon water tanker which was to be towed by one of the vehicles.

We travelled through the Nile delta; after driving through the desert, seeing the green flooded fields with the farmers planting rice or cotton was a wonderful sight and at intervals you also see donkeys going in circles bringing up the water from the sweet water canal to irrigate the fields. The only disadvantage of driving through the villages was that you could smell them from three or four miles away before you had even reached them. The reason for this was that as the farm workers were extremely poor, they lived in huts made from mud bricks with the roofs made from palm leaves and, in order to make the huts waterproof, they would throw all their rubbish on top of them, which rotted and then hardened in the summer heat. They also collected big piles of animal dung and left in the sun to dry hard, which they used as fuel for cooking and heating in the winter months. Because of all this, as you drove through the villages you would encounter huge swarms of flies.

We arrived at our company based in Alexandria late in the afternoon, but before going to our billets we had to do a final check on our vehicles for tyre pressure, water and that the fuel tanks were topped up, as we were to be leaving very early in the morning.

We left on our journey at 6.30a.m., and when all the vehicles were strung out on the road, the Captain and I in the Jeep went up and down the convoy with the Captain driving and me spacing the trucks. When the convoy was in a reasonable spaced out condition we moved to the point to lead it. Our first part of the journey was to travel along the military coast road leading to Tobruk about 220 miles away. It was a pleasant drive through the last part of the Nile Delta into desert towards El-Alamein, which would be our first stop and then on to Mersa Matruh where we would stage for the night.

When we arrived at El-Alamein, we were given permission to visit the British and German cemeteries with the monuments to the fallen. Then, a little bit further were the monuments to the minefields of the two armies which was as far the German army advanced into Egypt before the battle of El-Alamein. We then proceeded a little bit further to our staging area. The area we chose was near an Egyptian village and an old

German aerodrome, which still had a burnt-out fighter aircraft on the landing strip.

I didn't realise at that time that we had some very odd drivers who had been in the desert a long time and were a bit deranged. One of them was from my company, a Jewish boy from the East End by the name of Zuerer. He decided to go and have a look at the plane which was about 150yds from where we were standing. When he was about 20yds from the plane one of the drivers standing next to me noticed a board hanging on the barbwire with a skull and crossbones painted on it and written underneath "Achtung Minen" we stopped dead in our tracks and shouted to him to stop but it was no use for he was determined to reach the plane. When he reached the plane he rummaged around casually for a few minutes while the few of us that were near him stood petrified that he would set off a mine. He then turned around and started walking back in his own footsteps that were imprinted in the sand. As we did the same we called him all the names we could think of but all he did was to smile saying that his trip was not completely wasted and he pulled out a wristwatch which he found by the plane. One of the drivers looked at the watch and remarked that it wouldn't be much use to him as it had no glass covering the face, so he decided to go back to find the glass. By then I wasn't there to stop him as I'd been called away to other duties and I was only grateful that no one was hurt.

After that stop we proceeded to one more stop before reaching Mersa Matruh to stay the night. We always tried to stage near a village and pay the Headman with tea and sugar to supply us with personnel to guard our goods and vehicles throughout the night.

The following day we carried on our way to Tobruk where we arrived early in the afternoon without any further incidents. We staged outside the town behind a small hill which had been an old anti-aircraft base and depot right in the desert. After having our tea and having taken our salt tablets I gave instructions to the drivers that before they did anything to check their vehicles for fuel and water and make sure that the tyre pressures were correct, which was most essential to be ready in the morning for our next day's journey. While the drivers were doing their tasks, the C.O. and myself drove into the Tobruk garrison to see if they could supply us with a hot meal. When we arrived there we found out that the garrison was small and had no facilities to feed such a large body of men for we had over hundred personnel in our group, we drove back to our camp and gave instructions for everyone to be issued with tined meat, potatoes and tinned fruit. The cook supplied us with big containers of Compo tea; the tea came in 1/2lbs packets of tea, sugar and powdered milk mixed together and there was a standard amount that was put into each container filled with boiling water. For our meal we used our cookers. We used to be issued with tins of sweet potatoes, which very few of us liked and we used to swap them with the natives for eggs.

While we were cooking that evening, there was an incident that scared all of us. Out of nowhere there was an enormous explosion. When you stage in old wartime camps, before you start any fires you check for old ammunition lying about from the war that has been covered by sand. In the desert the wind blows and shifts the sand constantly and covers or uncovers anything that is left behind. Nothing rust through lack of moisture and thing deteriorate very slowly. What had happened was that one of the drivers, when setting up his cooker, had spilt some of his fuel which caught fire on the ground and when he lit it, not realising that under his stove there was a large quantity of 20mm shells covered by thin layer of sand, the heat of the fire exploded a few of the shells which destroyed his cooker and his meal. Everyone stood rooted to the spot, thinking that we might be in a minefield. Thank god no one was hurt but before we could continue with our meal we had orders to check the site thoroughly.

As we had time in the afternoon, some of us decided to explore the site. During the African campaign there was a great battle at Tobruk and the group that I was with found a dump of anti-aircraft shells left by the advancing British Army. They were about 4'6" high. In the desert, you soon learnt to acquire some sort of scarf to wear under your shirt collar, as the wind that blows all the time carries a fine sand which gets into your food, water, clothing and especially your shirt collar, which gets impregnated by it causing a sore neck. The best scarves for the job were silk or fine cotton. We knew that the shells had long silk bags full of cordite in them that would make wonderful scarves, but the problem was how we would get inside the casing. One of the men suggested that that there were plenty of large boulders around, on which we could knock the shells out of their casings, which we did. After a while, when we managed to acquire a couple of scarves each the C.O. came up and ordered us to stop immediately, shouting at us in a very strong language what fools we were. He stood up one of the shells and showed us the top, explaining that these shells had been primed and should we have hit the top the shell would have exploded killing or badly injuring us.

The C.O decided that as we had been driving for nearly a week that we would have two days' rest. Although there wasn't much to do in Tobruk, we all needed a rest, so it was decided to take it in turn to transport small parties of men to a small beach that had facilities to swim and shower in fresh water, which was a real luxury for us.

Our next destination was the Derna Pass, about 120 miles away. Most of us had heard from other drivers that been down it how dangerous the pass was. We had already driven through two passes at Mersa Matruh and Solum which were quite easy to negotiate. It took about six hours to reach the pass without any incidents. When we were at the top, as I looked out I realised that what I'd heard about the pass was not exaggerated; looking down to see a drop was terrifying, but the view from the top was magnificent. Looking to the left you could see the Sahara desert for miles and to the right the coast road with little patches of green vegetation. You could also see the Bedouin camp with their flocks of sheep and goats grazing on small patches of pasture. Originally there was a suspension road between two hills at a height of 600 or 700 feet built by the Italians when they occupied Libya, but during the retreat after the battle at El-Alamein the German army had destroyed t in order to slow down the British advance, but the British Army Engineers had managed to cut a zig-zag road down the mountain in just 72 hours. The road was very steep and had sharp hairpin bends. As it was late afternoon the C.O. decided to stage the convoy where we were for the night as it was too late to go any further. He then called a meeting with the two R.E.M.E. Sgts. and myself to discuss what would be the best way to get the convoy down the road. It was decided that I would drive down to the bottom of the pass in my Jeep, then the convoy would proceed down in first gear travelling at 5mph, one vehicle at a time.

The drivers were also instructed to keep their cab door open when going down so that should they skid on the sand-covered road and couldn't control their vehicle, they could jump to safety and let the vehicle go over the side. When a vehicle negotiated the last bend my job was to signal from the bottom to send the next vehicle down. We did manage to get all our vehicles down without a mishap. My drive down was the most terrifying I have ever had, but also the most exhilarating. The road was very narrow and very steep with no safety barriers or safety rails and, should one miss a turning, one would go right over the edge. When I reached the bottom and looked around there were great mounds of crashed vehicles each side of me that had gone over the edge which made me a bit apprehensive.

The whole exercise of bringing the convoy down the pass took nearly the whole day and it was decided that we would stage where we were for the night again and get over the trauma of the pass. The following day we moved on to Derna, to replenish our supplies.

The town of Derna was only a short distance from where we staged and as soon we loaded up our supplies we parked our vehicles just on the edge of the town near one of the army units. The C.O told us we would be staying here for two days to service our vehicles and those needing small repairs we had been unable to do on the road would be done by the local army workshop.

The town itself was quite small, but it appeared to be gradually returning back normal from the war. We spent some of our time exploring the town; it had a beautiful church but there wasn't much more to amuse ourselves with so we spent most of our time with our vehicles doing maintenance, going to the canteen or resting up as much as possible for the long journey ahead.

In the army, if you've been driving a certain amount of time with a companion you develop some sort of friendship and having driven with the C.O for the past two weeks we were on quite a friendly basis. But you must never overstep the line for the sake of discipline: he was called Sir and I was Sgt. Griebel.

When we left Derna on our way to Benghazi the landscape slowly changed with more patches of green vegetation, which made a pleasant change from seeing just the brown desert and the blue sea. When we were about 35 miles into our journey and on our first break the C.O. came over and asked me if I was interested in archaeology. It turned out that we were very near the ancient city of Cyrene and if I was interested in visiting, he would also ask the other two Sgts. to accompany us and we would go and visit the place when we reached our next rest stop. As we were an independent convoy there was no set time or miles we had to travel each day, as long we arrived in Tripoli on the on the correct day.

At the next stop after we had our drink and salt tablets, and we decided that we would stage there for the night. Then the four of us climbed into my Jeep and we were off to Cyrene which was about 20 miles away. During the drive the whole countryside was barren of people and animals. When we were nearing Cyrene I noticed every so often little round objects, which I recognised soon enough as German Teller Mines which had been dug out during Montgomery's offensive and had never been cleared. I pointed this out to my C.O. who was driving and suggested that perhaps we ought to slow down and watch out in case there were any others covered by the sand. From then on we drove very carefully and arrived at the site, which was right on the edge of the sea.

The site was completely deserted but we discovered that there many snakes on top of the ruins basking in the sun. The actual site was magnificent: there was a Roman temple with many of the marble columns stills standing, which at one time has been converted by Crusaders into a church and you could see where crosses had been carved on some of the columns. There was also a completely intact Amphitheatre and many remains of other Roman buildings and at one end of the site. If you looked into the sea when the sun was very bright you could see broken marble columns under the water and some ruins of the town which must have been destroyed when there was an earthquake. We spent quite some time walking around the site and marvelling at what sort of town it must have been when it was inhabited. But we couldn't get too carried away as we always had to watch out for the snakes. As the time was getting late we had to return to our staging area. In 2004, when on a cruise visiting North Africa, Aileen and I visited Cyrene, which hasn't been changed by the passage of time, but has lost some of its charm by so many tourist parties visiting the site.

The next day we resumed our journey to Benghazi, which took three days. There was only one major incident in the course of the journey. On the second day, when we had staged for the night and the last vehicle had arrived, I checked the total to see if all the vehicles were in. While checking one of the drivers informed me that that he passed one of our vehicles on the road which was stationery and the driver asked him to report to me that his engine had overheated because his water hose had split. He needed water to replenish his water tank before he could proceed. I went to see the breakdown vehicle Sgt. to ask why he didn't stop to help the driver and he told me he didn't see any vehicle that needed assistance. I reported to the C.O. what the situation was and suggested that I should go in the Jeep as it would be much faster than the breakdown vehicle, to which he agreed. I acquired a spare hose pipe and left on my journey to help the driver with his vehicle.

It was late in the afternoon and I was nearing the position where the vehicle was supposed to be and I saw, to my relief, it was only a short distance away. As it was already becoming dark, I parked behind his vehicle and straight away inspected his engine by torch light to see what repairs were necessary before it became pitch black. In the desert, like most places near the equator, there are only a few minutes between the sun setting and night starting. We change the water hose by torchlight. I went to the rear of the Jeep to get a four gallon Jerry can of water that I always carried and as I was undoing the straps to release it I looked down there was a part of a skeleton with the skull inside a steel helmet staring back at me with bits of blanket still around it. I stood transfixed looking at this sight, the other driver wondering what was holding me up with the water. He came closer and when he saw what I was looking at his comment was: "He is a good German and the helmet would make a nice souvenir for you." When I came out of my daze I realised what had happened; when I stopped and used my brake I must have disturbed the top of a shallow grave from the North African campaign. The other driver and myself got our shovels and reburied the bones, then filled the vehicle water tank, switched the engine on, checked for any leakages and, as everything seemed to be working, we drove to our staging area and reported to my C.O. that all the vehicles were in.

When we arrived in Benghazi we staged at a fairly large garrison which had space to accommodate all our vehicles and, best of all, they were able to feed us. The C.O. decided that as we had been on the road driving for the past 18 days we would have a three day rest.

Benghazi was quite a big town and must have been a beautiful city before being badly damaged by the war. My friends and I visited some of the ancient sites and the cathedral which was built in a beautiful Byzantine style which was magnificent. As this was going to be the last and the longest part of our journey – about 700 miles – we had to load up as many provisions and as much fuel that we could as we were advised that there were only small garrisons along our route and as some of them were being closed down.

The temper of our drivers was becoming very frayed and there were many disputes; there is nothing more boring than convoy driving. You drive hour after hour at a regulated slow speed and you see nothing except the desert and the back of the vehicle in front of you, which you must watch out for all the time and keep your distance. I have never heard of such a long convoy like ours to travel such a long distance in so many days.

Some of the drivers had brought footballs with them and our C.O. decided that we should form two teams who, when we stage in the afternoon for the day, would play matches against each other. The idea worked and soon the men calmed down. Backing one or the other team seemed to boost morale. When they played and there was the usual shouting, booing and clapping like in real matches, but it seemed to calmed their tempers.

On the second day of our journey I had a nasty experience which nearly cost me my life. We were staging near one of the smaller units and I was checking the vehicles to see how many were still missing. When the breakdown vehicle eventually arrived – which was supposed to be the last – the R.E.M.E. Sgt. in charge told me that they were late as they had to stop several times to do minor repairs to several vehicles that that had problems with their. I counted the vehicles again to make sure that they had all arrived. I discovered that I was still one vehicle short. I went back to the R.E.M.E. Sgt. and asked him if he was quite sure that he was the last vehicle in and didn't see any other vehicle on the road. He informed me that his vehicle was definitely the last one and there were no other vehicles behind him. I immediately reported to the C.O. that there was a vehicle missing and I would have to go back to find it, and asked him if he wished to accompany me. He agreed that I should go but he could not go with me as he had to write up his daily convoy report.

We had a few drops of rain not long before we staged and I decided to put up the hood on my Jeep, just in case there was some more rain to come. The sun was just setting and I knew that most of my journey would be in the cover of darkness. After driving for more than hour and a half – about 45 miles from where we had staged – I was just about going to give up my search and return to inform the C.O. that we would have to organize a full search in the morning when I saw a light flashing in the distance. Since the desert is a flat terrain and in the night you can see a light not knowing whether it is five or fifty miles away, I decided to drive on and about 7 miles later there was a light flashing from an old costal gun emplacement where I found the vehicle and the driver. I asked him what had happened and why he was off the road. He explained that his engine had overheated and he decided to get off the road while the engine was cooling off and brew himself a mug of tea. When the engine was cool enough, he would carry on and catch up with the convoy, not realising that he had in fact lost all his engine cooling water. When he started the engine he discovered his predicament. I was furious with him and told him in no uncertain manor that he has been told that if one breaks down, to remain where they were so someone can report their position to be able to find them. I fetched my Jerry can of water from my Jeep and discovered that I barely had enough water to fill his tank. He switched on his engine we checked if everything was working then I told him to go on while I turn around and follow him.

When the driver turned his vehicle around and started on his journey I then turned my Jeep around to follow him. After travelling several miles my engine spluttered and stopped. As I was checking the engine suddenly it dawned on me what was wrong. A Jeep has a tank that holds 10 gallons of petrol and the fuel consumption was 10-12 miles to a gallon of petrol. I realised that the last time I had topped up my tank with fuel from my Jerry can we were about 55 miles from the staging area and I had intended to fill up in the morning before proceeding with the convoy. Having travelled to the broken down vehicle 47 miles away I had used up all my fuel. Taking stock of the situation, the driver that I helped out would not be back to the staging area until 9p.m. He wouldn't report me missing but by 10p.m. the C.O. would inquire if I was back in camp and, realising that I was missing, he then would send someone back for me either right away or in the morning. I then realised that I had no food except four Oranges and a pint of water in my water bottle.

At that time I wasn't very worried as I expected someone to come back for me. I sat in the Jeep looking out for any lights in either direction that I could stop to help me. By one o'clock I was becoming sleepy and decided to make myself comfortable and get some sleep. One of the fears of being alone in the desert, especially at night, was wild dogs who carry rabies in their bite. I had no firearms as my Tommy gun was with my kit, stored in one of the vehicles for security reasons. I laid two blankets on the roof of the Jeep, knowing that it would be uncomfortable to sleep on, but at least I would be of the ground. I must have been very tired as I feel asleep almost immediately and when I awoke there was bright sunshine. It was becoming very hot. I climbed down from the roof and sat in the Jeep with the roof protecting me from the sun. I ate my oranges and drank some of my water, still expecting someone from the convoy to come back for me. The temperature was rising to about 100 degrees.

No one came and there was no traffic on the road. I began to be worried as I only had a ½ pint of water left in my water bottle, which I took small sips from to keep my mouth moist, but by midday I had none left. I tried to recover some water from the engine radiator but the taps were stuck and I didn't carry tools in the Jeep as they could be stolen, being an open vehicle. I then realised that I was dehydrating, getting cramps in my stomach and feeling sick. On the way to pick up the broken down vehicle I did pass a native village about fifteen miles away and I did think to walk back to it to ask for help, but I realised that in this heat I would never make it without water. When evening came and it was cooler, I climbed on top of the Jeep to lay down and rest, being very scared that I was going to die of thirst. Eventually I fell asleep, but kept waking up with cramps in my stomach.

In the morning I managed to climb down from the roof and into the cab of the Jeep to be in the shade. My thirst was so great that I would have done anything for a glass of water – even kill. I kept on falling asleep and at about 3 o'clock I heard a horn being blown many times, becoming louder and louder. At first I couldn't believe it and I thought I was hallucinating again. Then I saw a vehicle coming towards me, which I recognised as a 10hp Hillman, my C.O.'s car, which parked beside me. When the C.O. and his driver came up to me all I could say with difficulty was "water, please give me water" as my mouth was so dry and I was nearly passing out. The C.O. produced his water bottle and made me drink it in small sips and then laid me on the back seat of his car, instructing his driver to fill my petrol tank, pack all my things in the back of the Jeep and then follow his car back to our camp.

Once we started back the C.O. was very apologetic and explained to me what happened. The driver of the vehicle that I helped didn't arrive at camp till very late, thinking that I was behind him and, not thinking that there was anything amiss, didn't report me missing. The C.O. thought that I had returned from my trip very late and didn't report to him, not wanting to wake him up. As he was using his staff car the following day, which he did occasionally use, he thought that as usual I was spacing out the convoy. It wasn't until the second day morning, when they were staging for the first brake he realised that I hadn't reported to him the previous evening and, after enquiring if anyone had seen me, he realised that I had been missing for quite some time. He instructed the convoy to remain where they were and took his staff car with his driver to find me. They had to drive about 140 miles before they reached me.

That was how I nearly died in the desert. On the way back to our camp, while recovering in the back of car from lack of food and drink, the C.O. produced a corned beef sandwich and told me to eat it slowly with small sips of water. That was the best sandwich I ever ate. The journey back took just over three hours and when we arrived some of the drivers cheered that the C.O. had found me. The cook was given instructions to make me a hot meal but I couldn't eat much of it as I was still feeling a bit sick. After I finished my meal I reported to the C.O. who ordered me to go to sleep and have as much rest as possible and in the morning he would see if I would be fit enough to drive.

The next morning, when I got up I felt practically normal and after breakfast I reported to the C.O. to carry on with my duties, who inspected me and although he said I looked healthy enough, when we started our journey he would drive the Jeep and I would space out the convoy until he was satisfied that I was completely fit and capable of driving. We were in the fifth day of our journey since leaving Benghazi, driving past farms that were originally cultivated by the Italians when they occupied Libya. At every kilometre there was a small house for the farm workers and every ten kilometres there was a much bigger one for the manager and every hundred kilometres a fort which housed administrative offices and a small garrison.

The next day, when we were about to stop for our lunch, the C.O. pointed out to me a huge black cloud coming towards us. We weren't sure what it was until a very large insect hit our windscreen. At that time we were right at the front of the convoy and the C.O., who was driving the Jeep, recognised the insect and turned around. As we drove back along the convoy he explained to me that the black cloud was a swarm of locust and instructed me to shout to the drivers as we pass them to follow the Jeep no matter what and to shut all their windows. We in the jeep were not so lucky as, except for the windscreen, the vehicle was completely open. We were in for a very uncomfortable ride. We were back at the head of the convoy when the swarm hit us; it was a petrifying ride, the insects being between 4-5" long and, as there were millions of them, we had to drive through them completely blind. It was impossible to see anything through the windscreen being completely covered with squashed insect bodies. They covered us all over, they managed to get inside our shirts, up our sleeves and shorts. Although they are harmless, they were extremely uncomfortable. We drove right through them for about one and a half miles before stopping to clean ourselves and our vehicles off. All our engines and radiator air vents were blocked solid by the insect bodies, which were most difficult to clear, but it had to be done as otherwise the engines would overheat and seize up.

When I looked back at the sight it was incredible: as far as one could see there was this huge green looking carpet travelling at slow speed and leaving behind it bare desert. We also saw local people with large baskets collecting the insects, who I was told roasted and ate them as they were a good supply of protein.

We proceeded with our journey to our next staging area. As we were nearing the end of our journey, with only two hundred miles to Tripoli, our course took us past a place which was named by the forces as Marble Arch as it looked like the Marble Arch in London.[22] The reason for this arch being in the middle of Libya was that when Mussolini had defeated Libya in 1937 he built this arch over the main costal road, with bronze plaques in three dimensions honouring his forces for being victorious, which must have looked magnificent. Unfortunately many of the forces passing through had cut of anything protruding from the sculpted figures such as fingers, toes and heads as souvenirs. Although there was still an R.A.F. base and a small army base we decided to stage in the desert.

When we arrived on the outskirts of Tripoli the following morning we still had a day in hand. It was decided to leave Tripoli and stage in the desert nearby for the day to give us time for the vehicles to be checked for any missing tools or damage before we delivered them to their allocated units. During the inspection we discovered that we were in a little trouble. During our journey we had been drawing rations of food and fuel wherever we could, not knowing if the next supply depot had been shut down or didn't have enough stock to supply us. When we came to check what supplies we had, we found that we had two weeks' surplus of food and a surplus 2,000 gallons of fuel. The army has no system of returning supplies once they have been issued and it is a chargeable offence to have too much or too little. The C.O. called a meeting with the two Sgts from R.E.M.E. and myself to discuss what options we had to get rid of the surplus. There were several suggestions like burying the lot or to burning it, which would have be a terrible waste. Eventually it was agreed that two of us would go to Tripoli to see if we could find a Libyan buyer who would buy the goods.

One of the Sgts. has been stationed in Tripoli before and spoke some Italian. He asked me if I would accompany him. We took my Jeep and as we entered the outskirts of Tripoli we saw a

---

[22] There was a major battle there during the desert campaign 1941-42.

large Fiat garage with many large lories in front of it. We drove to it and asked one of the men for the proprietor. After waiting a few minutes a short middle aged Libyan gentleman appeared who luckily spoke English and politely asked us what we required. We asked him if we could speak to him privately. He showed us to his office and, once there, we informed him that we were there not in an official capacity but on a private matter. We explained to him that we had a certain amount of goods which we no longer required and no one would miss and asked him if it would be of any interest to him to buy them. The goods consisted mainly of tins of beef and fruit, but also some tins of potatoes and jam. After he asked us more questions about the goods he agreed to take all the food but only 1,500 gallons of fuel as his storage was not big enough to take any more. After bartering for a while we agreed on a price of £1,200 in £1 or £5 sterling and it was also agreed that he would follow us to the staging area in his large lorry to pick up the goods. He asked us if we would like some refreshments as he needed a little time to assemble the money.

Soon he returned with an enormous 10-ton Fiat lorry which would be big enough to take all the stores. When we returned to our staging area he inspected the goods which seemed to satisfy him, his vehicle was loaded and he then produced and handed to us two a big paper bags stuffed with bundles of notes, which were counted quickly. There were smiles all round, with both sides feeling satisfied with the deal. After he departed we divided the cash. Each driver received £5, the store drivers £10 and the C.O. and us three Sgts split the rest. My share came to about £120. Unfortunately we had to burn the other 500 gallons of fuel.

At long last we were coming to the end of our journey. When we hand over our vehicles our task would be finished. We had been driving for 29 days and had covered over 1,700 miles with only a few small incidents and accidents and we were relieved that all of us had arrived safely at our destination.

As I drove through the modern part of Tripoli, which was built mostly by Italians, I thought it was a very beautiful city with wide boulevards flanked by shops and apartments, everywhere decked with flowers, with the walkways covered with a roof resting on slender pillars to protect shoppers from the sun. We had no trouble finding the unit as there were many signposts giving us directions to different units. When we arrived at our designated ordinance depot we were directed to a space in a huge vehicle park where we were to stage our vehicles for inspection. There waiting for us was a Q.M. Sgt. and small squad of men to check our vehicles for any breakages, dents or any tools or tyres missing before signing over the vehicles. While observing the changeover I heard someone shout "Betty!" I turned around and I saw that the Q.M. Sgt. was one of my old Brummie friends Bob from my old company that I came out with to Egypt. He straight away asked me if I could join him when the inspection was over for a drink and a chat, but I explained to him that until I have details what billeting arrangements have been made for me and my men and what my orders were during our stay in Tripoli I couldn't do anything. As soon as I knew I would get in touch with him.

After all the vehicles were been signed over the C.O. called an informal parade and gave us our orders during our stay in Tripoli. The men that were been posted to Tripoli would join their units while the man from my 286 company would be given seven days' leave and would be billeted in one of the Italian villas that had been taken over by the army. When our leave was over we would be returning back to Alexandria re-join our units where the C.O. would be leaving us as he would be going home. We would be using our three 3-ton lories and the Jeep for the return journey and it would take us about 7-10 days.

After the other drivers were taken to their respective units we were driven to our villa which was situated only a short distance from the town's shopping area and when we entered the villa we had a most pleasant surprise. Throughout there were marble floors to keep the place cool, all the rooms had fans hanging from the ceilings, all of which were working, there were four bedrooms and an enormous bathroom with a bath and shower. In the back there was a large flower garden with a patio cowered with a canvas roof to give us shade while having our meals. Best of all we had a Libyan caretaker-cum-guard, who for a small fee would cook our meals, clean our rooms and arrange our laundry. I did manage to see Bob several times and caught up with all the news about our old friends. We spent most of our time having a rest, wondering around Tripoli to see some of the archaeological sites and soon it was time for our journey back to Alexandria.

The day before our departure, since I was still acting unpaid Sgt. until I returned to Alexandria, I had to check out our vehicles and collect our stores and fuel for our journey as we were leaving early the following morning. The day before leaving I developed a sore throat, of which I took no notice as it didn't worry me much. I took some aspirins thinking I had a mild cold and hoping it would get better by the morning. In the morning there was no improvement and I was advised to see the M.O., but I refused as he might want to keep me in the sickbay and I would miss going back with my men to my company in Alexandria.

We set off early in the morning on our journey back to Alexandria and my throat seemed to be a little easier and I was able to eat some bread and swallow some tea with some discomfort. We were travelling at a much faster speed, not having a convoy. On that first day we managed to cover 200 miles, hoping we could do the remaining 450 miles to Benghazi in the next two days.

The following morning my condition deteriorated even further and I wasn't able to swallow any food or even drink any water without suffering great pain. The C.O. was very worried of my condition and told me that as soon we came across any army post or unit that had an M.O. I would have to see him as I couldn't continue much further in the condition I was in. Early the following morning, while we were staging for our first brake a staff car stopped at our camp with a British Lt. Colonel and his driver from Cyrenaica defence force and asked if he we could share some of our tea with them, to which we of course agreed. While he was conversing with the C.O. it came out that he was also travelling to Benghazi, but he had to be there that night. My C.O. explained to him my situation and asked him if he could take me with him and deposit me at Benghazi hospital, to which he agreed. I was told to take only my small kit and to leave the rest on the lorry that I had been sleeping in and it would be handed to my company in Alexandria waiting for me when I returned. I quickly packed all my gear and joined the Colonel for our long journey of some 380 miles. On the journey we stopped several times to give the driver a rest and to take refreshment, but I could only drink a little water as it was impossible for me to swallow anything else. The Colonel took some turns in driving and although I offered my services he wouldn't let me drive as he didn't think that I was in any fit condition to drive. Our journey to Benghazi took eight hours and as soon we reached there I was taken straight to the hospital.

When we arrived at the hospital the Colonel asked to speak to the duty doctor and when he arrived he explained to him my condition and left me to drive to his unit H.Q. in town. The doctor called a nurse and they walked me to the consulting room where he inspected my throat, lungs, heart and all the usual places. Afterwards he told me that I had tonsillitis. He then asked me if I was in any hurry to return to my unit, which I thought was a bit odd. I was a bit worried and asked him why that was a matter of importance. He explained that I would be cured within a week by having a course of antibiotics and a lot of fluids to drink. He then went on to explain that the hospital was short of patients as so many troops had been demobbed and as they had 17 nurses and only 15 patients, which wasn't enough for them to receive full rations of spirits, cigarettes and chocolate, if I didn't mind he would like to keep me in the hospital until the new year, which was three months away. He wanted me to think about it and give him my answer in the morning. I was then taken to a ward and as I was still acting Sgt. I was to share a ward with three other Sgts. who were waiting to be demobbed at the end of the year, who like me had been asked the same as me to stay in the hospital. I discussed with them the pros and cons of staying in the hospital and in the morning I told the doctor that I would stay.

Staying in the hospital was like being in a first class hotel. It had been built by the Italians with all the floors in marble which kept it cool and the ceilings were very high which kept the rooms very airy. The bed sheets were changed every other day and the bathrooms had both bath and showers which was a real luxury. We were also issued with pyjamas which I hadn't worn since I had joined the army.

The food was excellent, served on china plates with proper cutlery. We had three meals a day, with elevenses and a snack for supper. In the next fortnight our number of patients swelled to about twenty-five, some with jaundice, some with malaria, some with small injuries and five who were circumcised. Most of the patients soon got over their illnesses and were asked to stay longer, those of us who were healthy used to go around the wards and chat to the sick patients. Going around the jaundice ward I struck a friendship with one of patients. By his bedside he had a picture of a very beautiful girl which I thought was his girlfriend, but during our conversation I discovered that it was his sister named Babs. I asked him that when he next wrote to her would he ask her if she would mind if I could write to her as a pen pal. A few weeks later he told me that he had received a letter from his sister and she was quite agreeable to correspond with me and asked me to send her a picture of myself and she would send me one of hers, but more about her later.

When the three Sgts. and myself became better acquainted, we started to go out together into Benghazi. The town in parts was quite beautiful, but best of all it had a beach where we could swim and, having money from my ill-gotten gains, I was able to afford to enjoy myself with them. The hospital overlooked the town and it was very interesting to watch how the natives went about their business in their daily life. There wasn't much motor transport and most of the goods were transported either on a donkey or donkey and cart. I marvelled at the amount of goods they could load onto the carts and the poor beasts. One evening one of the Sgts. called me over to the window and showed me a sight I had never seen before. Going past the houses opposite us there was an elderly man walking with a young girl, which wasn't an uncommon sight, so I asked him what was unusual and special about it? He told me to wait and watch.

As the man and the girl passed one of the houses they turned quickly behind it. There was a small patch of lawn behind the house where the girl lay down and the man sat a short distance from her. In a very short time there was a queue of about 13-15 servicemen who paid the man and then had intercourse with the girl, which lasted only a few minutes. Later I found out that this was a daily occurrence and that in some of the tribes the girls from the poor families who wished to get married and had no possibility of having a dowry prostituted themselves until they acquired enough money for a dowry. It seems there is no shame attached to the girls, as when they made enough money they could give it to their future husband to start a business or buy a house with a piece of land. It was a sight I never forgot.

As we were approaching the winter season the weather was getting colder and I suddenly realised that I had no winter kit as it was in my kitbag which I had sent back to Alexandria and I didn't have any other warm clothing. I asked in the hospital stores if they could issue me with some but they had no facilities for issuing clothing. Luckily one of the Sgts. in my ward took me to his unit where the Q.M. was his friend, who issued me the appropriate clothing.

The time in hospital seemed to pass quickly and soon Christmas was upon us. The nurses asked all the patients that were able to help making the decorations for the wards; hats, chains, stars and all the other usual ones, which we later helped to put up in the wards. As this was going to be my last ten days in the hospital before returning to my unit, I was looking forward greatly to my turkey Christmas dinner. We were informed that there would be plenty of food and beer to drink but no spirits.

On Christmas Day, soon after our morning break, beer became available and we managed to drink a couple of pints which put us into a merry mood before our dinner. When dinnertime came all the patients went into the dining hall, including the patients that had difficulties in walking and were being helped by the nurses. We were served with large portions of turkey and stuffing with the usual vegetables and while the meal was in progress we drank toasts to the King, Doctors,

Nurses and anything else we could think of. Then came this wonderful Christmas pudding with cream. After dinner we went to our wards to have a rest until teatime where we were served turkey sandwiches and large helpings of Christmas cake. Beer was still available to those that wanted it, we had a few more beers and although I gave up drinking in the army after seeing how much alcohol was being consumed by men in the canteen, which could easily turn one into an alcoholic, I made this Christmas an exception.

After tea, when we had returned to our ward, one of the Sgts. mentioned that he was fed up drinking beer and suggested that we all chip in some money and go into town where they knew a place that stocked spirits to which we all agreed. After a short rest we went into town. We bought a bottle of Cyprus Brandy, Whiskey, Sherry and a dodgy bottle of Gin. When we returned to our ward we opened the bottles to sample them and by the time it came to our evening meal we were very, very merry. When we returned to our ward we still had a lot of our drink left, including a bottle of Sherry and one of the Sgts. suggested that we make a Punch from remaining drinks to finish the day. We managed to get a hold of two large surgical bowls and some oranges from the dining room which we cut up and mixed the whole lot together. After we let it stand for a while we started to take small sips of the mixture which at first wasn't very palatable but after a while we became used to. We were all acting a bit silly and one of the Sgts. dared me to drink a mug full of the mixture without stopping to breathe.

I took on the dare and all I can remember after drinking it is passing out and waking up in bed very sick with my head throbbing and a doctor standing nearby who came over and said "Thank God you are conscious at last, you have been unconscious for the past 32 hours and nearly died from alcoholic poisoning." He then proceeded to tell me how stupid I'd been and instructed the nurse to give me as much tea that I could drink and to get me a light meal. When the doctor and nurse had left I noticed in the bed next to me was the Sgt. that was supposed to be travelling with me to Alexandria lying there all bandaged. He could hardly speak and the story was that he was so drunk after I passed out and the doctor had finished attending to me that he decided to go for the night to his billet in Benghazi. He was billeted in a three story building. He went into a room thinking it was his room, opened the French windows onto the balcony to get some fresh air, stepped out and fell two floors down as the balcony in that room had been destroyed during the war. He suffered a broken leg, collar bone, one arm, several cracked ribs and he was told that he would have to stay in the hospital for at least another month. That's how my Christmas and the year 1945 ended.

**11 - Portrait sent home on
the 1st September 1945.**

1946

Just before the New Year I received orders for my return journey to Alexandria. As I was already bored and fed up having nothing to do for the last three months, it was a great relief to be going. We were to be a small party consisting of myself, two sergeants from my ward and two privates. We would first be travelling about 400 miles by road to Tobruk, taking about three days, where we would board a train that would take us on the remainder of our 450 mile journey to Alexandria.

The journey to Tobruk was uneventful and the vehicle we were travelling in took us straight to the railway station where a train was waiting for us. As we boarded, we were issued with rations for our journey and we were given the opportunity to fill our water bottles. We were also informed that at certain stops there would be other refreshments of tea and soft drinks to keep us going, as the journey would be 8-10 hours long.

In North Africa there was no wood or coal to speak of, so our trains were all run on diesel engines. Our train consisted of ten carriages and three engines – one in the front and two at the back. The carriages we were in were very old, having wooden seats, very primitive toilets and no glass in the windows, just some sort of Venetian blinds that could be opened for ventilation and light. Sometimes they had to be shut to stop the sand blowing in.

The journey started well enough, but after travelling for about an hour and a half the front engine broke down and the engineers decided that, as the two back engines were only powerful enough to push the train at a very slow speed, they would creep along to the nearest depot where, hopefully, there would be a spare engine. Being just after the war, the rolling stock was very old and worn out, and often broke down like this. After several hours we arrived at the depot which was in the middle of nowhere, but they had no spare engines. Luckily, they had some spare parts which could replace the broken ones on our engine. The work on the engine took about four hours, and by then we knew we wouldn't reach our destination that day.

We decided to prepare ourselves to sleep on the train, but as there were about 250 army personnel, as well as some civilians, on the train there was very little space for sleeping. The five of us discussed the situation and came to the same arrangement we had used back when travelling from Calais to Toulon in France.

When the train got moving again we moved at a reasonable speed and our hopes were that we would arrive in

Alexandria the following morning, but it was not to be. After travelling for a further three hours we heard a large bang and the train slowed to a stop. We were again informed that another engine had broken down and we would be travelling slowly to Solum, where, thankfully, there would be a spare engine. It was quite late when we arrived at Solum, and so the army organized some food and hot drinks for us, which was most welcome as we had been running low on water. It was also good to be able to wash, as it was the first chance to have a good clean in two days. We knew that we would be spending another night on the train as there wasn't a spare driver and our one had to have a sleep.

Early the following morning, once again we proceeded towards Alexandria, hoping that there would not be any more mishaps, but again we had to stop for repairs, but this time we were lucky in that the repairs could be done on the spot, without having to drive to a depot. We finally arrived in Alexandria in the evening on the third day of our travels; at last our nightmare journey was over. In great relief we descended from the train and I said goodbye to my four companions, who had another long journey back to England. Meanwhile, at the station there was a 15cvt. vehicle waiting to take me back to my company. As we were travelling, I realised that we were not going to the company at Palm Court where our quarters were under canvas, but to our winter quarters which were situated right opposite the seafront overlooking the Corniche and Stanley bay, one of the most beautiful parts of Alexandria.

At that time the Corniche was kept clean and the roads fully repaired. To the right of us it lead to Queen Farida's palace and to the left, going round to the far side of the city, was King Farouk's palace. While staying at our winter camp we often used to watch King Farouk and his court travelling to visit the Queen. When that happened, the whole of the Corniche was cleared of traffic so that he and his entourage could travel in the limousines at high speed without any interruptions. The cars were painted red and black, which were the colours that could only be used on the King's vehicles; no one else was permitted to use them in Egypt. Most of the houses facing the sea were magnificent villas which are sadly no longer there; in 2004, when Aileen and I were on a cruise, we visited and the palaces remained but the villas had been demolished and replaced by ugly high-rises that looked very shabby and in need of repair.

When I arrived back at camp, I reported to the duty sergeant who told me to report to my platoon commander in the morning before walking me to one of the barracks, allocated me a bed and blankets and then left me. I had no other kit than that which I had left the hospital in and it was too late to retrieve my kit from the company stores, so I wouldn't be able to collect it until I had seen my company commander Capt. Foulks. In the morning I reported to the company commander, trying to look smart, which was an impossibility as I hadn't had a change of clothes for the past three days.

Tim ALEXANDRIA EGYPT 1946

12 - On my lorry in Alexandria, 1946. The message on the bumper was for my pen pal Babs back in England.

The first thing he asked me was where I had been for the past three months. In hospital, I told him, and then he asked what had been wrong with me. I said that I had been instructed to say by the doctors that I had Tonsillitis but they had decided to keep me for observations, which seemed to satisfy him. He then proceeded to tell me that he had no spare vehicles for me as the company was waiting on a delivery of new 10-ton Leylands to replace our old vehicles which had kept on breaking down and we had run out of spare parts for. He also told me that when we received our new vehicles there would be very little chance of me having one as they would be allocated to the drivers whose vehicles they would be replacing. Until then, we had a full complement of vehicles so there would not be a spare one for me, but he had two jobs on offer for me: one working in an office, which he knew I hated, and another that was most unusual in camp. The job that he offered me was that of camp refuse collector. I would be in charge of a Ceylonese private, one donkey and a cart. The Ceylonese private would be responsible for looking after the donkey, the cart and the stabling. He then proceeded to explain the job to me.

In the camp cookhouse there were large bins where all the waste food and slops were thrown. These bins had to be collected nightly after supper for sanitary reasons and disposed of at a local dump. During the day, we were to go round the camp and one other camp adjacent to ours and collect anything that was discarded from the workshops, like wood packing cases, worn out engine parts and any other metal bits, which also had to be disposed of. I would also be responsible for making sure the boiler was heating and supplying hot water, and I would be told how to maintain it. I was told that, although the Ceylonese private had been doing the job for the past year, it would be my responsibility to make sure it was done properly. The only disadvantage was that the job would be seven days a week. I would be excused of all other duties and I would still be part of my platoon. As soon as a vehicle became available it would be assigned to me.

I thought for a moment about what he had said; seven working days didn't worry me as I hardly did anything on my days off as there was very little to do in the desert and I realised that this was a little independent unit which would suit me fine. I told the company commander that I would take the job, starting the following morning.

After seeing Capt. Foulks, I went to the QM store to retrieve my kits and blankets. The private working there was new and I didn't know, as many of the drivers I knew before going on the convoy had left for home. I asked him for my kit and he went to look for it. After a while he came back and informed me that there was no record of my kit being handed in. I asked to see the QM sergeant and when he arrived I explained to him what had happened. He then checked his records and told me that there was no mention of my kit being handed in to the stores, but there was a record of my firearm being handed into the armoury. I asked him what the procedure was in such a case. He told me that he has to report this to the platoon commander to decide whether to report this to the military police, or he will give permission for a completely new kit to be issued. After lunch, I reported back to the QM and to my relief I was told that everything had been sorted out and that he had received permission. Luckily, I had taken all my personal possessions with me when I went to hospital otherwise they would have been lost. At long last, I was able to wash, shower, change my clothes and feel clean once again.

The next morning, wearing my overalls I waited at the company office for the Ceylonese private. He arrived punctually at 9a.m., and introduced himself. He gave his name, which I could hardly pronounce, but he told me not to worry as everyone called him George. He was about 5'6" with a huge smile. I asked him what job we would actually be doing. He explained that in the morning we would be going around the camps several times to collect all the packing cases of wood and cardboard. We weren't to pick up any rubbish outside the camps, as that was done by soldiers on punishment. After lunch we had to check the boiler house, before finishing at 3p.m. The rest of the afternoon was ours to do what we wished, but after dinner we would have to pick up the cookhouse bins and load them onto a large vehicle that would take them to a larger dump in the desert, but we wouldn't be going to the dump ourselves; the last man in my job had made a deal with an Egyptian carpenter who was willing to buy the wood and some of the metal and was willing to pay us £1 a day, which we would split between us.

I thought about it, and realised that it would double my army pay with no loss to anyone, so I agreed with the arrangement. We went around the camps, checked the boiler and then left the camp for a side street a short distance away, where we met the carpenter, who took everything but the cardboard and some metal he didn't require, paid us and then went on his way whilst we travelled to the dump to get rid of the leftover rubbish.

13 - Refuse collectors - myself and the Ceylonese private with the donkey.

At 7.30p.m. we did our cookhouse collection. When we arrived there were two large metal bins for us to pick up which were full of slops. They were very heavy and it took both of us to lift each one onto the cart. I asked George if we were going to the same dump, but he said that we weren't, and that he had forgot to tell me there was another arrangement for the disposal of the slops. It seemed that there was an Egyptian who had a food stall in a very poor part of Alexandria and was prepared to buy the slops for £1 a day, which I and George would also split. I asked George what the Egyptian did with the slops and he explained that the man boiled the whole lot with curry powder and other spices, before draining the mixture and selling it as a cheap filling for pita bread. The man had a little lorry when we met him on which he had some containers. We transferred the slops into his containers, he paid us the pound and on the way back I could only think how amazed I was that in a single day I had tripled my army pay.

Towards the end of March the company was preparing to move to our summer camp in Palm Court and I was informed by my M.T Sgt that a vehicle was becoming available, a ten-ton American Mack lorry, as one of the drivers was being demobbed and I could have it immediately if I wished. I accepted his offer as I was getting bored being a refuse collector; at long last I would have a permanent job. As soon as I could I went to meet the driver of the vehicle and, although it was old and slightly battered, I thought it was beautiful. I checked it all over, making sure it had all the tools, equipment and tyres before I had him sign it over to me.

When everything was completed, he asked me if I would like to have his dog, as he couldn't take it with him back to England. The dog, Percy, was about ten years old, a magnificent red setter with whom he had enjoyed the company of for many years. It would be a useful asset to have while driving on detail as he would act as a deterrent to stop the natives stealing from my truck, and feeding him would be no problem as there was always spare food being thrown out of the cookhouse, so I agreed to have him.

Our company didn't really do big convoys – most details only involved one to three vehicles. On ten-ton lorries you usually had a second driver and sometimes a German prisoner of war in the back to watch out for any thieves, but they were getting scarce as most were gradually being repatriated. Going on detail, we were always issued with rations, as most details were one to two days, depending on the distance. On some details there were occasions where you could make a little money, one of them being transporting the company's old and dirty blankets to be dumped and burned. The Army changed our blankets three times a year in the Middle East; the new ones were issued and the old ones rolled up like sausages, ten to a bundle, and taken on lorries to Tel El-Kabeer where they were incinerated. The blankets were a mixed lot, some manufactured in Britain, New Zealand, Australia, but the best were made in the US; green in colour, very thin and made of pure wool, they were prized by the Egyptians who made overcoats from them. A lorry usually carried 30-40 bales and as soon as we would leave the camp we would drive out of Alexandria to the desert where we would unload the bales one at a time, take out the American blankets, roll the bales back up and load them up back onto the lorries. Usually we managed to find 25-40 blankets in a load. On the way there were always men shouting to us, asking us if we had any American blankets to sell. When we stopped they would buy the lot from us for £1 each. When we arrived at the dump no one bothered to check the number of blankets and as long as we had the correct number of bales they were dumped and burned.

Another little scheme that we had was, when returning from a detail with an empty vehicle, there were always a lot of Egyptian men walking along the road shouting to us to see if we would give them a lift to Cairo or Alexandria. If we had enough time in our schedule we would let them ride in the back and charge them a fee of 10p to Cairo and 20p to Alexandria. Sometimes I had as many as twenty-five passengers. On one occasion, when I was on detail to Cairo, I had a pleasant surprise: I and my spare driver had to spend the night at Cairo HQ barracks and, when walking back to our billets from the mess hall, we passed the parade ground, where I saw an officer wearing a Black Watch regimental kilt walking across smoking a pipe in a way that I instantly recognised. Usually you were not allowed to walk across the parade ground so I took another look at the officer and realised that it was my old pal from my Army Cadet days Reggie Gold.

Without thinking I shouted "Reggie!" He turned around, not recognising me as all he could see were two soldiers in dirty overalls. He came over with a scowling face but as he got near me a big smile broke out on his face. We chatted about our families and what we had been doing since we had seen each other last. He told me he was second in command of the garrison company and, if I would like, I could be stationed in the Cairo garrison with the rank of Sergeant as he needed one and, knowing me, I would fit in nicely. I thanked him for the offer, but I told him I enjoyed the job I was doing. We said our goodbyes, and I didn't see him for another year (but more on Reggie later).

The driving job became a routine but was never boring, as I saw new things wherever I travelled. When I returned from a detail I had to check my vehicle to see if it was serviceable for the following day's detail or if it needed any repairs. I also had to check how far we would be travelling and for how long to work out what rations would be needed to draw from the stores and whether or not it was necessary for a second driver to come with. In the summer my working day started with reveille at 5.30a.m., leaving camp on detail an hour later and then I worked until 1p.m. before stopping for a rest until 4p.m., when I would work another two hours until 6p.m., as the temperature in the summer was between 95-105F and, in the canal zone where I was stationed, could reach up to 122F (50°c). The work that we did after 4p.m. was usually maintenance on the vehicle or, if it was urgent, a night detail.

As the situation in Egypt was getting more tense, our orders were not to go out unless there were at least four personnel in a group and we were issued with entrenching tool handles to carry on our belt in the bayonet frog[23] for our protection. The drivers had orders to under no circumstances stop driving and there was an unwritten rule that if you knocked down a native you made sure he was dead, as the Army paid a fixed sum of compensation to the family for any deaths but if he was injured they had to pay a pension for the rest of their life and the driver would be charged for injuring a person.

Driving at night was becoming hazardous and everyone hated it. There was one incident that made a lot of us sick, when one of the drivers from my platoon came back from a detail one evening. He thought that he had hit a boulder or a desert animal

---

[23] A webbing holder for bayonets that goes on your belt.

like a wild dog and, as we never stopped to check. When he got back to camp was his first opportunity to check, and when he crawled under his vehicle he quickly rolled out again and was violently sick. Those of us nearby looked under to see what had caused his distress and we discovered that he must have hit an Egyptian villager walking along the road and, being pitch black, he wouldn't have seen him. When the man went underneath he must have been caught by the rear wheel and spun around on the rear axle as he looked like a lump of meat on a spit. The body couldn't be identified and after seeing it many of us were queasy. The whole thing must have been hushed up as we didn't hear any more about it.

At the beginning of June we had some good news. At that time you had to serve abroad for three years to be granted any home leave, but suddenly the government announced that the period was being halved to eighteen months as the war was over and there were now more ships available to take people home. I worked out that I would be eligible for my leave just after Christmas. There was great jubilation among the troops as there were many of them who would be shortly going home to their loved ones and every day they started checking the notice board for the date of their departure. I carried on driving details in great enjoyment and I knew it would be another six months before it would be my turn.

A few weeks later I was instructed by my platoon sergeant to report to the Company Office in the morning before going on detail as the CO wanted to see me. When I reported there my CO Capt. Foulks told me that there had been a communication from the War Office selection board that stated that as the war was over and, with so many soldiers being demobbed, there was a surplus of officers in the force, and so they were interviewing mainly personnel in category A1 and in some cases A2, but in all cases if commissioned they would have to sign up for at least a further three years. He asked me if I would be prepared to sign up for this period of service. I thought about it and told him that I had gone off the idea of being an officer and I had no interest staying in the army for another three years in some base depot company office as I was having a much more interesting time driving to different places. Having looked through my service record he noticed that I had applied for British naturalisation, and asked me if I still wanted to proceed. I replied that I did as soon as possible. He told me to check the notice board for when the documentation arrived so I could sign it.

Things were getting quite serious in Egypt and there were many more attacks on British servicemen. We were informed that bases in Egypt were to be moved to the Canal Zone near the Great Bitter Lake in the Sahara Desert. The place where our company was to have a new base was called Thag which was very easy for me to remember as it was my initials. In August, our company was given the job of moving some of the units to their new locations along with other general transport companies. It was a very busy time for us and we had to drive much longer hours. In September, I had one incident that happened on one such detail. I was on a two day trip and, having delivered my load to one of the units and picked up another for delivery to my company, I was staying the night with one of the units based in the desert. I was going to sleep in the back of my vehicle, as it was more comfortable than the beds that you were usually allocated in camp, and I was very tired and couldn't be bothered to go to the cookhouse for my meal, so I decided to use the rations I had with me. The usual way we had our meal was to take a tin of meat and vegetables and put it on our exhaust pipe under the bonnet, switch on the engine and a few minutes later we had a nice hot meal followed by a tin of fruit.

Just before I could start my meal an orderly came running up to me and asked my name before telling me that I was wanted in the Company Office as a telegram had arrived for me. I rushed to the office thinking the worst, that someone close to me had died or was seriously ill, but when I reached the office the duty officer handed me the telegram with a big smile. I quickly opened it and the message said: "Happy 21st Birthday love from Mum, Dad and Rozia." It was the 14th September 1946. Dates didn't really mean much in the desert as one day was the same as the next and I really forgot all about it, so I celebrated my 21st birthday with a tin of meat and vegetables and a large mug of tea.

While stationed in Alexandria a funny incident happened to me involving a Jewish family. There was a photo shop a short distance from our camp that had just received a consignment of new Kodak cameras which were at a price that I could afford, so I decided to go and see if I could buy one. Whilst inspecting one of the cameras, the owner of the shop came over to explain the different functions of the camera. During the conversation he asked me if I was Jewish and when I told him I was he asked if I would like to join them for Friday night supper as they often invited Jewish servicemen for meals over the weekend. I accepted his offer and the following Friday he arrived at the camp gate in a large Hummer parked by the guardhouse where I was waiting for him.

We drove to his house which was situated in one of the nicest parts of Alexandria. It was a large villa with spacious gardens I was met and made most welcome by his family. There was his wife, his son, who was slightly older than me and a very pretty daughter, Hanna, who was slightly younger than me. We had a delightful Shabbat meal and as I was leaving, thanking them for their hospitality they invited me to come again to which I accepted.

After several visits I discovered that the family was quite wealthy, owning cotton mills and exporting cotton cloth all over the world. Besides that, they owned several other businesses of which the photographic shop was a side-line. On one occasion, when I was have an after dinner drink with the father he mentioned that the daughter had a dowry of £50,000 – which was roughly equivalent to £2m in today's money – and should she marry he would buy a house for the couple. He also mentioned that he and his son were thinking of moving part of their business to England and anyone marrying their daughter would be invited to join the firm. He then told me that Hanna liked me and, if I would like, I could take her out to get to know her better (but, of course, with a chaperone).

It was then that I realised that all the invitations to dinner were simply to find a husband for his daughter. I did go out with Hanna on several dates but I realised that our relationship would never work as we had very little in common. Hers was a very sheltered life, having everything given to her on a silver platter and knew nothing of the real world. She had very little interest in anything except getting married, having a home and starting a family and meeting her girlfriends. On the other hand, my interests when leaving the army were, being a young man, to meet a lot of girls and have a lot of fun and make my own way in life. Although she was a beautiful girl, I couldn't see a future for us. I had a talk with her father, explaining to him why I had to refuse his offer and thanking him and his family for their kindness, before leaving. I never heard from them again.

Just after my birthday, the task of moving the units from Alexandria and Cairo was completed and we were the last vehicles to leave Cairo with all our equipment. As we were leaving we were stoned by the natives, which was quite daunting and scary, but we managed to arrive at our new base at Thag without any injuries or serious damage to our vehicles. At our new base the only permanent buildings that had been built were the company office, the cookhouse, showers, toilets and boiler house. Our washing facilities we long tables with wash basins on top and a row of water taps above them, all in the open. Our accommodation were some very large tents with a double roof to keep them cool and slept eight to a tent, although they could accommodate twelve. With winter approaching, we were issued with extra blankets as the temperature could drop below freezing and often water left overnight in the basins would turn to ice by the morning. We still had to do small convoys to the Alexandria docks, but we went by a specific route so as to not antagonise and upset the natives. Most of our supplies now arrived at Port Said.

Incident March 1946, Canal Zone, Egypt

When we moved to the Canal Zone from where we were stationed in Alexandria the camp area was much larger, the distance from where we were to the Atlantic coast was 3,000 miles and all of it was the sand of the Sahara. We were on one end of the desert and across the other side of the canal was the Sinai Desert. The perimeter fence was still being worked on and didn't have all its barbed wire in position around it. During the night we had to post double the guards as in the previous month we had had two of our tents stolen. The tents we used were eighteen feet long, fourteen wide, with walls 5'6" high, made from canvas with two eight-inch-thick bamboo poles ten foot high to keep it up. It was no mean feat to steal a tent of such size, as each weighed roughly a third of a ton and they were quite valuable as, in the desert, they could house a large family.

Despite the extra guards posted, we lost another tent the following month, which was most embarrassing as the tent was near the guard tent. It was then decided to change the way we did our guard duty. In future, the guards would split up and each detail will watch a different section of the camp. There were to be extra guards posted from the men that were not on details, even those that were from the lower fitness category like myself. Our orders were that if you challenged anyone you saw and they didn't respond correctly, you were permitted to shoot. At that time there was a lot of unrest in Egypt through the Nationalist movement and there were many attacks on service personnel. During riots, which were quite often, several were killed including an acquaintance of mine.

One night, when it was my turn to be on guard duty, I was posted on a nearby sand dune so I had a bird's eye view of the fence. I thought I saw some movement by the perimeter wire opposite some empty tents. I watched the spot for a while but I wasn't sure if there was anything unusual going on. I quietly called out to the guard sergeant, who silently came over and sat down beside me so I could point out the spot where I had seen the movement, but there was nothing to see. Even so, he decided we should watch the spot a little longer. Suddenly, there was movement by the wire and at first it looked like it might have been a pack of wild desert dogs, but soon we realised the movement was being caused by eight or nine men crawling very slowly under the wire, making their way to one of the empty tents.

I asked the sergeant if we should call for backup and challenge them, but he said that we should instead just watch them to see what they were up to. We waited about twenty minutes, but nothing seemed to be happening. Then, we suddenly noticed that the tent was very slowly sinking to the ground; so slowly you wouldn't realise what was happening unless you were looking for it. The walls were carefully taken down and rolled up into bundles. When the roof was nearly down, the poles were slowly removed; it was quite a feat, as one pole was extremely heavy, so to take it down slowly in complete silence must have taken great willpower. The whole thing was rolled up into two parcels and the men then started crawling back under the wire with sections of the tent. The whole process took about two hours in total silence.

The sergeant called in extra guards and we started walking towards the men, challenging them to stop. Unfortunately they didn't and the order was given to open fire with our rifles. The thieves escaped over the wire, but had to drop their loot in the process. More guards arrived and we all went to the spot where the thieves had escaped to retrieve our tent. When we arrived we found that two of the thieves had been shot dead, but we didn't know if we had injured any others, and it was too dark to tell who had shot who. But, I knew that I was the best shot there that night.

Later, I asked myself if I had been the one that had killed one of those thieves. If so, did I have any remorse? No. If it was me I didn't want to kill him – I didn't want to kill anyone – but I was a British soldier protecting the camp and my friends in it, who could have been hurt or badly injured by people who certainly didn't care if they killed any servicemen. Would I shoot again? Yes, to protect my family, my friends and myself. At that time the feeling for the Egyptians was not great, although I didn't hate them and understood why they were restless. I knew several Egyptians stationed at Alexandria who I got to know very well, but with any country it was a mixed bag. They were stealing and could easily have been armed, which wasn't unusual, and if I was the man that shot them then they died for greed.

The sergeant notified H.Q, who in turn sent a Military Police officer and an Egyptian Police officer, who took statements from the sergeant, myself and two other guards that had opened fire, and informed us that there would have to be a court of inquiry, but we never heard any more about it. Soon after the incident a battalion of Ghurkhas were posted to the area, who took over the duties of guarding most of the camps which they did until the work securing the camps was finished. After that, we never had any more tents stolen.

***

Several weeks before Christmas my name came up on the company notice board. It said that on 2nd January I would be going on home leave, which was wonderful news as I'd been planning it for a long time. We were all looking towards our Christmas holiday dinner, as it was quite a big thing in the Army. On Christmas Day there were no duties or guards, and any duties that were necessary were done by non-Christian personnel including me, being Jewish, and all the meals were served by the officers with a lot of banter, which was great fun.

After Christmas, I started preparing for my leave. There were about a dozen of us from my company who were going on leave at the same time, and we all had to take all our kit except our firearm. I packed several hundred cigarettes that I had saved up from my rations for Dad and for me to smoke while on leave, and some chocolate for Mum and Rozia, which was very hard to come by back at home but we seemed to have a bit of in the army. The period of my leave was 46 days (28 days plus a further 18, one day for each full month on overseas service). We received our travel warrants and our rail tickets, that went from

Dover to London. I asked the Sergeant who was issuing the documents if he could change my rail ticket to one that went via Torquay, to which he kindly obliged and which saved me money as I could visit my pen pal Babs.

The journey home started by travelling to Port Said, where I boarded a boat that took me to Toulon, France. After arriving there, we boarded a train that took us the same route that we travelled on the way to Egypt, back to the port of Calais. When I arrived at Port Said I learned that the boat I was to travel on to France was a 5,000-ton American Liberty boat run by an American crew and, as there were 2,000 of us, again we had to share our quarters in eight hour shifts, but this time there was plenty of water for washing and drinking and there was a canteen where there were soft drinks and other bits and pieces.

The food on the boat was terrific: we had steaks, burgers, hot dogs and chips, followed by tinned fruit and lots of ice-cream. The weather was beautiful until we reached the Messina Strait, when it turned very stormy and from then on I was seasick until we reached Toulon and boarded the train. The journey to Calais was much improved from the last time I had been on it. The carriages were more comfortable and the journey took about fourteen hours to reach Calais where a ferry was waiting for us. I arrived in London on the morning of 9th January 1947.

1947

No one at home knew I was arriving and when I got to the family flat in St. John's Wood and mum opened the door and saw me she shrieked with joy and made a big fuss, hugging and kissing me. She couldn't believe how much I had grown and how healthy I looked. Straight away she worried that she hadn't prepared any food for me. I told her not to worry about food as I'd already eaten not long ago during my journey. I then gave her my food ration coupons which had been issued to me before going on leave.

Quickly she phoned Dad at work and he arrived home in a very short time. He asked me a million questions about where I'd been, what I'd been doing, how long was my leave and how long I'd been travelling. Rozia was home and I was surprised by how much she had grown and how pretty she had become. We had a long chat and I caught up with all the news. Dad told me that it seemed that all he could find out about our family in Poland was that they had perished in the Holocaust, but he was hopeful that maybe some of them had survived.

All together we lost between thirty-four and thirty-eight relations in the Holocaust. This filled me with a great sense of sadness, as I lost many people I had known and loved; uncles, grandparents, cousins had all gone. There was some good news, however, that Mum's brother that were in Poland – Zygmunt, with his daughter Dana, and Izydor – both survived, escaping to Russia and they were there in refugee camps. Unfortunately, they each lost a wife and child; Zygmunt lost his wife Zosia and son John and Izydor lost his wife Giza and Dora, with whom I and Rozia used to play when we were children. Sadly, when the families split up, the wives were caught by the Gestapo and sent to concentration camps where they perished.

Just after the war, Winston Churchill's son was in the same sort of business as my Uncle Joe, who was friends with everyone, and Joe was friendly enough that he could ask Lady Churchill if she could make some inquiries through the British Embassy about the surviving family's whereabouts. They were traced by the Embassy and arrangements were made for their release. Uncle Zygmunt received a visa for him and Dana to come to England and Izydor received a visa to travel to France where he had to wait for his visa to join the family in England. Zygmunt was now only living fifty yards away from the flat in a house on Abbey Road which Uncle Joe had bought for them. That evening Uncle Joe came over to the flat and after making a big fuss over me we went over to see Uncle Zygmunt, Dana and his new wife Tina, who he had met in Russia. They made us most welcome and we asked each other many questions. When he saw me last I was eleven and now I was twenty-one, so he was amazed by how much I had grown up, all the while my new aunt was all the time trying to stuff us with cakes.

The weather was extremely cold and, with a shortage of coal, I was grateful for my thick army overcoat and sweater. Although the flat had central heating it was only on for a short time during the day because of the fuel rations.

I managed to see some of my friends but the atmosphere seemed to be totally different to when I had left for the Middle East. No one had time for much fun anymore and everyone seemed to be chasing jobs or planning weddings, and with strikes and food shortages they were wondering what the future held for them; the spirit of friendliness and togetherness seemed to have gone.

I managed to arrange with my pen pal Babs to visit her in Torquay during my second week of leave. I travelled there in a very cold railway carriage on a train that seemed to take forever since it stopped at every station, however small, on the route. Babs was waiting for me on the platform and she was as beautiful as in her picture. She informed me that her parents had agreed to me staying in their house and dining with them during my visit, and she told me how much she enjoyed our letters, as well as how great it was to meet me in the flesh finally.

We went to her house for lunch and I met her parents, who welcomed me very warmly. Her brother was still in the Middle East and they asked me many questions about what the food was like out there and the conditions of living. During my chat with Babs she told me she was engaged to a bus driver and they were planning to get married in the summer. She was full of plans about her future, which rather put the lid on any plans that I may have had with her. She was a delightful girl to go out with. She introduced me to her future husband and we went to the pictures and several parties, which were most enjoyable, but soon it was time for me to travel back to London. I thanked the family for their hospitality and wished Babs and her fiancée all the happiness and luck for their future. We promised to keep in touch, but after she married it all fizzled out and I never heard from her again.

I still had over a month's leave left, but I found London a bit lonely. I always looked forward to my leave home thinking that things would be the same as when I had left, but they never were. I spent quite a lot of my time at my old club The International Youth, but there were very few old members that I knew from before joining the army. Most of my old friends had either gone back home to their countries, had been called up into the Army like me or had got married and moved away. Although I managed to go out on several dates, it was all platonic as they knew there was no possibility for anything else as they all knew I was only going to leave a few weeks later to Egypt, and it would be another year before I would be back again.

I did manage to visit the Abbotts, my second family, who had moved from Ewell to a small place called Burbage, near Hinckley in Leicestershire, through Uncle Charlie's job. The building they lived in was a lovely 300-year-old cottage, which had originally been three small cottages which Charlie had converted into one. It still had the original beams and leaded windows. It was next to a church and the whole thing was very picturesque, but the doorways were very low and I kept banging my head on the beams. I spent a very pleasant four days with them, in which we exchanged all our news. I told them about our family in Poland and they were very sad, especially about Zygmunt and Zosia, who Charlie had spent a holiday in Poland with just before the outbreak of war. I promised Aunt Sofie that as soon as I was demobbed I would come for a longer visit.

I returned to London not knowing what I was going to do for the rest of my leave. Then, one of my old friends from the International Youth invited me to a party where I met a girl called Joe (short for Josephine). We hit it off right away and I asked her to go out with me. On the first date I found out that she worked for the Cable and Wireless company and had just broken up with her boyfriend. From then on we managed to go out every other day, which made my leave much more enjoyable. Towards the end Joe and I agreed to write to each other regularly and keep up our friendship, which we did.

The day came when my leave was over. I went around the family houses to say my goodbyes and my two uncles had a discussion with me about my future. When I left the army, they told me they would like me to think about joining the firm again to train as a furrier. The next morning Mum and Dad came to see me off at Victoria Station, where I caught the train to Dover to start my return journey. I arrived back at my company camp towards the end of February.

On arrival I reported to the Platoon Sergeant to tell me about what vehicle I was to be assigned to and what details I was to do. He informed me that at that point there were no vehicles available and for the time being I would be helping other drivers with their maintenance, and when needed could act as a second driver. Otherwise, I was to report to the office every morning and make myself useful generally. I soon found out from one of my friends that if I acquired a paper pad and a pencil from the office and walked around with them in my hand, no one would bother me thinking that I was already doing something.

14 - The staff of the CRS, July 1947. Left to right top: VR. Martin, W. III Coy R.A.S.C (M.A.C), Dvr Harvey, J. 661 Coy R.A.S.C (St. TPT), Dvr. Ireland, 4th Air F Sigs Reg. Left to Right bottom: Dvr. Griebel, H. 286 Coy R.A.S.C (GT), Capt. Little, A. S., R.A.M.C., Capt. Parr, E. J. Parr, R.A.M, L/cpl. Langley, R.A.S.C.

Every camp had three or four civilian shops: a tailor who made civilian suits and shirts and altered your uniforms to fit better, a cobbler who handmade boots and shoes, especially desert boots and monk-style shoes, all with crepe soles which were extremely comfortable and became my favourite footwear, and were priced very reasonably (after some bartering). There were also two general stores that sold practically everything: sweets, chocolate, soft drinks, socks, picture frames, etc. I used to wander around trying to escape office work by visiting them and having a chat and usually being offered tea or coffee, which helped kill the time.

About two weeks after having this quite boring pastime, I bumped into a corporal from my old company (from when I had first arrived in Egypt) in the canteen. While having a chat I told him how fed up I was doing odd jobs and not having anything useful to do. He thought for a moment and then told me that he worked at the H.Q office and they had received a request from the Medical Inspection Room (M.I Room), which was situated about a quarter of a mile from my camp, for a replacement orderly as one of theirs was going home on demob. He asked if I would be interested in the job. I told him that I would be but I didn't know if I would be suitable, as the only knowledge of medical treatment was the First Aid training I had when I first joined the Army. He told me not to worry as I would be given training and instructions from the doctor, who would also be my C.O. He said if I wanted the job, he could fix it for me. What was interesting to me was that the M.I compound was in the adjacent camp for security reason, but was completely independent, with all the orders coming from the medical H.Q in Ismailia. After digesting all the information I told my friend if he could arrange the posting for me I would be most grateful.

Two days later my name appeared on the company notice board with my posting instructing me to report to the M.I Room where I was to report to a Cpl. Langley, who was second in command and who asked me for some details about myself and then explained that although sick parade took place at 10a.m., the doctor never arrived before 10.30 and I would meet him at noon after the sick parade was over. He then took me to the accommodation tent to dispose of my kit before showing me around the compound. Our accommodation was a very large tent that could sleep ten but, as there were only five of us when the orderly I was replacing goes home, there would be plenty of spare room. There was a table and chairs, two small easy chairs, a telephone on the table and Langley explained that it was an extension from the office in case of an emergency, so that if there was any personnel that was taken seriously ill in any of the units in the area, whoever was on duty could take the ambulance, pick up the doctor and take them to the patient straight away. He then pointed to a bed on the opposite side of the tent and told me that it would be my bed until the other orderly goes home. Then, I would take his place, which came with a large wardrobe.

In the meantime, I was to unpack and by the time I finished it would be noon, so the sick parade would be over and I could be introduced to the doctor. At noon Cpl. Langley walked me over to the M.I Room and introduced me to the doctor. His rank was Captain and his name was Little. He was 4" shorter than me and about forty years old. He asked me several questions about myself and a lot about football as it seemed that his pride and joy was that before he was called up into the forces he was the doctor for the Glasgow Rangers.

He was very curt and told me that I was to receive all my training, instructions and duties from Langley. My first impression of him was not a good one; I didn't like him very much but it didn't matter as he was going home in two weeks' time and he was counting the days until then. There was already a stop-gap doctor to take his place, a Capt. Parr, who would be going home two weeks after Little, and then we would be getting a permanent doctor, Capt. Girdadale. The corporal was going home two weeks after Capt. Parr. After my interview the corporal instructed me to report to him after lunch when he would introduce me to the other orderlies and show me the rest of the compound.

When lunch was over I reported back and we went around the compound area, which was about seventy-five yards each way. Beside our tent there was a smaller tent which had four beds which was used should we have any patients that had to be kept overnight for observation. There was also a much smaller tent in which there was a large cupboard with all the cleaning materials we would need. We also had an elderly Egyptian who was employed by the Army to clean the dispensary, the office, our tent and the ambulance. We paid him a further small sum to be a sort of servant for us, getting him to take and collect our laundry, clean our boots and, if we wished, to bring our lunch from the cookhouse for us to eat in our tent.

There were only three permanent buildings in the compound and a small car park for the ambulance. The largest of the buildings was split into two sections, the smaller a consulting room which contained a locked drug cupboard, the larger a treatment room and dispensary. The toilet was a huge hole with circular brickwork around it on which there sat a wooden seat, and the whole block could seat six with a small brick wall between each toilet for privacy. There were two showers for our use in another brick building. It was explained to me that we only treated service personnel and a few civilians for small injuries like boils, cuts, stomach ache or constipation. We also treated personnel for venereal disease. Any patient running a temperature was kept overnight in the small tent and if there was no improvement by morning, they were taken to the hospital in Ismailia.

Shortly after joining the M.I staff, which was just before the Jewish festival of Passover, I had a pleasant surprise: I was working when one of the orderlies told me that there was an officer outside wishing to speak to me. I went outside and I recognised by his badges that he was the Jewish Chaplain. He introduced himself (although I cannot remember his name now) and told me that since the forces had been moved to the Canal Zone, he had been making a list of all the Jewish personnel in the area and my name had come up. He then asked me if any Jewish organisation or another Rabbi had been in touch with me when I was stationed in Alexandria and if I had received any Kosher food. When I told him no one had he said I must have slipped through the net. Then he asked me, as the celebration of Passover would be soon upon us, if I would like a parcel of Kosher food to celebrate the occasion. I replied yes, of course, and we chatted a little longer before he left and I thought nothing more of it.

A fortnight later I was informed that there was a large parcel in my Company Office. It was my Kosher food parcel to celebrate Passover. It contained tins of chicken soup, gefilte fish, tins of meat, tins of fruit, a box of Matzos and a small bottle of wine. There was also a small copy of the Haggadah[24], which I kept for many years but was lost when we moved house. From then on I received a fortnightly parcel of Kosher food until I was demobbed, which I shared with my companions and made me very popular.

Cpl. Langley started my education by first giving me an Army First Aid book, which I kept hold of for many years, until unfortunately it was also lost with my other army souvenirs when we moved. He then took me to the dispensary, explaining the contents of the different bottles and boxes as well as where they stored all the bandages, splints, plasters etc. On the first day being on duty in the M.I Room I found the job quite easy, and if there was anything I was unsure of one of the other orderlies could help me. The only difficulty I had was trying to decipher what the doctor had written on the chit as to what treatment to give the patient as his handwriting was stereotypically terrible.

I found the work extremely interesting. The system that was in place involved all the patients we were responsible arriving at 10a.m., when they were lined up for inspection by the doctor when he arrived. The patients went in one at a time, controlled by the corporal. After being examined, they were given a chit describing what treatment was needed, which they then took to the dispensary to receive from one of us. Most of the complaints that we treated were for a fever, which we gave the patient Dover powders for, and which consisted mainly of opium

---

[24] The Haggadah is the prayer book used for Passover services held in the home known as a Seder.

(and is, of course, no longer used). For constipation we gave N9 tablets, stomach pain we gave Tincture of Belladonna, for headache we gave aspirin, for rashes Calamine ointment. Cuts we treated with Vaseline, a bandage and some sulphur powder sprinkled on it, and boils we had to put on a poultice and when it came to a head but didn't burst it had to be lanced and a wick put in to drain it. When it came to venereal diseases, gonorrhoea was treated in one of the corners of the room with a curtain pulled round, where there was a small tank filled with a mixture of potassium permanganate, with a thin plastic tube and small tap coming from the tank. The patient was shown how to wash out his penis with the mixture and then given M&B tablets[25] which usually cured him. For crabs, a common complaint, we gave the patient a tube of mercuric ointment which usually did the trick. Every night one of us had to be on duty for emergencies and to issue condoms to the servicemen, of which we always had a large stock, to prevent sexual diseases.

A few days after I joined the M.I Room we heard that the demob was being slowed down by several weeks, which meant that the two doctors and Corporal Langley would not be home until the beginning of July, but it didn't matter as Capt. Girdadale, our new C.O and doctor, had already signed over control of the M.I Room and the other two doctors were relieved until they went home.

Two weeks later we had a communication from our H.Q in Ismailia that because so many units had moved into the area, the M.I Room would be enlarged and would become a Casualty Reception Station (CRS). There would be an additional orderly posted to us and there would be a much larger tent to put patients in overnight. We didn't know who would be the replacement to Cpl. Langley when he went home, but a few days before they were all due to leave the C.O asked me to see him after the surgery was over.

---

[25] The common name for Sulfapyridine, an antibacterial medication no longer prescribed for treatment of infections in humans.

When I saw him he told me that he had been trying to find a replacement for Cpl. Langley but both his unit and my company had informed him that they had no Non Commissioned Officers (N.C.Os) spare. But Capt. Foulks, who was now second in command of my company, suggested that, as I have twice held the rank of Local Temporary Acting Sergeant, he could promote me back to that rank if he liked. He asked me if I would be willing to accept the position. I told him that I had only been in the M.I Room for a very short time and there were orderlies far more qualified than me. He told me not to worry, as if there was anything I needed to know he could teach me. More importantly, as we would be having much larger sick parades, what he needed was someone with experience with command as a sergeant, and it would be a lot easier for me to control the men on sick parade.

I accepted his offer, and his first order was for me to make a list of all the equipment, stores and medicines to be ready for the final signing that would take place when the other doctors went home. When the other orderlies heard that I was taking over from Langley, they were quite relieved as I was not a stranger to them, and congratulated me on the promotion. The next few weeks were extremely busy, and with the help of other orderlies I managed to have the list ready in time for the signing over.

The day came for Capt. Little, Capt. Parr and Cpl. Langley were leaving us for home, in the first week of July. Capt. Girdadale took a picture of our group and he said he would send a copy to them after the photos had been developed, after which they departed for Port Said and their boat home.

That afternoon I walked over to my company to see Capt. Foulks, who presented me with my sergeant stripes and for the third time I became a local unpaid temporary acting Sergeant and second in command of the CRS. I also acquired a very large Alsatian dog that had belonged to Cpl. Langley since he couldn't take it home with him. He was a friendly dog with which we all used to play and he was terribly spoiled. He always used to sleep next to my bed but he had this annoying habit of waking me up in the morning, waggling his large tail in my face.

Our sick parades were getting bigger and bigger, and we had to collect our supplies from Ismailia much more often using our ambulance. Capt. Girdadale said that this was not satisfactory, as each time the ambulance was away the CRS was left without any means of emergency transportation, and so he suggested that, as a sergeant, I was entitled to a motorbike. He made arrangements for me to be issued with one from my company on which I would be able to collect the supplies. When I went to collect the motorbike, I mentioned to the Motor Transport Sgt. That I'd not ridden a bike since my school days, and never on a public road. He asked me if I had ridden a push bike on a public road; I told him I had and he said I shouldn't worry as it's not different, expect you have an engine doing the peddling. He allocated me a bike from the pool and told me to try it out around the car park Seeing how well I rode he told me that he was quite happy and signed the bike over to me.

Using the bike for my first trip to Ismailia was not a great success, and although the road was quite straight, all the time it was covered with very fine sand from the desert that made it quite slippery. Twice while taking corners I skidded, the bike going one way and me the other, and as I was only wearing my summer uniform I grazed my knees quite badly. When I arrived at the medical stores I managed to acquire a roll of plaster and lint and dressed my injuries before collecting the supplies. On my return journey I only came off once which was a great improvement, but from then on I wrapped my Putties around my knees for protection and wear my long trousers and a pair of dispatch rider gloves, which helped a bit. I still used to come off the bike when taking the bends and I began to dread using the bike. I asked Capt. Girdadale if he could swap the bike for a 1500cwt General Purpose vehicle which would be much more useful to us, as sometimes the stores were too bulky for transporting on the bike. He agreed and, to my great relief, so did the company, and soon the two vehicles were exchanged. After my experience with the bike I swore never to ride a motorbike and since then I never have.

15 - Me with my motorbike.

After my experience with the bike, and having sustained damage to my shirts and trousers, I had to go to the Q.M stores, which were in our compound. When I arrived, to my surprise who should be the Q.M Sergeant there but my old pal from my original company, who I had last seen back in Tripoli. He greeted me like a long-lost brother, took me into the back of the stores and offered me a cup of tea whilst we exchanged stories of what had happened since we had last met. He then asked what I required from him, and I told him about my experience with the bike. He told me not worry as he had just received new stores of American K.D which were a better-quality fit, which he could exchange for my old torn ones. He then suggested that I should bring my Battle Dress uniform which he could exchange as well, as he had just received a shipment of New Zealand uniforms which were made of much better, thinner material and didn't make you itch like the English ones. From then on, whenever new stock arrived like vests, pants, socks etc. he would exchange mine for new ones. We met quite often for a cup of tea and a chat about where some of our old friends were, but more about him later.

Capt. Girdadale was much more efficient than the last few doctors in organising the CRS. First he told me that he wanted me to help assist him in the consulting room. In the Army, every year you had to have a booster injection for tetanus and typhoid, and as the number of personnel under our care grew he taught me how to give the injections to take some of the strain off him. He also taught me how to lance and treat boils, take patients' pulses and temperature; we had to keep thermometers in a glass of cold water because of the heat during the day. I also received instructions on how to administer ether to put a patient to sleep and how to use local anaesthetic, at which I became quite proficient.

In mid-August we received news from our H.Q in Ismailia that there was a cholera epidemic in Egypt and they gave us specific instructions about what procedures to follow and what precautions to take. The CRS received a serum to inoculate with and small container bottles to take urine samples from all the personnel in our area with, which was about 2,000 servicemen and 300 Egyptian civilians working in the various camps. As there was a shortage of serum, essential service personnel were the first to receive it and no civilian personnel would be permitted to leave the area and if they do they would not be allowed back in until the epidemic was over. Check points were set up to make sure that the orders were complied with. All the shops selling food and drink would be shut down for the time being. Any personnel that arrived at the CRS with stomach complaints or signs of a fever would be taken to the Ismailia hospital immediately, no matter what time of day and the serum was to be kept either in a refrigerator or a cool box, which was supplied every day with a block of ice from the cookhouse.

My first orders from Capt. Girdadale were to phone all the units in our area and get a list of personnel that needed to travel out of the area on urgent duties, as they would be the first that would have to be inoculated and tested. We worked out that we would only be able to inoculate 70-90 people per day, as we were responsible for driving around the camps to make sure no food or drink was being sold in the civilian shops and that the camps were complying with the quarantine. The sick parade was held once a day in the evening. We only had six syringes and thirty needles, so my job each evening was to sharpen the needles and then sterilise everything for the morning.

The team doing the inoculations consisted of the Doctor, myself and four orderlies. I and the doctor did the inoculations themselves, whilst the orderlies tended to the urine samples and the sterilisation of used needles. We worked six days a week and we estimated all being well and good it would take us four or five weeks to get the job done. During our patrols to check the civilian shops, they all complained about the orders but we told them they must stay shut until we could inoculate them or we would have to impound their stock. Nearly all the shopkeepers cooperated with the order except one; after he had another warning with which he didn't comply, Capt. Girdadale ordered me to confiscate his stock of soft drinks and sign for them. The total amount of bottles came to 389, which I signed for and the only place they could be stored was our little tent where we stored our medical equipment and cleaning supplies. Unfortunately, being the middle of the summer and they temperature usually reaching over 100°F, it wasn't the best place to store them and the bottles started to explode due to the heat expanding the gas inside them. I asked Capt. Girdadale what to do with them and he thought for a minute before saying that, as the owner of the shop had accepted my chit for 389 bottles, and as the contents are exploding, for safety reasons we would have to get rid of the contents. I suggested we do so by drinking it, so I put some of the bottles in the cool chest and made sure there was enough for all of us to have cold drinks during the day. I told the boys the good news and they were delighted, as we would have free cold drinks for at least a month.

One evening, about ten days into the epidemic, while I was sharpening and preparing the inoculation needles for the following day, one of the orderlies came into the surgery and informed me that a Major had arrived in a staff car and was wishing to speak to me. As the sick parade was over and the doctor had already departed to his mess, I thought before I phoned the doctor I would better see what the major required. When I saw who the major was I had a pleasant surprise: it was my old pal Reggie Gold. He greeted me like old friends do and after having a chat and a catch-up I congratulated him on his promotion and he told me he had also become an adjutant to the area commander. I asked him why he had come to see me and what I could do for him, as I didn't want to phone for the doctor as we were all extremely tired, having been on duty since 8.30a.m.

He asked me why we had been shutting all the food shops in the area and I told him that we had received orders from the Deputy Director of Medical Suppliers (D.D.M.S) that until all the service personnel had been inoculated against cholera and their urine tested we had been told to keep the shops shut. They had been shut for so long because the serum we needed to inoculate with was in short supply. I then asked him why it was a problem to him. He then explained that the problem was that the shop owners pay the area H.Q for a license enabling them to have a shop in the camps, and since we closed them down they were demanding their money back and the area C.O was not much pleased. I suggested that if he or his C.O were to get in touch with the D.D.M.S in Ismailia to ask them to supply us with extra serum for the civilians working in the camp shops, stressing the urgency of the matter, as soon as the serum arrived we could see to it that the civilians were inoculated and tested so the shops could open as soon as possible.

We chatted a little longer and then he departed back to his H.Q. The next morning I informed the doctor of Reggie's visit and what arrangements I had made; he was glad that I didn't phone him as he was already in bed by then trying to get some sleep. Ten days after that we had a communication from H.Q that extra serum had been allocated to us and was ready for collection. I didn't see Reggie again until eight years' later, just before he emigrated to the US where he became a very successful osteopath.

One evening, a couple of days after Reggie's visit, I had another visitor to the CRS, a Captain Bob Watson asking for the doctor. I asked him if perhaps I could help as the doctor wasn't available. He explained that since we had moved to the Canal Zone, for security reasons the N.A.F.F.I and camp canteen supplies were being stored at the army supply compound of which he was in charge. He knew that we were only inoculating essential army personnel, his problem was that he employed civilian labour at the depot and one of them had to travel with an Army lorry driver to collect stores from the dock and distribute them to different units. He also had another civilian working in the compound who had been injured when one of the boxes dropped on his toe. Since the civilians were responsible for food shipments, and it was possible they could spread the disease if not inoculated, he asked me if we could help. As we had received serum for the paid civilians I was sure that we would be able to squeeze an extra one in for him. I told him if he brought the two civilians the following evening after the sick parade, I would ask the doctor to inspect the injured one and I would inoculate the other. In the morning I told the doctor of the arrangement with Captain Watson and he agreed.

When Capt. Watson was leaving, he asked me if we could use some chocolate in the CRS, as if I sent one of the orderlies to his depot – which was only a short distance away – he would give us some chocolate to bring back. I thanked him for the offer but the only day that it would be possible would be on a Sunday as we were working a six day week. He suggested I come and have lunch with him and then pick up the chocolate, to which I agreed.

On Sunday, when I arrived Capt. Watson showed me around the depot, which was huge, and told me how grateful he was for my help. We went into his office where, at the back, there was a small dining room where we had a marvellous lunch. It seemed that he had an Egyptian servant who was also a cook. After lunch he took me back to the warehouse, to a stack of small boxes weighing 28lbs, full of chocolate bars. He pointed at them and said: "I promised you some chocolate, so help yourself." I asked him how many I could have and he said as many as I wanted. It turned out that they were part of the last shipment and when they had been unloaded they were placed on an uneven surface. In the heat they melted so that one end was thin and the other thick. They could not be sold in the condition they were in and the whole shipment would have to be burnt if it wasn't taken. I took three boxes, as any more would be a waste, thanked him for the lunch and as I was leaving he said that we must have lunch again and that he would give me a call.

We became quite good friends and whenever I came for lunch he always had goods for me to take back to the CRS that would otherwise be destroyed: toothbrushes, toothpaste, shoe brushes, shoe polish, notepads and pencils etc., which I always shared with the doctor, the orderlies, friends from my company and, of course, my friend the Q.M Sergeant who had been so kind to me. Everyone appreciated the chocolate and, as there was so much of it, we all made parcels which we sent to our families in England where there was a great shortage.

The cholera epidemic lasted eight weeks before the area curfew was lifted and everything went back to normal. We went back to our routine of two sick parades a day and things not being so hectic gave us time to rest and relax.

There were two incidents that happened during my time at the CRS that are worth mentioning. One of the civilian workers, who worked in the camps doing menial jobs and who we always thought was a hunchback, always walked bent over with this big hump on his back. One day he came to the CRS, complaining of pain in his back. I took him in to see the doctor, who asked him to take his shirt off and when we looked at his back there was this incredible sight: the lump on his back wasn't through curvature of the spine, but an enormous cyst with seventeen heads, most of them ready to burst. The doctor took one look at it and told me to get one of the orderlies to take him to hospital. We didn't hear any more about him until several weeks later when an Egyptian came to the CRS. I was just about to ask him what he wanted when I realised that this was the same man we had sent to the hospital. He looked much younger, walked upright and was 6'7" taller. I took him to see the doctor who was as surprised as I was seeing the change. The man told us he had only come to thank us for what we had done for him, as now that he could walk upright and was perfectly fit he was being given a much better job with a pay increase.

During this time, in our area there was a company of Danish soldiers stationed and one day one of their trucks brought one of their soldiers, dead. He had been shot in the head, so a report had to be made regarding the circumstance of his dead. We were told that there must have been a cartridge left in the chamber of his rifle and while cleaning it he must have accidentally pulled the trigger. The doctor made a death certificate and the body was sent in an ambulance to the hospital for an autopsy and then burial. We didn't think much more about it, but then in the course of the next ten weeks we had two more deaths come in from the Danish camp in similar circumstances, each time with the person shot accidentally in the head. We became suspicious and the doctor decided to send a report to the Military Police special branch to investigate. They acknowledged our report but we never heard anything more about it, however there were no more accidental shootings.

Some time later we had a sergeant from the Danish company come to us for treatment. The doctor and I asked him about these deaths. At first he was very coy about speaking about the subject, but as we pressed him on it he agreed to tell us off the record what had happened. He made us swear on our honour that what he was to tell us would not go any further. It seemed that when Denmark had been liberated there were many Danes who were Nazis and during the war collaborated with the Germans. In order to escape revenge from the members of the resistance movement, they volunteered for the army to avoid retribution. Several had been in this company and it turned out they were responsible for the deaths of some resistance fighters during the war. No one knew who shot them but justice had been done. We never spoke of this matter again.

Towards the end of September, I had a communication from my company that my naturalisation papers had been processed and shortly I would be becoming a British subject. On 13th October I had a call from my company to report to the office of Capt. Foulks the following day, who would be finalising my naturalisation documents. When I arrived at his office he explained the procedure to me. I had to read my allegiance to the crown and country aloud to him, which I did, and after that he signed and handed me the document, congratulated me, shook my hand and welcomed me as a British subject, informing me that I could now take my Polish flashes off that were sewn onto my uniform. We had a little chat and he asked me what difference naturalisation would do for me. I told him that I was now the first member of my Polish family to have British citizenship and that it would come in useful if dad should start a business, as he would be able to have me as a British national on the board of directors (which was a requirement).

He also informed me that the company had received news that all service personnel with the same demob number as me would be going home at the beginning of January, but that actual date I would not receive until a week before I was due to go. He suggested that, as the time was getting closer, I should attend a seminar at the education compound which could tell me about what my options were for training for civilian life and what income I could receive whilst training or studying. I thanked him for all that he had done for me and returned to the CRS where everyone was waiting for me, wanting to see my naturalisation certificate.

I told Capt. Girdadale about the seminar that I was attending and he suggested that, as I had done very well as a medical orderly, if I were to sign up for a further three years he would recommend me to go to the army medical college to study medicine. I thanked him for the offer but explained that, as my father had lost all his family in the Holocaust, and being the only male family member remaining in my generation, I ought to go home. Also, since I had a great difficulty in remembering names I would never make it memorising all the Latin words. I did go to the seminar where I was given many options for training or study, but the best bit of all was that the government would give me £250 a year for two years if I went onto a training or study course.

One other incident that happened to me was whilst walking outside of our perimeter in the desert where I tripped over a small rock, grazing my ankle. I took no notice of it, cleaned it and put a plaster on it thinking it would heal up without any more attention being required. But it didn't, and soon it had turned into an ulcer. I showed the doctor and he suggested putting a penicillin dressing on it. At that time, everyone thought penicillin could cure any infection. The only penicillin available to us was in cream form, with which a dressing was made, but to no avail. The ulcer just wouldn't disappear no matter what dressing was put on it, but more about my ankle later.

One of the last things that happened before I was demobbed was when my friend, the Q.M Sergeant came over to see me, telling me he had a problem. There was to be a major inspection of his camp and he had too much surplus stores which he had to get rid of. In those days, you could be reprimanded if you had too much of anything, as there was no such thing as returns in the Army and it was seen as a waste, but mistakes inevitably happened. The Q.M Sergeant asked if I could take 100 tins of cigarettes off him, each containing 50 cigarettes. (In Egypt, we used to be issued with 50 cigarettes for free each week.) I told him that I would be able to get rid of them if he brought them over and, if he wanted, he could bring over one of the large tins that biscuits came in.

The following afternoon he arrived with a huge box containing cigarettes and the tin that I had asked for. Soon after he departed, I distributed the cigarettes among the orderlies and some friends who made parcels to send home, but I still had 1,500 cigarettes left. I made several parcels of about 200 cigarettes which I sent to Dad, and the remainder I filled the large biscuit tin with, about 1,000 cigarettes. I put the tin in my kit bag but I found that they took up so much room that the kit bag would not be big enough for my gear and the cigarettes. I took a couple tins of cigarettes to the company workshop and gave them to the canvas fitter I knew in exchange for him making me a kit bag that was 6" longer and 4" wider, which did the job.

At the beginning of December, at long last, I received the exact date of my departure. I was to report to Port Said on 7th January where I was to board a ship. I informed Capt. Girdadale of the news so he could arrange a replacement. He told me he didn't know whether one of the orderlies would be promoted as he may be able to get another N.C.O from my company. In the meantime he and I should take stock of our stores and equipment and he will get whoever takes over to sign for them. He then told me he would also give me a letter of recommendation saying that I was a fully qualified orderly, which would come in handy if I should ever want to carry on in the medical profession.

When Christmas came we were invited to my company camp for the festivities, as it was going to be mine and some of my friends' last one before we left the Army. There was joy and some sadness for some of us, as we had all been together for two years, sharing times both good and miserable. As usual, we talked only of the good times, we exchanged addresses, promised to keep in touch, and said goodbyes to those we would be leaving behind.

1948

On the morning of the 7th January and Army lorry fitted out for transporting troops arrived at the guard house to pick me up with my gear and transport me to Port Said for my journey home. When I climbed aboard there were some other boys from the company accompanying me on the same journey and we were to pick up some more on the way before reaching Port Said. Eventually, when we reached our destination, we were taken to the base depot, allocated tents and told to await further orders.

The next morning we were told that the ship would not be sailing for another three days as there were many more servicemen that needed to arrive from other parts of the Middle East. As there were several personnel and friends that had served with me, we managed to acquire a tent for ourselves that we could all be together in and we made sure that was always someone in the tent looking after our kit.

While being in camp I found out a little more about our ship and our journey. Her name was the Otranto, she was a 20,000 ton passenger liner who before the war used to do the England-Australia run. We would be sailing to Cyprus first, then to Malta, where in both places we would be picking up more service personnel. Then we would sail to Gibraltar which would be our last stop before home. When the ship finally had the full complement of passengers, we would again be sharing the sleeping accommodation in eight hour shifts.

Eventually, when we left Port Said for Cyprus the weather was excellent and when we arrived at our first stop we were told that we would be docked there for two days. While in dock someone pointed out the famous ship, the SS Exodus, which had taken Jewish refugees to Palestine. From Cyprus we had a pleasant passage, and we stayed a further two days in Malta before sailing to Gibraltar and then Southampton.

When we reached Gibraltar, the weather was becoming slightly stormy with a strong wind blowing in from the Atlantic. Two days' later, when we left the Mediterranean Sea, we hit a bad storm which made me seasick and it only became worse when we went through the Bay of Biscay. The storm became a gale, one of the worst I have ever known; I was so sick that I decided to go down below to lie down in my bunk, but it only made me feel worse as the smell of the vomit from so many other people being sick was thick in the air. I went back to my spot by the mast on the deck where I stayed for the rest of the voyage. I was so sick that if someone had chucked me overboard I would have been grateful. Friends tried to persuade me to eat but the only thing I could stomach were bread, which was plentiful, and sips of tea with sweet condensed milk.

The weather conditions were becoming worse and there was torrential rain so we all wore our anti-gas capes, which were waterproof and gave us some protection from the rain. The storm was so fierce that, during the second night of the storm the ship went through a huge wave and came right out of the water and then came down again with a tremendous bang. The foghorn sounded and we were all ordered to put our lifebelts on and go to our allocated lifeboat stations as they were worried the ship might have broken its hull. After the ship was inspected we were allowed to stand down, but we had to travel at a reduced speed, so the whole journey from Gibraltar to Southampton lasted for four and a half days.

We docked in the morning and very shortly afterwards we started to disembark. At last, when I was on firm land I swore to myself that I would never again sail in a ship except if necessary across the English Channel. I never did until 46 years' later when I took my wife, who was recovering from a cancer operation, on a cruise of the Mediterranean in a ship that was much larger and fitted with stabilisers. Before the army personnel disembarked we were told that we would be going through customs and were warned that if we had any bayonets, swords, pistols or any other unauthorised arms or equipment, we should get rid of them as there would be a proper search by the Military Police and Customs Officers.

Eventually, after waiting a while on the quayside, we were allowed to proceed through customs. The customs officer ordered me to remove all my gear from my kitbag before inspecting my kitbag, where he found my tins of cigarettes. He asked me what was in the large tin and I told him. He opened the tin and mentioned that there were far too many than we were permitted to bring in. I explained to him that I had been saving up my free issue rations so I could have cigarettes while on leave. He put his hand in the kitbag, took out of the small tins that contained 50 cigarettes and asked me if it was alright for him to take it. I told him I hadn't seen anything, he quickly put it in his pocket and told me to go on my way.

When I had left customs there were trains waiting to take us to our demob centre. I don't remember the name of the place, only that it was a huge place that at some point must have been an aircraft hangar. Inside there were counters with racks of underwear on one side, in the middle racks upon racks of all sorts of clothing for us to choose from as our civilian gear, and on the other side tables and chairs for signing documentation. We queued up in line, first to hand in our firearms, then all our other army equipment, our canvas packs, ammunition pouches and webbing, except for our kitbag and army belt, both of which I have to this day. We kept our uniforms, as having been in the Army you were automatically a reserve until the age of 50.

First, I went to the counter where I was issued with a civilian vest, pants, shirts, long johns and socks. Then I proceeded to the rails where I was fitted out with the rest of my civilian clothing. You were allowed either two suits or a suit, sports jacket and flannels; I chose the latter. Similarly, we had the choice of either an overcoat or a raincoat; I chose a raincoat as I still had my army overcoat which I could use if the weather became too severe. The last thing I chose were shoes, a tie and a hat. There were many changing rooms where we could try on our clothing to see if the fit was right. When everything was satisfactory, I packed all the clothing away and went to the documentation tables.

16 - A photo taken of me just as I was demobbed in my Army uniform.

I was entitled to 86 days demob leave – 56 days plus 30 days, one for every month of overseas service – for which I was paid just over £25. The I was given my travel warrant, clothing coupons, rations book, national health and employment cards. The last document was my discharge papers, which wouldn't come into effect until my leave was over. When the documentation was finished we were driven to the railway station to catch the train to London. Before I boarded the train I managed to get the chance to phone my mother and tell her that I was back in England and that I would be home in about three hours.

I arrived home on 18th January, 1948. It was bitterly cold and I was glad that I was wearing my thick army uniform. Mum, Dad and Rozia were waiting for me and, after all of them giving me welcoming hugs, as it was early evening, Mum started preparing our supper. She suggested we all sit down and wait for her so we could share all the news together. While waiting for her, Dad told me all that had happened whilst I had been away. He was no longer working for Uncle Joe as, since Uncle Zygmunt had joined the firm, he couldn't get on with him and, after several serious arguments, he decided to leave and start his own firm with a partner. They had premises in Old Bond Street on the 1st floor above what is now a Cartier; the name of the firm was Grie-Belle. Dad asked me if, when I was in the West End, if I would come to his firm and see what it was like and, perhaps, if I should decide to start again learning to be a furrier his partner, who was a very skilled craftsman, would be willing to train me.

I told him that, having just arrived and having three months' leave, it was too early for me to start thinking about my future. For the news few weeks I am only going to eat, sleep and have a good time after three years in the desert, after which I will start thinking about my future.

The other news Dad told me was that he had bought the five story house, No. 28 Abbey Road, which was next door to Uncle Zygmunt's house and that he had fitted out the rear room on the ground floor for me to have my own place. Uncle Izydor had received his visa to travel to France and was now living in Paris while waiting for the family to receive permission to bring him to England.

After supper, Uncle Joe phoned asking if I'd arrived, and when I spoke to him he asked me so many questions about my journey, and if I would call in at the firm as he and Zygmunt would like to see me. After we had our coffee I was beginning to feel very tired as it had been a long day and I hadn't had much sleep on the boat. I asked Dad to take me to his house to my new room. The room was very large, about 22' by 18', with a huge window overlooking the garden. It contained a bed, table, chairs, some cups and saucers and a big easy chair. There was also a gas fire with a small gas ring connected to it so I could heat the room and make myself a hot drink. On a small table there was a phone which was an extension from his small office he had in the house. Next to my room there was a small room, that must have been a kitchen, where there was drinking water and where I could wash in the mornings, but I would have to go to their flat to bathe as there were no facilities to heat water.

I told Dad how pleased I was with the room and if there was anything else I needed, I would acquire it myself. I thanked him for everything and he left. I was so tired that I just undressed and went to seep immediately. My first day home was over.

The following morning, after sleeping in late, I had a quick wash and shave with cold water, which I was quite used to but in a warmer climate. I decided to wear my uniform as it was much warmer than my civilian suit, and also because I was still on active service. It was extremely cold and the gas fire took too long to heat up the room, so I went over to my parents' flat for breakfast and to see if I could have a bath. Dad had already gone off to work, so Mum made me some breakfast. While eating she explained what the position was with the hot water and the central heating; the two were only on twice a day for three hours in the morning and three hours in the evening. This was because of the coal miners' strike, which was also affecting electricity, meaning there were frequent power cuts. So, if I wanted a bath, I would have to have it either in the early morning or evening. Lots of firms at the time were suffering through the strikes and many of them could only work a three-day week.

After breakfast, I told mum that I was going to go into town and that I would not be back until the evening, so she shouldn't worry about preparing food as I would eat in town. She asked me where I was going and I told her that I wasn't going anywhere in particular, I just wanted to get the feel of the town, see some of the old places where I used to go out with friends and maybe I would by chance bump into some of them. If I ended up near Bond St. I would call on Dad and see his firm.

When I left the flat in St. John's Wood, I decided to walk to Marble Arch. The walk reminded me of my first day in England when I had come from Poland, but the comparison between the two walks in the same part of town, ten years apart, was tremendously different. When I had walked through London on my first day it had been just a month after the coronation of King George VI, and there had been such a sense of gaiety and contentment, with buildings and shops freshly painted, decorated and stuffed with merchandise. People had been in high spirits, but now the streets were drab, with many spaces between the buildings where bombs had been dropped. On the whole, most of the shops looked very bleak, with some of their windows still boarded up, as the materials to repair them were in very short supply. There had been a great shortage of goods for sale and I discovered that more and more things were rationed and that the rations of food that people were receiving had grown smaller and smaller than what we had been receiving during the war.

After having wandered around for a while, and being near Bond St., I decided to see Dad's firm. When I arrived, I walked through an impressive entrance to the lift, which took me to the first floor where his firm was. I rang the bell and Dad opened the door, surprised to see me. He introduced me to his partner, Mr. Kay, straight away, and then to the rest of the staff. Besides Mr. Kay, who was a fur cutter, there was a machinist, a finisher and a liner. There was also a receptionist, but she was running errands for the firm. He then showed me around the place: there was the workroom, which had two huge tables, one for cutting furs and another for finishing, two fur machines and a Singer sewing machine. There was a mall table with a kettle for tea. The reception room was also used as a showroom, and there were two other small rooms, one of which was an office and another a stockroom with a security door, for the furs. As it was lunchtime,

Dad took me to a nearby Lyons for lunch and afterwards I left him and carried on walking.

I decided to visit my old club, the International Youth, in Pond St., but when I arrived it was shut with a notice on the door stating that the club had moved to new premises near Paddington Station. As it was getting late, I decided I would visit the following day and I travelled back home to my parents' flat to wait for Dad to come home so we could all have supper together. My long journey home to a civilian life was over.

The following morning I managed to have a bath, which for me was a luxury as I had not had one since a year ago when I was home on leave; in the army we only had showers. Over breakfast Mum told me that Uncle Joe phoned asking when I would be calling in at the firm as he and Uncle Zygmunt were eager to see me. I told her that I was going to the West End and I would call in at the firm to see them, and I won't be needing any lunch in the near future as I would be spending most of my days in town. I travelled to Bond St. and then walked down Grafton St. where I had been on my previous leave. Uncle Joe had told me that there had been plans to refurbish the firm so I was curious to see what had been done to it. When I arrived at the building it was quite a surprise. The front of the building had been completely cleaned, all the windows repaired and painted, and on the side of the steps leading into the entrance there was a big sign in blue with white letters that said: 'DEANFIELD FUR MODELS'. I didn't know that the firm's name had been changed from the old name Vienna Fur Models or that while I was away my uncles had changed their surname by Deed Pole from Diestenfeld to Deanfield.

As I walked through the entrance I couldn't believe what a transformation had taken place. The building was seven stories high, five from the front and seven in the back with a door into the Mews where there were spaces to park cars. The last time I was in the building, if one wanted to reach the top floor, one had to walk five flights of stairs. Now there was a brand new lift facing you travelling from the basement right to the top. When I opened the showroom door, I was met by a showroom that had also been completely transformed from the old one. The partition wall had been taken out and in place of it in the back of the room there was a small area which has been partitioned with glass walls to be used as an office by the secretary-cum-model to see when a customer entered. The whole area was huge, painted in pale blue with a carpet to match. On the wall to the right there was a beautiful antique mirror and above the mantelpiece of an Adams fireplace a big raised circle, inside which was a scene from ancient Greece, all painted in white. The furniture, two sofas, two easy chairs and two desks with chairs were all Louis XVI. It was a showroom that could have graced any of the big fashion houses.

My two uncles were sitting in the little office and as they say me walk in, they both came over, embracing me while asking me questions about my journey and what I was intending to do with myself now. I told them that for the next few weeks I was going to try to get used to being a civilian again, as well as try to meet up with some old friends, meet some girls and generally have a good time. After *many* more questions, they said that before I decide on anything, to think about joining them working in the firm, as that was the original plan for me when I first came to England. I said I had a few options available for me at the moment, but I would consider their offer and speak with them again before I made any decisions.

After our talk, Uncle Joe took us on a tour of his firm. In the past year it had been completely transformed and had grown considerably; the basement had been split into two parts – one a stock room and the other a cold storage with huge, thick steel security doors – and the half-basement had been turned into a fur cleaning department with all new equipment imported from America. The first floor had two cutting rooms and a design and pattern cutting room, the second floor had another cutting room and a finishing room, and when we reached the third floor I had a big surprise: the firm had become not just a fir company, but had another business by the name of Joedon (named after my uncle), which produced couture dresses, suits and coats.

The top floor had now become a proper canteen, with a cook and a small flat that was occupied by a caretaker-cum-cleaner who was also a night-watchman. After the tour, Uncle Joe took me to the canteen for lunch, where we chatted some more and he told me that whenever I was in town to come see them and some of the old staff from when I had worked there last. As he was seeing me off, he pulled two lovely white fivers out of his pocket and gave them to me, telling me to have a good time and enjoy my leave, hoping to see me when he next came to dinner.

After leaving Uncle's firm, I walked towards St. James's Place, which was only a short distance away from where the Overseas League, nowadays known as the Royal Overseas League, was situated. During the War I had tried to join, but was told that only British, Commonwealth or Colonial subjects could join. Now that I was a British subject, I thought I would try again. I went in and asked at the reception desk if I could join; I was told that there was a long waiting list, but members of the British Forces that had served in the war could join immediately. I was asked to fill in a short form stating my name, rank, unit, etc., pay two pounds and then I was given my membership card and told about the facilities that were available. It was a large place with accommodation available for overnight stays, a gym, a games room, a restaurant, two bars and a dancefloor, where dances were held every Saturday night. I was very pleased that I had my membership, as from then on, whenever I was in town, I had somewhere to pop in if I wanted a drink and a sandwich, or if I had a companion to go for a drink with.

I decided to have a drink at the bar and while sitting there I had a tap on my shoulder. A voice from behind me said: "Hello, Tim!" I turned around and standing there was an old friend from my engineering days, Edward, with whom I had worked with for nearly two years before going into the Army. I asked him what he had been doing since I saw him last and he told me that soon after I had left he too had been called up to the Army, but had been turned down on medical grounds. When the war had ended he was released from war work and, along with his father who had worked in the Ministry of Supply during the war, they began a wholesale cloth business. When he asked what I was doing, I told him I had been recently demobbed, but that I hadn't decided what I wanted to do with myself yet. Edward then said: "Tim, we worked together and I know that you are very capable. Our firm is expanding rapidly and now we are quite a large export business. How would you like to join our firm?" I told him that I didn't know anything about cloth and I wasn't all that good at dealing with customers, but he said not to worry as they would teach me all that. We had another drink and he gave me his card and asked me to take my time thinking about his offer. I never took the job but we often saw each other at the club and had a drink and a chat together.

I spent the next two weeks going to museums, art galleries and cinemas. I managed to meet my pen pal Josephine; she told me she was in a serious relationship with a Swiss boyfriend that she had met while I was abroad and she would not be able to see me anymore. I visited my old club, the International Youth, in their new premises, but it wasn't the same as when I had been a member before. It had become very political and there were many Young Communists that had taken over the running of the club, with communist posters stuck on the walls, which wasn't for me.

While leaving the club, walking down a flight of stairs, someone called out for me and, as I turned around, I slipped and fell backwards, hitting the back of my head on a concrete step. I must have been knocked unconscious because when I came to, some of the members were lifting me onto a table. There was a lot of blood on my uniform on my uniform and on the floor. Someone swabbed the back of my head and told me that there was a deep cut; they were going to bandage it and take me to St. Mary's Hospital. When they had bandaged me up, I was helped off the table and asked if I was well enough to walk down to the taxi that was waiting to take me to the hospital, to which I answered "yes."

Two of the members of the club accompanied me to the hospital casualty department and stayed with me until I was seen by a very young doctor and a nurse, who took me to one of the dispensing rooms where I was told to lay on my stomach. The doctor then told the nurse to shave the part of my head where the cut was and prepare some stitching equipment while he administered a local anaesthetic. After trying twice to stitch the two edges together, I turned around and said to him: "You haven't done this before, have you?" He confessed that he had only just qualified as a doctor and this was his first week at the hospital, and only the second time he has had to do stitching (the first time being in practice on a dead animal).

I told him that there was nothing to it, just take the forceps, clip them onto a curved needle, thread the catgut and then gently catch the two sides of the cut and bring them slowly together. Make a knot and then snip it about the knot, and do the same every half inch along the cut. He looked at me and said: "Have *you* done this before?" I told him that I was a qualified Army medical orderly and I'd been taught to stitch small wounds, which I'd done several times. It took him another twenty minutes before he was finished.

The nurse put on a dressing, gave me some aspirin, as I had a headache, and told me to come back in seven days' time for a check-up and to have the stitches removed. When I came out of the dispensing room, I didn't realise but the two boys who had brought me were still waiting for me, and when they saw me, they asked if I would like them to see me home. I told them that, apart from the headache, I was perfectly alright, but thanked them for the offer.

When I arrived home, Mum saw the state of me and I thought for a minute she was going to pass out with shock. I told her that the wound looked worse than it was and that when I wash the blood off my body and uniform I would look much more presentable. All that I wanted was a hot drink and a lay down in my room, and if possible, some sleep.

For the next few days, while my head recovered, I decided not to go wandering and stay at home, at least until my stitches had been removed. However, I soon grew bored at home, with nothing to do expect read the newspaper or a book. While in the house, I discovered some floorboards in a cupboard that had been left from repair jobs done after Dad had bought the house. There were also some tools and a few sheets of sandpaper. I decided they would make some excellent shelves in my room and so I asked Dad if I could use them, to which he agreed. They were the first piece of furniture I had ever made and it turned out exactly as I wanted; it made me very proud, especially when Dad commented on how well I had made them. Later on, especially in my retirement, I took up the hobby of woodworking and became very good at furniture restoration.

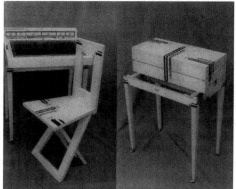

17 - A writing desk I hand crafted in my days woodworking.

Uncle Joe visited me several times to see how I was doing, pressing me to come and see him and Zygmunt as soon as I was able to discuss my future. I told him that until my stitches were removed I would not be going into town and that I still wanted to explore all my other options before deciding. After his last visit, I realised that it was time to give some thought about the options that were available to me, to start working on my career. First, I made a list of my qualifications and my options. I had offers from both Dad and Uncle to join their firms, I was a qualified driver holding a heave goods license and had experience driving many vehicles, from a Jeep to a tank transporter and amphibious vehicles. I had a letter from my C.O saying that I was a qualified medical orderly, which I could use if I wished to study to be a male nurse. I had training in engineering during the War as a jig and tool maker and a machine setter. I had some small experience in the fur trade, having worked for my uncle's firm for a while. I had the option to go to study as a professional photographer and, should I be successful, I could apply to work for a newspaper or magazine. Or, I could try and acquire an apprenticeship to become a plumber or heating engineer.

After looking at the list, I started to think about what would be the best choice for me. To take a job as a heavy goods driver would mean being away from home most days of the week. This would be very tiring and boring, especially in winter when it was cold and wet, which wasn't very appealing. To train as a nurse was a possibility, but I would want to find out more about the profession before I committed to anything. To go back to engineering appealed to me as most of the large firms' staff were members of a union, and after the experience with the unions I had had during the War, it was definitely not for me. To become a professional photographer or a plumber was potentially a nice option, especially being paid £5 a week by the government to study. To join Dad learning to be a fur cutter wasn't practical, as with only one cutter to learn from, I wouldn't gain the overall knowledge that I would need to be a top craftsman. The final option was to join my Uncle's firm. The last time I had worked for him it was a rather stormy relationship, so if I took up his offer I would have to be very careful of what I wanted and what was being agreed upon.

However, I always like working with my hands, doing craftwork, and I enjoyed the atmosphere of a large workroom, and the last time I had worked for him it had been on the whole very enjoyable. Towards the end of the week, I decided to phone my uncle to ask him when it would be convenient for me to come to the firm and discuss their plan for me. Of course, I thought, if the talks were not satisfactory, I still had two options left. When I phone the firm, the secretary informed me that Uncle Joe was abroad for eight days, informing me that he had travelled to the

Paris branch of the firm; this was the first knowledge I had of a second branch. Before the war, Uncle had had a small agency in Paris, which was just an office, but now it had a showroom and a stockroom as well. I told the secretary to inform him of my call and, if she would be so kind, to ask him to call me on his return.

The following Thursday I went to the hospital to have my stitches removed. I was seen by a different doctor who, after removing the stitches, told me that my wound had healed up nicely. He asked me if I had had a tetanus injection and I said that I hadn't, but I had one eight months ago in the Army. He told me that, to be on the safe side, he would give me a booster shot, which he administered straight away. He then told me that if I should experience any repetitive headaches or nausea, to come back to the hospital straight away and an x-ray of my head would be taken.

It suited me that my Uncle was away as if gave me more time to think about whether I was making the right decision, and to let the hair on my head grow back where it had been shaved so I looked more presentable. Over the weekend I had a discussion with my Dad, where I told him about my decision to work for Uncle Joe and not for him, explaining why, to which he agreed that perhaps it was a better choice for me to get what I wanted. During our conversation, Dad asked what civilian clothing I had. I told him I had what the army had given me when I was demobbed, as all my other clothing from before going into the Army was far too small for me now. He told me that I would need at least six shirts, and knowing how fussy Uncle was about appearances, he would like me to try on my civilian suit so he could see me in it. I went and changed into my civilian clothes, which felt a bit strange as it was the first time in three years I had worn them. When Dad saw the suit he said that it didn't look good; it looked cheap and didn't fit me all that well. He still had a few lengths of suit cloth from before the war, and on Monday, if I was free, we would go to the family tailor (where he and Uncle had their suits made) and have two made for me. Then he went to fetch the cloth to see which colours I liked; the ones I picked were a medium grey pinstripe and the other a dark blue pinstripe.

On Monday morning, Dad and I travelled by tube to Aldgate where the tailor's workroom was just opposite the station. It was a very tatty looking building, like most of the buildings that were there at the time. The workshop was on the first floor, occupying several rooms. We met the tailor, whose name was Mickey Stitcher, which I will never forget. He took my measurements and told me to come for a fitting in a week's time and, if the fit was satisfactory, the suits would be ready for collection a week later. After we left the tailor, Dad took me to Gamages and bought me four white shirts and said that now I had sufficient clothing to start my job.

Uncle arrived back at the end of the week. I called him and told him that I was ready to come to the firm that Monday to discuss his proposition. He said that Monday was not suitable as he had too many appointments, but Tuesday would be perfect, so we arranged for me to come at 10a.m. on Tuesday. When I arrived, both my uncles were there waiting for me in the showroom, from which we went to Uncle Joe's large office on the first floor. When we were all seated, Uncle Joe asked me to tell him my decision. I said that before I did, I must know what their offer was exactly. Uncle Joe told me that he wanted me to join the firm, learn to be a cutter and then learn about the other departments, so I can eventually be part of the management. Then he asked me what I wanted. I said that I would like to join the firm, but on certain conditions: I wanted to learn the fur trade and become a mink cutter (which was a job at the top end of the trade), I wished to work either with Mr. Steiner, with whom I had worked with before when I was in Leeds, or Mr. Federman, whom I knew to be one of the best craftsmen in the business, and I would like to be able to make my first coat by the end of my first year in the firm. If I was not capable of accomplishing that, I would leave the firm and try a different industry, rather than waste everyone's time. Finally, I wanted to be treated the same as any other junior cutter would; I didn't want to be treated as if I was special and I wouldn't report what was happening in the workroom, otherwise the staff would never accept and trust me.

I think both my uncles suddenly realised that I was no longer a boy, but a man who knew his own mind. Uncle Joe thought for a while, then told me that some of the things I wanted were not possible: both Mr. Steiner and Mr. Federman were leaving the firm to start their own firm called Chamber Masters, but he had hired a new foreman, Mr. Jones, to replace Steiner, on a two month trial and I would be assigned to work with him. There were also two other junior cutters training in the firm, with whom I would have to share some of the duties so as to not show any favouritism, like cleaning furs and occasionally delivering items to the customers. As for making a Mink coat in my first year, I had set myself a tall agenda, Uncle continued, telling me that not many cutters handle mink unless they have been in the trade for at least three years.

I told him that he didn't know much of what I had been doing in the past seven years. When working in engineering I learned to make jigs, tools and set machines before I was seventeen. By the time I had been doing it a year I was a charge hand responsible for thirty drill operators. In the Army I took my driving test after four lessons. I held a heavy goods license for up to 10-ton lorries, and I had had various leadership jobs in which I was in charge of up to seventy men at one point. In my last job I had become a fully qualified orderly in five months. If I was to work here, I had every intention of being able to make a mink coat in a year.

After my little speech, I think Uncle began to realise how serious I was. He said 'OK' and told me we would give it a try. He asked if I still had my tools from the last time I was in the workroom and I said that I wasn't sure, but I would look in our store cupboards at home where Mum had put all my stuff when I had been called up. He told me not to worry about it too much, as any tools I was missing the firm would supply me with. There was a whole box of tools that, over the years, had been left behind by other cutters who had moved on that I could take from, and Uncle would supply me with some new fur cutting knives from Sweden, which the firm was trying out and were supposed to not need sharpening. The firm would also supply me with two white overcoats, which I would have to put one in the firm's laundry once a week. The reason we had two overcoats was so that, when a client came round, we could change out of our dirty overcoat that we worked in and into a clean one.

Over the years as a furrier I developed a few tricks of the trade that made life easier. Every so often we would have some well-to-do woman come in, who would have recently bought a coat from us, complaining that one sleeve was an inch too long or something of the sort. I would tell them to wait in our showroom and I would take the coat back to my workroom, where I would hang it up and change back into my dirty overcoat to carry on working on whatever it was I was doing. After twenty minutes I would change back into my clean overcoat, take the coat back to them and ask them to try it on. "Oh yes, it fits much better now," they would say, and off they'd go none the wiser. It always worked.

Then, he asked me if I had enough civilian clothes, as he expected me to be smartly dressed for clients, when occasionally we will have to come down and meet them in the showroom. I told him about the two suits and when they would be ready, so I would be able to join the firm in a fortnight. We then discussed pay: the starting pay for a junior cutter was £4 a week. I told him that this was not acceptable for me as under a government scheme I would be able to study and receive £5 a week. If I could start on £5, with the possibility of pay rises when I progressed to other roles, I would be happy to take his offer. Uncle Joe thought about it before agreeing to my terms.

I was told the working times were 8.30a.m. to 6p.m., with an hour for lunch. If necessary to work overtime or half-day Saturdays during the fur season, I would be paid extra. After we finished discussing all this, we had a drink and we all relaxed, them asking me many questions about what sort of jobs I had been doing during my time in active service. I told them some of the experiences I had received, and before long it was time for me to leave.

That Saturday, I decided to visit the International Youth club to thank all the members who had helped me when I had had my accident, and to say goodbye as I had decided to depart the club since it had changed so much from what I remembered. As I was leaving I had a stroke of luck. There was another member there that I knew from the old days who was also leaving. We had a chat and I asked him where he was going and he told me he was going down to Marble Arch, to Speakers' Corner. I asked him if I could join him, to which he agreed, saying he would be pleased to have my company.

When we reached Speakers' Corner, his friends were already there and he introduced me to them. Two of the boys were identical twins, Jack and Harry Simler; we got talking and we seemed to take to each other. I found out that they were a year older than me, and that Jack had been in the R.A.F during the war and on being discharged had become a flying instructor at a flying school near Stonehenge. Harry was just finishing with his studies as a Chartered Accountant and had just started working in a firm. There were six of us in total. We listened to one of the speakers for a while, who was a bit boring. Harry then asked me if I was staying on with the others, as they were all going to Leicester Square to see what pictures were showing. He asked if I would like to join, and I replied that I would be delighted.

When we reached Leicester Square there were no films we wanted to see showing, so I asked them if they would wanted to join me at the Overseas League for tea or a drink, which they all readily accepted, surprised that I was a member there. We had a most pleasant time finding out that all our families had similar backgrounds. That was the beginning of a lifelong friendship and those of us still alive are still in touch sixty years on. There were two other friends – one an Assistant Director of films and the other a solicitor – and we became a group of five and we were inseparable for the next seven years until I met my wife, Aileen.

On my last week before starting work I went to the tailor for my suit fitting. There were some small adjustments to be made, but Mickey told me that the suits would be ready for collection on that Friday morning. When I had collected them and brought them home, I decided to wear one that evening, as I was going to my parents' flat for a Sabbath meal and so I could surprise them with my new look. When I arrived at the flat, Mum told me how good I looked in my suit, as it was the first time she had seen me properly dressed in three years out of my uniform. During the meal, Dad asked me how I had got on with my uncles. I told him about our agreement and the pay of £5 a week. Dad said it wasn't overly generous, but it should suffice me for the time being. Out of my wages, I would have to give Mum £2 a week for food, laundry, dry cleaning and any other expenses, which I was happy to contribute.

On Monday, I arrive at the firm a few minutes early. Uncle Joe was already there; it seemed that he was usually at the firm a bit earlier than the staff to do some office work. He told me how pleased he was to see me and took me down to the stockroom where he issued me with two white overcoats and gave me two new pattern fur knives, then pointed to a wooden box full of fur working tools and told me to help myself to whatever I needed. He then said that, as I was so serious about becoming a furrier, he suggested that I inquire at the Northern Polytechnic, who did a course in pattern cutting and fur cutting, which might be of help to me. I sorted through the tools and took the ones I would need, and then Uncle Joe told me to go to the main workroom to report to Mr. Jones.

I went to the workroom and introduced myself to Mr. Jones, who asked me what experience I had. He said, as I was to be his assistant, he had some sleeves which were ready for nailing[26], so he will start me off with that to see how well I do, and then we would carry on from there. He came over several times to see how I was doing, and after I had finished, he said that at least he could see that I could nail. During a tea break I met the other two junior cutters; they were both slightly younger than me and were called Bernard and Tony. There was also a young apprentice named Tom, who was about two years younger than us. I found out that Bernard and Tony were sons of big skin merchants with

---

[26] The process of tacking them out.

whom the firm had dealings with, and Uncle Joe was doing them a favour having their sons learn about furriery, so they had some knowledge of how furs made when they eventually joined their families' businesses. They came from Jewish families that were quite wealthy, and so they were very spoiled. They were quite pleasant to be with, but didn't show a lot of interest in their work.

Working with Mr. Jones didn't work out as I had expected. Every time I wanted an explanation of what he was doing, he would say he would show me late when I had had more experience. He was an old-fashioned type cutter and I came across people like him in a fur firm that I had worked for just before I had left for war work. Every time I came around to his side of the table to see what he was doing, he would turn his back on his work so I couldn't see what he was doing and told me to get on with some other work. I mentioned this to Uncle Joe, and Joe told me not to worry as he himself wasn't all that please with Mr. Jones' work, and he would be leaving at the end of his two month trial period. An old friend, with whom Joe had worked in Vienna, a Mr. John Prusha, and who was considered as one of the best fur cutters, would be taking over as the overall manager of the workrooms and I would be his assistant.

When Mr. Prusha took over and I was introduced to him, I saw that he was the same age as Uncle Joe and straight away I felt that we would get on with one another. He asked the usual questions about experience, and then said that if I was to be his assistant, we were to start from scratch and he would teach me how *he* wanted his skins stretched, trimmed and anything else I would be doing.

He picked up the fur knife and gave me a lecture in how to use it, and some advice which stayed with me all my life (later in life I gave the same lecture when I had my own apprentices): "I know you are eager to start cutting, but that is the last thing you do. Anyone can cut and be a fur mechanic, but I am going to teach you to be a craftsman and a cutter. As I am just starting a mink coat, you will start learning from scratch. You will first learn how to split open a skin, then stretch them, trim and sort for colour, size and depth of hair. Then you will learn how to study the pattern and how to calculate which skins will be used in different parts of the garment. One of the most important things is to be able to visualise the garment; how it will look when it is finished. Not many people can do that, but I think you will be one of them." He then picked up one of the skins and slid inside it a special tool used for opening skins.[27] He then explained to me that the skin has to be open exactly in the middle of its belly and instructed me how the top paws had to be cut open. After he opened a dozen skins, he dampened them and proceeded to instruct me how he wanted them stretched. He gave me some of the skins to stretch, occasionally coming over to my station to check on my progress and correct any mistakes that I might have made. After a while he just let me to get on with stretching without any corrections.

When all the stretching had been completed, some of the skins were already dry and it was possible for him to start trimming them. He picked up a skin and explained that we had to look for any damages or imperfections on the hair side. He then started trimming the skins, instructing me all the time as to what he was doing. After he trimmed a few he marked a skin for me to try trimming. I picked up my knife; it was the first time I'd cut a mink skin. He gave me some more skins and told me to mark them out where they needed to be trimmed, and after inspecting what I marked out, and except for a few corrections that needed to be made, he told me to trim them. I learned more in that one day than in the two month that I was assistant to Mr. Jones. From that day on, when I woke up in the morning, I was eager to go to work to see what new things I could learn, for every day I seemed to acquire some new knowledge.

My progress with Mr. Prusha was quite rapid, as he encourage me and gave me instructions all the time. He asked Uncle for me to become his permanent assistant when I didn't have other duties to perform. One of the duties I had was cleaning

---

[27] It is a piece of wooden board about 25in. long, 3/8th in. thick, and tapered from 2½ in. at the top to 4½ at the bottom.

furs, which all of us junior cutters had to do. It wasn't that difficult; we had to use sawdust mixed with chemicals and, although we wore masks and we had a brand new cleaning department with all the latest equipment, it was still dusty and smelly work. We wore white coats and head coverings, but the dust still used to get into our clothing.

One of the other things that I had to do was delivering garments to our clients. One of my favourites was to Sir Winston Churchill's daughter, who was married to Vick Oliver (a famous comic and musician). I never forgot their address: 66 Westminster Gardens, Pimlico. When I did my delivery, he was always kind to me offer me a cup of tea and gave me a 10/-(50p) tip which was very useful. (Uncle had connections to the Churchill family through doing some business with their son Randolph.) One of my other favourite deliveries was to passenger liners at Southampton. After the war, the tax on fur was 80%.Wealthy customers that travelled to America used to avoid the tax by asking American friends travelling with them to pay and take the delivery of their garment on board the ship as their own, which meant that the garment was being exported without a tax having to be paid. For the firm it was quite legal. If a foreigner paid in foreign currency and the export licence was in his name it was all right, but it had to be delivered to him at the customs at the time they were leaving the country. There was a special boat train at Victoria Station strictly for passengers travelling to the boat, which went directly to the dock at Southampton where the liners were moored. There were customs officers at the entrance to the platform to check the passengers boarding the train. I used to go to the Victoria Station and go to customs asking for permission to deliver an export parcel to the customer on the train. Of course, I knew they were not on the train but on the ship, as they used to have so much luggage that they usually travelled by Limousine directly to the ship. After been given permission to board the train I bought a platform ticket and went straight into the dining car, telling the Steward that I was waiting for a customer to deliver a parcel.

Just before the train left I would pop into the loo and wait until the train left the station. I would emerge and go back in to the dining car. When the steward appeared I told him that as the customer was not on the train, I would have to travel to the ship, and when the ticket officer comes around I would pay the fare. As it was a non-stop train the journey it didn't take long. Arriving at the docks I would go straight to customs with my export certificate and ask permission to board the ship. When I boarded the ship I saw the purser and asked him to direct me to the customer's cabin, where the customer would be waiting for my delivery. I took the garment out of the box, let the customer try it on to make sure that everything was satisfactory, and then I had the delivery note signed. After which I was usually given a £5 tip. When I left the ship, I normally went into town to have a meal and return by a normal train to London. These trips usually used to take most of a day.

Working with Mr. Prusha I progressed quite rapidly; I was able to do his work without him having to check on me, knowing that the work would be done to his satisfaction. After three months came the day when he let me cut a small strand of Mink. A Mink coat usually has two skins in length, invisibly joined by cutting the head of the bottom skin and then cutting a small piece of rump from the top one, which were sewn together by the machinist. Then the two joined skins were cut in a special way to make a strand the machinist would sew them to the length of the coat. There was always a surplus of heads and rumps, some were used to make parts for under collars or under sleeves. The piece I was to cut was for an under sleeve. He showed me the pattern, where the strand had to fit and told me to work out how many cuts would be necessary for it to be the correct in size and then, when I was completely ready, to cut it. I had previously practiced cutting on cheaper furs, which was a much coarser kind of cutting, but this was in a different class. After I worked out what I had to do, I cut the skin and gave it to the machinist to sew for me, keeping my fingers crossed. It seemed that my hard studying with Mr. Prusha had paid off, as after being sewn and stretched, the strand was exactly the size that was required.

After he inspected the strand and seemed satisfied that it was to his standard he gave me several more to cut. After these were cut and sewn and were as he wanted them, he said "I think you are good enough to start cutting skins. I shall give you skins to make one of the sleeves." Making the sleeve was a success, and from then on I worked with him on mink coats more or less permanently and was given more responsibility by him. I was tasked with jobs like marking out and trimming garments for the finishers and the same for machinists when the coat was put together. As he was the best craftsman in the firm, he worked on the most expensive fur coats, and as I worked with him I gained knowledge working on sable, beaver, fox and many other exotic furs.

Just after Easter I enrolled at the Northern Polytechnic to do a course in furriery, pattern cutting and design. I soon gave up on the fur course as I already knew much more that course taught, and instead I did two courses in pattern design which would be more use. My social life consisted of meeting my friends over the weekend, going to the Overseas League for a few drinks, seeing if we could meet some girls to go to the pictures with, but nothing too serious. Being Jewish and nearly 23, the family was urging me to join the synagogue's social club, which was situated just across the road from me, to meet some Jewish girls. I met three that I went out with, but it was always was the usual thing. As soon we had gone out on a couple dates, there was an invitation to tea to meet the parents. And, as usual, beside the parents there were other members of the family. During the tea it was like a quiz show, being asked "What do you do? What does your family do? What are your prospects? What synagogue do you belong to? Etc., etc., etc. The girls, although good looking, pleasant and liked to go out with me, had this habit of mentioning that this or that friend was getting married or another one getting engaged, which made me feel that I was being pressurised to have a serious relationship with them before I had even thought of having one. Through these meetings I realised that in the last ten years, going to a boarding school, being told not to speak Polish and learn to be a Englishman, living with an English family, with so little contact with Jewish culture and family that I had lost the feeling of Jewishness and my outlook on life was totally different to theirs. I felt much more at ease with non-Jewish girls.

As the year was nearing autumn, the pressure on the workrooms to produce more was hectic, as not only did we have to produce customers' orders for Christmas, but the firm produced a collection of furs in conjunction with other Couture fashion houses, which was shown in St. Moritz, Switzerland for the annual show there. As the volume of work increased, so did the amount of overtime we were doing. Many customers demanded the garments for a certain date as they wanted it before they went away for Christmas. Sometimes, so that the finishers could start working first thing in the morning on some of the garments that needed to be finished urgently, I had to stay in the firm overnight with the heaters on in the workroom to dry off the furs that had been tacked out. I would sleep on one of the boards, get up at 6 o'clock, take the nailing pins out, mark out and trim the fur and have it ready for the finishers at 8.30a.m. It seemed that Uncle Joe was satisfied with my progress at work, as by the end of the year my salary had doubled and my pay was now £10 a week plus overtime, which in 1948 wasn't a bad wage for a 22-year-old. When Christmas came, I received an extra two weeks' wages, 200 cigarettes and a bottle of Whiskey, which me and my friends put to a good use when we celebrated the new year.

1949

After New Year's we were still extremely busy at the firm, as the fur season lasted until Easter. I was very lucky to have to have a use of a car, as with Uncle Joe spending more and more time abroad he gave me permission to use his car when he was away, which was a big plus when going out with girls.

As we were entering the month of February, I was getting a bit apprehensive as my year with the firm would be up soon, and I still hadn't made my mink coat. I decided to give it a little more time. I felt that I was ready to make a Mink coat of my own. Should I not be given one in next few weeks, I would have to think of going into a different type of work. I think that Mr. Prusha realised how I was feeling and must have mentioned it to my Uncle, as just after the Easter holidays, when we started work again, Uncle Joe came to the work room with a bundle of Mink skins and a coat pattern which he put on my bench, saying "I think it is time for you to make a coat on your own. Should you have any difficulties you must ask Mr. Prusha for advice." When Uncle departed, Mr. Prusha came over looked at the pattern and said; "You shouldn't have any trouble making this coat, just take your time, work out each piece as you did for me and you will be all right."

The coat took four and a half weeks to make which, was about a week longer that Mr. Prusha took, as I was most careful not to make any mistakes, knowing if the coat didn't turn out all right it would be a long time before I would get another one to make. After the coat was finished and ready for the customer to have her fitting, Mr. Prusha came over and said to me: "I am proud of you. I've been watching you how you have been working and I've inspected the coat, and you should be proud of yourself, as the coat is as good as any I've seen." I said to him that I wanted to thank him for teaching me and all the patience he had when instructing me, and that it was a credit to him of my success. It took me fourteen month of training for me to be able to make my first mink coat, which was two month longer that I originally estimated. After this coat I was given more mink garments to make, and after a while I was surprised that, like Mr. Prusha, I was given other expensive furs to make on my own, like sable, beaver and fox. I also acquired knowledge working Chinchilla fur, which is *very* expensive. I was given another rise to twelve pounds a week. I didn't find out until many years later that Uncle Joe used to tell mum that I had golden hands and was becoming one of his top cutters. I wish I knew that at the time, as I would have asked him for more money.

Several things happened this year that are worth mentioning. I wasn't all that happy living in Dad's house, as he had this habit of coming into my room at awkward times, when I was entertaining friends for instance, to ask if I would look after his fur garments overnight. I decided to look for a place of my own.

Although it was very hard to get accommodation, I read in the local paper that Westminster Council was going to build a non-subsidised block of flats in Wellington road, with some of them being bachelor flats, which was very near to my parents' place in Abbey road. At that time, ex-serviceman who had served during the war were given priority to housing. I went to the Council to inquire about the flats and put my name down for one. First I was asked how long I'd lived in St. John's Wood. Then it was explained to me that, as the flats were not being subsidised, the rent would be at a commercial rate of £3.17/6 (£3-85p), which included all essential services. I would have to have an income four times the rent, and on signing the lease I would have to produce my P60 as proof of my income. I was told I would be notified when I could view the flat sometimes beginning of 1951.

This was also the year that my sister, Rozia, got engaged. At that time she was studying at the London College of Fashion and Design, where she had met a boy called Ronnie, fallen in love and got engaged, with the wedding planned for 1950. I liked Ronnie very much and we got on very well.

Dad had a small workroom at the top of the house where he used to employ a fur cutter, machinist and a finisher, who he had employed when he had a business in the West End. Now they worked for him in their spare time. Having a lot of orders, dad asked me to make some mink coats for him, for which he would pay me £150, which was quite a lot of money. At that time I was friendly with several girls, but nothing was serious, so I agreed to do it. I decided to work for him four nights a week, starting after dinner until 10p.m. The arrangement worked out very well and, although it was a bit tiring, I managed. The extra money came in very useful, and the work gave dad a chance to accumulate money for to pay for Rozia's wedding.

I used to spend a lot of my leisure time at the Overseas League, where I made a lots of friends. One of them was Bill Williams, who was an ex-Indian Army Colonel. I got to know him through being friendly with a very attractive girl called Jean, who he was trying to get to know. I introduced him to her. Jean and I got talking one evening in the League bar; she was quite an interesting girl. She was about three years older than me and told me that she was a mistress to Brigadier Walters, Chairman of Walters Palm Toffee[28], and when he was away liked a bit of fun and company of other men. She came from quite a well-to-do family, her father being in the diplomatic service, but she enjoyed the life that she was living. Through this introduction I was myself introduced to Indian food. Bill was so grateful that I had acquainted him with Jean that he asked me to dinner in an old Indian restaurant called Shafis, which was in Soho, where Chinatown is now. We had a wonderful meal, being served a variety of dishes, each one with different, unique flavours. I, in turn, introduced the restaurant to my other friends, who had also never tasted Indian food before, and it soon became our favourite restaurant. One night we had an incident which made us favourite customers of the restaurant owner.

My friends and I were having a late supper and, as it was closing time with only one other table where there were five guys drinking, we asked for our bill. The owner, with whom by now we were quite friendly with, came over and speaking softly, asked if we could stay until the party at the other table had departed. We asked him why and he said he would tell us later, but he would be much obliged if we could. Of course we agreed and he right away he brought us a bottle of wine on the house for us to drink while we were waiting for the other party to depart. Eventually, the other men left and the owner came over to us thanking us for staying. We asked him what that was all about. He explained that he had been informed by the other restaurant owners about the men at the other table, who had been operating a racket in other areas. They would come into a restaurant shortly before it closes, wait until everyone had departed, and when presented with the bill they would complain that the food was terrible and had made one of them fell sick, demanding money as compensation. If the restaurant did not give them any money,

---

[28] At the time, a famous sweet firm.

they said they would wreck the place. Through us staying they got fed up waiting and left. From then on we became one of his favourite customers, always having the best table and always served a glass of liquor on the house after our meal. During summer, when it came to me taking my week's holiday, I was asked to forego my holiday and take holiday pay instead, as we were extremely busy. It was O.K. by me as I wasn't going anywhere and the money would come in useful going out in the evenings. We had a very busy season and I was glad when Christmas came to have a few days' rest. I received another rise and the usual bonus of two weeks' pay, cigarettes and whiskey which I used with my friends to celebrate the New Year.

1950

At the beginning of January there was great excitement with the forthcoming marriage of Rozia to Ronnie. There were many discussions about the wedding dress, what we were all going to wear, and all the arguments about who we should send wedding invitations to. Our family was very small, but Ronnie seemed to be related to half of the East End and there had to be a big sort out of which of his aunties, uncles, cousins, second cousins and friends should be invited. Also, which of dad's customers and friends from the synagogue should be invited had to be decided. Jewish weddings usually concentrate more on food than drink. There would be a reception after the ceremony and later tea would be served for about 120 people, with a late dinner for the family at Hendon Hall for about 80 people and, of course, everything had to be strictly Kosher. There were long discussions about what sort of menu we should have. Eventually it was decided that it would be a traditional dinner of eight courses. Soup, Hors d'oeuvres, Vole-au-vent, followed by Lemon Sorbet, then chicken with all the trimmings, desert, Petit fours and Coffee or Tea. I was asked by Rozia and Dad to be the best man, but I wasn't keen on the idea as I hadn't done it before, but they kept on asking and in the end I did a deal with Dad. I would be best man on the condition that I could have all the opened liquor bottles that remained after dinner, to which he agreed. At such functions the bar is usually separate from the caterers and you have to pay for the whole bottle that has been opened and they then become your property. I had enough liquor for entertaining my friends for the next three years.

In June, one evening I was in the Overseas Club when a friend of mine came in with a party of friends. He was a manager of one of Ford's car depots. They had just been to the 100 club in Oxford St. Among the party was a beautiful girl called Jean, who I thought was about sixteen. I got talking to her and I found out that she was actually twenty. During our conversation she told me that only this week had she arrived in London from a finishing school in Switzerland and as she didn't know anyone in London, her brother had asked her to come with him to the Jazz club where she met my friend. I straight away asked her if she would like to come on a date with me tomorrow, to which she agreed. We chatted a bit longer about where to meet and then joined in conversation with the rest of the party. After a while my friend took me to one side and asked me not to start anything with Jean, as her father was the motoring correspondent for the *Daily Telegraph* newspaper and he was trying to get some publicity for the Ford Motor company. I told him he was too late as I had already asked her on a date, but not to worry as my behaviour would be that of a gentleman.

Jean and her parents lived in Bentinck St. near Harley St., so we arranged to meet in Baker St. near Selfridges. When we met I asked her if she would like to go to pictures or dinner and drinks at the Overseas League? She chose the dinner, saying that way we would get to know each other better. During the meal she asked me questions about what I did and where I worked and I, in turn, found out that she had been in Switzerland for two years in a finishing school where she was learning to become a Debutant. Her family used to live in a big house in Ammering near Worthing with a tennis court and a big garden. Their neighbour was Jack Cotton, who was a top band leader at that time, and their car used to be a Bentley. But all that changed when her father came out of the R.A.F. where he was a Squadron Leader and went into a business with a Swiss partner and lost all his money, around £60,000. Now she had just finished a modelling course and was on one of the agency's books. She had also worked as an extra in films and was a stand-in for one of J. Arthur Rank's stars.

After dinner, when I took her home I asked her if she would like to come out with me again, she gave me a big kiss and said "yes, please." She gave me her telephone number, I said to her: "This being Monday, how about Tuesday, Wednesday, Thursday, Friday and the Weekend?" Jean said: "Not Friday or Monday as these are the days I wash my hair and do other things, but the rest is O.K with me, only call me before you meet me in case I am not ready." When I called the next day Jean asked that instead of meeting her outside, would I come and pick her up from the family flat where she was living and have a drink with her family, which was fine by me.

Their flat was in an old mansion block, in the semi-basement consisting. It was very large and consisted of a u-shaped passage, from which there were doors going into three bedrooms, two lounges, and in the centre a big kitchen and scullery. In the past, when I'd been invited by a girlfriend's for tea I always took a bunch of flowers for the mother, which I found was a wise thing to do, as the mothers always used to mention to the girl what a nice man I was. This time as I'd been invited for drinks and wanting to make a good impression, I took a box of chocolate for the mother and a bottle of Whiskey for the father. The gesture seemed to pay off, as after meeting her mother Elsie, father Mac and brother Alistair we had a drink and a chat to get acquainted, after which Jean and I decided to go to the club to meet our friends. On the way Jean told me that her parents were impressed with me and that I was a suitable boyfriend for her. As our romance progressed, I was seeing Jean at least four times a week. Sometimes, when we wanted to go and see an early film, I would pick Jean up from her place straight from work; her mother would make a snack for us knowing that I didn't have a chance to have a meal. As we became more intimate I started to think that this maybe was the girl that I would like to marry. She was terribly naïve, having had such a sheltered life and hadn't had much experience of real life. I asked Jean would she like to be my permanent girlfriend. She said yes, but for time being she didn't wanted us to be too serious and soon we became very intimate.

Her family accepted me as her boyfriend and I became extremely happy. I entered in a new phase of my life. Most of her friends were either in the entertainment industry, professional occupations or worked in the city, and her father Mac being a motoring correspondent had many friends in the same job working for other papers, especially Basil Cardew from the *Daily Express*, Charles Fothergill who I think was from the *Observer* and other journalists. In all the time I knew them I never saw them sober. Mac's other friends were from the car industry, especially the motor racing side. He used to go to all the motor races like Silverstone to do a story on them, and soon I was being invited with Jean to accompany him to the races, where I was introduced to many of the famous racing drivers of the time, like Fangio, Sterling Moss, Hawthorn, Allard and several others. Allard, who was not only a racing driver, but also built racing cars and very fast sport cars, had a showroom in Park Lane. During one of these races he invited me to accompany him to do three laps around the Silverstone circuit. I found it petrifying travelling at 120-150mph, but also exhilarating. Most Saturday nights Jean's parents gave a party for friends and neighbours, one of them being Alicia Markova[29]. Occasionally Humphrey Littleton, the Jazz band leader who was also a cartoonist on one of the papers, with his friend George Melly the Jazz singer and his sister Andrea, came these parties. These parties used to go on into the early hours of the morning. Jean and I used to join the party late after we'd been to the club, pictures or my place. One had to be a bit careful with some of these friends as some of them were spongers, who occasionally tried to borrow money from

---

[29] Alicia Markova was an English ballerina and a choreographer.

you, never expecting to be asked for it back. They would come up to you and say: "Tim, I am a bit short of the Readies this week, could you lend me couple of Pounds?" I soon found out who was who, and I would answer: "Sorry, old boy, I am short of the Readies myself."

Using my Uncle's car became not very practical as he was spending more time in London, and some of the times when I needed to use the car at the same time as him he took precedence. I decided to save up to buy my own car. It would have to be a second-hand one as there were no new cars available and anyhow at that time I didn't have enough funds to buy one. I already put my name down for an Austin 10, which was just starting coming off the production line, but it would be two years before one would be available to me.

I'd always kept in touch with Abbotts, and Auntie Sofie kept on asking me to visit them. I hadn't seen them since I went into the army and it was time that I should pay them a visit. I had a few days off work, so I decided to visit them. In the morning I caught the train to Leicester, arriving there just before lunch, where Uncle Charlie picked me up in his car. We then drove to little village called Burbage near Hinckley, Leicestershire, where they lived. Their house was three cottages, three-hundred years old, which Uncle Charlie had converted and restored into one; it was named Archers Cottage. He travelled all over the countryside to where there were old cottages being demolished to build new homes, and salvaged old beams, floor boards, windows and slate tiles. The cottage was next to a church and the whole effect was stunning. When I arrived, Auntie opened the door and as I walked in I bashed my head on the top beam of the doorframe, nearly knocking myself out. When I recovered, Auntie said that she should have warned me that all the doors in the cottage were very low and to make sure that I bend my head when walking through them. They made a big fuss over me, saying how much I had grown and changed over the past three years. We had lunch, during which they asked me many questions: where I've been and what I have been doing in those far-off lands. After lunch, Auntie took me upstairs to show me my bedroom, which was a struggle as the wooden steps had warped through passage of time and none of them were level. Also, I forgot about the doors and bashed my head again, not quite as hard as first time. While I was unpacking Auntie asked a lot more questions about my social life and if I had a girlfriend.

I told her all about Jean and straight away she asked for us to come to stay with them for a weekend. During the conversation I told her about me trying to save up for a car. She asked me how much I needed to save. I told her £200. She thought for a minute and said: "Tim, I will lend you the money, I have money sitting in the bank, doing nothing and it would be good you for you to have a car which will enable to visit us more often, and you can pay me whenever you have a bit of spare cash, but there is no hurry." I was overwhelmed by the offer and I told her how grateful I was by her generosity and, of course, I would accept.

During my stay, Auntie and Uncle Charlie took me sightseeing all over the local area, where I was introduced to many of their friends. They also took me to Leicester market where I bought a pair of Victorian wine decanters. I hugely enjoyed my visit and, as I was leaving, Auntie gave me the cheque for the £200 and asked me to visit them soon. I told her that as soon as I had acquired the car and had a spare weekend, I would come up with Jean.

When I returned to London I went straight round to Jean to tell her all about my visit and how generous Auntie was. Mac was there and I asked him if he would be kind enough to advise me about how to go about buying a car. He asked me what sort of car I was thinking of buying. I told him I would like a sports car, something like an M.G. or something similar. He said: "I don't think you have enough money for an M.G., but we will go to a car showroom on Finchley Road that I know that stocks sport cars tomorrow and we will see what they have on offer." The following Saturday we visited the showroom. The owner, who knew Mac, showed us his stock. Mac was right that an M.G. was out my reach and after trying several sports cars, we settled on a B.S.A Scout with a canvas roof, four-seater sport car, 1929 model in black. It had a detachable boot like a large trunk which could be detached to pack for long journeys.

Although the price was more than £200, as the owner knew Mac and as we had a little bargaining, he accepted my offer and I became a proud owner of my first car. Having a car made a big difference to me as I no longer had to rely on using Uncle's car. I was able to travel to work, where I could park at the back of the firm's building where I had a parking space, and often I was asked by Uncle Zygmunt to give him a lift home, which wasn't very far from me, but he never offered to contribute to the cost of petrol. Jean and I could now go further afield to visit friends which was marvellous. A month after I purchased the car, I made arrangements to spend a weekend with the Abbotts using the car, so that I could show Auntie what I'd purchased, also to introduce Jean.

When we arrived at Archer's Cottage, I had several presents to give them, as Uncle Joe had given me cigars for Uncle Charlie and stockings for Auntie Sofia. They made a big fuss of Jean and told me how lucky I was to have a girlfriend like Jean, saying in jest that she was much too good for me. As it was nearly lunch time, Auntie showed us to our rooms and I did remember from previous visit to bend down when walking through the doorways. We had a most enjoyable weekend and before we left I paid back some of the money I owed to Auntie, also promising to come for another visit as soon I had another long weekend. Travelling back to London the car developed a fault with the brakes; it wouldn't stop properly and the brakes felt very spongy. I knew quite a lot about maintaining a car and, as there was no maintenance book with the car, I pulled up at the nearest garage to see if they could help. The mechanic asked me to drive the car over the well.[30] After he inspected to see what was wrong he said: "You have a real old car here, I haven't seen one of these for years. Your trouble is that this car has a system

---

[30] In those days lot of garages didn't have hydraulic ramps. Instead they had a long well where the mechanic could climb down and see under the car to do repairs.

that that has only one brake in the front which is fitted on your drive shaft with the oil seeping down from the joint above. To make it to work properly the whole unit will have to be taken down, cleaned and the shoes washed down with spirit to get rid of the oil. I asked him if he could do it for me, but he said no, that the earliest he could do was the next day in the afternoon. I then asked him if the brakes would hold up driving back to London, as I had to be there that night. He said what he could do was give the brakes a clean which would make it safe enough for to reach London if you don't drive too fast, but you must have them seen to when you reach home. We arrived home safely without any more trouble.

18 - My first car and my first serious girlfriend.

The following morning I telephoned a local garage at Swiss Cottage that had been recommended to me about whether they could do the repairs on the car and make arrangements for me to bring the car. It was a small garage with only the owner and one other mechanic doing all the work. After agreeing on the price for the work and time for collection of the car, I left them to it. When I collected the car, the garage owner accompanied me on a test drive and explained to me what they had to do to the car, and then he advised me to think about changing the car for another one. I asked him why, and he explained that, with the car being very old, he had found when working underneath that there were several parts that would soon have to be replaced and that it was very difficult to find new parts. He also explained that the brakes would have to be cleaned every 8-10 weeks. I paid him and thanked him for the work and the advice he gave me. On the way home I thought about the advice that I'd been given and decided that although the cost of cleaning the brakes wasn't that great, the best option for me would be to exchange the car for something better.

That evening, when I was at Jean's we decided to go to a pub with her parents for a drink. While drinking, Mac and I had a chat about the car. I told him of my decision to change the car sometime later in the year, when I'd finished a couple of jobs that I was doing for my Dad and I would have sufficient funds to maybe buy an M.G. Mac said he would have words with the Dealer who sold me the B.S.A. If he should have an M.G in stock would he will be willing to take my car in part exchange with cash for the balance.

Just after Easter we had a letter from Germany with the news that the dad's second youngest brother, Uncle Gustav, had survived the war, the only one from the whole family. He was living in Munich with a wife and daughter, and wished that the family would come to visit them, as for the time being he couldn't come to England as he only had a Stateless Passport which made it very difficult to get a visa. Dad had the same problem as he was waiting for his naturalisation papers and a British Passport. We had a family conference, and it was decided that I would go to visit them for a week later in the year, travelling by train, as I was the only one in the family with British citizenship, except for Rozia who was a British citizen by marriage.

At work one thing happened that year that later on had a big influence in my future working life. The firm employed a Polish-Jewish man called Wladek Kimerman who before the war was a fur machinist in Poland. He was an excellent machinist and had five years' experience as a fur cutter in the cheaper end of the trade, but his goal was to become a Mink cutter. Mr. Prusha and I were asked by my Uncle Joe if we could use him as one of our machinist whilst teaching him, to which we agreed. He was a remarkable man. In 1939, when Poland was invaded, he escaped to Russia, joining the exiled Polish army, wherein he reached the rank of Sgt. When the Polish army was realised by the Soviets, they were sent to serve in Italy. He was fanatical of his hatred of the Germans. Whilst his unit were fighting at Monte Casino, they sent his Platoon (of thirty men) with him in command to a position in the mountains, to hold a pass to stop the Germans getting through until reinforcements arrived. The Germans sent a company (110 men) to clear the pass. He held his position for three days, and by the time the reinforcements arrived there was him and four of his men left alive, all of them wounded. For that he received the highest decoration for valour, the Vilituti Military, which is equivalent to the Victoria Cross. As far as I know he was the only fourth or fifth Jewish soldier to receive it. He was demobbed in England, and that was how he came to work at the firm. His big problem was that he was very arrogant and had a terrible temper. He was a quick learner and in five months he was given a Mink jacket to do, which with a bit of help was satisfactorily made. After which he thought that he knew everything and started to question and argue with Mr. Prusha and me when we were trying to instruct him. His temper and arguments came to a head, when through his bad temper we lost us two very good machinists, which at that time were very difficult to replace. Mr. Prusha told Uncle Joe that he didn't wanted him in the workroom as he was too disruptive, and he was moved to a smaller workroom on to the next floor, where we manufactured the cheaper end of our business, where he was able to cut and sew his own work without using other machinists. But more about him later.

In the autumn the family received another letter from Uncle Gustav in Germany inquiring about when someone from the family would be coming for a visit, and it was decided that I should go next year after Easter. As it was nearing the end of the year there were preparations for Jean's parents' Christmas party, which they gave every year to which all their and Jean's friends were invited, and I was looking forward to it very much. When Christmas arrived the party was a great success, but I drunk and ate a little too much for which I suffered the following day. New Year's Eve we had another smaller party and I started the New Year, again, with a hangover.

1951

Just before Easter I started to prepare for my trip to Munich to visit my uncle. I hadn't seen him since 1937 and I didn't know if I would even recognise him. As I was travelling by train, Dad wrote to him giving him the date and the time of my arrival and asking him for details of how we should meet once I arrived there. Once I had arrived and left the station, there was a big club opposite called the Casanova Club, which he owned. I was told I should go in and ask for him, and he would be waiting for me there. I left London a week after Easter early in the morning for Paris, where I had to change trains to Munich, arriving there at 5p.m. I followed the instructions that I had and, sure enough, looking across from the station was the sign of the club. When I walked in the place was full of American servicemen. I found out later that it was the largest one in Munich for the American forces. Suddenly a man ran over to me and started hugging and kissing me; it was my uncle. I didn't recognise him straight away, as although he was only eight or nine years older than me, we both had changed a lot and when I left Poland he was about a head taller than me and had been working several years and I was a school boy. Now I was half a head taller than him and he looked much older than he should have. The first thing he told me was to call him Gustav, which wasn't the name by which I had called him in Poland.

We went into his office where Uncle told me that he had a little paperwork to finish and as soon that it was completed we would go to his apartment to meet my Auntie Jenny and my cousin Rosita, who was 5 years old. Soon we left the club and drove in his Mercedes to his apartment which was a short distance away. Munich was very badly bombed during the war, and there were huge gaps where buildings used to be everywhere. His apartment was in a three story block in the middle of a bombsite with a small car park in front where three were three Mercedes cars parked to be used by his staff. He explained to me when he had arrived in Munich there was no accommodation available. He and his friend and their families were all living at another friend's house, which was not suitable and so they had decided to buy a plot of bombed-out land where, with the help of some builders, they built their accommodation. His flat was on the first floor and when he opened the door Auntie Jenny made a huge fuss of me and straight away told me to sit down and have some food and tell them all the news about the family.

After we had some food, Uncle wanted to know all the news about our family, how we survived the war, if we needed anything, what I was doing, and many, many more questions. Then it was my turn to ask him about his survival and if he had any news about whether any of the other members of the family had survived. His was a very interesting story. When the Germans occupied Poland and started to round up Jews, he managed to escape near the west border of Poland, where he acquired papers of a dead fascist Pole, which allowed him to have some sort of existence. In 1943, there was a conscription of Fascists Poles into the German army and he was conscripted. His unit was sent to serve in Romania as a reserve unit to the German army fighting in Russia. Towards the end of 1944, the Gestapo found out about his false identity. He was arrested and while being interrogated they smashed his hand. He was put in a concentration camp awaiting transportation to an extermination camp in Poland.

Luckily, the Russian army advanced so rapidly that they liberated the camp before he could be deported, and all the prisoners were freed. It was at that time that he met Jenny, who became his wife. They had to use their camp for accommodation, for food and security till the war was over, but there was no restriction on their movement. When the war came to an end they were allowed to leave to wherever they wished to go. They were given identity papers, outfitted with clothing, pair of boots and 10 kg of flour, some tinned food and a little money. Not wanting to be under the Communist rule, he and a couple of his friends decided to travel to Vienna. Being summer, they decided to walk all the way to conserve the little money they had and sell their food on the way to give them a stake to start some sort of business once they arrived there. In order to preserve their boots they tied them around their neck and walked bare footed to their destination.

When they reached Vienna they managed to acquire Stateless Passports and being in the American Zone enabled them to travel freely between Austria and Germany. Jobs were very hard to acquire as no one wanted to hire refugees, especially if they were from camps, and most of them went to be black marketers to earn a living. The big business was cigarettes. My Uncle had a partner who was his friend from the camp, and acquired another partner who was also a refugee from a concentration camp to their enterprise of selling cigarettes on the black market. They managed to make arrangements with an American Q/M to acquire cigarettes by the wagon load. They kept their spare cash and their books and their working capital in a safe which was in my Uncle's flat, and by the end of the first year of trading they managed to acquire over 250,000 Dollars. One night their new partner came to the flat with another man and once inside produced guns and robbed them of all the money. That wasn't the worst of it, for they gave the names and addresses of my Uncle and his friend to the police as black marketers.

Luckily, they had one or two friends on the police force who tipped them of which enabled them to escape to Munich with some money that they still had. In Munich they were able to acquire new names and identities and start all over again. Once there they had to start some sort of profitable business and they must have had connections with the local authorities to be able open an American service man club. Now he and his partner owned three American forces clubs; Casanova was the biggest and it was strictly for American whites, one was strictly for American blacks, and the third one was mixed. He was also owner of two Perlon stocking factories, one that was having its machinery installed and would be in production in very short time, the other one was waiting for the remainder of it machinery to arrive from Switzerland. I suddenly realised that I had quite a wealthy uncle.

We chatted some more and he informed me that as the flat didn't have a spare room he had arranged for me to have a room at a nearby hotel but I would be having my meals with them. He was allocating me one of the Mercedes Benz cars for my personal use while I was in Munich. And then he asked me if I would help him. It seemed that to run his businesses he had to start working at 7a.m. by opening the Casanova club. He asked me if I would be willing to open the club for him while I was in Munich, so that he could have couple extra hours of sleep. He would take me to the club in the morning, introduce me to the staff and his partner, and of course I would be paid. I told him I would be delighted to help him but I would not accept any payment for helping him. Shortly after we left for the hotel, which was only short distance away. It was newly built. When we entered the foyer the owner greeted us; it seemed that he was a friend of my Uncle's. I was shown to a very comfortable room while Uncle made arrangements of where I was to park the car and for how many days I would require the room.

I then drove him home in the car that was allocated for my use, and before I left him we made arrangements for me to be at his flat at 6.30a.m. for breakfast before we left for the club. When I returned to the hotel I was extremely tired. I went straight to bed, for it has been a very long day and I had to be up so early in the morning.

The next morning, after having a quick breakfast in my Uncle's flat, we drove to open the Club, where there was already a large queue of American soldiers waiting to enter, most of them carrying little parcels. (I found out later that these parcels contained goods that they bought after being paid on Friday. After spending all their money on booze and women, by Monday they were so broke that they didn't have enough spare cash for a drink. The parcels contained expensive cameras like Leica, Contax etc., all sorts of expensive watches, gold cigarette cases and lighters, and many other expensive goods which they sold to the Germans, or to anybody else that wanted to buy them, for about a tenth of their value. I managed to acquire a Contax camera with a built in light meter for £30 which sold in England for over £200.)

While working at the club I found out it was a great money-making machine. Uncle and his partner bought large barrels of German Schnapps[31] at three Marks a litre and sold it in the bar to the serviceman in ½ litre bottles for nine Marks, which was a 500% profit margin. The place was full all day and night; their biggest problem was acquiring the ½ litre bottles. There was also a kitchen which supplied simple hot and cold meals at reasonable prices, so the customers didn't leave to look for places to eat.

When I had some spare time I managed to walk around Munich, which was a real eye opener. Whereas in England we still had food and cloth rationing and, here there was no rationing at all. All the commodities were in plentiful supply: beefsteak, real meat sausages, bacon and cheese was available here in as large a quantity as you wished, compared to the pitiful amount we received on our ration books back at home.

My week with my Uncle passed very quickly and soon it was time for me to depart home. Before I departed, Uncle bought many things for me to take back to the family, some which I declined as I would had to pay a hefty import duty on them. I did managed to bring home three watches that he gave me for myself, Mum and Dad, which were gold (mine being gold plated instead), some nylon stockings and one of the new transistor radios which were coming on the market from America, which he probably

---

[31] A very strong German alcoholic drink.

acquired from an American soldier. We then went back to his flat where I said my goodbyes to Auntie Jenny and Rosita. Uncle then drove me to the station, where just before I boarded the train back home he gave me a sealed envelope to open when I reached home. We said our goodbyes, I boarded the train and as soon we left Munich I opened the envelope that Uncle had given me. In it was a bundle of Marks equivalent to £70, which I calculated would enable me to part exchange my car for an M.G. I arrived in London on Sunday evening and went straight to my parents flat to give them all the news about Uncle Gustav and his family, and to distribute the presents.

The following evening I went to see Jean to tell her and her parents all about my trip. I gave Jean and her Mother several pairs of the nylon stockings that I had brought back with me, which were much appreciated. I asked Mac if he could phone his friend the car dealer to see if he had an M.G in stock, as I was now in a position to acquire one, to which he agreed to do the following day. Mac was true to his word and the following evening he phoned me and told me that he had spoken to his friend and the dealer did have an M.G. in stock. It was the same age as my present car, but it has been completely restored and was in my price range. I asked Mac if he could arrange to see the car the following Saturday, as I wouldn't be able to before then, being extremely busy at work.

Mac phoned me the following day to tell me that he had spoken to the car dealer and he was willing to hold the car for me to inspect until Saturday afternoon. He arranged for us to be there at 11.30a.m. I could hardly wait for Saturday to come, and when it did we travelled to the car showroom on Finchley Road where I was shown the M.G. As soon I saw the car I fell in love with it. It was the Magna model with a six cylinder engine, of which very few were made. The engine was the copy of the one that was used by Col. Cobb to establish many world records. The bonnet was much longer and the car was faster than the standard M.G. Its colour was red with red leather upholstery to match. It has been completely restored and newly respired, the price being £300 which was a little bit more that I wished to pay. After a little bargaining we settled on my car in part exchange, plus a further £80. After all the paper work had been completed, Mac and I drove back to his place so that I could show Jean the car I'd purchased, and take her for a spin; she seemed to be as thrilled as I was with the car.

In the beginning of May I had a message from Westminster Council to get in touch with them regarding taking possession of a bachelor's flat in Reynolds House, one of the new blocks of flats build by the council in Wellington Road, St. John's Wood. I made an appointment to see them the following day, where I was asked a lot more questions about my job and my salary, which seemed to satisfy them. I was told that one of the office staff would be going with me to show me around the flat to see if it was satisfactory for me, and if it was, to bring me back to the office and sign the lease, which would be for seven years. The man from the office and I travelled in his car to the block of flats and parked at the rear of it where there was a small car park. He showed me a door and explained that the door only opens from the inside for security reasons, so if you parked your car you would have to walk around to the front entrance to access your flat. We walked to the front entrance and there was a lift to all the floors. My flat was No. 8 on the second floor.

When the door opened and we walked in I thought the flat was absolutely wonderful. The first thing that was noticeable was that the flat had parquet flooring. There was a corridor from which there were two doors, one leading to a bathroom, the other to a kitchen which was complete with a gas cooker, a larder and fitted cupboards all around, with glass cupboards above them. The end door lead to the main living room which was extremely large - approximately 22' by 22' – and as you walked in, facing you there were French doors opening onto a very large balcony, with another large window beside them overlooking Wellington Rd. To the left of the room there was another large window that overlooked the back of the flats and the small car park. There was also a service hatch between the kitchen and the room. The whole place, being newly built, was very well decorated and all looked superb.

After the inspection we went back to the Council office where I signed a 7-year lease and became a very happy proud owner of a flat. I told Jean the good news and she decided that she would help me furnish it. Dad let me have the bed that I'd been using in his house. It wasn't really a bed, but more of an Ottoman which was wider than a standard single bed, upholstered and went against a wall and turned into a settee. One of the first things Jean and I bought from an auction house was a very big red carpet for the main room. Jean liked antique furniture, so we hunted around the second-hand shops behind Baker St. where I bought a Georgian Sheridan table that was slightly damaged which I had restored, a Georgian writing desk, a Victorian reproduction glass cabinet to match and four Edwardian upholstered dining chairs. I didn't have a wardrobe as there was a large built-in cupboard in the hall which was large enough for my clothes. My sister Rozia bought me some cutlery, cups and saucers, a tea pot and a packet of tea, and frying pan, saucepan, and I bought some modern design plates with scenes from Paris drawn on them in black and white from Woolworths, which my daughter still has in her collection of pre- and post-war china. I don't think I used these things more than four or five times as I use to eat out most days and I still had the original packet of tea when I met my future wife.

Having my own flat my life became much more settled, as I didn't have to worry about my Dad suddenly walking in or knocking on the door asking me to do some sort job for him when I was entertaining friends or having an evening with Jean. Of course, Mum worried all the time that I wouldn't eat properly being on my own, so I promised her that I would come every Saturday for lunch. Jean was getting fed up with the haphazard job of modelling and part time film work and took a secretarial course, and after passing it acquired a job as a secretary with a Greek shipping company in Park Lane, which gave her a bit more money.

In June, as it was coming to the holiday season, I asked Jean if she would like to go on a touring holiday with me in the M.G. to Devon and Cornwall. She thought that it was a marvellous idea and it would be a lot of fun doing it. I asked her if her parents would approve of such a thing, but Jean said that now she was over 21, they didn't have much say in the matter, and that in any case they thought that I was good for her and trusted me to look after her. We told her parents of our decision to go together on our holiday and they took it quite gracefully. The only thing Mac said was to be careful, and discussed with me what the best routes were to take and some of the places where one could get reasonable accommodation.

In the beginning of August we started to organise our holiday; we could either go the last week of August or the first week of September, as after that the fur season would be starting and I wouldn't be able to get away. We decided on the end of August, and this time I didn't leave an address at the firm where I would be staying; in the past four years I had only managed to have nine days of holiday, as every time I went on one I was recalled back to do some special job, and this time I was making sure I would have no interruption.

In those days you couldn't book in a hotel or a B&B as a couple unless you were married, so you bought a cheap gold wedding ring, which I did from my pal Harry Simler (who at that time was working as an accountant for a jewellery firm), and you usually registered in a hotel as Mr. and Mrs. Smith or Jones. We left for our holiday on the last week of August with our first stop over being in Exeter. Our journey went off without a hitch and the weather was glorious; we booked in the Rougemont Hotel without any bother under the name Mr. and Mrs. Grant. We stayed there a couple nights, exploring the town's cathedral during the day, which was magnificent.

From there we travelled along the coast to Torquay, stopping on the way and admiring the beautiful countryside. Just before we reached Torquay my car stopped. Thinking back to my last car, I thought the worst. It seemed that my battery was completely dead. I couldn't understand how that had happened as

I made sure that the battery was fully charged before we left London. I called the A.A. and when the mechanic arrived he told me that my dynamo wasn't working and he would have to tow me to a garage in Torquay which repairs M.G.'s. When we arrived at the garage, the mechanic working there told me without even looking at the fault that the seal above the dynamo was worn and the oil was seeping into the dynamo, which was the same problem I had encountered with my last car. Then after inspecting the condition of the fault he informed me that the dynamo could be part exchanged for a reconditioned one, but they could not replace the seal as they didn't have one in stock, but that I could get one from the main M.G. garage when I returned to London. In the meantime they could do a temporary repaid to stop the oil seeping, but advised me to have it checked every couple of days just to make sure that there was no damage to my new dynamo. The car would be ready the following afternoon. After agreeing the cost of the job, I asked them if they could suggest a B&B where Jean and I could stay, which was quite near to the garage.

I collected the car the following afternoon, after checking the repairs and that everything had been done to my satisfaction, I paid the repair bill and went back to the B&B where Jean was waiting for me. We discussed where we were going to go from Exeter, and we decided to start early in the morning and travel towards Torquay, where we would stay for couple of nights, stopping on the way to visit Teignmouth, which we were told was worth a visit. The weather was very kind to us and it was warm and sunny all the way; having the roof down on the car and driving along the wonderful Devonshire coast with a beautiful girl, you couldn't wish for more.

When we arrived in Torquay, I went to the tourist office which directed us to a very pleasant B&B near the cliffs, where we booked in for two nights. From Torquay we travelled to Kingsbridge, which was another beautiful place, staying two nights, and being summer the yacht clubs were having their annual races, which we were able to watch from the cliffs while having a picnic. From there we travelled through Plymouth, where we had lunch, and then onto Penzance, where we booked into a hotel for four nights before returning back to London. At the hotel we met another couple who were touring Cornwall and we decided to team up to do it together. It was a lot of fun; we went to Land's End a couple of times. In those days, it wasn't as commercialised as it is today and you could picnic anywhere along the cliffs without having to listen to music blaring out from a nearby fairground. We found a lovely old pub, where in the evening they served extremely good meals. They produced their own Scrumpy[32] and the first night I drunk a little too much of the stuff, not realising what a high alcohol content it had. Waking up the next morning I found I had a terrific hangover. Soon the holiday was over and it was time for us to return to London. We said our goodbyes to our new friends, exchanged addresses, but they lived near Newcastle and although for several years we exchanged Christmas cards, we eventually lost contact with them.

We left Penzance for London early Saturday morning, taking the more direct route and staying the night in Exeter at the same hotel we had on the way down. We arrived in London on Sunday evening. After dropping Jean home I went home to check my post and prepare myself for work. On Monday, when I arrived at work there were several jobs waiting for me. Uncle Joe asked me if I had enjoyed my holiday, and why I hadn't kept in touch about where I was staying. I explained to him that Jean and I were touring, not knowing where we would be staying, and for once I didn't wish to be recalled halfway through my holiday. He smiled and seemed to take it in good grace and walked away.

My dad had been suffering with ulcer for several years, and a couple of weeks after returning from my holiday he started bleeding while sitting on the toilet and lost nearly five pints of blood. He was rushed to the New End Hospital in Hampstead and while he was being attended by the doctor, Rozia phoned me to tell me what had happened. I left the firm straight away for the hospital to be with Dad and to find out in what sort of condition Dad was in. Arriving at the hospital I managed to speak to the

---

[32] A rough, strong cider, especially made in the West Country.

doctor that was attending on him. He told me that his ulcer had burst and was having a blood transfusion to replace the blood that he had lost. They wanted to operate on him straight away, as if they didn't he would die, but they had a problem as dad was insisting on a second opinion and they didn't have another doctor to attend to him. The doctor asked me if I knew another doctor that he would trust. I asked the doctor if I could see Dad and try to persuade him, to which he agreed. When I saw Dad he was the colour of parchment and very weak. I explained the situation to him, but he was adamant to have a second opinion, being an incredibly stubborn man. I thought for a moment and told him that I was going to call Dr. Odens, who was a cousin of Mum's, if that would be satisfactory to him, to which he agreed.

We managed to get hold of our cousin, who came to the hospital straight away and explained to Dad that if he didn't have the operation immediately he would be dead in an hour. After that he took his advice and was rushed straight away to the operating theatre. While Dad was being operated on one of the nurses asked Rozia and me if they could test us for our blood group. If it matched with Dad's, it would be possible to give some of our blood to our father. We both agreed to give blood and they prepared two beds for us to lie on before extracting our blood. Then the nurse came with a bottle, a rubber tube with a needle at the end of it, which must have had a diameter of a 2" nail, and after five goes she was able to find a vein. My blood seemed to flow very slowly and it seemed to be very frothy; it took about twenty minutes to extract a third of the bottle, at which point she stopped extracting the blood, taking out the needle putting a plaster over the hole and bring me a cup of tea.

The nurse had the same problem extracting the blood from my sister. After we had our tea the nursing sister came back to take our medical history of our past illnesses. When I told her that I had Malaria, she told me that they couldn't use my blood, took the bottle and poured all my blood down the sink. To this day I cannot understand why the nurse didn't ask me my medical questions before she took my blood. Dad was in hospital over three weeks before he was allowed to return home with a strict diet sheet and no more smoking. He wasn't allowed to eat any red meat or fried foods, so Mum cooked only boiled chicken, which I hated, so when I came for dinner she always cooked a piece of roasted duck or beef for me and the family started calling me 'the chosen one'. Dad recovered very quickly and soon was back to normal. The firm became very busy as it was a very good year for the fur trade and we had to employ more staff. We did a lot more overtime; it became very difficult for me to see Jean during the week and we crammed all our social invitations into the weekends. As the year came to an end we had a great Christmas party at the firm, to which staff family members were invited; I invited Jean. Everyone received a bonus in their pay packet, chocolate, a bottle of drink and some of the senior staff received a turkey.

1952

The year started with the sad news that King George VI was seriously ill, and then that he had died on February 8th and Princess Elizabeth became Queen. The King laid in state in Westminster Abbey until his funeral, which was held on the 15th February. I tried to see him to pay my homage, but there were thousands of others trying to do the same and I just didn't have sufficient time to do so. I felt very privileged to be given British citizenship and to fight in the British army, so even though I wasn't born here I felt he was my King. I did see the funeral procession, standing in the street with thousands of other sad people, and it made me think and remember how much had happened to me since I had the honour of seeing him the year I had first come to England. The funeral was one huge pageant with dignitaries and servicemen from the Empire, Colonies and Foreign countries, who came to pay homage. It was very gloomy but at the same time very exciting.

The firm had a branch in Paris, where we had a lot of customers, and although the making of the fur garments was done in London, after fitting they were exported to Paris for finishing and lining. The branch there had only a showroom and a small workroom where the finishing was done. Towards the end of April, Uncle Joe asked me if I would be willing to go to Paris for a year to organise a full workroom there by employing a cutter, machinist and an apprentice and teach them to work to same standard as we did in London. I told him I wasn't interested as I had a girlfriend, a flat and a car, being very happy with my life as it was. He then said that if I took on the job it would serve as good experience for my advancement in the firm. My pay would be increased to £16, I would be provided with a room in a hotel which was opposite the firm in Rue du Faubourg Saint-Honoré, lunches I would have at the firm, my evening meals I would have with him when he was in Paris. As for a car, I would have the use of his when he was not in Paris. Then he told me to think about it and we would have another discussion later in the week.

When I met Jean that evening I told her about my conversation with Uncle and asked her what she thought of the idea of me being away for a year, only coming to London occasionally on short visits. Of course, she didn't think much of the idea, as it would have a serious effect on our relationship. Before having my next meeting with my Uncle I thought hard about what to say to him and decided that I only had one option that would work. I discussed it with Jean and she agreed to it.

My Uncle Joe was a regular flier from London, travelling two or three times a week mainly to Paris, and from there quite often to Zurich or Frankfurt. He always bought an open return ticket, which he seldom used and he kept them in a basket beside his office desk to be used whenever he needed one, and it was also available to anyone going to Paris for the firm. When we had our next meeting he asked me what I had decided regarding his offer. I told him 'yes and no', and explained to him on what conditions I would be willing to go to Paris. Firstly, it doesn't take a year to set up a workroom, six month at most, and I wanted to be back in London for good by Christmas. I would want air tickets for me to fly to London every weekend, as I know there were sufficient spare tickets for me to do so, and I would want to be able to take and bring back goods for the firm. The only trouble I could foresee was that I hardly spoke any French and I don't know at all any technical words referring to fur manufacturing. He told me not to worry about that as it isn't any more difficult than when I was learning to speak English, and there was a young lady pattern cutter who worked in the firm who speaks perfect English, and would be able to help me explain all the technical instructions to the staff in French until I was be able to do so myself. He asked me if wouldn't consider staying until Easter, but my answer was 'no', as I thought six months would be plenty of time to setup a workroom. If I couldn't do it in that time then I wouldn't be much use to him. After thinking it over, he agreed to my terms, and told me that we would be leaving for Paris the second weekend of May.

I had a letter from Uncle Gustav in Germany asking if or when I would be coming for another visit. I wrote to him explaining my position and that it would be impossible for me to visit him since I would be working in Paris, but I would definitely come for a visit next year.

Uncle Joe informed me that we would be going to Paris by train overnight on the Golden Arrow and He had booked a place for us in a sleeper carriage, as with the goods that he was taking and the amount of luggage that I would have it would be much more practical than flying. We left London on a Friday, catching the train at Victoria Station leaving at 9p.m. and arriving in Paris at 7a.m. When we had settled down in our compartment we decided to lie down to get some sleep, but when we arrived at Dover we were woken up by the sleeping carriages being unhooked from the train and transferred onto the boat for the channel crossing. The whole crossing and exchange to the French railways took about two hours. I hadn't been to Paris before, except when I was coming to London as a boy when I had to change trains from the Orient Express onto the Calais train and having heard so much about the city I couldn't sleep anymore with the excitement of seeing it. We arrived on the outskirts of Paris about 6.30a.m. Paris has no trains running through the town; all the stations were on the outskirts around the town, and the trains had to travel all around the town to reach the appropriate station.

As we were travelling half way around the town to our station it was a beautiful sight; being a sunny morning one could see the Sacré-Cœur church on the highest part of Paris with the Eifel Tower in the distance. When we arrived there was no Customs as all the passport control was done while travelling on the train and we could disembark with our luggage, acquire a Porter who took our luggage to a taxi rank where we acquired a taxi who drove us to my hotel.

When we arrived at the hotel, the manager who knew my Uncle took us with all our baggage that we had to my room. The room that I had was tiny, and with all our baggage there wasn't any room even to turn around. Uncle suggested that we go and have some breakfast at the Bistro that was adjacent to the hotel, and by the time we had had it the firm should be open and he would be able to go and send someone to my room to pick up the goods and his luggage, which would give me a chance to unpack.

When I finished I was to come up to the firm which was right opposite on the first floor, to meet Odette, his fiancée, and inspect the workroom. The breakfast consisted of several croissants and a strong large coffee, after which I returned to my hotel room waiting for someone from the firm to pick up Uncle's goods. After a short while a young boy arrived who couldn't speak much English except for few words, who explained in sign language that he had come to pick up Uncle's things. I found out later that he was my apprentice. When he had left and I had put away all my luggage, I still found the room slightly claustrophobic, but it would do for the time I would be in Paris. I crossed the road to the firm and when I entered I received a very warm welcome from Odette, and then I was introduced to finisher who had come in to finish a job on a coat that we had brought from London, and had to be delivered later that day. She was the only staff member there as the firm didn't normally open on a Saturday during the summer. We sat down to discuss what would happen on Monday morning when I started my work.

Uncle explained that Odette was in charge of the firm and I would be in charge of the workroom. There was a bundle of Mink skins waiting for me to make into a coat. The firm had employed another cutter who had previously worked for Dior and a machinist whom I would have to train that their work was to the firm's standard. Joe wanted the cutter to work with me for a while until I was satisfied that his work is good enough to let him work on his own, and to make sure that the machinist's work was as fine as ours in London. Should I require anything for the workroom, I should tell Odette and she would acquire it for me. Sometimes, when Joe was not in Paris, I would have to help Odette with the customers as there were quite a few English people living in Paris who came to us for their garments.

After discussing few other matters connected with work, we went for an early lunch at a nearby Bistro. During lunch, Uncle mentioned that in the evening he was entertaining some friends and customers at the nightclub Lido in Champs-Élysées and he wanted me to accompany him. I was to meet him and his party in the club foyer at 8.30p.m. and have dinner there, which included along with a half bottle of Champagne and the show in the price of the ticket. This was the beginning of one of my duties when Uncle was in Paris: to help him entertain his friends and clients. In the time that I worked in Paris I must have visited every top night club. There was Patachou, which was run by Madam Patachou, who didn't join in singing when you were in her club. She would creep up behind you with a pair of scissors and cut of your tie which was then pinned on one of the walls. There was a Madam Fred, whose club was mainly for lesbians, where they gave a show dressed as men, Carousel for Gay Men, who when appearing on stage were made up as most beautiful women, Eve, Moulin Rouge, Follies, Berger and several others. Most of the owners seemed to know my Uncle and Odette as we always seemed to have one of the best tables. By the time I left Paris for good I was sick and tired of night clubs.

I had a funny incident happened to me before I met Madame Fred. About the three weeks after I started work in Paris, Odette told me that there was a very important customer, a Madam Fred coming that morning to order a very expensive mink coat. After the style of the coat had been agreed, she wanted me to calculate the amount of skins that will be required, so she could cost the coat. We waited in the showroom for her and when the doorbell rang, Odette went to let in the customer. In walked a beautiful girl with a very good looking young man. I was introduced to them as the nephew of Uncle Joe who had come from London to run the workroom. I went to fetch some bundles of different colour Mink skins and started to discuss the coat with the lady. Odette, who was standing behind them, started frantically waving to me and pointing at the man. I suddenly realised that Madam Fred was a lesbian dressed as a man. Luckily, there was no damage done and we had an order from her to make her a mink coat exactly like a men's trench coat with lapels and belt and buttoned on the main side.

On the Monday that I started work, I was introduced to the full staff as 'Chef de Atelier' and then with the help from Uncle I explained to them how the workshop was to be organised. I didn't have much for the Machinists to do, and I explained to them that for a little while they would have to help the finishers out until I had done some fur cutting. When the staffs were leaving for lunch, which was two hours, they shook hands with me and again when they came back and once more when they went home; as I had a staff of nine, this meant I shook hands thirty six times a day. This went on all the time I was in Paris. In the afternoon of the first day the finisher came up to me with a collection box asking me for some for money. I asked her what was it for and not being able understand I asked the pattern cutter if she would translate. It seemed that during their afternoon brake the staff didn't have tea, they had a glass of wine, and we all put in a shilling (10p) which was enough to buy two bottles of wine. I thought it was a marvellous idea. The apprentice was sent out for the wine and when the afternoon break came they poured out the wine, not in wine glasses, but in water tumblers which we drunk during our fifteen minute brake. I must say that that the atmosphere in the workroom was always much jollier before we went home.

When it came towards the end of the first week, I realised that it would not be possible for me to go to London that weekend as I had too much to do organising the workshop. I phoned Jean to tell her the bad news, but I told her that should there be other occasions like this, I would organise tickets for her to fly to Paris and spend the weekend with me. Altogether she came over three times during my stay in Paris.

During my third week I had a bit of a surprise. Early Tuesday morning, before I had even had a chance to have a shower, there was a knock on my door. I opened it and standing there was Harry Simler, who at the time was my closest friend, and Ian 'Teddy' Krempel, who was our Polish friend. They, knowing that I was working in Paris, had thought they would come over and give me a surprise visit. When I got over the shock, they suggested that I get dressed and we all have some breakfast, and then I could show them around Paris. I told them that I would take them to breakfast somewhere, but as I had to work on a workroom that needed all the time I could give it, I couldn't take the time off to show them around. I suggested that they go exploring on their own, giving them directions to several good restaurants that I knew for their lunch, and then told them to come back at about 7 o'clock when we could go out and enjoy the evening.

When they came back in the evening, we went out to a local restaurant that I knew where we had a jolly time, having drunk a couple of bottles of wine. After the meal I asked them what they wanted to do next. They said that they wanted to meet some girls and have a good time with them. I told them that there were hundreds of girls on the Champs Élysées and I asked if they would like me to take them there. They though that it was a good idea, so I drove them up and down the Champs Élysées, but no one seemed to be to their taste. As it was getting late and I had to be up early for work, I told them that the only other place that may be suitable was the Place de la République, and then I would have to leave them as I had a hot date with my pyjamas.

I drove them there and, again, they couldn't find any suitable girls. I was getting a bit desperate and I said that the only other place where they might be lucky would be in Pigalle, near the Moulin Rouge, but then I would definitely have to leave them. I drove them around Pigalle, but again no luck. I stopped to discuss what they wanted to do as I couldn't stay with them any longer, when two beautiful girls approached us and started to chat us up. They spoke English and my friends took a fancy to them straight away.

We chatted with them for a few minutes and the all seemed to get on very well, so told them that I was going back to my hotel and that I would see them in the morning before I went to work. But, no, the four of them arranged to go to a nearby hotel for the night and insisted that before I went I must have one last drink with them. After a lot of persuading I agreed to have one drink.

The hotel was just across the road. When we were in the room waiting for our drinks, Teddy was talking to me in Polish about the girls and how nice they were, when suddenly one of the girls turned around and said to me that nice to hear men talking pleasantly about them. Teddy and I looked at her surprised and I asked if she was Polish. She said no, but that she had a Polish boyfriend who had taught her. She told us that she also spoke Italian, Spanish, German and Russian. I also found out that they were actually not prostitutes, but worked in the Eve nightclub as showgirls, but the pay was so bad that, to supplement their income, a few nights a week they would go out and if they found a couple of fellows they liked they would chat them up and, for a little money, spend the night with them. Then she suggested that I stay and when they were finished with my friends, she, her friend and I could have a threesome.

I thanked her for the offer, but told her that I had a beautiful girlfriend at home. But I said that I would do a deal with her: I would phone her to have dinner, but in return I wanted her to teach me French so I could converse with the workers in the workroom and anyone else I encountered in my daily life reasonably well. She agreed to the arrangement and we went out several times.

In the morning I went to my friends' room to see if they were back. Finding them fast asleep, I woke them up and asked them how the night had ended. They told me that after I left they all went to their beds. About four hours later the girls said they were hungry, so they all went to an all-night restaurant for a meal. During the meal, the girls excused themselves to go to the toilet, and they never saw them again. I asked them how much the evening had cost them. £50, they said. I had a really good laugh, but they thought that the money was well spent.

There were several other incidents that happened to me while I was in Paris. One Monday, while flying back from London, there was a passenger on the plane sitting next to me who struck up a conversation with me, asking me if I lived or worked in Paris. I told him I was working for my firm setting up a workshop in Paris. He informed me that this was the first time that he had flown and the first time he had been abroad. He was in the antique business and he was hoping to buy a few pieces to take back for his firm when he returned to London.

While we were chatting, he asked if I had some spare time and if I would be willing to show him around Paris. I told him that for the next two days my evenings were free. He then asked me if I could recommend a reasonable hotel. I suggested that my hotel was quite reasonable and was situated in the middle of Paris and, if he liked, I could take him there when we arrived and speak to the manager to see if any rooms were available. When we arrived at the hotel, I spoke to the manager, but unfortunately he didn't have a spare room as Paris at the time was crowded with people that had come to watch the horse races at Longchamp, but he said that he would phone some nearby hotels to see if they had a room.

After several calls he managed to find a room a couple of streets away. I took my acquaintance in my uncle's car and got him settled into the hotel. Before leaving we arranged to meet later at his hotel after I had finished work at 8 o'clock and have dinner together. When we met that evening, we had a meal at a local restaurant that I knew. During our meal we chatted mostly about which places he should visit, and I suggested that after we finished eating I could take him round to some of the places, but then I must be off to have some sleep as the following day was to be very busy.

When we left the restaurant, I drove him around to Sacre Cœur, from which you could get a magnificent view of Paris, and after parking the car we wandered around, me showing him some of the landmarks. After a while I told him that I must leave to go back to my hotel and explained to him that it was quite easy to get around Paris using the Metro. He said that he would go back with me and he asked if I would be so kind as to drop him off at his hotel as he was very tired too.

When I dropped him off at his hotel he asked me if it would be possible to repeat the evening tomorrow, by having dinner and seeing a bit more of Paris. As I hadn't been out much as I didn't know anyone in Paris and he was quite pleasant, I told him that I could and that I would pick him up at the same time tomorrow. This time we had our meal and I drover to Montmartre, where we had a bit of a walk around, and the on to the Rue de Italiens, where there was a night marked all along the road selling a variety of goods. We walked up and down the market, where we both bought several things to take back to our hotels.

As he was leaving the following afternoon, I was wished him a safe journey, but he said that, if I was free, he would like to take me out for lunch as thanks for taking him round Paris. I told him it wasn't necessary as I had enjoyed his company, but he was most insistent, so I agreed to meet him at his hotel at 12.30p.m. the following day. The following day, when lunchtime came, I walked to his hotel, expecting him to be waiting for me, but he wasn't there. I asked the concierge where he was, and they told me that he must still be in his room as his key was still hanging on the wall. I went to his room and when I entered he was still in bed. I asked him if he was ill. He said no, but that he just didn't feel like going out and then asked me to sit beside him to discuss what we were going to do. As I sat down next to him he grabbed me, trying to kiss me and pull me into the bed. I pushed him off me, shouting that I wasn't interested and made an extremely quick exit. I never saw him again.

There was one other incident that is worth mentioning as it changed my relationship with Uncle Zygmunt forever. On one of my weekend visits to London, I met an old friend and during our conversation I told him that I was working in Paris, but that I was having a fairly lonely time there as I didn't know many people. He mentioned that he had a cousin in Paris studying at the university, and if I had some time free I should give him a call. On my return I did give him a call and we became quite friendly, going out in the evenings for drinks and a meal.

Several weekends later, when I was in London, he phoned me on Sunday night to ask me if I would purchase a car radio for him as they were very expensive and difficult to acquire in Paris, to which I agreed. As it happened, I wasn't leaving London until 11a.m., as I had to call in at the firm to take some goods back with me, and since I only had a couple of pounds on me, I thought I would be able to borrow the money from the petty cash and pay it back the following weekend.

Before arriving at the firm, I visited a business that sold electrical goods and found out that the cost of the car radio was £14. I then went to the firm to put up the goods for Paris and I asked Uncle Zygmunt for a loan of £14, explaining that I had no English currency and my chequebook was in Paris. He refused on the spot, saying that he couldn't lend me the money. I asked him why, as I worked for the firm and I would be back the following weekend when I could repay him, but he was adamant and told me that the only way he would lend me the money was if I signed a banker's draft to draw the money from my account. After a lot of arguing I signed the transfer and acquired the radio. When I returned to Paris I told Uncle Joe about the whole episode, who was at once on the phot to London, shouting at Uncle Zygmunt, telling him that should I need a loan again to give me one out of petty cash. I never forgot that episode and I still have that cheque to remind me.

During the last two weeks of my stay in December, I started preparing for my journey back to London. Uncle Joe tried to persuade me to stay on another three months, but I refused, telling him that I'd had enough of Paris; I had done my job, the workroom was running smoothly, so there wasn't any necessity for me to stay any longer. This time I would be travelling by train on the Saturday before Christmas and, as I had more luggage than when I had first arrived, I had to buy an additional suitcase.

A few days before leaving, Jean phoned to ask me if I would buy some cheeses for the Christmas party. I thought it was a marvellous idea and I told her I would buy some extra ones to give to our friends as presents. I had a little suitcase, which I used for carrying documents, which I took to a shop that only sold cheeses. I knew the owner and asked him to fill the case with different cheeses that he thought would be suitable for my friends, and to label them so that I would know what they were. He wrapped them all very nicely for me – there were about a dozen parcels and the whole lot weighed about 3kg.

On Saturday, I boarded the day train at Gare du Nord Station, which would arrive at Dover, where everyone had to go through customs before boarding the train for London. Those days most people had their luggage checked when going through customs. When it came to my turn the customs officer asked me the usual question: "Have you anything to declare?" I told him that I had the usual allowance of duty free, then he asked me what the contents of the little suitcase were. I told him there was cheese in it and he gave me a funny look and asked me to open it. Having been travelling in a fairly warm train, when I opened the case the smell of the cheeses poured out of the suitcase and wafted over to him. He swiftly moved back, telling me to shut the case. He didn't bother checking my other cases, just marked them as passed to be able to board the train to London.

When I arrived at my flat, I phoned my parents and Jean, who both wanted to see me, but I refused, telling them that I had been travelling for the past nine hours, which had been very tiring, and after I unpacked all I wanted to do was have something to eat and drink before I sleep. I said I would phone them in the morning and arrange a time to see them all. After I had unpacked and put the cheeses in the fridge, had a cup of coffee and sat down, I looked around the flat and just thought how happy I was to be back in London for good.

The following morning I sorted the cheeses into which ones to give to Mum and Dad, which to keep in the fridge for friends and the remainder I returned to the suitcase to take to Jean's home where I would be spending the evening. Mum phoned me to tell me to come over for lunch, which I did and, luckily, the cheeses I gave her were ones they liked. That evening, when I visited Jean and opened the case with the cheeses, they were all delighted with the selection and started tasting them straight away. A week later, on Christmas Eve when there was a small party at Jean's, some of the cheeses were used to make a lot of tidbits, which were very successful. The remainder were used at the New Year's party.

1953

After New Year's, when I arrived back at the firm, I found that my old bench was still there and with work waiting for me with it. Being a coronation year, everybody wanted fur coats, jackets and stoles. There was also a tremendous amount of remodelling and alterations to be made for the titled clientele, who wanted their ermine capes and cloaks altered so they could wear them to the coronation ceremony in Westminster Hall. I was told the firm would be working full overtime, which included Saturdays. I soon found myself working till nine or ten at night.

At the end of March I heard a rumour that Wladek Kimmerman was leaving to go to another firm and I thought this might be a chance for me to run his workroom, as I had already run one in Paris. I didn't say anything to Uncle Joe until I was sure he was leaving, but more about him later.

As the coronation was approaching, the whole country was getting excited and talk of Britain having a new Golden Age like the last Elizabethan era was all over the place. Everywhere, on buildings, in stores and on the street there were decorations being put up with flags and bunting. The pub opposite Jean's flat acquired a large television, which they installed in a very large room on the first floor with chairs, allocating their regulars tickets to watch the coronation for a small charge, which included refreshments at lunch. Jean's mother was allocated four tickets and I was invited to join them.

When the great day came, we arrived at the pub just before 11 o'clock and found our seats. Mac and I bought some drinks and placed them on one of the little tables provided. The television was switched on and we all eagerly waited for the show to start. Although it was raining on and off, it didn't seem to make any difference for the thousands of people with their children that had lined the parade route with their flags, waiting for the procession to start from Buckingham Palace. When, at last, the procession started, the Queen and Prince Philip travelled in the golden coronation coach with their personal escort of guards riding on their magnificent horses with their swords and breastplates shining like silver and gold.

After the coach came through, then followed the Landau carriages with all the dignitaries, consisting of Kings, Queens, Presidents, Prime Ministers and other important state members from the colonies and dominions. Unfortunately, as it was raining, they all had the roof covers on and so it was very difficult to recognise them, except one who was the Queen of Tonga, as her Landau was not covered. As she drove by, smiling all the time, she seemed to enjoy the rain and received a tremendous ovation from the crowd.

I am glad that I was able to see such a great spectacle, as I don't think there will ever be another one as grand as that one, as most of the colonies have become independent nations in their own right.

At the firm we were still very busy as there were many post-coronation function and balls, and that continued until our season started in the Autumn. About two years previously, the firm had hired an Austrian cutter and his wife, who were give the old caretaker's flat, with the wife becoming responsible for our canteen. We had quite a friendly relationship and we had many discussion about MG cars, as he owned one as well as me, but his was a later model than mine. He had bought his at a very reasonable price and, having been damaged, he received permission to keep it in one of the firm's cellars that was not in use, where he was able to completely restore the car. I was having a lot of trouble with my MG and I was thinking of changing it. Jean's friend, who was married to an American sailor to whom I was the best man at their wedding, kept on asking me to sell him my MG to take back home with him to America, where he could have it completely restored.

My predicament was solved at Christmas. Just before the festivities, Uncle Joe told me that he was so very pleased with what I had accomplished in Paris that the firm had bought the MG from the Austrian cutter as a thank you gift for me, which was a wonderful gesture and completely solved my problems. I sold my old car to my American friend and I received a much better, younger car instead.

1954

The year started quite bleak, with snow, rain and cold. I wanted to try out my new car by taking Jean for a long drive, but we couldn't until the weather improved. Eventually, we had some reasonable weather and managed to do several trips to Ferring and Angmering near Worthing, where Jean used to live and still had many friends. The car was in a very good condition and performed without any trouble, which enabled us to make many more trips to visit our friends throughout the year.

Just after Easter I received a letter from Uncle Gustav in Munich asking me to visit the family there, as I had promised I would. I checked which dates would be the most convenient for me to go with the firm, which turned out to be the third week in May. I phoned Uncle Gustav to ask if those dates were suitable, which they were. I left London in the car on the Saturday of the third week of May, allowing myself two days for the journey, staying the night in Frankfurt.

I arrived in Munich at Uncle's flat early in the afternoon on Monday, where he and Aunty Jenny made me most welcome. Uncle told me that he had booked me a room at the same hotel as last time and, as before, I would be eating with them. Then he asked me if I was willing to open the club early in the morning as I had done on my last visit, to which I said of course, as one of the reasons I had come was to help and give him a rest. On Monday morning, I opened the club at 7 a.m. as before, but this time I only had to stay on duty until 2p.m., by which time Uncle and his partner arrived, with each of them doing alternative nights, one staying until 3a.m. and the other being able to leave at 6p.m., which allowed uncle to take his family and myself for some relaxing entertainment.

A few nights after I arrived, Uncle received an invitation from a friend, who was also a club owner, to an opening of his new club called Intermezzo. He accepted the invitation, telling his friend that there would be eight people in his party. The following evening we arrived at the club and were greeted most warmly by the owner before being shown to a table in the most prominent position to be able to see the show. The place was absolutely packed. While we were waiting for two members of our party to arrive, a waiter informed Uncle that they had phoned to say that they were unable to come.

We were supplied with some courtesy drink, and while waiting for the show to start, in walked Ingrid Bergman with her husband Roberto Rossellini. There wasn't a single table or a place to put another table in the club, so Uncle's friend came over and asked him if we wouldn't mind sharing our table, to which my uncle agreed. When they were seated, I looked over at Ingrid Bergman and I discovered that she was much more beautiful in person than she looked on the screen.

They both spoke German and English and told us many amusing stories about Hollywood. We had a memorable evening full of laughter, which I will never forget. Sometime later, I heard from Uncle that there was a whole write up in the newspaper about the opening of the club, with my picture and a caption calling me a famous furrier from London visiting Munich and mentioning Ingrid Bergman and her husband at the party. I asked him to send it to me, but he said that he would keep it for me when I next came to visit as he wanted to show his friends. When we met again I asked him about the clipping and he was most apologetic as he had lost it.

Towards the end of my stay, Uncle told me that his company was in the process of changing the four Mercedes cars that were for staff use and he wanted to give one to me. He told me I could try them out to see which one I liked. I thanked him and told him how delighted I would be to own one, but I would have to find out what the procedure was for bringing a second-hand car into Britain. It went to the offices of the German AA, who were affiliated with the ones in Britain to inquire about the cost. They were most helpful and explained to me that the duty was 40% and the purchase tax was 80% of that of a new car, which worked out that I would have to find nearly £1,000 to bring the car to England. I explained all this to my Uncle, saying the cost would simply be too great, and I suggested that it would be better that when he part exchanged the cars to send me the money of whatever the car I chose fetched and with the money I could buy myself a new car in England, to which he agreed. I never heard anything more about it and when he came over to England to visit the family, I never mentioned it to him as it seemed that my uncles were all very good on promises and very bad at keeping them.

When I returned back from Germany, Jean's father told me that he had been offered a factory maintained Jaguar 120 sports car to compete in the Monte Carlo rally from Jaguar, and asked me if I would be willing to be his co-driver, which was a great honour. I told him that I would have to think about it as I would have to see how it fit in with my commitments at work. After I worked out how much time I would have to take off from work and the expense of going, it would be more than I could afford, so I told Mac I had to decline.

In June, Uncle Joe asked me if I would take over making a mink coat that Wladek was working on as he had left the firm. I said no, as the way he worked was quite different to mine. He was insistent that I take over the job as Mr. Prusha had far too much to do to make this coat in time for its expected export date. After a lot more arguing I told him I would make the coat, but that I wanted a £2 rise, making my weekly pay £18. He agreed after grumbling about me asking for too much money for a young man.

We went to Wladek's workshop to check how far he had progressed with the coat, and after calculating the work, I discovered that he had overestimated by seventeen skins. I picked the skins out that I didn't require and gave them to my Uncle, telling him that by making such a saving on the coat should cover the cost of my rise for a year. Then I asked him if I would be taking over Wladek's workroom, having been successful in setting one up in Paris. But uncle said no, explaining to me that his workroom consisted of much older craftsmen than me, and it would be unfair on them to put me in charge. The firm had already employed someone to take over, but uncle said: "Your time will come." It was a great disappointment to me, but there was no point arguing as I could see his mind was already made up.

Towards the Autumn, I had a serious talk with Jean about our future. We had been going out together for nearly four years and we should have been thinking of making our relationship on a serious basis, perhaps even getting engaged and married. Jean knew that I would have trouble with my family, especially my father, so she suggested that we get engaged, but not tell my parents until we had decided to get married. She said she would not marry me until I was earning at least £1,200 a year, hoping by that time my parents would find our relationship more acceptable. Her parents had always accepted me, so we had no problem there.

I contacted my pal, Harry Simler, who at that time was working as an accountant to a diamond merchant and a jeweller, telling him the good news of our engagement, and asked him if he would he me acquire a good engagement ring. He asked me what sort of ring Jean wanted, and I told him that she wanted a single diamond solitaire ring. He suggested that my best bet would be to but the diamond from his friend the merchant separately, and then have the ring made up by his other friend the jeweller. He told me he would speak to both of them and phone me if they were agreeable.

Two days later he phoned me to tell me that he had arranged for Jean and I to see the diamond merchant, and when we had chosen a diamond he would arrange to see the jeweller. When we met the diamond merchant, who was an extremely pleasant chap, in his office in Hatton Garden, he explained all about the quality and sizing of diamonds, and then asked me how much I wished to spend. I told him my financial limitations and then he went to his safe and brought out a small chamois bag and poured a handful of cut diamonds out onto some black velvet cloth. He picked out several diamonds which were 1 to 1 ¼ carat, and told me they were in my price range.

They all looked extremely small, which made me hesitate about whether we shouldn't think about maybe getting a different precious stone. He then picked out a larger stone and, although it looked like a 2-carat stone, it was in fact a 1 ¾ carat diamond. He explained that he had trouble shifting it, as it looked like but wasn't a true 2 carat diamond. It was in my price range and cost £170 (about £4,500 today).

Jean said straight away that she liked it, so I bought it. After we left the diamond merchant, Harry walked us to his other friend, who was only a short distance away, who was to make the ring. The jeweller offered us a cup of tea while discussing the detail, and after he had taken the size of Jean's finger, told us that the ring would be ready for collection in a fortnight, and would cost £24 to make. After we left the jeweller, and being lunchtime, we took Harry out for lunch to thank him for all the help he had given us in securing the ring.

Two weeks' later we collected the ring. Jean was delighted with it and we rushed to her home to show it to her parents. They were delighted that, at long last, we were engaged after which, over the weekend, they arranged a small party for us and I became officially an engaged man.

After our engagement, Jean and I started having discussions about what preparations had to be made if we were to be married. Like all young couples in love, you have a perfect vision of your wedding and marriage. Although it would be possible for me to acquire a larger flat in my block, I could not ask for one until we had a firm date for our wedding, as my flat was for bachelors, and my lease firmly stated that it was only allowed that one person occupy the flat.

We decided that we would have to start saving money to buy things that couples required for their wedded life. Although Jean worked for a Greek shipping company, earning quite a good salary, she could never manage her money very well, always being broke and forever buying herself makeup, clothes, but most of all: shoes. We discussed the problem of her buying sprees, and she promised faithfully to curtail her spending and start saving. Of course, it didn't last, and a few months later she had blown most of her money on some silly hat and dress. Luckily, I was earning a reasonable wage, as in the evenings I was still doing private work for my Dad, and I was able to save up a sufficient amount of money to buy the things that we would need, and store them in the storage that came with my flat.

As it was getting to the end of the year, I kept pressing Jean for a date for the wedding, telling her that we could manage quite well on the salary that I was earning at the time. In the end she agreed that we would marry when my salary reached £1,000 a year, which would be when I received my next raise (which I expected in the following ten months). For the remaining part of the year, we seemed to spend a lot of our time visiting many of Jean's relations, who wished to meet me as I would be becoming the latest addition to the family.

1955

The year started with Jean's brother, Alistair, being demobbed from the R.A.F. We had a party to celebrate the occasion, with many of his friends arranging their own one for him too. It was a quiet time for us, as I was working very hard to save money and I didn't have a lot of spare time.

In May, Mac told me that he had again been asked by Jaguar to participate in the Monte Carlo rally, which he had accepted. He asked me again if I would be his co-driver, as his wife, Elsie, and Jean both wanted to go to Monte Carlo to meet him when the race was over and have a few days' holiday together. I declined again, telling him that I really couldn't spare the time as I was working very hard in the firm and then in the evenings for my father to save enough money for the wedding, but I thought that it would be good for Jean to have a few days' holiday.

When I saw Jean, she asked me if I minded her going with her mother to Monte Carlo to meet Mac, but I told her I didn't as I thought it would be a good idea for her. After Mac left for the rally, Jean and her mother left a day later, and I expected them to be back the following Saturday. When I phoned their house that Saturday evening to find out if they were back, Mac answered the phone and told me that while they were in Monte Carlo they had met up with some very old friends who were there with their yacht. Unfortunately he and Elsie could not stay, but they persuaded Jean to stay the week with their friends on the yacht.

When the week was over and Jean still hadn't arrived, I asked her parents if they had heard from her, and if so if they knew what she was doing. Mac told me that Jean had been in tough the day he had to go away and that she had been invited to stay on the boat a little longer and she had told him that it was too good an opportunity to miss, but he said that she would be sending me a long letter explaining everything.

When Jean arrived back she explained to me that the reason she couldn't arrive earlier, as when they were returning from their cruise their engine had broken down and they had to sail to the nearest port in order to fix it. When they arrived there, the Chandler didn't have the required spare part in stock and they had to order one. With the waiting and repairs they didn't return to Monte Carlo until Thursday from which she returned back to London. She was very loving, making a big fuss about how much she had missed me, wishing that she could have been back earlier. What Jean didn't know that my Uncle Joe had taken my mother to Monte Carlo for a few days' holiday, having been invited by Prince Rainier III, who was his friend. (His firm made all the furs for Grace Kelly, who was marrying the Prince.) While there, Mum and Uncle – who knew Jean – while strolling along the seafront had seen Jean frolicking with couple of young men on one of the yachts, which Mum mentioned to me when she came back. I was hoping that Jean might tell me about it, but she didn't and I didn't want to have a row, especially since she was fully captivated by our marriage plans, but a seed of suspicion entered my head.

When autumn came I had the disappointment being told that I wouldn't be getting my rise until the beginning of the next year. I told Jean, who said that we should carry on planning for our wedding and when I receive my raise we would set the date of our wedding.

1956

This was the year that changed my life completely. In January, Jean sprung a surprise on me. The family had received a letter from their cousins in Vancouver, Canada – with which they kept in touch but had never met – inviting them to come for a visit. Her Mum and Dad couldn't go and they suggested that she should go for a month instead of them. She said that her close friend Pat wanted also to go with her as she wanted to see Canada and she would be her chaperone. They intended to go around the beginning of May, and she asked me if I would mind. As we wouldn't be getting married until the end of the year, it would be her last chance to do it. I told her I did mind and I didn't like the idea as it was not long ago that she had been away five weeks and we were trying to save money. She told me that her father was going to pay for her trip to help her out with the expenses. I thought about it and I wasn't very happy but eventually I agreed, but I told her that I want her to leave her engagement ring in case she loses it, which would be waiting for her when she arrived back, to which she agreed.

We carried on as before making plans for our wedding, she also being excited to her forthcoming trip. Two weeks before Jean and Pat were to leave for Canada we had a big party for them at Jean's parents' flat. Her brother wasn't there but came in about 10p.m. with three friends who he knew from the Jazz club; they were all about my age. After introductions and a drink we seemed to take to each other as if we had been friends for years. Their names were John Wynn (a Dentist), Peter Tobias (a Jeweller and silver merchant) and John Levy (who was a manager at the Times furniture store). We ended up becoming the closest of friends and stayed so all our lives until Peter and John Levy died. John Wynn lives in Cape Town who is ill and has Alzheimer's, and we still keep in touch. They all had some sort of influence in my life, but more about them later.

Jean and Pat left the first week of May. The night before they were leaving we all had a dinner together and after Jean gave me her engagement ring for safe keeping. I took the following day off work to be with them to see them leaving. We boarded the boat train to Southampton. When we arrived there it was an emotional departure with tears and kisses, making promises to write every week. The porter took the luggage aboard with the girls following. We waited until they came on deck, waving to us until eventually the ship set sail. We then boarded our train for our journey back to London feeling very sad. Coming back to London I felt very empty, fed up and lonely. Jean and I had been together five and a half years and it felt strange in the evenings not to phone her to have a chat or go out for a meal and to the pictures, visiting friends or going to the club.

Two weeks after Jean left I had a call from my pal Harry Simler telling me that we had an invitation to dinner by his friend Sidney Bernstein at his home, who wanted to meet me. I asked him why, and he said "I know that you are not too happy working for your Uncle's and he has a proposition for you that might be of interest." I agreed and asked him to make the arrangements, which he did for the following Saturday. When we arrived at Sidney's house in Southgate, I was introduced to his wife Barbara and his two sons.

We went into the lounge where Barbara served us coffee, after which she and the boys left us for us to have a chat. Sidney started off by telling me that he was the Managing Director of a fur firm Witte Ltd. He asked me if I knew of it. I told him I knew of the firm, but not much. He then said: "I know that you knew Wladek Kimerman, but did you know that he was our factory foreman?" I said. "No, he was a very difficult person to work with, arguing with everyone and I had no interest in what he was doing."

"Well," he said. "That is our problem, Wladek no longer works for us and Mr Witte."

We had a jolly nice meal and after Sidney said to me "I would like you to come to see the firm and then put a proposition before you. Would you be interested?" I told him whether I am interested or not I wouldn't know until I heard what the proposition was. "I know where your firm is and if you like I can come up on Monday at 6p.m. to discuss it." I said. He was agreeable to that arrangement and he said he would phone me on Sunday to confirm, which he did. On Monday, after work I proceeded to the firm which was situated on the third floor of No. 1 Hanover Street, facing Dickens and Jones. As I entered I was greeted by Sidney, who took me straight to an office where I was introduced to Mr. Witte.

When we were all settled, I was offered a drink. After, Mr. Witte started by saying that he knew quite a lot about me, the quality of my work and also about me setting up a workshop for my Uncle in Paris that had been very successful. "Our problem is that that Wladek had so many big rows with our staff, that we have lost all our staff except for one finisher, one junior cutter and a machinist. We want you to take over the factory as a working manager, completely reorganize it and be responsible for all the work produced in the workroom."

The offer took me by surprise, as I'd never heard anyone in the industry, especially at only thirty years of age, receiving such an offer. "First we would like to take you on a tour of the premises and after we would talk further," He said. The firm was a lot smaller than what I'd been used to as it was all on one floor. There was Mr. Witte's office which led to the main office, which was used by Stanley, one of the company Directors, who was in charge of company books and finances. From the office there was a passage with three doors, one lead to a showroom, one to the stockroom, which was well stocked, from which there was a door leading into the factory. The factory had six large windows overlooking Regent Street, with workbenches running alongside of them with places for five fur cutters. There were eight fur machines in one row which were placed behind the cutters, and in one corner there was a very large table where the Finishers and Liners worked. The whole place seemed to be very well laid out, and after the inspection was finished, we all went back to Mr. Witte's office to continue our discussion.

I told him that I was interested in the offer, but I would like a couple of days to think it over. If I accepted, I wished in the evenings, after I had finished working at Uncle's firm, to come to Witte's to cut and make a garment for them so that they could see the quality of my work. I would come on Wednesday evening to give them my reply, and if they had prepared skins for a garment that they wished for me to make I would prepare and cut the skins. On Wednesday evening, when I came up to the firm both Sidney and Mr. Witte waiting for me in the office, and as soon I sat down they asked me what I had decided. I told them that I would like to take the job on, but before we go any further I still wanted to make a garment. Mr. Witte said that he had prepared things for me, and we proceeded to the stock room where he showed me a pattern of a large stole and a bundle of fourteen mink skins in a silver blue colour, of an excellent quality. I did a quick estimate of whether there was sufficient materials and told him that there was one skin too many. He said that they always used that amount of material for that pattern and asked me to keep the extra skin should I need it. We agreed for me to work every evening for an hour and a half, which would enable me to cut the skins, which could then be sewn by the machinist during the day and the garment would be ready in two weeks. This suited me fine what with Jean being away.

Towards the end of the following week, in the evening, I came to the firm again to check whether everything was sewn correctly and ready to be lined. Everything seemed to be correctly done, so I picked up the leftover skin from the job and gave it to

Mr. Witte, saying it was very seldom that I am wrong in my estimate and I don't believe in taking Cabbage[33], whereupon he called Sidney into the office for us to have a drink. Then, when we were altogether he said to me: "we are very happy with your work and we would like you to join the firm in the position that we discussed, so let's talk business. Firstly, what sort of salary do you want?"

I said: "before we go any further, there are two things I want to establish and get sorted. I understand that you make all the designs and patterns, so before we issue the jobs to the cutters, we should discuss them together so that I know exactly what you require, and so I can do the estimate of how much material we would be using. The other thing is that if you have any complaints about the staff or that the work that is being done, you complain to me, as it would be my fault if things are not right, and it would be my job to sort it out. The salary that I require is £1,500 a year and three weeks' holidays."

He looked at me with some surprise, saying "that's a bit high." I said to him: "you wanted the best, and you also want me to establish one of the best couture workshops in the country for you. He and Sidney looked at each other and there must have been some sort of non-verbal communication between them, after which he said: "alright, we agree to these term, but we would also expect you to work overtime during the season, for which you would be paid in a lump sum at the end of the year. There is one more thing: do you want a contract?" I said no, as they usually don't mean much, as if I am not suitable for you can sack me and if I am not happy with the firm I want to be able to leave.

Witte then asked me "When can you start?" I said not for five weeks, as I would have to give four weeks' notice to my Uncle and finish a Mink coat that I am working on, and then I must have a week's holiday. Mr. Witte asked me if I could forgo my holiday, but I told him no, as I haven't had one for a year, and I wanted to come and start working in my new job with a fresh

---

[33] Cabbaging was a common practice in the trade that if you had any materials left over from a job, you considered it to be yours to take home.

outlook, but should they have any special important jobs that needs doing I would come and work in the evenings. After having another drink to celebrate our deal, I went home elated, as not only had my pay increased by 75% but I was going to have my own workshop with full control and responsibility for building up the firm's reputation.

When I returned home, the first thing I did was to write to Jean giving her the good news. My increased salary would give us a fairly comfortable life, and I asked her if she would tell me the date when she intends to return. On the following Friday morning, I told Uncle Joe that I would like to speak to him before we departed from work for the weekend. Before meeting him in the evening, I was a bit apprehensive as I loved my Uncle very much, and although we had our differences in the past, he has been very good to me. I didn't want to upset him, and after thinking over, I thought the best way to tell him was to be honest and be straight with him.

When we met I told him that I'd decided to leave the firm and that I was giving him a month's notice. He asked me why, so I told him that I had been working for him for eight years, and had become one of his top cutters, I've set up a factory in Paris for him which is very successful, and since I'd been back I seemed to be stuck in a rut. I didn't get on with his brother Zygmunt, so I didn't see any possibility of further advancement. I had been offered a job by a firm as a workroom manager in charge of all the firm's production with a decent salary. I am only doing what he did when he came to England, starting out with a firm from Vienna and then branching out on his own. He said: "O.K. I had some plans for you later on, but if you want to try on your own I can only wish you the best of luck. You know that if you change your mind I would always want you back. Incidentally, who is it you are going to work for?" I told him Witte Ltd. and his manor change slightly.

I didn't know at that time that he and Mr. Witte hated each other over some incident that happened before the war. "The only thing I ask of you that you don't divulge any information about workings of the firm or try to persuade any of the staff to leave with you." I told him I already discussed that with Mr. Witte and that we agreed that I would not divulge anything about Uncle's firm and I wouldn't do the same with Mr. Witte. During the week Sidney phoned me to tell me that the firm had advertised for new staff, and asked which evenings would be convenient for me to interview them. I told him any evening during the week. In the following two weeks we interviewed and managed to employ two cutters and three machinists, which gave me a nucleus of staff. The cutters started the same day that I would be taking over the workroom, which enabled us to prepare work for the machinists which were to start a week later.

The last week before departing from my Uncle's firm I spent nearly every evening going to my new place of work, discussing with Mr. Witte patterns, calculating how much material each job would require so that it would all be ready on the day that I would start. During our discussions Mr Witte asked me what would I like him and the staff to call me. Mr. Griebel or Mr. Tim? I told I have never been big on being called Mr. anything; everybody always calls me just Tim. Then I asked him "What do I call you?" He said some people call me Mr. Witte, some call me Nat, and some call me 'Governor'. I asked "What does Sidney and Stanley call you?" He said 'Governor', so I said I would call him Governor too, but to the staff you are Mr. Witte. We managed to prepare everything for the workroom for me to start when I came back from my week's holiday.

My months' notice was coming to an end and I had to think where to go for my holiday. I saw an advert in a paper that Butlin's were starting holidays in hotel accommodation at Margate instead of chalets and camps, so I thought I would try it. It was an unusual holiday; I didn't realise that they didn't have single room accommodation, so when I arrived there I was told that I would be sharing accommodation with four other young men. I wasn't keen on the idea but as there was no other accommodation available, I accepted it.

It turned out to be quite a pleasant holiday. The four men were French, all about my age and able to speak English. They were a team of architects from Paris who had come over to

England quite often for a week's holiday as it was so much cheaper than in France. We decided to ask the catering manager if we could sit together for our meals, and every evening after dinner we went to pubs in Margate, trying to see how many different ones we could visit during the week of our holiday. It was great fun. We were a merry crowd and no one got seriously drunk. On Saturday, when my holiday had come to its end, I drove back to London, arriving late in the afternoon. I notified Mr. Witte that I was back and would be starting Monday as planned. I asked him if he could arrive a quarter of hour earlier so that we could sort out any last minute instructions before our staff arrived, to which he agreed.

On Monday, when I arrived at the firm there was a young man with Mr. Witte. He introduced him to me as his oldest son, Alan, who had just returned from America where he was with a firm learning to cut Persian and Broadtail coats, and Witte wanted me to have him as one of my cutters so I could teach him to be able to cut mink coats. It took me by surprise as he had never mentioned anything about his son during our talks. I asked him why he didn't mention about him during our negotiations. He told me that Alan had decided only last week that he was returning to England while I was away. I told him I don't like those sorts of surprises and although I don't mind teaching him, I know personally how difficult it is for a member of the family to work in a workroom, having had that problem working for my Uncle; there had to be certain rules. One was that he would be treated as any other member of the staff, keeps the same working hours and never talks to you or Sidney about what happens in the workroom, as if that happens either he or I would have to leave. The staff gets very uncomfortable when member of the family is present and it would take time before they would accept him and trust him. They both agreed to these terms. Alan and I work together for the next 33 years.

I discussed with Mr. Witte a few more minutes any last instructions, and then with Alan I went into the workroom to meet my staff. The night before I had to think of what I would say to my staff. As the firm was on the third floor we had no windows to display our goods, with the exception of advertising in the fashion magazines, all our trade was done by recommendation and the whole firm relied on how good our garments were produced in the workroom. It was much more worrying than setting up a workroom in Paris, as if I didn't succeed in Paris the garments could be transferred to be made in London workrooms. When I entered I found myself with seven of my staff. There were my two new cutters: Bob, who was seven years older than me, and Derek, who was five years younger, Alan, who was seven years younger, and Eddie the junior cutter, who was about the same age as Derek, one machinist, one finisher, one liner and a tea lady. They all greeted me, some calling me Mr. Tim or Mr. Griebel. I straight away told them that I didn't think much of being called Mr. They could call me Tim and I would call them by their first name.

Then I explained to them about the workshop and the work we would be doing. I told them: "We are starting from scratch. Mr. Witte has given me the task of setting up a workshop which I intend to be one of the best workrooms and one of the best firms in England, but I can only do it with your cooperation. We haven't a lot of time as the season starts in three months, by which time I hope the workroom would be fully operational. This is not the first time I've set up a successful workshop. You are not quite the whole workforce; there will be three more machinists joining us next week and eventually we will have six machinists which will be assigned to each cutter. We will also be employing two apprentices to learn from and help the cutters. I know that you are competent cutters, as I know the firms you worked for, which have much larger workrooms and you developed your own individual style off cutting, but as this is a fairly small workroom, as most of you will be working on mink garments, and as there is the usual difficulty of someone being ill or absent and is working on an urgent job, I have developed a way of tacking out the skins and calculating the job so that we can work a similar way and take over other cutters' jobs in an emergency. If any of you are working on a job and have a better ways of doing it, speak to me. I am a good listener, I have a lot of patience, I am always willing to learn and I would always discuss it with you. But we will speak about this later."

Then I introduced Alan, explaining to them that although he is the boss's son and will be working with me as I am to teach him mink work, he is part of our team and has nothing to do with the office. He is to be treated the same as anyone in the workroom. I then issued everyone with their jobs, discussed with them the patterns and how I wanted them done individually and told them that I would check in on them from time to time. As we only had our one and only machinist, Yvonne, who would sew repairs or anything that we required to prepare for cutting, all other work would have to be done for the staff that would be joining us next week.

My own job was to make a full-length coat in beautiful, very dark mink. When I was given the bundle of eighty skins, I estimated the job and told the 'Governor' that there were ten skins too many. He said we always used that many on that particular pattern so keep them in case you need one or two extra. Three weeks later when I finished the coat and returned the ten skins I didn't need that were left over. Sidney came up to me and told me that the coat I had made was one of the best he had ever seen and it had never been made with the amount of skins that I had used.

Most days, by the end of the day, I was completely shattered; I was glad the day was over. Before leaving the firm, the Governor started to asked me into his office with Sidney and Stanley for a drink to discuss the day's events, lasting about half an hour, which became our daily routine, and after having a couple drinks I used to be a lot more relaxed and ready to go home.

The following Monday my three machinists arrived. I gave them a little talk about what was expected of them. During this one of them spoke up and said: "I know all about you as there is a machinist at your Uncle's firm who is a friend of mine and they told me they call you 'The Perfectionist'." I replied: "As you know so much about me, you can be my machinist." Her name was Mary, she was a lovely lady, a little bit older than me and one of the best I've ever worked with. We worked together for nearly twenty years until she very sadly died of cancer. She was replaced with a friend of hers with whom I worked with for the next fourteen years until my retirement. Except for the apprentices, who were joining us the following week, we were now able to start production. When I retired thirty four years later, of the original staff that had started with me, all that were left was Allan, a cutter called John who started at the firm as one of the apprentices, one finisher and a liner. The rest of the staff were either replacements for those who died, retired or I had to get rid of for different reasons. In all the years that I worked at the firm I only had to sack three of my staff.

I was worried about Jean as she hadn't answered my letter for nearly a fortnight and I wondered if she was alright. I decided to telephone her in Canada to see if anything was wrong. When I eventually got through, a man answered, asking who I was and to whom I wished to speak to. I told him I wished to speak to Jean and to tell her that it was Tim. When Jean came to the phone she was delighted and surprised that I had phoned. I told her that as she hadn't written her usual weekly letter I thought that she might be ill and then I enquired who the man was that had answered the phone. She told me that everything was well, that she and her friend Pat had taken a flat on a short lease and the man that answered the phone was her cousin helping her to settle in to their flat. She had acquired a part-time job to help her with the rent and I should receive a long letter explaining everything in few days' time.

The letter didn't arrive until ten days' letter, explaining in great excitement what had been happening to her since she arrived in Canada. The firm she had a temporary job with had asked her if she could stay with them until the end of July. She asked me if I minded, as the extra money would come in useful when we were married. I quickly replied her letter telling her that I do mind, but if that's what she wanted to do it was fine by me, but she must let me know what date she was coming back. Again, I didn't hear from her for three weeks, and when I phoned her as before, the same man answered the phone before. When I spoke to Jean, she was very apologetic about not writing but she had been extremely busy, but she was in the process of writing a very long letter explaining everything. I told her that I won't be phoning her again as the cost of the call worked out about £7 a go, which would be better used by putting it into our savings.

After that conversation I had that suspicious feeling again that thing were not quite right between us, especially about the so-called cousin in Jean's flat. When I met Jean's parents for a drink, I asked if they heard from Jean. I felt that they were a bit evasive with some of their answers. I began to think again that she may be cheating on me, but then I thought it might be my suspicious mind; I was getting a bit disenchanted with the whole idea of us getting married and I couldn't keep on worrying all the time about what Jean was doing. I decided to stop worrying, concentrate on my job, which was very important to me to, and make a success of it; I couldn't allow anything to go wrong for it. All I could do was wait and see what Jean would write in her next letter, and although everything in the workroom was going according to plan, there were still one or two things that had to be sorted out.

After I finished my first coat, Governor called me to the stockroom where he was waiting for me with a pattern and a bundle of blue mink skins, one of the best colours I'd ever seen. He explained to me that each year there was a most prestigious competition arranged by the Scandinavian fur association (or S.A.G.A.) for the best workmanship, design and style. The firm had competed for the last few years and never won. We had a month before the show, which would give me sufficient time to make a coat that the firm could enter into the competition. We spent a little time discussing the pattern and the style and after we sorted out one or two things that might prove to be a problem, I returned to the workroom and started the job, which I finished in plenty of time to enter the competition.

I didn't know how we had done as the show was in the evening, but the following morning when I arrived at the firm,

Governor came up to me shaking my hand and showing me the trophy for winning first prize. I didn't realise at the time what a big thing it was, as the publicity that we received in all the leading fashion magazines that were sold all over the world was great for business. In the thirty four years that I was with the firm I made twenty nine coats for that competition and won twenty seven times.

My routine during the week became: go to work, have a meal in the evening in a nearby restaurant after leaving work, then proceed to my club at St James's where I met a few of my friends and have a drink or two, then go home to bed. It was a bit monotonous and very lonely, but I couldn't do much until I heard from Jean about what she was planning to do. I came to a decision. Jean wasn't acting as a women eager to be married and if I didn't get a full and reasonable explanation in her next letter I would write to her that it was time that we go our separate ways as I was completely disenchanted with her the way she was behaving.

In the middle of August, on a Friday, when I came back from my usual visit to the club I had a late telephone call. When I answered the call a voce said: "Tim where have you been?" I didn't recognise the voice so I asked: "Who is it?" It was John. I knew several John's so I asked which John, and he replied that it was John Wynn, the one I had met at Jean's going away party. Then I realised he was the dentist that I got on with so well. I asked him what I could do for him. He told me that he and Peter, whom I had also met at Jean's party, had been to a fashion show given by Alexon, which was a huge fashion wholesale firm, where they met the show models and invited them to an all-night party on Saturday which was being held at one of his friend's flat in Goldhurst Terrace, Swiss Cottage. He told me that I had been invited and asked if I could come. I straight away accepted and thanked him for the invitation, looking forward to see him on Saturday. On the Saturday, in the afternoon, I started to prepare myself for the party. First I went to the Off-licence and bought a bottle of Johnny Walker, my favourite whiskey, to take to the party, then I laid out my clean shirt and best suit before I shaved and showered. While I was dressing, John phoned me asking me if I could come over a bit earlier as they needed my help. I agreed to be over at 6.30p.m. and when I arrived John propelled me towards one of the rooms telling me that they had collected the five models from Alexon but as they were preparing the food and drink for the party there was no one there to entertain them.

I opened the door and that's when my life changed for the next fifty years. In the room there were five girls, four were facing me, all were extremely good looking. The other girl was facing away from me sitting on a chair, talking to one of the other girls and all I could see was a marvellous pair of legs and glorious long chestnut-colour hair. I said hello and when she turned around I was completely captivated by her beauty. I have met many beautiful women through my job, but this was something else. I quickly managed to get some drinks for the girls, and then I plonked myself on the floor beside this beautiful girl's chair and started chatting to her. We introduced ourselves; her name was Aileen MacCullum. As we were chatting, the room filled up as more and more people arrived and became very stuffy, so we moved into the hall and sat on the stairs. We swapped information about each other. I told her that it is only a short time since I was appointed as a factory manager at a firm in Hanover St. W.1. and I lived in Wellington Rd, and Aileen in turn told me that she came from a small place near Gosport, in Hampshire, and had been in London for a year and a half working for Alexon in Conduit St. as head showroom model, which was only two streets away from where I was working. The other information I gathered was that she had just come back from a week's holiday in Monte Carlo, she was a fan of Frank Sinatra and I told her that I was a fan of Sammy Davis Jr. and had a large collection of records by both singers, and if she wished, over the weekend I could collect her and bring her to my place for an afternoon tea or an evening meal or both where we could listen to them, to which she provisionally agreed to. I also found out that she was sharing digs with another girl in Hamilton Terrace. While we were chatting, John came over asking me if I had any eggs in my flat. I told him yes, but asked why. He told me that as this was going to be an all-night party and so many had accepted the invitation, they were going to be short of food for breakfast. I agreed to go back to my flat to bring back the eggs and any other food I had spare, but before I left I asked John to look after Aileen until I came back and not to let anyone other man near her. He said to me: "thanks, she's my date."

I got up, took John to one side and asked him why he didn't warn me when he pushed me into the room. He told me that he had only met Aileen the day before and she agreed to be his date for the party. I asked him if he minded that I'd already asked her for a date. He replied not at all, as he didn't know her all that well and there was someone else here that he wished to meet, but he would look after her until you come back.

I raced back to my flat, cleared my fridge of all the food I could spare and raced back to the party where John was still looking after Aileen. The party was a great success and everybody seemed to have a good time. There must have been between seventy or eighty people with plenty to eat and drink. The music was provided by playing LPs on a Hi-Fi player or by one of John's old friends who was a dentist but also leader of an amateur five-piece jazz band who used to play at charity do's.

At about two o'clock in the morning, Aileen said that she was tired and had enough of the party, and asked if I could I take her home. I told her I would be delighted to as I also had enough. I got Aileen's coat, we thanked John and Peter for the invite to the party, I told John that I would give him a call during the week and perhaps he and Peter could come over to my place for a drink the next weekend, and then we left. It was only about a ten minute journey to where she he was living. When we arrived there I asked her again if she would like to come to my place in the afternoon, I could pick her up about four o'clock for tea. We could either go to the pictures or play some records and later go for a meal, to which she agreed.

I drove to my flat to get some much needed sleep and in the late morning the following day, after dressing, I made a big effort to tidy up the flat to make a good impression when Aileen came. After lunch I managed to acquire a cake from our local supermarket which was attached to our flats. At four o'clock I picked up Aileen from her place and we drove back to my flat. When we arrived Aileen seemed quite impressed with my flat, the position of it and all the facilities I had. I asked her again whether she wished to go to the pictures or stay in after tea. She decided that we would stay in have tea and listen to the music. While having tea I explained to Aileen the situation that I was in regarding Jean. I also told her that Jean wasn't behaving like somebody who was looking towards marriage and I felt that things have gone wrong between us, and I am only waiting for a letter from her with her usual excuses before I write to her calling the wedding off. I asked Aileen if she was going out with anyone particular. She said no, the only boy she occasionally sees is a boy she grew up and went to school with in Alverstoke, the place where she lived, otherwise she had gone on a few dates, all platonic in nature, as she promised herself that she wouldn't have any serious relations until her twenty first birthday, which was next April. I was a little surprised for she acted older and I thought and there might be a problem, as there was a ten year age difference between us. We chatted some more about things that we had in common, like travelling and archaeology. I told her that I was having a lonely time and asked her if she would occasionally be willing to come out with me. She said that we would see how we get on today before she agreed to anything. After tea we made ourselves comfortable to listen to the music.

After a while, Aileen said something remarkable: "Tim, when were your net curtains last washed?" I was taken aback a bit by that question, but I answered that they hadn't been washed since Jean made them about three years ago. She didn't say anything until the music stopped and then said that it was time that they were washed and that she was going to wash then. Before I could say anything she had got up and started taking the net curtains down. I didn't stop her, but I thought it was a little strange. Then Aileen asked me if I had any washing powder. I told her that there was some in the cupboard in the bathroom. She took them in to the bathroom and suddenly I heard her shout: "Tim, you better come here and have a look."

I rushed into the bathroom and Aileen was pointing at the bath where she had soaked the net curtains. I looked and there were my net curtains in pieces, having disintegrated. I told her not to worry, I would have some new ones made up. She said "No, I'll measure how many yards you would require and if you buy the netting I will make them up for you for. I feel responsible for taking them down." We argued a bit but eventually I agreed for her to make them. After that we carried on listening to the records till it was time for us to go for meal at a nearby restaurant and both of us being tired from the party I took Aileen to her digs, but before I left her I asked her if she thought any more about us going out together? She said yes, but it has to be platonic for the time being. I said that's all it can be for the time being until I sort out my situation with Jean. We made arrangement to meet on the Tuesday. John phoned me during the week to inform me that he Peter and Mike Plant had managed to acquire a large flat in Ladbroke Grove over some shops with the neighbours above them being Australians, which would be great for parties. The house warming party would be Saturday and I was, again, invited. I took Aileen to the party and we had great time. From then on it sort of became a routine: party Saturday night, then on Sunday we met the boys in a pub for a drink and we all went and had lunch together. Usually after lunch, Aileen went back to my place to listen to records and have tea, after which I took her to her digs so she could rest and prepare for work on Monday.

I still hadn't heard from Jean, but I wasn't worried as I had more or less given up on her. I was seeing Aileen three or four times a week. One of the models who worked with Aileen called Judy, who came from Tiptree where her father had a farm growing 70 tons of strawberries each year for jam manufacturing. Each year she used to invite the five models from Alexon with their boyfriends on a Sunday middle of September to her father's farm. After lunch, for the afternoon and high tea, Peter, who became a close friend and was going out with Aileen's friend Ann, suggested that we travel together in his car, a Sunbeam

Talbot, instead taking two cars, which was agreeable to us. On the Saturday before we were going we went to our usual boys' party. As we were leaving quite early and it was impossible for Peter and Ann to get any sleep at the flat, he suggested that we all sleep at my flat and, although it would be a tight squeeze, we could manage by the girls sharing my bed and Peter and I sleeping on the carpet. We left the party quite early and when we arrived at my flat, there were several letters for me one from Canada.

I opened the letter with some apprehension. It was from Jean, but when I read it a big smile appeared on my face and it was as if a big weight disappeared off my shoulders. It was a very short note, on a single sheet of paper, which stated that that she had changed her mind about getting married as she thought we were not compatible. I thought it was a bit strange that after nearly six years she only just discovered that. When I finished the note I said quite loudly "THANK GOD!" Aileen asked what the matter was, seeing the big smile on my face. I passed the letter to her which she read and understood what I meant. I explained to Peter and Ann why I felt so happy and Peter said straight away that we must have a drink to celebrate the occasion. Those days I used to enjoy having a few drinks in my leisure time, especially whiskey or brandy. We never drunk too seriously, but that night we were just very merry.

Peter, who by now had become a very good friend, knowing how unsettled I'd been for the previous few weeks, looked in my drinks cabinet and spied some wine and a full bottle of brandy. He poured wine for the girls and turned to me, saying: "Come on, Tim, let's have a proper celebration: let's drink bottoms up." That meant drinking the brandy in small tumblers in one go like you would vodka. The girls tried to persuade us not to as Peter was supposed to be driving us to Tiptree in the morning, but by that point we had already drunk almost the whole bottle and were quite merry, so we told them that we were ok. Aileen kindly made us a pot of coffee and went to bed with Ann while Peter and I finished the bottle.

The following morning we had to pay for the drinking the night before, as we both had terrible hangovers and we both still felt a bit tipsy, which worried the girls who thought Peter was in no condition to drive. He insisted that he would have no difficulties driving. Halfway to our destination we stopped at a small village pub that served coffee, which we bought for the girls, and at the same time asked the barman if had anything for hangovers. He told us that he had one of his own recipes, if we would like to try it. He took some time to mix the drinks – I don't know what he put in them but while sitting there with the girls we found our headaches disappearing. When I went to pay, I had a chat with the barman, who I discovered was also the owner of the pub, and asked him about the drinks. He explained that before he had bought the pub he used to be a barman in one of the luxury hotel in the West End, where he had clients come in every morning looking for a hangover drink after they had been out clubbing.

We carried on with our journey, stopping for lunch before we eventually arrived at the farm. The other models and their boyfriends were already there, plus about fifteen people who were either local friends or family. We were most welcomed by Judy's parents and, after having a cup of tea, her father took us around the farm. There was a large kitchen, about thirty feet long and fifteen wide, which had a large ladder attached to the side and three enormous freezers. Hanging from the ceiling were sides of beef, pork, bacon and venison, as well as rabbits, pheasant and wild duck. As it was a beautiful sunny day, most of the girls wanted to go back to the garden where they could lay on the grass and sunbathe.

Before they all left, Judy's father asked if anyone was interested in antique furniture. There were only two of us that showed interest and when the rest left he took us on a tour of the remainder of the house. When he opened the door to the dining room I couldn't believe what I was seeing; the whole room was completely furnished in Louis XVI furniture, including some tapestries, pieces of porcelain and carpets. Then we went into the lounge which was furnished in a similar style. I asked him how he had acquired these fantastic treasures. He explained that not far away there was an old country mansion which was damaged during the war and which needed a lot of repairs that was going to be demolished. The cost of repairs to the owners would have been too much, so they decided to sell the contents of the house by auction and the developers would then be able to demolish the property. At that time, soon after the war, it was very difficult to sell antique or old furniture as everyone wanted the new Swedish style of light colour furniture. The auctioneers had great difficulty selling the contents and would practically accept any offer for it. He put in a bid for all the contents of the rooms, plus several other pieces, except the paintings and other pieces that the family wished to keep.

When I joined Aileen and the others lying on the lawn in the garden, there were a couple photographers from the local press. It seemed that the tea party was a yearly doo with some of the guests being local councillors. They took pictures of the dignitaries and of the girls lying on the grass. Soon it was time to have our tea. We all trooped in to the large dining room; at the far end there was a full size billiards table which was piled up with all manner of food. There was roast beef, gammon, ham, chicken, turkey and pheasant, there were also Scotch eggs, grilled sausages, bowls off potato and mixed salad. We were asked to help ourselves and move to the other side of the room where there were several large tables with chairs, which were all laid out with cutlery and drinks. There were spirits, wine, beer, cider and soft drinks. It was a very jolly party where everyone enjoyed themselves. When everyone finished eating and the tables were cleared, there came the piece de resistance. Judy's mother came in with one of the biggest strawberry cakes I've ever seen. I was told that they had used six pints of double cream and eight pounds of strawberries; I must say we all had second helpings.

19 - Newspaper clipping of the day at Tiptree. Aileen is pictured centre.

Soon after tea, most of the guests departed, except for a few family members that lived locally and our small party. We returned to the garden where we made ourselves comfortable to catch the remainder of the sun before we had to return to London. After a while Judy's father asked us if we wanted to take home some strawberries. We all said yes, so he took us to one of the fields and told us to pick only from these two fields where there were dessert strawberries that had the best flavours, and to fill as many punnets that we could pick, as it was the end of the season and they wouldn't be picking any more strawberries until next season. He explained to us that the bulk of his strawberries that he grew were for jam making and they must be neutral in flavour, as when the jam is manufactured, flavouring syrup is added so that wherever you buy, that brand of jam it always tastes the same. These strawberries were literally too tasty to use.

We picked about fifty punnets of strawberries between us, which we packed in the boot of the car. Soon it was time for us to depart home. We thanked Judy's parents for this marvellous day, who in turn invited us to come again the next year. We made good time driving back to my flat where we divided the strawberries and after which Peter left us to take Ann home. We managed to carry our share of strawberries to my flat, which we stored them in my fridge until Aileen decided what she wanted to do with them. Then, she made herself ready for me to take her to her digs.

20 - All of us relaxing at Tiptree. Aileen is pictured second from left, with her model friends Judy, Sylvia and others from Alexons. I sit in a deck chair, far right.

Before Aileen left I asked he to sit down for a minute as I wanted to discuss something with her. I asked her, now that all my commitments to Jean were finished and I had no regrets, would she consider being my girlfriend permanently? She thought for a minute and said she would like that, but we would have to take it slowly, as she wanted to make sure I wasn't just on the rebound. I told her I am not on a rebound and that by the way Jean was behaving, I had decided there was no future for the two of us. From then on we started going out four or five times a week depending what commitments we had at work.

I gradually was able to find out a bit more about her and her family. The family originated from the west coast of Scotland, from a place called Skipness. Her father Duncan (although everyone called him Mac) was a coppersmith foreman and worked during most of the war in the Gibraltar dockyards repairing ships until he was invalided out with a heart condition and given only given a year to live. He bought a set of Home Doctor books and had so far managed to live a further eight years. He and Aileen's mother, Elsie, lived in Alverstoke in a small rented house – a two-up-two-down – where Aileen was born. Their income was very limited as all they had was Duncan's pension, which wasn't very much. Aileen was an extremely good swimmer, Olympics standard, but the family didn't have the means to buy her swimming costumes or equipment and in those days there were no sponsors. She had to give it up and started to compete in beauty contests. She became Miss Gosport in 1954.

21 - Picture of where Aileen grew up.

At that time, from what I've been told, the beauty pageant producers produced a show for the public and went into competition with other towns that held contests and the best ten town shows were shown on television in a program called Top Town. Gosport was one of the towns that was chosen. Aileen was a marvellous dancer and did several shows on the television, her speciality being the Can Can. She kept the dress from the show all her life. I still have it and it will be handed over to our little granddaughter when she is older, who just started drama classes. After the shows finished, she decided to base herself in London and become a model.

22 - Aileen in her can-can outfit, before I knew her.

She then asked me about my family, life in Poland and then moving to England. She was a bit envious of me having travelled in some of the countries that she would liked to have visited, as I discovered that she had great interest in history, archaeology and travel, but so far only been to Monte Carlo, which had been her first time abroad. We seemed to have many other things in common except ballet, serious theatre and dancing. She loved dancing and was extremely good dancer. I explained to her that though I could dance badly, through an injury to my knee that I had received playing rugby in school, it was very difficult for me to dance as my knee kept giving way. Luckily in our group there were several friends who were good dancers.

Aileen changed her digs to large flat which she shared with three other girls and it was much nearer to me, only ten minutes' walking distance. The only disadvantage with it was that it only had one bathroom and with three girls sharing it, it became a bit crowded, especially when they were going out on their dates and she asked me if sometimes she could use mine. I had a spare set of keys that Jean us to use and gave them to her to use whenever was her need. We used to go quite often to eat in Soho and one of our favourite restaurants was Que Vadis which was frequented by artists, who several times sketched Aileen without us knowing. On leaving the restaurant, they would present them to Aileen, complementing me on how lucky I was being with such a beautiful girl, which made me feel very proud. Most of the sketches were not that good and Aileen destroyed many, but one was excellent and Aileen framed it, which I still have.

23 - Sketch of Aileen at Que Vadis. The caption reads: 'She's beautiful. Cost you a fortune?'

As the year was coming to an end, I started to think of what to buy Aileen for Christmas. At that time, Italian sweaters in very fine wool were in fashion and were in very short supply. Aileen often admired them when we were window shopping in Bond Street. As it happened, one of my Uncle's friends was importer of Italian fashionable sweaters and had a showroom in Regent Street, which was only a short distance from my workplace. As Aileen and I quite often met for lunch, I arranged with him for me to come to his showroom during our lunch break. When we met, I didn't tell Aileen of my arrangement, I just told her that before

321

we had lunch I had to meet a friend in his office for a few minutes on a business matter, as I wanted the whole thing to be a surprise.

When we arrived at the showroom he had about a dozen different styles of sweaters for Aileen to choose from. I told her chose whichever she liked, but that she wouldn't be able to wear it until the end of the year, as it would be her Christmas present. She was surprised and excited, tried on half a dozen of them, after which she chose one that she liked which was wrapped up nicely for us. I thanked and paid my Uncle's friend, leaving with the thought that I managed to buy Aileen a present that she would enjoy. She was going to stay with her parents over Christmas and I made her promise that she wouldn't open her present until Christmas day.

Aileen quite often had to do shows over weekends to which often when I could, I would drive her to. After a few times, she complained that my M.G wasn't quite the car for her to travel to the shows in, as the firm always arranged for all the models doing the show to have their hair done in advance, and travelling in my car, the wind undid all their hard work and took her ages to get right again. I told her that Peter was thinking of changing his car for a newer one, and I had been thinking of changing my car as well, so when that time comes I will make him an offer for his.

At work the season was in full swing and our order book for Christmas was completely full, with me having to work a lot of overtime, sometime not getting home until 8p.m. Often Aileen, having keys to my flat, would let herself in, have a bath, make herself a cup of tea and wait for me until I came home, when I would have a wash, change my shirt, have a drink and rest for a while after which we would go out for a meal, before I took her home. Aileen went home a day before Christmas, whereas I had to work right up to three thirty on Christmas Eve, after which we cleared the workroom so we could hold a party arranged by the firm for the staff and their families and also at which Christmas presents from the firm were distributed among the staff. Before the distribution took place, the Governor thanked us for our effort completing all our orders on time and how pleased he was the way we had progressed as a unit. Each staff member received a week's wages and a £10 National lottery certificate, a bottle of wine, 200 cigarettes or a big box of chocolates. Alan and I received Brandy and wine, and instead of cigarettes I received fifty Dutch Panatelas cigars and Alan had an extra box of chocolates. All the staff gave Alan and me a present and we in turn gave each of them a present. The biggest surprise for me was that, before I left for home, Sidney asked to see him and the Governor his office. When I entered they invited me to sit down and have another drink with them. Then they told me how happy they were the way that the workroom progressed and gave me a thick envelop telling me that that was my Christmas bonus. I thanked them for it and after chatting for a while about what we were all doing over the Christmas break, I left them as I had made arrangements to have a drink with my old friends from my Uncle's firm.

Before I left the firm, I was curious what was in the envelope so I popped into our toilet and when I opened the envelope I was stunned: inside were sixty new, crisp white £5 notes and that was on top of my extra week's salary that I that I already received, which equalled 20% of my salary. I then realised when the Governor said I was a valuable member of the company, he meant it. I also received my overtime pay which was accumulated during the year and paid to me at the end of each year, which came to another £235, which gave me more money that I had ever had before. In my Uncle's firm senior members of staff never received more than £50 for a Christmas bonus.

I went to meet some of my friends from my Uncle's firm for a drink in nearby pub. Everyone was quite jolly as we had all had several drinks in our respective firms before meeting. Hector Hunter, who was my Uncle's designer and pattern cutter, with whom I'd been friends ever since I worked for my Uncle, asked me if my firm had given me a good bonus. I told him yes, but did not tell him how much, as I didn't want him and others to jealous and dissatisfied with theirs. Peter and John were having a party which I went to, but I didn't enjoy it much, as I was missing

Aileen as she wouldn't be back until the afternoon of New Year's Eve. She would be meeting a boy with whom she went to school with for a drink, after which she would phone me at John and Peter's place to pick her up to join me at their party. When the evening of the party came I told both Peter and John that I was expecting a call from Aileen for me to pick her up. I waited but there was no call. I was disappointed and worried that maybe something happened to her or that she had decided to stay with her parents for the New Year. There was no way I could get in touch with her as they didn't have a phone.

24 - A picture of Aileen in the first couple of months of knowing her.

Early the following morning, Aileen phoned me saying that she was sorry that she missed the party but she phoned three times to speak to me, but every time she phoned, Peter took the call and he was so drunk that she couldn't get any sense out of him. She thought of asking her friend to drive her to the party, but he also was drunk and she didn't feel safe. Eventually, later on she managed for someone who lived in St. John's Wood to drive her home. I asked why she didn't take a taxi. She told me there were very few about, being New Year's Eve and she didn't have enough money on her. I told her never to worry about fares for taxis when coming to me; I will always pay the fare. She came over later and we celebrated the New Year by having lunch, then spending the afternoon in my flat having a rest and tea before meeting our crowd in the evening for dinner to celebrate the New Year. So ended the wonderful year of 1956.

1957

After New Year's, when we returned to work, we were still extremely busy and had to work a half day on Saturdays, as our season didn't finished until after Easter. We now had orders that had to be delivered by that date, especially to our Jewish clientele, so that they could wear their new coats when going to Synagogue during Passover.

One day, I was called to the stockroom by the Governor to estimate two mink coats using the same pattern, telling me that these were for one of our most important customers, a certain Lady Hughes, and he wanted me to make both of them. I was a bit surprised, as usually he would just hang the different jobs on the rail for me to distribute to whoever I thought was capable of doing the work. They were both identical patterns, but each was in a different colour of mink. I asked Sidney about this lady and he taught me something. He told me that this Lady, who was about fifty, was a widow who had been married to a very wealthy man who had left her a fortune. She would come to the firm several times a year and order sometimes a jacket or stole, but every two years she orders two identical mink coats in different colours. I mentioned that she must be very wealthy, spending about £4,000 at a time. He said that everything is relative; she's on her last £4,000,000. To us, spending that sort of money is a fortune, but to her it is like spending £1.

I made the coats and, after they were fitted, Sidney told me that although Lady Hughes was one of our best customers, she could sometimes be difficult when it came to her fittings, but this was the first time that no alterations were required, which made me very pleased with myself. Then he said: "Tim, the Governor and I are very pleased with your work and how you run the workshop. We know you've been approached to join another firm. You are not thinking of leaving us?" I told him that as long as the Governor and the firm treats me right and keeps to the agreement we have, I would stay with the firm as long as they wanted me.

Easter was approaching and Aileen was going to spend it with her parents, her 21st birthday being on the 15th. I asked my friends if we could arrange a party for her and I would supply a cake and couple bottles of Champagne, to which they agreed to. I thought of what would be an appropriate present for her and decided to buy her a gold watch. I asked Peter, being a jeweller, if he could a acquire one for me. He was more than happy to and brought me five to choose from, of which I chose one with a gold bracelet. When the party was in full swing and after we had sung Happy Birthday, I presented her with the watch, with which she was overjoyed. She kept that watch all her life and, although she had several others, she wore that one most of the time and kept it even after she lost one part of the bracelet.

The following weekend, Aileen went home for her birthday. I was to pick her up on her return from the railway station to drive her back to my flat from where we would go for an evening meal. On the way back she was telling me what a marvellous time she had seeing her old friends and family, and then mentioned that he parents would like me to come for a weekend next time she visited them. I asked her that next time she writes to her parents to thank them for their invitation, and to say that I would be delighted. After she had a rest and refreshed herself I took her out for dinner and after we returned, I suggested to her that I should probably drive her back to her digs after such a busy day. She looked at me and said: "I have decided to stay the night." I was so surprised and overjoyed, but I couldn't quite believe of what I was hearing and I asked if she was sure, to which she said yes.

The next morning, when we arose, I asked her if this meant that we are now going to have a serious relationship. She replied that we haven't known each other for very long and, although we feel love for each other, let's take it slowly for a while and see how it goes. From then on we became an item. I still had Jean's engagement ring, which I showed to Aileen and asked her if she would like it or if I should keep it. She said to me: "Keep it if you wish, but I don't like diamonds or Platinum, as I prefer Sapphires and gold." I found out later that she preferred gold to any other jewellery. I didn't want to keep the ring and soon after I asked Peter to value it for me to get an idea of what it was worth; he valued it at £175. It was a few weeks later that Peter decided to change his Sunbeam Talbot car and asked if I still wished to buy it, telling me that he wanted £225 for it. I told him that it was a bit more that I wished to pay, but asked him if he would exchange the car for Jean's ring. After thinking for a minute he accepted my offer, but told me I wouldn't be able to take possession of the car for two more weeks, as his car won't be ready until then and he needed the use of his car for travelling to Birmingham where he had business interests. That suited me fine, as it gave me a chance to sell my M.G.

I knew someone who was keen to buy my car and we completed the deal on the Friday before Peter was to hand over his car to me. That Sunday morning, Aileen and I waited for Peter, as we had decided when Peter delivered the car we would drive to Richmond for lunch and at the same time test the car. We waited but by lunchtime there was still no car. We were worried that he might have had an accident. I'd been watching out for him, looking through my back window on to the car park behind the flat. At 4.30p.m., a breakdown vehicle arrived, towing Peter's car. I rushed down to see what had happened to my car. Peter descended from the car, saying it could be fixed and he would pay for the damage. When I examined the car, the whole front of the grill and both wings were completely crumpled and bent out of shape; the bonnet and windscreen were completely caved in. I asked Peter what had happened. He explained that he was late leaving Birmingham and as he was driving through the Downs, which weren't lit back then, a Pony walked out in front of him. He couldn't stop and hit it. The Pony landed on the bonnet and went straight through the windscreen. The pony was killed, he was slightly bruised and lucky not to be killed also.

He knew that I used a local garage only a short distance from my flat and told me to phone them on Monday to give me an estimate the cost of the repairs. On Monday, I phoned the garage owner, who I had grown to know quite well and who quite often use to pick up my car from my car park for servicing. I asked if he could come down and tow my vehicle to his garage, inspect it to see if it could be repaired and if so, to give me an estimate of the cost and I would phone him in the afternoon for his answer. When I phoned him he gave me the details of what work that would have to be done and the cost. He couldn't find a new grill, but there was a firm in Chalk Farm which specialized in rebuilding and re-chroming all car metal parts. He would be able to purchase a second-hand wing from a breaker's yard, whilst the other wing and the bonnet can be rolled out and the windscreen replaced. The total cost would be £90 and the car could be ready Friday, or at least not later than Monday. I accepted his estimate and price with a proviso that he would make good any rust places and scratches that were necessary on the car, to which he agreed. I phoned Peter to tell him of the estimate and He paid me the money over the weekend.

On Monday evening I picked up my car at the garage and I couldn't believe what a marvellous job the garage had made on my car. The paint work and all the chrome was in pristine condition, and having been polished, it looked as if it had just come out of a showroom. I thank the owner for the marvellous job he done, paid him and drove back to my flat where by now Aileen was waiting for me. She was delighted with the car and we decided to finally go for a meal and test the car, which we found to be satisfactory. Now I had a car in which I could take Aileen in comfort to her shows.

Soon after a marvellous thing happened to me. Aileen needed to change and register with a doctor, as hers was still in Gosport. There was a new surgery being started by a Dr. Charkin just a few yards from the flat. I suggested to her that we register together with him. I hadn't been happy with my doctor, so I thought it I would change from him at the same time. We went to the surgery to register and whilst I was there, I asked for an appointment for him to look at my ankle. I'd been suffering with an ulcer on my ankle since just before I left the army in the Middle East, where I had grazed it on rock nearly eight years ago and it wouldn't heal. For three years I had tried to get treatment for it, first from my doctor, who twice had poisoned me with Penicillin, not realising that I was allergic to it, and later at the hospital for tropical diseases, who tried all sorts of ointments, none of which would work. Eventually, they tried a new treatment and applied radioactive ointment, which lasted four month, but after testing me for radioactivity they found out I was so hot that I wasn't allowed to have any more for the next four years. Instead, they gave me bandages impregnated with ointment which wrapped round my ankle and made a soft cast. When I showed my ankle to Dr. Charkin, telling him the whole history of my suffering, he examined it and said: "You don't need treatment, you need an operation for varicose veins." I told him when I was in the army I'd already had had an operation on my veins. "Well," he said. "You need another one and I will make an appointment for you at the Middlesex hospital."

My appointment came three weeks later for me to be admitted on the following Monday. Mum and Dad wanted to come with me to the hospital, but I refused, telling them that I was quite capable of getting there on my own. When I reported to the hospital, all my details were taken down by a nurse, then I was taken to a ward where I was allocated a bed, given a gown and told to undress and then get into the bed, after which the nurse left me. When I was in bed another nurse came, who took my pulse, then my temperature and explained to me the procedure before my operation. She told me that my operation was scheduled between four and six. I was to have no food or drink, except for sips of water and an hour before the operation I would have an injection to help with the anaesthetic. They wheeled me to the operating theatre just before 5p.m., and after the operation, still unconscious, they wheeled me in into the ward to recover.

When I came to, the nurse gave me some water to drink, after which I straight away fell asleep. I was woken up at 6.30a.m. and the nurse got me out of the bed to walk me around the ward, explaining that I had to walk around for a while in order to stop the blood in my legs clotting. I found out from the nurse that the operation was successful and that I had thirty-five stitches in my right leg and twenty seven in my left one. After a while, I was taken back to the ward to wait for my breakfast. Soon after breakfast we all had to get up while for the orderlies made up the beds. Then we were ordered to lay on top of the bed ready for the Matron's inspection and the Doctor's rounds.

Visitors were allowed between 12p.m. until 2p.m. I expected that I would have one or two visitors, but when they opened the door for the visitors to enter twelve people came around my bed. Everybody in the ward looked on, wondering who I was, as there was Aileen with three of her model friends, four of my close friends, Mum and Dad, Alan representing the firm and Uncle Joe. My small bedside table was completely covered with fruit, chocolate and bottles of cordial, the firm sent me a basket of strawberries, which I gave to the nurses. As I was introducing them to each other the matron appeared and told them that I could only have two visitors at a time and the rest would have to wait outside.

On the Thursday, which was my fourth day in the hospital, after the Doctor's rounds, the surgeon that operated on me came to check up on me and, after inspecting my legs, told me that that the cuts were healing well and I would be able to go home after lunch, but I would have to return next Tuesday morning to have my stitches removed. When at home he instructed me to walk around as much as I could in order to stop the blood clotting. I asked him when I would be able to return to work. He advised that I should not start until the following

Monday. After lunch, before leaving the hospital, the nurse gave me a supply of pills to take for four days. When I arrived home, I phoned Mum who asked me if I needed anything and insisted on seeing me and bringing me some food.

When she arrived, I told her that I had plenty of food and I could manage as I could walk and that I would come to see her and dad after I had my stitches out. After mum left, I phoned the firm to tell them that I would be able to return to work on the following Monday. Then I phoned Aileen to let her know that I was home and she told me that she would come over to spend the evening with me. On Tuesday, when I arrived at the hospital, I was taken by a nurse to her office where she removed my stitches, then called the duty doctor who checked the cuts, informing me that they had healed up nicely and that he was discharging me. I wouldn't have to return for any further treatment, but should I have any problems to phone the hospital and I would have an instant appointment. I still had a bandage on my ankle in order to stop the ulcer rubbing against my trousers.

Then the miracle happened; ten days later, when I took the bandage off, there was no ulcer. It completely disappeared. There was no scar or any sign of anything ever being there. I then thought, I'd been suffering for the past eight years, seen six or seven doctors and it took a young doctor, just starting his surgery, to cure me within two weeks. I went round to his surgery to thank him and he was my doctor until he died thirty one years later.

When I went back to work, everyone was kind to me and the Governor told me to take it steady and should I get tired, to go home early. By the end of the second week I was back to normal with all the stiffness gone from my legs. Soon after the operation, Aileen was going to visit her parents and she told me that they had again invited me to come with her and spend the weekend. Of course I accepted. I found out from Aileen that her mother liked Terry's All Gold chocolate and her father liked Whiskey, which I bought to take with us. We decided that we would leave on Saturday at 5.30a.m. so that it would give us two whole days there.

When we left London it was one of those wonderful, warm sunshine mornings with hardly any traffic. We were travelling on the A3 and, after we passed Richmond, it was more or less a straight run to Portsmouth. Those days the A3 was much more winding and narrower than it is today, with trees and flowering bushes nearly all the way. Just the other side of Devil's Punchbowl, just before Hindhead, there was parking place with a snack bar that also had a doughnut making machine, where you could purchase freshly made doughnuts to take home. I always stopped there for them on the way to and back when visiting Aileen's parents.

You had to turn off at Gosport for Alverstoke onto to a secondary road, which led you straight there. The main part of it is quite old, with one narrow road going through it, with paving in some places only on one side, leading to a square with a tree in the middle and small local shops around it. The house that Aileen's parents lived in was in the middle of a terrace of very small houses, which I believe we originally built to house workers working at the Portsmouth and Gosport docks. They were two-up-two-downs, with no bathrooms and the toilet was outside in the back, adjacent to the house, which also had a fair sized garden. The church was right opposite their house, which I found out later rung the bells quite often, which were very loud, and when I heard them the first time they made me jump. They didn't bother Aileen or her parents as they were used to them. We arrived at her home just after 9.30a.m. having stopped on the way for breakfast and in couple places to admire the wonderful country and scenery.

Her mother opened the door with great excitement and Aileen introduced me to her, before leading us into the kitchen, which was also their dining room, where I was introduced to her father. He greeted me warmly and we took to each other right away. I presented them with my gifts, which delighted them greatly and asked me to call them Elsie and Mac. After we sat down to have a cup of tea, we were asked about our journey what the weather was like and if we had any problems coming to them. Aileen caught up with all the news about her family. Her mother mentioned that in the afternoon we had all been invited to her Aunty and cousin's house for high tea.

After we finished our tea, Aileen's mother asked me to take my small weekend case into the front room where I would be sleeping. The room that I walked into was about 10' by 10', there was a two seater settee, a small table and two small easy chairs. I looked and wondered how I was expected to sleep on the settee. I called Aileen, who had a good laugh, telling me that she forgot how small the settee was as they very seldom used that room. I asked her if her mum could spare another blanket and I would sleep on the floor, which I had done many times before, where I would be much more comfortable. After all, it would only be for one night. After I got myself sorted, Aileen decided that we should go for a walk while her mother prepared lunch for us. Aileen showed me around the village, took me to the beach where she used to swim and the woods where she used to play with her cousin Gay, who I was going to meet later on.

Soon it was time for us to return to her house for lunch. After lunch we had a rest until 4'oclock and then it was time to go to her aunt's for tea. Her Aunt lived only a few streets away, and when we arrived, again there was excitement; everyone talking at the same time, I was introduced to her Auntie Aggie, her cousin Gay, her husband Douglas and son Nigel. They all wanted to know all about Aileen and her time in London. They seemed to know quite a lot about me as it seemed that Aileen wrote quite often to her cousin, mentioning me in her letters. It was a beautiful afternoon and we all sat in the garden and had a proper English tea, being served ham salad, jelly, homemade cakes and, of course, tea. Usually family do's can be a bit boring, but everyone was so very friendly towards me and I really enjoyed myself this sort of tea; I hadn't had it since before the war, when I had come to England and lived in Ewell with the Abbotts.

We left Alverstoke in the late afternoon for London and, after thanking Aileen's parents for a wonderful time, we only stopped on the way at Hindhead to have a rest and buy doughnuts for us to have back at home. On the way back Aileen told me that her parents liked me and would like me to come down for a visit again. From then on, we visited her parents three or four times a year. I also introduced Aileen to my sister Rozia and my brother in law Ronnie and from the start they became friends, and quite often we use to go out together. Rozia told me that Aileen was a much more suitable girl for me than Jean and told me that mother, who met Jean several times, didn't like her. I never knew whether it was that she wasn't Jewish or for some other reason. I asked Aileen if her parents knew that I was Jewish. She answered that she had informed her parents in a letter about me some time ago and it didn't matter to them as long she was happy. I then explained to her that although she met my parents at the hospital, the reason I hadn't invited her to meet my parents officially at their home was that dad and mum were orthodox Jews and at present they would disown me if were to marry a non-Jewish girl. If and when we became serious in our relationship, which I very much wanted, I would take Aileen to them and tell them that she was the girl I wished to marry and it would up to them to decide what they wanted to do, but it wouldn't alter my decision. I had to make my own decisions since I was fifteen, and although I was brought up in the orthodox religion, I'd grown out of it. I observed all the high holidays but to me religion was a personal thing; I am very liberal in my outlook on religion, so orthodoxy didn't suit me personally. We all believe in God in our own way, and should our relationship become serious and we decided to get married I would take Aileen, and should we have children, they would be able to decide for themselves when there were older what religion they wished to follow. After hearing what I said, she told me that a couple of her friends had experienced that problem, but one was now happily married and the other was thinking of getting engaged, and as to us she was happy to be as we were.

At the end of May, some friends of John and Peter's came back from a holiday in Tossa Del Mar in Spain and told us how marvellous and cheap the place was, with the sun shining all the time. This was at the beginning of package holidays and a huge number of English people started going there for their holidays.

John and Peter decided that they would go at the end of June to Tossa by car and find out what it was like. When they came back they confirmed that although the place was very crowded, it was also very cheap; a bottle of wine costing about 10p and cigarettes 5p for a pack of 20. I asked Aileen if she would like to go to Spain by car and at the same time do a small tour of France on the way to Spain, on the way back taking a different route and spending a couple days in Paris where I could take her to all the places I knew from when I was working there. We could synchronise our holidays to go away at end of August just before our seasons started and spend the two weeks together. Aileen got very excited about going abroad. She had always wanted to, and right away she started planning what clothed she would need to take with her. That was the beginning of our adventurist travelling, spanning the next fifty years until her death, which took us all over the world.

Aileen managed to acquire a road map of France from the French Tourist Office and we started to plan our journey. We decided that we would allow ourselves three days touring France down to the Spanish border, which would give us the opportunity to explore some of the places we would be travelling through, then a week in Tossa and, on the way back, three days in Paris. We found out that the best way of crossing the English Channel would be from Folkestone to Dieppe and, once in France, we would visit Rouen, Chartres, Orléans on our journey and stay the night at Tours. The second day we would continue our journey to Poitiers, Limoges and Toulouse and stay the night there. The third day we would reach the Spanish frontier, by travelling through Carcassonne to Perpignan staying the night there before crossing the border into Spain. We left London for our holidays the last week in August.

Those days, going from Folkestone to Dieppe, there were no combined passenger and car ferries; you went on one boat that took only passengers, and the cars and the rest of the vehicles were loaded by crane onto another boat in the hope that they would arrived at Dieppe at roughly the same time as you. We left London very early in the morning as our ferry was leaving

Folkestone at 7a.m. The weather was fine and the Channel was smooth, thank goodness, as I am a very poor sailor. When we arrived at Dieppe, we received the good news that the ferry with the cars was only half an hour behind us and it would be docking shortly, giving us enough time to have a cup of coffee at the quay side. When the car ferry arrived it was unloaded very quickly and by 9.30a.m. we were able to proceed on our journey. The following day we continued our journey to Limoges. After exploring Limoges, where we walked quite a lot enjoying the sights, we proceeded on to Bergerac.

About halfway there I began to tire. I mentioned to Aileen that the next hotel that has a room with a bath or a shower we would stop at and spend the night there. The first hotel that we tried didn't have any rooms available, but after driving another ten miles we came across a little country hotel called Hotel de Paris, which was on the main road in the middle of nowhere with some barns behind it. I went in and asked if they had a room with a shower, a place to park my car and, if possible, if we could still get a meal. The answer was positive and the patron, who spoke English, directed me to one of the barns to park my car in, suggesting that, as we were only staying the night, we could leave most of our luggage as the barn was lockable and would be locked until we departed. When we returned to the hotel he showed us our room on the first floor, which was large with old French furniture, a sink and a huge mirror with a light above it, a small table beside it and a couple bedside lights; I don't think the wallpaper had been changed since the Napoleonic times. The shower room was next door to our room.

After the patron left us, we decided to have a shower to refresh ourselves before having our dinner. When we came down to have our meal, there was loud music coming from the dining room and the patron explained that there was a wedding party having a wedding feast, but he had arranged for us to have a table on the other side of the room. We went up to our table and one of the waiters came with a menu for us to order our meal. Neither of us was very hungry and didn't really want a big meal so we ordered a Veal escalope with vegetables, a couple glasses of wine, some French pastries and coffee. While having our drinks, the waiter came up to our table and told us that the bride and groom wished for us to join their wedding celebrations. Aileen and I were very tired and I went up to the wedded couple, thanking them for the invitation and explaining to them that we had driven a long way, were very tired and all we want to do was to eat and have a good night sleep. The groom then suggested that we at least have the meal with them before retiring to our room, to which Aileen and I accepted.

It was a very merry company and luckily quite a few of them spoke English. The ones that didn't I could just about converse with them in my poor French. The meal was a lengthy affair, starting with soup, vol-au-vent, chicken, a sweet, cheese, Petite Fours, and of course wine, finishing with liquors. First, we drunk a toast to the bride and groom, and then after each course we toasted their mothers and father, grandmothers, uncles and auntie and few other member of their family. Luckily, the celebrations had to finished around nine, by which time Aileen and I were quite merry and, after thanking them all for their hospitality, we went up to our room and, after quickly undressing, right away fell into our bed and fell asleep.

In the morning, my travelling alarm clock – which was a gift from my Uncle Joe and had been with me on all our travels – woke us up at 7a.m., as we planned on an early start. We quickly finished our ablutions and went to the dining room for our breakfast. We had the usual continental breakfast, after which I asked at the reception counter to have the barn unlocked and prepare our car to continue our journey. When I received the bill I had a pleasant surprise as the whole stay had only come to £3, which included the wine that we had drunk, several soft drinks, the accommodation and breakfast. I was so astonished at the price, after paying the previous hotel at least three times as much, that I left a 20% tip, making a note to stay there on the way back. We resumed our journey to Toulouse, where we stayed only for a short brake to have coffee, as we wanted as much time that we could spare to explore Carcassonne, of which we had read up on before we left London.

Driving towards Carcassonne we could see the town in the distance and already it looked magnificent; we couldn't wait to get there. When we arrived there, about 11.30a.m., we had a quick snack, and soon started exploring the place. We walked all around the town on the old defence walls, stopping to examine the battlements and defensive towers. After we came down from the walls we walked in the narrow cobbled streets, admiring the old houses, the church and many other buildings where they still reproduced the old crafts. We spent so long there that we left ourselves a bit short of time to reach Perpignan, meaning we arrived there later than we had wanted to. When we arrived in Perpignan, there was music and dancing everywhere; it seemed that there was sort of fete going on in honour of some Saint, and the place was packed with people. We discovered that during summer there was a fete nearly every week.

We tried several hotels to find accommodation, but to no avail, each one telling us that there wasn't a single room available in the whole place. Then we had a little luck. We decided to have a meal in a nearby bistro before proceeding in our search for accommodation. While eating, I spoke to the Patron, telling him of our difficulties and he confirmed that the all the hotels are booked up but, if we were not too fussy and since we were only staying for one night, he knew someone who might be able to help. He directed us to a house that was just a short distance away and when I inquired about a room we were told the only room they had was a room that was used as a stockroom, but it had two beds and we could use the bathroom and toilet which was next door, which we could have for £2. He showed us the room, which had a lot of boxes and baskets in it. The room and the beds were clean and I asked Aileen what she thought. She said we didn't have any option and decided to take it. In the morning we did our ablutions, we dressed, thanked the man for helping us out, paid for our room and we drove back to the Bistro for breakfast. While there I thanked the Patron for helping us with the accommodation and then we proceeded on our journey to Spanish border.

When we arrived at the border we first had to go through the French customs to check our passport and have our Carnet stamped, and a short distance away were the Spanish customs where we had to go through the same routine and then we were in Spain. I made a slight mistake of asking one of the officials what was the best route to Tossa. He asked me if I wanted the scenic route or the straightforward one. Both Aileen and I decided we would travel on the scenic route which went along the coast. In those days the roads in Spain were absolutely terrible with huge potholes, in many places the tarmac missing altogether; you noticed the difference when you crossed the border from France into Spain. We only had to travel a short distance to reach the coastal road. I didn't know at that time that the locals use to call it Route 365 as it had 365 bends and turns from the border to Tossa. There had been a bad storm a few days earlier and in some places the road had partly washed away. There were gangs of men under guard, working to repair and widen the road, which we discovered were convict labourers. The road was only one car's width and you had to drive with your foot on the brake and your hand on the horn; the bends were all blind so every few yards when you neared one you sounded your horn and the driver coming toward you would do the same so you didn't crash. You had to slow down completely to see who had space for one or the other to pass. It was one of the two most petrifying drives that I've ever had, the other being the Derna pass in North Africa.

Eventually, when we arrived in Tossa, all we wanted to do was to find a hotel to have a rest after the horrendous journey. Tossa back then was a very small place, there were very few hotels and it was very crowded. We stopped outside one of the new hotels that had only recently been built and I managed to acquire a room with full board. When we entered our room, which was quite pleasantly furnished with a sea view, we just dumped our luggage on the floor and collapsed on our bed. After having slept for a couple of hours, we unpacked, had a shower and got ourselves ready to go and do a bit of exploring of the resort before our evening meal. We wondered around this small town, which was extremely crowded with people, and as we walked along the promenade we couldn't see the beach for the amount of people playing or lying on the sand. When we returned for our meal we were directed to the dining room and were shown to our table where we had a pleasant surprise, discovering that we would be sharing the table with two other couples from London that had arrived a day before. They were very friendly towards us and soon we were swapping stories; we seemed to get on very well together, and during the meal they suggested we join them to spend our holiday together. I asked Aileen what she thought of the idea. She thought it would be great and, since all of us had our own cars, if we wanted we could always do our own thing. After the meal we went to the lounge to have some coffee and drinks and to discuss what to do the following day. We decided that Tossa beach was much too crowded, and one of the boys said that they had been told that there was another holiday resort not far away called Lloret del Mar, which was practically empty and, although it was on the same road that we came on to Tossa, he had been told it's in much better condition with not so many bends and suggested perhaps we ought pay it a visit. We discussed more the pros and cons of travelling there and we decided to go next morning each couple taking their own car.

The next morning we left for Lloret and as we were not having lunch at the hotel they supplied us with a packed lunch. Although it was the continuation of the road that we arrived in Tossa on, it was in much better condition. When we arrived at the beach it was completely deserted with only one family playing with their children, ourselves and a Spanish doughnut seller who sold the most delicious long pastries stuffed with custard and soft drinks. We made ourselves comfortable under a shady thatch umbrella and had the most wonderful time on this extremely clean beach, playing ball, swimming and sunning ourselves. When it came to lunchtime, we opened our packed lunch and discovered that it consisted of two rolls with no butter, a sliced tomato in it, a piece of plain cake, an orange and a bottle of orange juice. We looked at our lunch and decided when we returned to our hotel we would have a word with the manager. When we returned to our hotel we did have a word with the manager and our packed lunches greatly improved, except they used olive oil in our rolls instead of butter. From then on we travelled to Lloret every day.

Tossa, being a small town had very few roads that you could use your car as most of the side roads were only wide enough for a donkey, so in the evening when we went out we would wander around to do bit of shopping and have a coffee and a drink. Opposite our hotel there was a one of the narrow roads where we found a bar that served fantastic tapas with our drinks where we spend most of our evenings if we weren't shopping. One of the evenings, when we were there, the bar advertised that a new night club was opening opposite the bar, a day before the other couples were leaving for home, which was a day before us, and we decided that it would be a good idea to spend our last night together there. The tickets were at a special opening price of £1.50 each, and you also received a bottle of Spanish sparkling wine with each ticket. When we arrived at the night club we presented our ticket and were shown to our table and the waiter brought our six bottles of Champagne and started opening them. We asked him just to open two as we didn't know how they tasted and whether we would drink all of them. After tasting one of the bottles we found it wasn't too bad; a bit sweet but drinkable. We discovered that we would have to wait a little while for the cabaret to start which, when it eventually started, consisted of a guitar player and a pianist accompanied by two Spanish dancers doing traditional dances. The act lasted about three quarters of an hour, after which the pianist remained playing dreary tunes, after half hour of this one of the boys took a bottle of champagne over to the pianist and asked him to play some Jazz or Boogie. It took him a while to understand as he couldn't speak any English. After he understood what we wanted and started playing, we found a couple of bongo drums and cymbals sat around the piano and began accompanying him. After a while other customers joined us by singing some of the tunes and kept on bringing us glasses of whiskey or brandy. Everyone was enjoying themselves and the whole place was one big party. By 2'oclock we were extremely merry and the manager came over, asking us to stop as he only had a licence permitting him to be open until 2 o'clock and he might lose his licence if he kept it open later for us. By then we were either very merry or drunk that no one took any notice. By 2.30a.m., the manager was getting so desperate that he threatened to call the police if we didn't leave. After a few minutes we dispersed but some of us went across the road into the bar opposite to have some coffee or another drink, buy our duty frees and say our goodbyes, wishing everyone safe journey home and swapping addresses.

Walking back to our hotel, Aileen had hysterics laughing at me as the road was very narrow and, being very unsteady on my feet, I was walking with my two bottles of spirits in a zigzag fashion, bumping into the walls of the houses each side, and when we arrived at our hotel I had difficulty finding the entrance and Aileen had to guide me through it and help me into our room where I collapsed on our bed and fell asleep. I woke up in the morning with a terrible hangover and thank goodness we didn't have to leave until the following day, as it gave me a day to recover and do our packing for our departure early next morning.

We still had three days left of our holidays and our plan was for me to drive on our first day as near to Paris as we could so that we would be in Paris the following day by 10a.m. This would give us nearly two days there for me to show Aileen all the sights. We departed for our journey back about 7a.m.; it was a glorious morning, being slightly cool which was ideal for driving. We were going to travel from Tossa to Girona and then through to the Spanish border and on to Perpignan where we would stop for a snack before taking the main road to Paris. Everything was going well until 10 miles past Girona.

Driving up a hill the car spluttered and stopped and our nightmare journey began. I stopped to open my bonnet, trying to figure out what was wrong. I checked all the plugs, leads and fuel pump, but everything seemed to be in order; all that was left were the fuel lines and the carburettor. I undid my fuel lines and filters, blew through each one to check if there was any blockages, but everything seemed to be in order; that left the carburettor. All my previous cars that I'd owned had S.U. carburettors; the Sunbeam Talbot was fitted with a Stromberg one, of which I completely ignorant as to how it worked. I checked it, but it seemed to be working with the fuel passing through it, so I connected everything back and continued on our journey and having travelled about a mile the engine stopped again. I again took the fuel system to pieces and put it back together; the engine started and again and cut out after travelling a mile. I told Aileen that we would have to go to a garage to have the fault sorted out. I had a look in my AA book and there was a garage listed in Girona that repaired Talbot cars. I managed to flag down an English driver going that way who kindly offered to ask the garage to send a breakdown vehicle to us. While waiting a civil militia policemen came over asking what the problem was. I couldn't understand him as I didn't speak Spanish, but luckily he spoke French so I was able explain to him in my bad French that I had something wrong with my vehicle and I had asked a passing driver to asked a garage in Girona to send a breakdown vehicle so that the garage could fix my problem. He then asked me how long I'd been waiting. I told him about two hours and he said the break down vehicle should have arrived an hour ago; he then stopped the first Spanish vehicle going toward Girona giving the driver instructions to go to the garage and send the breakdown vehicle straight away. He then stayed with us having a chat about our holiday until the breakdown vehicle arrived forty-five minutes later. The driver, who also was the mechanic, got out and came over to the car and tried to start the engine but to no avail. He informed me that problem was Benzene and started to undo my fuel pipes, but I told him I'd already done that. He insisted to check them blowing through them putting it all together and trying to start the engine which didn't start, informing me that that he would have to tow the car back to the garage in Girona. The breakdown vehicle was the oldest I'd ever seen; it must have been built in 1919 or 1920, as it was completely rusty with a small crane in the back. The driver took out a thick steel chain with which he connected my vehicle to his giving me a distance between his and my vehicle about 3 ½ ft., explaining that I would have to control my vehicle when he was towing me.

I was a bit apprehensive with that idea as the distance between the vehicles was a bit short to travel on winding mountain roads, but I had no choice. I asked Aileen to sit with the driver as I was worried that if I suddenly had to brake sharply Aileen could injure herself on the windscreen, as at that time there were no safety belts fitted in cars. Although the distance to Girona was only about 10-12 miles and we were travelling at between 18-20mph, it was one of the hairiest rides I have ever had. This road was one of the worst of the Spanish roads. Being in a mountainous region, driving uphill wasn't too bad, but going down I had to have my brakes on all the time, as the tow rope was so short that one mistake I would crash the front of the car into the back of the breakdown vehicle.

Eventually we arrived at garage in Girona. The foreman, who luckily spoke English, came over, and after explaining to him that we were on our way home, asked if the car could be fixed today. He told us to leave everything in the car and go and have some refreshments and come back in a couple hours while he will inspected the car and do the necessary repairs. We found a bar only a short distance away where we had a coffee and a sandwich and, when we returned to the garage, the foreman informed me that they found that the fault, which was the fuel system. He told me they had changed the cork washer on the fuel pump, changed the plugs and the electrical leads and then he opened the cover plate on the carburettor and shoved me a slightly bent lever with a pin on the end of it, explaining that the pin controls the flow of petrol and should the car stop again, to open the cover and bend the lever a little bit more. When we arrive home, we should take it to my garage to have the part changed as he didn't have any spare parts. He then started the engine to show that it was working. I thanked him for fixing my car, paid the bill which came to about £3.50 and we were off again.

Everything was working fine until we came to the hilly part of the neighbouring area. Going up the hill the car stopped again. I opened the bonnet and it smelled of petrol fumes, which I didn't take any notice of, thinking that they were from flooding the carburettor. I adjusted the carburettor as instructed the car started and we were off again. This happened every time I had to travel up a steep hill. Altogether, I had five stops, the last of which was in pitch black before we reached the Spanish border. At the border we had to have the passports and documents checked before the barrier was raised. After everything was found to be satisfactory we proceeded in the No Man's Land to the French frontier post. I stayed in the car to keep the engine running while Aileen went into the office to have our document stamped, and as Aileen was about to enter the office, the engine spluttered and stopped. I jumped out of the car waving my arms and shouting to Aileen to come back. She came back to the car asking what was wrong. I explained to her that before we have our documents stamped I will have to ask one of the officials to help me to push the car near the barrier so that, as soon the documents were stamped, I would be able to push the car over the border and we would be in France. Otherwise we would be stuck in No Man's Land for a long time.

A very kind border guard help me with the car to the barrier, Aileen had the necessary documents stamped the barrier was raised. I managed to push the car through the barrier and we were back in France. Aileen and I managed to push the car to the side of the road where I was able adjust the carburettor for us to get going once more. We were still travelling through mountainous country and the road we were travelling on was all uphill, with me worrying all the time that I might have to stop again before we arrived at the top. Unfortunately, luck was not on our side, and it did. By now it was pitch black, but luckily I had had my small torch, which I always kept in the car, the light of which allowed me to adjust the carburettor and we reached the top of this small mountain. From there it was only a short distance to Perpignan and I remembered from the previous journey that this road sloped all the way to Perpignan, so I told Aileen that I was going to try to coast down all the way to Perpignan without using the engine, hoping that it would start when we arrived there. As there was very little traffic, I was able to drive down at a reasonable speed to give the car a decent momentum and we coasted all the way, arriving at Perpignan in very short time by about 9.00p.m.

Once there I prayed that the engine would start, which it did. The town was in process of another fete with music and people celebrating another saint's day. Aileen and I discussed what we should do and decided that, as we hadn't eaten since we left Girona, food would be our first priority, after which we would look for somewhere to stay the night. I remembered that there was a big garage opposite the Bistro we had eaten in when we were on our way to Spain, which was only a short distance away from where we were now. I checked in my AA book if they repaired Sunbeam Talbot cars, which they did, so we decided to drive there and maybe the patron would again be able to help us to find accommodation.

When we entered the bistro the patron, recognising us from our previous visit, directed us to a table, asking us how we enjoyed our holiday. I told him our holiday was fabulous but our journey home had been terrible, explaining to him the problem I'd been having with the car. We ordered our meal and I still remember what we had: Aileen had veal escalope and I had peppered steak with chips, which to us tasted like one of the best meals we had ever eaten after the day we'd had. Aileen had some wine but all I wanted was water as I was still sweating profusely. During the meal I must have drunk about 1lt of water and I bought 2lt more as I was still feeling extremely thirsty. After our meal, I asked the patron at what time in the morning did the garage open. He told us it would be open at 7.30 the following morning, then I asked if he could help us again to find accommodation. He explained to me that this fete was much more popular than the one last week and as far as he knew there hadn't been any rooms available for the past two days, but that we could drive 5 or 6 miles further on where they might have some rooms.

I discussed the situation with Aileen, asking her if she wanted to take the chance to look for a room further away, but if she wouldn't mind, she could alternately sleep in the back of the car and I would sleep in front and we would stay here allowing me to be first at the garage in the morning. Without hesitation, Aileen thought that this was our best option, so I asked the patron whether it was all right if we stayed parked in front of his establishment, explaining that we decided to spend the night sleeping in the car. He was quite agreeable and he even offered to lend us some blankets, but I thanked him for the offer and told him that we had everything we needed and all we wanted was to get some sleep.

By then it was after 10p.m., the music and traffic died down and we got in the car. Aileen settled down with a blanket and cushion in the back and I in the front passenger seat. I slightly opened the top hatch to let in some air, locked the car and we settled in for the night. Aileen fell asleep almost immediately; I was still very thirsty and sweating, drank some of the water that I had bought and tried to sleep. I don't know what time I dozed off but I woke up at 3a.m. unable to sleep. It was just beginning to get light, so I opened the door to see what the weather was like. It was a beautiful morning with a slightly cool breeze and, with me still perspiring, it felt glorious against my skin. I sat down on the bonnet of the car, lit my pipe and had a smoke, but I still didn't feel sleepy, so I locked the car with Aileen inside and went for a walk. There were quite a lot of small shops in that road, so I did a bit of window shopping, all the time keeping my eye on the car. When I returned back to the car Aileen was awake wondering where I had got to. I told her where I'd been and told her that there were several shops that may be of interest to her to look at while we waiting for the garage to repair the car.

At about 6a.m., the patron, who lived above his establishment, opened his door, sweeping the pavement, putting out his tables and chairs and preparing them for his morning customers. He came over to us and asked if we would like to use his toilet and do our ablutions, for which we were most grateful. Afterwards we sat down to breakfast to coffee and some wonderfully fresh croissant. Then, after breakfast I drove to the forecourt of the garage to wait for it to open. The garage opened right on time and a man emerged, who I later discovered was the foreman, seeing a British registered car asked in English what the problem was with the car. I explained to him the problem I'd had with the car, also telling him what repairs were made by the Spanish garage. He asked me to leave the car with him and come back in an hour, giving him time to assess the job.

Aileen and I decided to kill the time window shopping at the local shops which were still shut, and when we returned to the garage the foreman came over and said: "Your car is all fixed, but you are very lucky not to have been blown up and burned to death. The repairs they did to your car in Spain were criminal. All the parts that they fitted were unnecessary; the new washer that they fitted on the petrol pump they left leaking, the new plugs they fitted there was probably no need to change and the new leads they fitted without suppressors, which are there to stop sparking." He then lifted the plate on the carburettor and removed the little lever that I'd been bending that had now had been straightened and said pointed to a brass component on which the lever with the pin rested on and said: "This was your trouble with your valve. Driving on the rough roads the vibrations loosened the thread on the valve and it started unscrewing, tightening on the pin on the end of the lever which stopped the flow of petrol and caused the petrol to be sprayed all over the car. All you were doing by bending the lever was relieving the pressure on the valve until it tightened again and that's why you could smell petrol all the time. A single spark from your unsuppressed leads would have caused an explosion, probably killing you both, when all the mechanic had to do was to tighten the screw." I thanked him for the explanation and work, paid the bill and we were off to Paris.

Before we collected the car I discussed with Aileen what we were to do now that we lost one day of our time. I told her that I still want to show her around Paris if the repairs didn't take too long. Looking at the map, which we always carried with us, I worked out that we were 565 miles from Paris, with two sections of the route being motorways and the rest A1 roads. If she was agreeable, I reckoned I could do the journey in 10-11 hours but we would have to take sandwiches and some drinks with us as we would only be able to have very short rest breaks, to which she replied that if it wasn't too much for me we should do it. We bought baguettes, filled one with cheese and tomato and one with ham and tomato, some plain French pastries, fruit juices and plain water to transfer to my large thermos flask to keep cool.

We left the garage about 8.45a.m. The route I worked out with Aileen, who was very good at map reading, was from Perpignan via Carcassonne to Toulouse on the Route National, then on A1 road through Limoges to Poitiers where we picked up again on the Route National going through Tours, Orleans and then all the way to Paris. The weather was very good, the car was running beautifully and the road had very little traffic and no speed limits and I was able to average between 60-65 mph. The A1 roads were not crowded and in a very good condition, the only except being the hold-ups when going through towns, but I could still average a good mileage.

We stopped every two hours for a short break, and everything was going to schedule. We were expecting to be in Paris by 7.30p.m., but when we were about 85 miles from Paris, my rear tyre blew out. I managed to change the tyre with the spare one and drove to the next garage that I could find to see if I could buy another tyre as the blown one couldn't be repaired. At the garage they didn't have my size tyre, even a second-hand one, as at that time tyres were still in very short supply and they didn't know anywhere locally where I would be able to acquire one. I told Aileen that I would have to drive at a much slower speed as I didn't want to take the chance of another blowout, but with luck we would be in Paris by 8.30-9.00p.m.

We arrived in Paris and I drove to my old hotel Faubourg St Honoré where I had stayed for six months while working in Paris without any further mishaps just before 9.00p.m. When we walked in, the same concierge was at the desk from when I had previously stayed, who recognised me and greeted us warmly, asking me what we required. I told him that we wanted a room with a bath and shower for two nights and asked if it would be alright to leave my car parked outside during the day while we stayed. He told us that wasn't a problem as tomorrow was a Saturday, there were no restrictions on parking. He then gave the key to the porter, who took us and our luggage to our room. The room was much larger than the one I had when I lived there. Although we were extremely tired and smelly from our journey we decided before we did anything to have a meal and a hot drink as we hadn't eaten since lunchtime, so we dumped our luggage and went to the bistro adjacent to the hotel where I used to eat when working in Paris.

There was the same Patron and his wife running the bistro and when they recognised me, they rushed over to us, the wife kissing me on both cheeks, asking me if I'd come back to work in Paris. I first introduced Aileen as my fiancé and told them that I'd moved on and that I no longer worked for my Uncle and we were in Paris on the way from Spain. We were hoping that being late that we could still have a meal at their place. The Madame replied that that, although they had just started clearing up in the kitchen they could provide us with a meal. There was no steak but she could make a veal escallop or grilled trout. We ordered the veal escallop and to celebrate that we had finally reached Paris, a half bottle of vine Chateauneuf-du-Pape, which was Aileen's favourite wine.

After the meal we quickly went to our room. We didn't bother to unpack, I had a quick shower while Aileen was taking her makeup off. When we had finished I jumped into the bed and I was asleep before Aileen had finished her bath. I woke up at 5a.m., very hot and still sweating, went into the bathroom to wash myself down to cool off, trying not to wake Aileen. I couldn't sleep anymore, so I lay on top of the bedding until Aileen woke up at 7a.m. We sat up and decided that before we went down to breakfast we would look at our Paris map and discuss which places she would like to visit. I suggested that we would first go to Sacre Cœur, then Moulin Rouge, and then wander around Montmartre. From there we could go to Place de la Concorde and the Élysée Palace, after which we could stop somewhere for lunch. After lunch, we could visit the Eiffel Tower and the left bank to see some of the artist's pictures and prints. To finish the day, I would ask the Concierge to book us a table at the Lido nightclub. I asked Aileen if the tour wasn't too much for her for, as it would be a lot of walking, but she agreed that it would be a wonderful tour, as she always wanted to see these places but she was worried that it might be too much for me after the tiresome journey. I told her not to worry as I had had a good night's rest and I felt fine. We dressed quickly and on the way to our breakfast I got the Concierge to book a table at the Lido. After breakfast we returned to our hotel room, we collected our map, cameras and off we went.

We started our tour by walking up to Sacre Cœur. It was a lovely summer's day, without a cloud in the sky, so we had a most wonderful clear, panoramic view of Paris. Aileen was rapturous being there and I soon discovered that she knew more about the places that we were visiting than I did, as she always borrowed books from our library to read up on the places that we were to visit. We followed our itinerary to Moulin Rouge and then decided to explore Place Pigalle. We hugely enjoyed wandering around the artists that were painting panoramic views of Paris for the tourist market, but our favourite were the quick sketch artists that could do a quick caricature of you. We could have spent much more time there but as we had a lot more to see so we walked down to a Russian restaurant Ches Yar, just of Champs Élysées, where I used to eat sometimes with my uncle when he was in Paris. We ordered some of their specialities which Aileen had never eaten before and I was glad that she enjoyed them as I love Russian food.

After lunch we followed the rest of our itinerary and went down to the left bank of the Seine. There we wandered around, looking at the stalls, browsing through the antique books, water colour pictures and prints. We bought some limited edition prints to give as presents and for us to keep, which we framed and I still have hanging on the walls in my hallway. When we returned to the hotel, the Concierge informed us that our tickets to the show at Lido had been booked and would be waiting for us at the entrance of the club. There were two shows at the club, one at eight and the later one at ten. As we were booked for the earlier one and, being very tired, we had a quick snack, allowing us to have some rest before we went out again. Although the club was only short distance away, we still took a taxi as we had had enough walking for the day.

At that time the Lido was one of the most popular night clubs in Paris and people were queuing to go in but, as promised, our tickets were at the entrance waiting to be collected and paid for. Once inside, we were shown to our table and informed that the two half bottles of Champagne were complimentary and included in the tickets. The place filled up very quickly and the show started on time. I don't remember much about the show except two acts; one was the group of beautiful girls in fantastic dresses opening the show, dancing and singing, the other a movable ice rink on which a couple did a most marvellous dance routine in ice skates.

I was so tired that during the show I kept on nodding off and Aileen had to nudge me to keep me awake. We managed to see rest of the show but, with both of us being so tired, we decided to return to our hotel straight after it finished and have a good night sleep. Although we didn't have to leave in the morning until 9.30a.m. to catch the Calais to Dover ferry, it was still many miles of driving before we reached home. In the morning we had a good breakfast as I didn't want to stop on the way for refreshments; all I wanted was to get on to the ferry without further mishaps. Once on board there was the usual stampede to reach the shop to buy your duty free allowance. In those days you allowance was 2 bottles of spirits, 4 bottles of wine, 200 cigarettes or 50 Panatelas cigars. By the time we got to the front of the queue and bought our full allowance it was time to disembark.

It took a while to clear the customs at the other end as they were very thorough in checking for any contraband, but once we were through we were off home and due to be arriving about 5.30p.m. On the way home Aileen was talking all the time how much she had enjoyed the holiday and how much fun we had, but not a word about the break downs and all the uncomfortable time she had to endure, and I thought what a wonderful girl she was. I was then I decided that she was the girl I wanted to marry. But, I told myself, I wouldn't push it as she had made it quite clear that at present she wanted our relation to remain as it was. I had to bide my time and try to gently persuade her. I didn't know till after she died, from her cousin, that just before we went on our holiday, when visiting her parents, she told her that I was the man she was going to marry. I wish she told me; we could have two more years of happily married life.

Poker Games

On the Sunday, two weeks after we came back from our holidays we invited Peter, John and Mike with their girlfriends to my flat for drinks before going Kenwood for tea. Peter's girl Ann, who was Aileen's best friend, came with Peter but the other two were coming straight from the suburbs and would be a little late. While Ann and Aileen were having a good natter we were getting bored waiting, Peter asked me if I played cards and if I had any at home. I told him that I had several packs and played friendly gambling card games for many years. After we found out that we all had played poker, he suggested while waiting for the girls to arrive we could have a game. We didn't have any gambling chips, but I had a big Whiskey bottle half-full of sixpence pieces that I'd been saving, which we decided we could use to play with. We were enjoying the game so much that no one minded that the girls were two hours late. As soon they arrived we went to Kenwood and while having tea we discussed how much we enjoyed our game and perhaps we could have another one soon. After discussing the game a bit longer we decided that we will try to have a poker game at the boys flat starting 9p.m. We four would be the permanent members and invite some of our friends to make to seven, which is ideal number for poker. I asked Aileen if she minded. She said no, as it would give her a chance to dust the flat, wash her clothes, her hair and have a good night sleep.

During the week we managed to invite three of our friend for our game on Friday. We acquired a set of poker chips that Bob got from his gambling brother John Aspinall, and we all chipped in to buy some drinks and cakes to have during our break. Friday evening, I waited in my flat for Aileen so that we could have a meal together before I left. After eating, she shooed me out so that I wouldn't be late for the game. I told her that so I don't wake her up I would sleep on the floor on the slim foam mattress that I kept in the flat for visitors. I arrived at the boys' flat early, enabling me to help out with preparations for the game. Our guests arrived a little bit early, so we could have a drink and a chat with them before the game started at nine o'clock. We used two packs of cards: one for dealing and one for shuffling. We also had certain rules so that there were no fallings out, such as a maximum bet, so that no one would lose more that they could afford. The type of poker we would play would be the dealer's choice, the length of time playing was decided before the beginning of the game – usually we finished between 2 and 3a.m. – and the players had to be on time. The evening was a great success; most of us smoked cigars when playing and had a drink of our choice, which made for a very jolly atmosphere and, when the game broke up at 3a.m., our guests asked if it would be possible to arrange another game the following Friday. We told them that we would have to check our work schedule and we would let them know.

On Sunday, when Peter, John and I met for lunch with our girlfriends, who all worked with Aileen as models at Alexon, we discussed the idea of having a poker game every Friday night at the boys' flat. We asked the girls what they thought of the idea. They all thought it was great as that was the evening that they would do as Aileen did, preparing for the party on Saturday night. It seemed that the word got around among our friends about our poker game and we had several calls from them wishing to join. We decided to make a list of who we would like to join our game, make a rota and invite them in turn. They would also have to contribute a small sum of money to help out with the cost of food, drinks and two packs of cards. We told our friends that our decision was that there would be a game organised on Friday every week at 9p.m., there would have to be a small contribution of money to help out with our expenses. There would be a box for the contribution money and any surplus after a year we would all decide what to do with. Then somebody suggested we ought to have a name of our card school. After long discussion and laughter trying to think up a name, we settled on the Knightsbridge Literary and Debating Society'.

The games were a great success and soon we were getting more of our friends on our list. On the original list there were five dentists, three doctors, two army Officers, three jewellers, two solicitors, two accountants, a publisher of books, a cloth merchant and a Furrier.[34] Occasionally, especially during the summer holidays when a lot of people were away at the same time, some of them asked if there was a place for one their friends to play with us. Through accepting some of them, we met some very interesting people, one of whom was Johnny Goodman, who at that time was directing the Saint series with Roger Moore, who also joined our game. Another was the editor who wrote Hickey gossip column in the *Daily Express*; one of the articles that he wrote was about Kensington in which he mentioned our game. He wrote: "as the evening draws near and the lights beginning to come on through one of the windows you can see the boys from the Knightsbridge Literary Debating Society lighting their cigars and settling down for another session of Poker." The next day, Lord Astor, who was a family friend of Bob Aspinall, phoned him wanting to join. Bob had to gently explain to him that it was a friendly game and the stakes were small compared to the ones he was used to. Towards the end of the year, the four of us with our girlfriends met to have our Sunday lunch at a hotel in Sloane Square to see if it would be suitable for our members of our poker school to have a yearly dinner. On the way we stopped at a nearby pub, the Stag's Head where something remarkable happened. As we were ordering our drinks, Stanley Baker, who was a big film star then, walked in with four young friends and they proceeded to the Salon bar. As we were having our drinks at the bar, a young man appeared, walked straight into Aileen and said: "Mr. Baker would like you to join him for a drink."

Aileen looked down at him and said: "How dare you to interrupt our conversation. I don't drink with strange men. I am

---

[34] Through pure coincidence, five of them were South African.

here with my boyfriend and friends, we already have our drinks so please tell Mr. Baker I am not interested." I then knew that she really cared for me and I walked around for the rest of the day with a big smile on my face. Several times during the summer we used to hire 32' broad boats on the Thames from Friday night until Sunday night that could sleep six to have a weekend of poker. The rules were that we took turns in cooking, rotated our beds as some were uncomfortable, no shaving to conserve water and cut cards who would empty the chemical toilet. We usually picked up the boat, sailed down to Cookham where we would eat a late dinner at the Bell and Dragon, then board the boat and start playing. The play would stop when the first duck quacked in the morning, which usually was about 3.30a.m. Sunday evenings the girls came down to meet us at Cookham where we all had dinner at the Bell and Dragon before returning to London. Walking into that pub on a Sunday evening, unwashed and unshaven, we must have been a sight for sore eyes.

Our Knightsbridge Literary and Debating Society meetings lasted for 15 years. I stopped playing for two and half years between 1963-1965, after we bought our first house as we were completely broke and I didn't have any spare money to play with. In all the years that we played we never had a disagreement and we only ever suspected one member of cheating, who was never asked to play with us again. As we all got married – I was the first, then Peter, then John – and we moved into our own houses, we took turns to play in each other homes. It eventually broke up when John married a South African girl and emigrated there and Peter died from cancer five years later. While it lasted, it was a lot of fun and we all had most wonderful time. Last time I played poker with John was in 1991 when I visited him in South Africa and he arranged two games with the boys that played with us in London.

1958

A week before Easter, when our crowd were having our usual lunch, we discussed what we were going to do over Easter as we weren't going to have a party that weekend as so many of our friends were going to be away. John mentioned that he had read in the paper that there was going to be a big Easter Sunday parade in Hyde Park and, if the weather was fine, maybe we should join it. We all thought it was a good idea and decided to meet at the boys' flat on the day with our cars at 10a.m. John, Peter and Mike had sports cars and were going to drive with the hoods down. Ann, Peter's girlfriend, didn't like being driven in an open car asked Aileen if she could change places with her and be my passenger. Aileen would go in Peter's car, to which she agreed.

On the Sunday, when we met at the flat, all the girls looked gorgeous; they had persuaded their boss to let them wear the latest styles as models for the parade, which would be a good advert for their firm and, of course, we were as always in our best suits when going out on a date. We then left for Hyde Park, hoping that leaving early enough we would be able to find a parking place and then join the crowds. As we drove along the traffic got denser and denser, and we suddenly realised that we were at the back of the parade. When we arrived at the park, the gates were shut and the policemen were directing the vehicles in front of the parade away from the gates so that there were no vehicles in front when the parade made its entrance. As soon all the vehicles in front were cleared they opened the gates and they let the parade through, with us following the parade and the police, seeing the beautiful girls in our cars, thought we were part of it and waved us through, shutting the gates behind us. There were many celebrities on the parade floats and as we passed there were thousands of people waving and cheering, so the girls sat on top of the sports cars waving back. The parade, after travelling to the end of the road, let the celebrities off, who were mobbed by people wanting autographs. We followed the parade vehicles, still hoping to find a parking place. There was a place just behind the parade vehicles where we parked and went to join the crowds to see what else was happening in the park. When we reached the crowd, I don't know if they recognised from the parade and, thinking that we were celebrities, suddenly surrounded us asking for our autographs. We tried to tell them over the noise we were not celebrities, but they wouldn't listen, so John said: "Sign any star's name that comes to mind." After signing about twenty-five pieces of paper as John Wayne, we started edging away from them, but they still followed us before they eventually gave up. We managed to find a place to have lunch, then we picked up our cars, went back to the boys' flat to have a rest, and in the evening we went for dinner at our favourite Indian restaurant. It was a memorable Easter.

25 - A picture I took of Aileen in the back of my friend's car, waving to the crowd during the Easter Parade.

Soon after Easter, Aileen and I started thinking of where to go for our summer holidays. We didn't want to go to Spain again, and after discussing the different countries that were available to us, we decided on Italy, as we were both keen to visit Venice. Package holidays were in their infancy and not knowing much about them, I decided to pay a visit to a tour operator named Swans that was just opposite our firm. When I entered, and after being asked what I required, the assistant brought me a whole load of brochures and maps of the region that we wished to visit, explaining the pros and cons of the area. He then suggested that the best place for us to make our base for visiting Venice would be Venice Lido, as it is the nearest island to Venice and only 10min by ferry to the mainland with a frequent service.

There are two luxurious hotels on the island: a very famous hotel called The Excelsior and the other Hotel De Banes. There were three apartments, of which the largest one the company rented for it clients. This was just before cheap flights and people tended to travel either by train, coach or car. Then he informed that the journey would be an overnight train in a sleeping carriage leaving London at 9p.m. arriving at Venice about 11a.m., where we would be met by their representative who would deliver us to our hotel, should I wish to book. The price in August to mid-September was £37.50, which included a room with an en suite and full board. I asked him if I could borrow his phone to call Aileen and when I got through to her I gave her all the details and asked her if she would like to go on this holiday, and if she could take the time off for the dates suitable for us. She said one word: "Booked."

George and René, who lived above me and were our very good friends with whom we would dine with quite often. A few days after we had booked the holiday, when we all went out for a meal, I mentioned to George that we had booked a package holiday to Venice. Right away they were interested, as they had discussed themselves the idea of going to Italy for their holiday. George wanted to know all the details, and when I told them our itinerary, George said that, if we didn't mind, he and René would be interested in joining us. Aileen and I looked at each other and we both told them we would delighted, especially since George spoke fluent Italian having spent three years there in the Polish army.

Our holiday was booked for the last two weeks in August. George and René could only spare twelve days so we wouldn't be traveling together as the travel agent could only arrange that they would travel there a day later and leave a day earlier than us. On the day that we were leaving for our holiday, Aileen came over early so that we could have a meal together and to leave for our train by taxi at about 7.50p.m., allowing ourselves plenty of time for boarding the train. When we arrived at the station we acquired a porter who knew to which platform to take our luggage, where our train was already waiting. On the platform there was a steward who, after showing him our tickets, directed the porter which sleeping carriage to take our luggage to and told us that our names are on the window of our compartment. We got to our carriage, which had our name and another couple's names on, with whom we would be sharing as it was a four-berth compartment. The bunks were already made up so we stowed our baggage away and waited for the other couple before settling down for the night.

The train left on time and we arrived at Dover two hours later where the sleeping carriages were transferred onto the channel ferry for our crossing. This process took about an hour and the journey across about 1½ hours. After we left Victoria Station we settled down to sleep, but when we reach Dover sleep became impossible with the shunting of the carriages to load them on to the cross-Channel ferry and we stayed awake until the same process finished at Calais. The whole process took about two hours and once we were connected to the French train and had started moving again, at last we were able to sleep. In the morning we went to the dining car to have breakfast. When we returned to our compartment the steward has taken the bedding, tidied the carriage, put down the bunks, making it comfortable for our journey towards Switzerland, where we would be crossing into Italy and then on to Venice. We stopped at both borders where our passports were checked and stamped. We arrived in Venice station at 11.30a.m. and, being outside the town we were meet by courier who had a water taxi waiting for us, which took us across to the town. When we disembarked, there was a horse and carriage waiting to take us to a ferry stop on the other side of town where we caught boat which took us to Venice Lido. Once we arrived there another courier was waiting with another horse and carriage which delivered us to our apartment.

It was quite a large building, with about thirty rooms and a huge reception and lounge run by the husband and wife owners. They greeted us warmly with a smile and, after signing in and giving them our passports, the wife showed us to our room, which overlooked a beautiful garden but no sea view as the pension was a short distance from the beach. The room was big, very well furnished and comfortable. After we had unpacked, we went down to the reception where we were informed of the times of our meals. We were also given information about the beach – the two hotels owned their own part of the beach which was private, the rest was a public beach, of which each pension rented a part of for their clientele, where there they had built chalets and were available for customers to have for a day or the week for a small charge. One of the things that was good was that if one rented a chalet, that there was a phone connected to the pension and if one wanted to spend the whole day on the beach, one could phone and lunch would be delivered to the chalet.

I told the patron that we would decide about whether or not to rent a chalet when our friends arrived the following day. We were then showed to the dining room where we had very good lunch. At lunch we decided that as we had such a long journey and were very tired that we would have a shower, then sleep until dinner time and, after dinner, have an early night and leave the sightseeing until George and René arrive. The next morning after breakfast, having time before George and René arrived at lunchtime, we went sightseeing around the lido, which we found with no motor vehicles very quiet. There was delicious ice-cream, with the sellers being very friendly, and a wonderful beach. When we arrived back at our pension we were just in time to greet George and René, having just arrived. We waited for them to finish all their formalities and had lunch together. During lunch, we told them of what we had seen of the place during our walk and, being such a beautiful place, we were bound to have a good holiday.

Whilst eating, George told me that having spoken to the patron he had been given information about where to catch the ferry, the opening times of the casino and the other places that we would be visiting. After lunch we had our coffee in the lounge where we planned how we were going to spend our holiday. We decided to book one of the larger chalets for ten days, which would be big enough for us as it had table, four chairs and four loungers. We would take an early ferry every other day to Venice for half a day, where we would visit the interesting sights, especially the Doge's Palace, the Cathedral and on one day to visit Murano Island to see the manufacture of glass, and maybe buy one or two pieces. Occasionally, if we overran on our expeditions, we would have lunch there rather than at the pension.

The following morning we left early for Venice. As we got near to the landing, which was by San Marco square, Aileen and I were completely enchanted by the magnificent of the town, the Doge's palace, the cathedral, all the churches with their bell towers and the large square with the shops and cafés with their table and chairs outside running along the three sides of the square where people were sitting having their morning coffee.

We decided to visit the Doge's palace first. In those days, there weren't so many tourists as there are today and it was pleasant to wander around without bumping into massive tours that you have today and having to stand in a long queue to enter any of the interesting sites. After paying a small fee for our tickets, we entered the palace. We marvelled at the size of the rooms, painted ceilings and the pictures on the walls. There were no restrictions on taking pictures and in those days, being a keen photographer, I laid down on the floor and took pictures of the ceilings. None of the staff or anyone else objected; they took it as if it was a normal occurrence and the same thing was true of the cathedral and churches.

After our visit to the palace, we decided to have a coffee in the square and enjoy the atmosphere of the place and then wander around and visit some of the shops. Those days in the square, the price of a cup of coffee was about 20p. The last time I was in Venice in 2011 it cost 7 Euros. Returning to our pension we were just in time for our lunch and, after having a short rest, we met up in our chalet to enjoy the beach and swim in the warm sea. That evening, after dinner, we decided to visit the Casino and have a little gamble in which we had some success and won a little money. Coming out of the casino, there was a stall selling individual pizzas and that was the first time Aileen and I had one and enjoyed it immensely.

Our next trip was to the island of Murano, where we visited several of the glass factories and saw several different demonstrations of glass blowing, after which we were encouraged to buy some of their wear, of which I still have one or two pieces. One of the fascinating places that we visited was the first Jewish Ghetto, which originated in Venice. The entrance still had the original gates and a guide that was taking a small group of people around, explaining to his group that these gates were locked during the night to secure the area with a guard posted to it, not because of anti-Semitism by the government but because of a section of the residents that were and often attacked by other Venetians. How true that was I never found out. Aileen and I were so taken up with Venice that we decided to visit again and we did altogether seven times during the holiday.

As our holiday came to an end, René and George left the day before us and we spent the last day preparing for our departure in the evening. We spent most of the day on the beach, resting for our long journey. The courier picked us up at 6p.m. to take us to Venice railway station, allowing us plenty time to settle in our sleeping compartment for our journey. We arrived in London on Saturday at my flat just before lunch. I asked Aileen what she wanted to do, whether she wanted to freshen up before we went out for lunch or go for lunch first. That's when she dropped the bombshell: she turned around to me and said "I am going back to my place and I am not going to see you anymore." For a minute I was absolutely stunned and I asked her: "Is it another man? Or is it something I've done." She explained we had now been an item for over a year and we hadn't progressed any further in our relationship. I replied that when we became an item and I had asked her if she wanted us to be engaged, she had said that she wanted to carry on as we were, and I didn't mentioned it again, fearing that she would think that I was pushing her and instead waited for her to tell me that she wanted our relation to go further. I said: "You know I love you and I know you love me. Do you want us to get engaged and then married?" She said: "Yes, but what about your family, especially your father; they are orthodox Jewish and I've been told that they would disown you." I said that that would be up to them; I'd been living my own life for the past twenty years and although I love them very much, I have to live a life that suits me. Then I asked her: "What about her family?" She told me there was no problem, both her parents were very fond of me and thought we were well suited and as to religion, they had no objection; her father who a keen student of the Bible and always thought that the Jewish religion was a much truer religion. "In that case, I will arrange for us to have a meal with the family and I will introduce them to you and tell them that you are the girl I am going to marry." I said.

She then said something very strange: "Don't do that yet. Let us be unofficially engaged for the time being. I have spare ring that I can wear on my third finger until such time that I want us to be officially engaged and meet your family." I found it very mysterious and tried very hard to find out why she wanted it that way, but all she said was to be patient and trust her and everything will work out. I didn't argue with her as I was so happy that she was willing to marry me, so we left it as she wanted.

That year was a very good year at work. We were both very busy; what with Aileen doing fashion shows outside London and I working long hours we had very little time to socialise except for on weekends, so we were both looking forward to our Christmas holidays. Aileen was going down to Alverstoke for Christmas to tell her parents what we decided about our relationship and would be coming back in time for the New Year's party at the boys' flat. In October, my family had a surprise visit from my Uncle Gustav and his wife Jenny from Germany. He had to see some people on business so he decided to bring his wife with him and introduce her to my parents, as they had never met. They were staying for three days and, of course, mum insisted that they come the following night to have a family dinner.

The dinner was a great success as mum cooked dishes that we had in Poland and he hadn't eaten like that since before the war. It was a jolly evening, reminiscing about the times we were altogether in Poland, but it was also a sad evening as dad and Gustav were the only two who had survived the war from our very large family. Grandma, who also survived the camps, was killed by the Poles when she came back home to claim her property. When the evening was over, I offered to drive them back to their hotel. On the way uncle told me that tomorrow night he and Jenny wanted to go somewhere where they could have a good meal and had dancing facilities. I suggested to them to book a table at Café Royal in Regent St., which was only a short distance from their hotel. He then said that he would like me and Jean to join them, as he had met Jean three years before when he was here on business. I told him Jean and I had finished our relationship over two years ago and since then I have a new girlfriend name Aileen, whom I hoped to marry, so if they wanted us to join them when they have booked the table, they should phone me later at my flat at what time to meet at the hotel.

When I returned back to my flat I phoned Aileen, telling her about our invitation and asking her if she would like to go. She said yes, and we agreed to meet at my flat straight after work and travel from there to meet my uncle. The dinner was great successes: the food was good, and we all enjoyed the dancing and although I am a very poor dancer, I tried my best. During dinner, Uncle invited us to come and stay with them in Munich, but I had to explain to him that as Aileen and I are both in the fashion trade, our season doesn't finish until after Easter, but we would think about it and maybe it would be possible during our summer holiday. We walked them back to their hotel and took taxi back to my flat. On the way, Aileen told me how much she enjoyed the evening with my uncle and she would like to go to Munich to stay with them. I told her it was bit early to think about it, as it was some time before our holidays, but that we would keep that as one of our options when we came to discuss our holidays. The following morning, I phoned Uncle as he was leaving back home in the afternoon. I couldn't speak to Auntie as she was out doing her last minute shopping, but I thanked them for the most enjoyable evening and told him we are thinking about their invitation. His only comment was referring to Aileen: "She is very beautiful and you suit each other, so don't lose her." The day before Christmas, Aileen went down to see her parents to tell them how our relation had progressed, and told me they were delighted, wanting us to spend a weekend with them at Easter, which was fine as we both had a week off at that time. We had a great New Years' party, but I was getting frustrated, waiting for Aileen to make up her mind for us to be officially engaged.

1959

The New Year started with the firm having a lot of orders, with everyone working overtime. The time went quickly and soon it was Easter and time for us to visit Aileen's parents. While having tea with them, they told me how delighted they were that we were now in serious relationship and I mentioned that I was a bit frustrated that Aileen, for the time being, didn't wish to be officially engaged. She said to me with a smile: "Don't worry, Tim. Be patient, you will see everything will turn out alright." I thought that she must know something that I didn't, but she wasn't telling me as they were the exact words that Aileen had said to me when I had asked her for us to be officially engaged.

When we returned back to London we started planning for our holidays. We decided that spending our holiday with my relations in Munich was not much of a holiday. We wanted to go to some warm place by the sea where we could relax and lay on a nice sandy beach and take one or two trips to see interesting places. We couldn't make up our minds where to go, then out of the blue Uncle Gustav phoned me, telling me that he, Jenny and three of his friends with their wives were going to Alassio for their holidays for the last two weeks in August, and he and Jenny would like us to join them for a week. The hotel, food and everything else will be paid for; all we had to do was to get there. I told him I would have to speak to Aileen so see what she thought of the idea and I would phone him the next day. When I discussed the proposition with her, she was a bit lukewarm about the idea until I suggested we travel by car and spend the week with them before touring Northern Italy, which has a few places that we wanted to see. She agreed that we should accept their invitation, so phoned I Gustav accepting his generous offer.

When our holiday time came I had my car completely serviced and checked for everything that could possibly go wrong after the disastrous journey from Spain. We set off on a very early sunny Saturday morning to Dover to catch the earliest ferry crossing to Calais. Before going we both discussed our route and the interesting places that we would like to stop to have a look around, and if everything went to plan we should arrive in Alassio early Sunday evening. The crossing was excellent as the sea was calm; it was the first time that I didn't feel sick crossing the channel. Once we left the Calais docks we took the major road to Reims and then to Dijon where we would spend the night. We arrived at Dijon just before five and driving to the hotel, we passed a Bistro which was packed and had been recommended in the AA book. We could hear dance music playing and could see people dancing and eating. I mentioned to Aileen that after we settled down in the hotel and had a shower and a rest, if she felt like going out it would be a good place to go for our meal and bit of fun.

The hotel was just around the corner from the Bistro; it was a four star one and they had a room available with a shower and bath. We quickly had a shower and a short rest. We decided that as we were tired from the journey we would go out to the bistro early, listen to the music a bit, have a meal and an early night as we had another long journey the next day. After we rested and dressed, we left the hotel at a quarter to seven for our meal at the bistro. As we neared the place, people were leaving and when we reached the entrance the music stopped, all the people disappeared – including all the staff – leaving the place completely empty. We were bewildered as to what had happened; it was like boarding the Mary Celeste. We didn't know what to do so we sat down at one of the tables to discuss what to do, hoping that someone would soon appear. After about eight minutes, a man appeared and walked behind the bar started polishing the bar top. I went up to him, asking what had happened, did we smell or something, as everyone had disappeared. He was most apologetic and explained that the Bistro has a dance every afternoon which finishes at 7p.m. for the staff to leave and the new staff to be able to prepare the place for the evening dancing session which starts at 8p.m. I asked him if it was possible to have a meal. Of course, he said, and suggested that we have the peppered steak with chips and peas followed with the desert of pancakes with orange liquor. I also asked him if we could have a half bottle Chateauneuf-du-Pape, which was Aileen's favourite wine.

While waiting for our meal, enjoying our wine and watching the people in the street passing by, customers started filling the tables around us, the music came on, playing some French romantic songs. Our meal arrived with a large steak, about 8oz, beautifully cooked and the sauce was the best I've ever had; it was a most satisfying meal after our long journey. We had a short dance and afterwards we went back to our hotel and to our bed.

In the morning we left our hotel very early as we hoped that we would have time to stop at Grasse to by some perfume for my Auntie. We were travelling through beautiful countryside on uncongested roads, which meant we were able to travel at fair speed through Lyon then Grenoble, before a break at Digne-les-Bains and then on to Grasee. About seven miles from Grasse we started seeing fields of Lavender and as we got near the town the aroma from the plants was getting stronger and stronger. We discovered later that Lavender and Jasmine are the two basic materials used in the manufacture of perfume. We stopped at one of the small perfume factories to buy some of their goods and they were kind enough to show us around and show us the method of manufacturing the perfume. Afterwards, we went on with our journey, crossing the French border at Menton and arriving at Alassio in the early afternoon. I drove straight to meet my uncle at his hotel, where he was waiting for our arrival. He took us to our hotel and invited us to meet him and his friends at his hotel for dinner, to which we agreed.

When we meet for dinner we were introduced to uncle's friend, who luckily all spoke a fair amount of English, as I was a bit worried that it would be boring for Aileen as she didn't speak German and that made it a very pleasant evening. I discovered from my uncle that the men were all millionaires living in Munich. Uncle's hotel had a private beach and he arranged for us to use it. With two deckchairs and an umbrella, it was very useful as the other beaches were very full. We had a wonderful holiday, but like all things, soon it was time to go home. Uncle gave me presents to give to mum and dad and asked that, knowing that I was going through Munich on the return journey, if I would deliver a baby pushchair which was not available in Germany, to which I agreed.

On our journey back we travelled through north Italy, stayed at Trento than we travelled on to Munich to deliver the chair, where we stayed for two days to show Aileen around the town. Then we carried on to Heidelberg, where we spend another two days before driving to Calais for our ferry home, arriving on the Sunday. When we got back into London, we decided to have lunch out before I took Aileen home. When we returned to the flat, I told that I was getting frustrated by her not wanting to be officially engaged and I would like her to make up her mind. She looked at me and said: "Everything will be alright; you'll see. I want you to wait another two weeks. Will you do that for me?" I said: "O.K." I wondered why the two weeks were so important, forgetting that it was my birthday soon.

On my birthday, I was waiting for Aileen for us go out. When she came, took her jacket off and asked if we could have a drink before we went out. While having chat and our drinks she took an envelope from her bag and gave it to me. I opened it, thinking it was a gift voucher for my birthday; I couldn't be more surprised, as it was a certificate of her confirmation to Judaism at the Liberal Jewish Synagogue in St John's Wood. I wouldn't have been more surprised if someone told me that I'd won the lottery. I said to her: "Why? I never asked you or discussed if you would change your religion, for it never mattered much to me as long it didn't matter to you." She then explained: "Do you remember last year when we came back from our holiday and we were unofficially engaged, I went to visit my parents to tell them about it. Dad asked me what sort of wedding we would have. I told him we would have to have it in a registry office, as we are both of different religions. But he worried that when we have children, there would be a burden of choice as to what religion to follow would be would put on them. He said: "Tim loves you, but he was brought up in a strict orthodox Jewish faith and it would be very difficult for him to change. As you know, I've been a bible scholar for many years and I have always thought that the Jewish religion is a much truer religion, so I would suggest that when you go back to London, go to the Liberal Synagogue, speak to someone there and see if you could go to a Saturday service and see how you like it. It would make your life easier if you were both of the same faith." I thought about it and when I came back on the following Saturday, I went to the synagogue and enquired about attending the service. I was introduced to Rabbi Rayner, who was most welcoming and asked me some questions about why I wished to attend the service. He then introduced me to one of the ladies to sit with me and guide me through the service. After the service, the lady explained about the Kiddush, where Rabbi Rayner and the congregation will say a prayer for bread and wine. After we had our Kiddush, the Rabbi came over and asked if I enjoyed the service. I told him I did and if it was possible, I would like to come to another one next Saturday, to which he agreed. After the second service was finished, walking to do the Kiddush I met the Rabbi again and asked him if I could speak to him about me converting to Judaism. He told me that if I phoned his office in the synagogue, the secretary would make an appointment.

"When the appointment was sorted out I met him at the Synagogue where he asked me a lot of questions, one of which was why I wanted to change. I explained to him that I was going to marry a Jewish boy and I want us to have a Jewish home and should we have children that they should grow up in the Jewish faith. He then explained that I would have quite a lot to study and some of it would be on Sundays in the Synagogue, but most would be at his home in Golders Green. The conversion course would take about a year. I told him I was quite prepared to do it. I had to learn the Shema[35] in Hebrew by heart, the prayers for the bread, wine and candles for the Sabbath and why it was we celebrate different festivals, as well as some of the Jewish history. I finished the course two weeks ago, had to pass a short exam and was presented with my certificate of confirmation. I shall be joining the Synagogue as a member just before the Jewish New Year."

I told her that when she went, I would go with her and we could take out a joint membership, so that we can belong to the same Synagogue and go to services together. Then I asked her if we could now be officially engaged and if I could buy her an engagement ring. On Saturday, when I see Peter, I would ask him to bring a selection of Sapphire and diamond rings for Aileen to choose from, as she had always said that she would like one for her engagement. Meanwhile, I would phone my mum and dad to see if we could come over next Saturday for lunch and to introduce you to them, to which she agreed.

I phoned mum straight away to ask her if I could come on Saturday for lunch and to tell her that I would be bringing my girlfriend for her and dad to meet. She was delighted that I was coming for lunch and straight away asked if there was anything special I would like her to cook; I told her not to fuss, just a normal lunch would do. I phoned my sister to tell her the good news, and asked if she and her new husband Peter Gregory could also be at mum's for lunch, as I thought, knowing dad, I would need some moral support. She was delighted and said she would definitely be there because she didn't want to miss the occasion. The week went very quickly and before long it was time for us to go to my parents' for lunch. We were both a little apprehensive as to what my dad would say. When we rang the bell, mum and dad were both waiting for us. Before they could say anything, I said that this was Aileen, she belongs to the liberal synagogue and that's the girl I am going to marry.

---

[35] One of the most important, if not the most important, prayer in Judaism.

What happened next surprised me. Dad walked over to Aileen, put his arms around her, kissed her and said "welcome to the family", then mum kissed her and as we were walking into the dining room. All that mum said was "Isn't she tall." Everyone at lunch was a very happy, with many questions being asked of Aileen. I think mum and dad had practically given up on me getting married by this point, as the previous few years they had been urging me to do so. I think they were eager for grandchildren, and mum insisted that from now on Aileen and I come for Saturday lunch when we were not working. I couldn't believe how everything went so well. A week later, Peter called at the flat and brought a large selection of engagement rings for Aileen to choose. She chose a beautiful large Sapphire and diamond ring. Peter also had a selection of antique men's signet rings in his case and when Aileen saw them straight away bought one for me. I now felt that we were fully engaged. Now we seemed much more contented and we could start planning for our wedding. We decided that we wouldn't decide anything until after Christmas, as we were much too busy at work being our season and couldn't spare the time.

Aileen didn't want a shop-bought dress; she wanted to design her own, and asked me if I could speak to my marvellous liner finisher, Edith, who was also a dress maker, about her making one to Aileen's design. I spoke to Edith and she was delighted to do it, having met Aileen several times when Aileen used to come up to the firm to meet me when we were going out. She wouldn't be able to start until after the season was over, but she would be able to come to my flat to discuss what Aileen had in mind. We were both very, busy but we also had to start thinking about getting larger shared accommodation, as my lease stated that my flat was only for single residency; married men couldn't live there. It was still very hard to find suitable accommodation and knowing that Aileen liked the area, we decided that I should try to see if I could get a bigger flat in my block. She liked the idea and we left it at that as I didn't have the time to go to the letting office until after New Year's, when we celebrated the Jewish New Year by both attending the liberal synagogue as a couple. After we walked to my parents' house to meet the family for a traditional New Year lunch, which mum prepared, and as usual there was enough to feed an army.

During lunch, questions were asked, like when we were thinking of getting married. I explained that first I have to find somewhere to live. We hadn't discussed wedding dates as at the time the synagogue was being refurbished, but we were thinking sometime before the next Jewish New Year. Dad suggested that if we couldn't find new accommodations we could always have a flat in one of his houses. Neither of us was keen on the idea and thanked him for the offer but told him that we were sure we would get a bigger flat in my block, being a tenant of long standing.

After lunch, we all made arrangements for breaking the fast on Yom Kippur, as it was one of the big celebrations in the family. Usually, I used to meet dad in the synagogue for the service at about 9a.m., stay until 1p.m. and return about 5p.m. for the memorial and evening service. Dad was very religious spent the whole day there as most of the very orthodox community did, but I didn't because I used to get a terrible headache when fasting so used to go home, take aspirin and go to bed to relieve the pain. After the service, Rozia met me and we walked with dad home, where Mum greeted us, usually with a glass of borscht and latkes to break our fast. This year, of course, everything changed. Now belonging to the Liberal Synagogue, I wouldn't be going with dad, but instead Rozia, I and Aileen would still meet him after the service.

We all enjoyed our lunch, but I couldn't get over how fond my parents became of Aileen. On Yom Kippur, we both fasted, went to the service at the synagogue, and left after the morning service finished. In the early evening, we went to mum's, who was preparing the meal for breaking our fast. Rozia was already there, but we had a surprise for my Uncle Joe and his wife Odette had come over from Paris and were going to joins us for the meal. I hadn't spoken to my uncle since I had left his firm, as I think he was very disappointed that I had left his employ. I introduced Aileen to them; they congratulated us on our engagement. The time seemed to have mellowed him, as when I asked them if they would they come to our wedding once we had decided a date, he replied that when they know the date they will definitely make sure that they would be there.

26 - My mother, Jozefa, at our engagement party.

When the time came, I left them to join dad for the memorial and concluding service. When we arrived back at dad's house, mum as usual greeted us with borscht and latke to break our fast before we sat down to our meal. The meal was a jolly affair; there was eight of us in all and, as always, mum cooked far too much so we were all stuffed, and when Aileen and I left she told me how much she enjoyed the whole evening with the family and meeting uncle Joe and Odette.

Before Christmas we were invited by Aileen's parents to come down to them to spend the festivities with them. We arrived at their place on Christmas morning, as we had both had to work up to Christmas Eve. We met more of her relations, all the women admiring Aileen's ring. We arrived back to London to join our friends to celebrate the New Year.

1960

Towards the end of January we started to discuss plans for our wedding. We found out that the refurbishing of the synagogue would be finished by the beginning of September and we thought it would be nice to be married in a newly refurbished synagogue.

We agreed to make an appointment with Rabbi Rabi and Rabbi Rayner to discuss what dates would be available in September. After I had the date I would make an appointment to see someone in the council housing office about acquiring a larger flat. We also decided that we wouldn't go for a honeymoon because of our work, but go on an extended honeymoon of three weeks the following year.

When we spoke to Rabbi Rayner about our wedding, he informed us that that the only date that was available was Sunday, 2nd of September, as it seemed that there were several other couples hoping to be married in the newly refurbished synagogue, which may or may not have been refurbished by that time. We couldn't marry at a later date, as at work it would our busiest time of the year and we didn't want to wait any longer. We booked our wedding for that date, after which I made an appointment with the housing officer.

The housing officer was a lady whom I had never met before, and when I explained to her that I was getting married in September and as, under the condition of my lease, my flat is only for single habitation, I would need a flat for two people. That was when came the Catch 22. She told me that it wasn't until I was married that I could apply for a larger flat. So than I asked her if I would be able to live in my flat after our wedding and until they allocated me a bigger flat, but she said no as it would be against the policy of the lease, so I asked her if she expected me and my wife to live separately. She replied that as the rules stand, there is nothing more she can do for me, but she sympathised with my predicament. I asked her who the manager of the department was, as I would like to book an appointment to see him. She very kindly gave me the telephone number of the manager's secretary and when I phoned, I was told that he was on three week's leave but she would book an appointment for me and send me a letter of confirmation when he had come back.

Three weeks later letter of my appointment arrived with the date and time. I arrived at the manager's office, where I met a most charming man to whom I explained my problem and the ridiculous situation. I also motioned that I knew that the tenants on the next floor are soon vacating their flat which would be suitable for us. I also told him that there are several couples that are not married who have a bigger flat, but whatever happens I intend to live with my wife in the flat and the only way we would leave would be for the council to acquire a court order. If that happened, I would make sure that the whole story would appear in the national newspapers, having friends working there, which wouldn't show the Conservative council in very good light. He looked at me with a hint of a smile and said: "You are very determined about this. Leave it with me and I will see what I can do about it. In two weeks' time you will receive a letter from me regarding what the council have decided about your problem.

Two weeks later I had a letter from the council that flat No. 15 in my block will be available to me in three months' time but I will have to settle the question of council deposits and decoration with the present tenants. The sum that you had to deposit with the council was £250 which was written in the lease agreement. I phoned Aileen with the good news and wrote to the council right away my acceptance letter thanking the housing manager for his effort of obtaining our flat. Now we were able to start planning our wedding.

From the start, when we decided to get married, knowing that her parents had very little money as they only had a small pension, I told her that she must tell them that they mustn't worry about the cost as I will pay all the bills. Aileen told her parents of my decision but they insisted that they must contribute something towards the wedding and we agreed they would provide the cars and flowers. As it was going to be a formal white wedding, Aileen had already bought white satin material and matching shoes and she had spoken to Edith to arrange a final discussion about her dress. For me it was easy, as I would hire the whole outfit, including top hat, apart from my shoes and shirt, from Moss Bros. Next we had to decide who to invite; both of our families were small, totalling about 25 guests. Then there were my firm's staff, and Aileen's model friends with their partners, all the boys from the poker school and many of our friends from our parties. By the time we finished the list we had 85 names on it.

Next, we had to booked a place for our reception. We tried several places, some couldn't do the date that we required, and others were much too expensive. Eventually, we settled on the Kensington Palace Hotel in Kensington, who were most helpful. We decided that for lunch we would have salmon as a lot of our guests were kosher, and later on tea, a dance with a DJ. The catering manager suggested that, often on such occasions, they use a small four-piece band who charged very little for their services, and that it wouldn't cost much more than hiring a DJ. We both agreed that it was wonderful idea and paid a deposit for the whole lot with the proviso that, if some of the guests couldn't come to the wedding, or if there were any extra guests, we would notify the hotel no later than two weeks before the wedding and the price would be adjusted accordingly.

Aileen arranged with my sister to be her Maid of Honour, but when it came to the Best Man, I had a slight problem. John and Peter were my very close friends – we were more like brothers – and I didn't want to offend either of them. I spoke to them about it and they decided to cut cards and Peter won. I spoke to the couple that we were taking the flat from that we should have a meeting to sort out the financial arrangement and they kindly invited us for tea so that we could inspect the flat. I knew them by sight as they had moved into the block at the same time as me. We knew the layout of the flat as it was the same size as that of our friends René and George, but as we went around it we knew that it would have to be completely redecorated. For a start, it had never been painted since they had lived there, except for the kitchen and bathroom. The kitchen was painted a sickly mustard colour and when we walked into the bathroom we had never seen anything like it: it was painted completely black, including the ceiling, with transfers of fish and sea animals all over the walls. The only good thing about the flat was that, in the bedroom, there was a large built-in wardrobe which they told us they were leaving behind would save us the expense of having of one built.

We agreed that that I would notify the council that we were satisfied with the flat and the day the council handed over the tenancy to me, they would return the deposit to them and I will pay in the new deposit. At the end of May I had a notification from the council that the tenants of No. 15 were moving on the last day of the month and I would have to make an appointment to relinquish the tenancy of my flat, which would be inspected before I received my deposit back, sign the lease for the new flat and pay a new deposit which was slightly higher than the old one, being a bigger flat. I straight away made an appointment, which was with the same housing manager that I had dealt with before, signed the official documents and paid the deposit. I moved in to the flat 30th May 1960.

Aileen and I started to discuss how we wanted decorate the flat and what furniture and kitchen utensils we would need. Aileen liked the furniture I had in my flat, the only things that we were lacking was a double bed, a chest of drawers and bedside tables in the bedroom. In the kitchen, we only needed a set of cutlery as the kitchen came fitted with the flat but we would change the cooker as it was very basic and I already had a large fridge. As for crockery I already had some and we were expecting some from friends who had asked us what we would like as a wedding present and we told them that Aileen was collecting whet pattern Denby ware and there was a list in John Lewis. I still have the set.

On decorating the flat, I knew a good painter who had decorated my last flat and he came to the flat to discuss what colour skim we wanted and the price of the job. The skim we chose was pale blue in the lounge and everywhere else white emulsion, with doors, window frames and kitchen walls in white gloss. As for the bedroom furniture, my sister knew a carpenter who worked in Wembley Stadium and had done some work for her and he agreed to build a chest of draws for the whole length of one of the bedroom walls. We bought the double bed from John Lewis and curtain material from Dickens and Jones for

Aileen to make the curtains. The last room the painter finished painting was the kitchen, which was in the early afternoon. As soon as he had finished we started cleaning the flat so that we could move the furniture from my flat to the new one. I arranged with our block porter to help us.

When we finished we were very tired and decided not to go out for a meal but have fish and chips from the shop which was just behind the block and some tinned peas with it, which I had in my larder. And then when we had a mishap, as when I returned with the fish, Aileen was laying on the bed fast asleep. I decided to let her sleep whilst I warmed up the peas. I put the tin in a saucepan on the gas stove with water and lay beside Aileen to have little rest while waiting for the peas to warm up. I was so tire I must have fallen asleep. Suddenly, there was a big bang from the kitchen. We rushed in to see what had happened and we were greeted with a green kitchen, peas on the walls, ceiling, all sticking to the still-tacky paint. I had forgotten to pierce the top of the tin. We looked at the mess and burst out laughing.

We decided to have our meal first – minus the peas – and then phoned the painter. He had a good laugh and told me not to worry; he would come round right away and, as the paint was still tacky, he would wash everything down with white spirit to get the peas off and leave it to dry overnight, then come back in the morning and repaint the kitchen, which he did. The last thing we bought for the flat were carpets. We visited the Cyril Lord showroom in Kilburn and chose two carpets with underlay, one for the bedroom and the other for the lounge. I was going to lay them myself. I wanted the bedroom carpet to arrive first so that the bedroom was ready when our bed was delivered. The bedroom carpet was delivered as promised and I laid it in time for the bed delivery. When it came to the lounge carpet I was informed that there would be a few days' delay as they were waiting for new delivery from the factory. When it was eventually delivered it arrived without the underlay. I phoned the showroom, enquiring about the underlay, and after they checked the invoice, they were most apologetic for their oversight and promised that the underlay would be delivered within the next two days. Unfortunately, what was delivered was not the underlay but another carpet. This time, I went to the showroom myself to see the manager, who again was apologetic and assured me that he would personally see that an underlay was delivered to me in the next two days, but no, they delivered another carpet. So now I had three carpets but no underlay. I was furious and phoned the head office, demanding to speak to the Area Manager who, after I explained to him the whole episode of the carpets, assured me that he would personally see to it that the underlay would be sent to me right away and the other two carpets collected. At last, the underlay arrived the next day, but they still didn't collect the spare carpets, so I put them in my storage room and it was another three month before they collected them, but at least I was able to finish our flat.

Now that the flat was furnished, all that was needed were curtains. On one of our shopping trips to Selfridges, I asked Aileen to choose which sewing machine she wanted and after a long conversation with the sales person and trying several of them, she chose one which I bought for her.

As the date of our wedding was getting nearer, Aileen started to move some of her clothing and stuff to the flat and, a month before the wedding, we decided that she ought to move in permanently in order that she had the flat ready when her parents arrived, who were coming from Alverstoke a couple days before the wedding and staying with her in our flat whilst I stayed at my parents' place.

On the Monday before the wedding, when Aileen came home for us to go out for a meal, she said to me that her firm had been chosen to represent England in a big fashion show which European Free Trade Association (E.F.T.A.) was putting on in Norway and that she had been chosen to be the model representing England. The show was leaving for Norway on the Friday after our wedding and she would be away a week. She asked me if she should I accept. I said to her "I don't see why not; we already decided we weren't going away for a honeymoon, so accept."

27 - The models in Norway, with Aileen representing the UK, far right. The picture was reproduced in several articles in the Norwegian press, and a piece about the trip featured Aileen in the *The Star*.

Two days before the wedding, we picked up Aileen's parents from the station and brought them back to our flat. They were impressed with the flat and her mother kept on telling Aileen how lucky she was having everything on one floor, with such large rooms, a fitted kitchen and bathroom. After they had unpacked, we all went for them to meet my parents. They seemed to get on very well together and, of course, Mum asked them to stay for lunch. Unfortunately, I couldn't stay as I had to get back to work. When I got back to the flat in the evening for us all to go out for a meal, Aileen told me that Mum had phoned and invited us all for supper. We had a wonderful meal, everyone swapping stories about the families, after which I took them back to the flat and I went to sleep at the boys' flat.

On the Saturday night, Peter and John decided that we would have a quiet stag night. Two other friends joined us and they took me to my favourite restaurant in Kensington, the Chanterelle. The five of us had a fabulous meal with quite a lot of wine. Afterwards we went back to their flat where they organised a poker game with two more friends who joined us so that we could have a full school. I told Peter that that we mustn't play to late as we were due at my parents' house very early the next day, where we would bathe, shave and change into our morning suits to be ready when the cars arrived at 10.30a.m. to take us to the synagogue. Of course, it didn't work out that way. Every time we suggested stopping the game, someone wanted to play another hand and the game didn't finished until 3a.m. Luckily the flat had enough beds and settees so everyone found somewhere to sleep. I told Peter that we must leave for my parents flat no later than just after eight, so if he wakes up before me to wake me up, but of course we overslept and I woke up just after 8.30a.m. As we were sleeping in our clothes, I woke Peter up, got him out of bed, told him we will have our cup of tea when we arrive at my parents' house, got in the car and arrived at my parents' house just at 9a.m. Mum was frantic, asking where we were; she had been phoning everyone to find out. I told her not to worry. All we wanted was a cup of tea and a clear bathroom and we would be ready on time. Peter and I managed to do our ablutions, get dressed and have a sandwich with another cup of tea just before the cars came. We arrived at the synagogue with ample time for my wedding.

The wedding was being held in the Liberal Jewish Synagogue's Montefiore Hall at 11.30a.m. The hall was usually used for plays and concerts, and had a large raised stage on which the wedding ceremony would be held. The staff at the synagogue did a marvellous job of arranging the Chuppah, the flowers, and below, a mass of chairs for the guests. When we walked in, the place was already half-full, and as we walked to the front seats, on the way we were greeted by friends and Aileen's relations who had travelled from Gosport and Portsmouth, who I introduced to my family. Then we all sat down, waiting for Aileen with her mum and dad to arrive. A few minutes later, the Rabbi arrived, and walking to the stage asked mum, dad, Peter and myself to join him on the stage.

Just before 11.30a.m., the organ started to play; Aileen's mum came in and was escorted onto the stage to join my mum and dad. Suddenly, the organ started playing Mendelssohn's Wedding March, the doors at the back opened and in walked Aileen on her father's arm with Rozia behind her. As soon as I saw her I was excited and exhilarate; I had waited so long and now I was going to marry the girl of my dreams. They walked down the aisle and then onto the stage for the service to begin. When Aileen lifted her veil, she looked stunningly beautiful and I thought how lucky I was to have such a wonderful girl to be my wife.

28 - Myself and Aileen after our wedding ceremony, on the steps of the Liberal Jewish Synagogue.

The service was performed in both Hebrew and English by a guest Rabbi from America, who at that time was holding services in our synagogue for the next year before emigrating to Israel. When the service was over, I broke the traditional glass and we walked to the side of the stage where the registrar was waiting for us and our witnesses to sign the wedding certificate. Most of the guests had already left for the reception and by the time we arrived most of them were sitting at the tables waiting for us to arrive. We took our places at the top table; there was the Rabbi, mum, dad, Aileen's mum and dad, then Aileen and I, Peter and Rozia. As soon we sat down the waiters started to fill the glasses with Champagne and, as there were several speeches, they kept on refilling them. As my sister doesn't drink, Peter drank hers as well his and when the time came for his speech he was so drunk that he couldn't stand up, so I had to do the speech, thanking Aileen's parents for accepting me as their son-in-law and thanking my parents for my upbringing.

29 - From left to right: my best man Peter, myself, Aileen and my sister Rozia.

After the speeches, the Rabbi said a prayer and our meal started. During the meal, several of my friends gave funny and slightly embarrassing speeches and the four-piece band that the hotel had provided, who were very good, played pleasant soft tunes for us. The hotel did a brilliant job; the table flower arrangements were beautiful, the meal was excellent and the waiters gave us a very good service. One of our wedding presents that we had from Aileen's friend Ann and her boyfriend Peter, who was a press photographer for the *Daily Express*, was that he would do our wedding pictures. He took pictures before, during and after the wedding ceremony.

The hotel also provided us to a small room adjacent to the reception room where we could change straight after the meal from our wedding clothed, for Aileen into a less formal dress and I into a lounge suit specially made for the occasion. While we were changing and the band went for a break, the waiters rearranged the tables and added several others for the guests that hadn't managed to come to the wedding ceremony but were able to come for tea and, when the band returned, to dance. The whole reception became like one of our weekend parties and many friends told us afterwards that they had so much fun at our wedding that it was the most enjoyable they had ever been to. The wedding came to an end at five thirty when the band stopped playing and the guests started departing. We stood by the door to wish everyone goodbye.

30 - From left to right: my father, my mother, Peter, myself, Aileen, Rozia, Aileen's mother Elsie and Aileen's father Mac.

Since we were not going on a honeymoon just yet, we had booked a room in the hotel for the night, as well as one for Aileen's parents, since they were not going home till the following day. Peter got us to have drinks with our friends that couldn't make the lunch – there were ten of them that included three girlfriends, and Bob Aspinall announced that he was taking all of us for dinner at Que Vadis in Soho. Aileen and I told him that we had had a long day and were very tired, but he insisted and said we won't be going there until 8.00p.m., so we had enough time to have couple hours' rest. He was so insistent that eventually we agreed to go. Peter was supposed to pick us up at eight, but it was John who picked us up instead, explaining that Peter was under no condition to drive. When we walked in to the restaurant, they gave us a big cheer that made all the other diners look around to see what was happening.

31 - The whole wedding party.

s ready | MODEL WEDS FURRIER

Fashion model Aileen McCallum after her wedding to Mr. Tim Griebel, master furrier, at St. John's Wood Synagogue, St. John's Wood.
Aileen has been chosen to represent Great Britain at an international fashion show in Bergen, Norway, later this year.

32 - Newspaper cutting about the wedding from the *Evening Standard* 5/9/1960, p.10

We had a fabulous meal, recollecting some of the silly and funny times we had done together in the past. After the meal was over and we were having our liquors and coffee, Bob wanted to take us to a night club, but both of us told him we were much too tired and all we wanted to get some sleep. We thank him for the dinner, got a taxi back to the hotel, booked an early call, went to our room and we were so tired we dumped our clothes, jumped into bed and were asleep almost immediately.

In the morning, after breakfast, I paid the rest of the bill, thanked all the staff for the marvellous job they had done. The doorman hailed us a taxi and we arrived at the flat in time to take Aileen's parents to the station for their journey home. When we entered they were both ready to leave, but before we left they commented on the wedding: how much they enjoyed themselves and how they thought how great everything had been. Her father, who had a very bad heart condition, said that he always wanted to live long enough to walk his daughter down the aisle on her wedding day, and yesterday was one of the happiest day of his life.

I drove us all to the station and, after they had boarded the train and it had departed, we drove back to our flat, had a cup of tea sit down; our longest day was over. We had known each other for four years, minus two weeks to the day when we were married, and we were married forty six years, two months and two days to the day Aileen died so suddenly.

Forty six years later, on a Sunday evening, Aileen wasn't feeling very well, and told me that she thought she was getting a cold. On Monday morning, I brought her a cup of tea as I usually did and she told me that she still felt that she had a cold and she herself felt cold, so I gave her another blanket and a hot water bottle. I told her that if she didn't feel any the better by the following morning, I would take her to the doctor. The next morning her condition hadn't improved. I phoned the doctor, who arranged for her to come right away to the surgery, which was only a mile away. She dressed quickly and we took the car.

About halfway to the surgery she started choking and collapsed in the car. I drove as quickly as I could and was there in five minutes. As I tried to get her out of the car I shouted to someone to get the doctor. I held her; she was unconscious. I was still holding her when the doctor arrived two minutes later. He looked at her, took a syringe from his bag and plunged it into her and tried to resuscitate her. An ambulance was already there, and the paramedics started attending to her all the way to St. Mary's hospital. We arrived there in a very short time where there was a trolley, two doctors and an orderly waiting to take her into the surgery. I waited whilst she was in surgery. After a while the doctor came up to me and told me that Aileen had died; they couldn't do anything, as she must have died when I was holding her at the surgery. After, they held an autopsy, which revealed that Aileen had died of a heart attack caused by clot in her heart. After her death I went into shock and depression. All I could think of was how I had lost this wonderful woman. It took eight months with counselling before I started to get used to the fact that I lost Aileen forever. I often think how happy our life has been, all the wonderful things we have seen and done during our holidays and travels, which still brings tears to my eyes, for I miss her so much and I will miss her for the rest of my life.

1961

In March, dad approached me with a proposition. He told me that he had inspected a house in Abbey Gardens in St. John's Wood, which was opposite his houses on Abbey Road and was on the market at a very reasonable price of £5,000. It had four floors and could easily be split into two maisonettes. He wasn't interested but Uncle Joe was and had asked him if I would be interested to buy it with him; I could have one half and he would rent the other. I went with dad to look over the house, and after inspecting it I found it to be in a very good condition. I phoned Uncle to make an arrangement for us to meet and discuss how we were going to buy the property. We decided we were each to put up a deposit of £1,000, the house would be bought in my name as I would be arranging the mortgage with a building society, of which he would be contributing half of all the expenses each. We arranged with our solicitor to get in touch with the vendor and his solicitor for the deeds of the house to check if everything was in order and, if it was, we would pay the deposit of £2,000, with a proviso that if I couldn't acquire a mortgage, it would be returned.

After everything was checked out to our satisfaction, I started looking for a mortgage and that's when my troubles started. In those days, the only place you could acquire a mortgage was a building society. I tried all the large ones and I received the same answer: they don't do mortgages on any property over two floors as it was considered to be commercial. Banks lent money on commercial properties, but only for 10 years and you had to have collateral, which I didn't have since I rented my flat. I was getting desperate as I did want the property. At that time my bank was Barclays in Bond Street. Although the manager, Andrew Macbeth, was a friend, he couldn't give me loan without collateral, and then I had a bit of luck. My brother in-law Peter suggested that I go and see his bank manager a Mr. Bill Hatchard, who was the bank manager at the Barclays bank at Queensberry, with whom he has use the services of the bank many times in his business. He would phone him and arrange an appointment for me and maybe Mr. Hatchard would be able to help me.

On the appointed day I met Mr. Hatchard at his bank. Straight away we seemed to take to each other and after having a pleasant chat with him, in which he asked me about my financial position and what position I held in my firm, he ordered coffee. While having our refreshments he asked me if I would be willing to open an account in his bank and if so, for how much. I told him that I could open an account for £100; would that be sufficient? His reply was that would be sufficient: he could write out my check for the £3,000 but the loan can only be for three months and the bank will have to hold the deeds of the house, which would then become the collateral. He would also speak to Mr. Macbeth, telling him that now that I have collateral, he would be able to, in three months' time, lend me the money for three months to pay off my debt. I went to see Andrew Macbeth and he was quite willing to lend me the money against my collateral, but only for three months and soon I found myself in the unique position of having two Barclays banks branches paying off my loan to each other every three months and all I had to do was pay the interest. This went on for nearly a year, with me trying to arrange a mortgage all the time, but to no avail. My Uncle got fed up waiting for us to acquire the house and decided to pull out the deal and my father decided instead to buy his share. Just before the end of the year we had an offer for the house of £8,500 and we decided to sell, as it gave each of us a profit after expenses of £1,500, which was a lot of money.

The year had started well for the firm and we had orders well after Easter; we were becoming quite well known for our workmanship and quality, and were exporting to many countries. Just before Easter, coming back from lunch, as I was walking through the entrance to the firm I was stopped by two very large gentlemen, who asked who I was and what my business was in the building. I asked them who they were and one of them showed me his warrant card. I realised they were Special Branch, but I still didn't know why they were in the building. After I explained to him that I was the manager at Witte's on the third floor they let me through and as I went up in the lift I saw there were two policemen on each floor. As I entered the firm I again was stopped by one of the two policemen and I heard Sidney shout "He is one of us!" and walked me into the workroom, explaining what this was all about.

It seemed that King Hussein of Jordan and his wife Princess Muna were our customers and had paid the firm a surprise visit. All the policemen were part of his security detail provided by the government, his own men were outside the firm. Soon after, Governor walked in to the workroom with the King and Princess Muna, walked over to my bench and introduced me to them, telling them that I would be the one making his wife garments whilst at the same time praising me on for my craftsmanship. I met the King and his wife several times when they were visiting London and for her fittings. One of the disadvantages of having them for customers was that only the Jordanian royal family could purchase garments from us as it seemed that other Jordanians were not allowed to shop at the same place as the King.

In July, Aileen and I started to plan our honeymoon. After Aileen read dozens of brochures we decided that, as we were going to Italy for three weeks, we would stay in Positano for two weeks which would be our base from which we could visit Pompeii, Capri, Herculaneum, Salerno, Sorrento, and Naples. We would be travelling to Rome by train in a sleeper carriage, arriving there in the morning, where there would be a coach waiting for us to take us for the rest of our journey to Positano. All this was arranged by our travel agent who was most helpful and gave us some more information, brochures and tips on how to get around that area. The second week of August we left London in a very comfortable sleeping train compartment, sharing it with another very pleasant couple who were travelling to Rome. There was a very good dining car, so we were alright for food and, with very few stops on the way, we were able to have a good night's sleep, arriving in Rome quite refreshed.

As promised, the coach was waiting for us and it seemed we were the last passengers. The coach was only half full and we had a choice of seats. We settled in, made ourselves comfortable for our six hour journey to Positano. The road that we travelled on was an Altostrati which Mussolini had built whilst in power, which was very similar to the Autobahn in Germany. We arrived at our hotel in Positano just after five absolutely exhausted. The hotel was a four star one with a magnificent entrance. It was situated in and cut out of the cliff face, about two hundred feet above sea level. After filling the register and giving in our passports we were shown by the Porter to our room, which was on the ground floor. When we walked in we couldn't believe our eyes; it was enormous, beautifully furnished with a huge double bed and French windows that opened onto a large patio overlooking the whole bay with Capri in the distance. We quickly unpacked, had our showers, changed into our holiday clothes and went to the hotel desk to find out a bit more about the place. The manager, who spoke excellent English, explained that with Positano being a very small town where artists come to paint, there are several galleries where they sell their paintings; otherwise tourist only come mostly to visit Capri and Pompeii. He then gave us the details about the beach and explained that there were two ways to reach it. From the hotel there were 247 steps to the beach or, walking right round by road, a distance of about a mile. He then gave us what other facilities were available, the times of the meals and informed us that we would be sharing our table with an American couple who were the only couple in the hotel that spoke English and, if we wished, we could have our breakfast served on our terrace with no extra charge, to which we readily accepted.

In the evening, when we walked into the dining room the waiter showed us to our table where the American couple slightly older than us were already sitting enjoying their drink. We introduced ourselves – I think their names were Bob and Judy – we sat down and the waiter took our orders for our meals. We started chatting and during the meal we found out that they had arrived three days before us and they had been relaxing for a few days before touring around the area. While having our coffee in the lounge we discovered that they also wanted to visit the same places that we did. Bob told us that they had hired a car for the week and as we both wanted to go to the same sites, we could join them touring and share the cost of petrol. Aileen and I looked at each other and we both said "yes". I offered to pay my share towards the hire, but Bob absolutely refused. I thought how lucky we were to meet such a nice couple and not have to worry about transport to the sites.

In the morning we took the steps down to the beach. They zigzagged down and at each turn there were little shops that had been cut out from the cliff selling homemade cakes, drinks, children beach toys and souvenirs. We met our new friends who were there before us and started planning which sites we would visit first whilst relaxing on the beach. We decided that we would first do a day tour of Sorrento and the countryside around it, which was not far from Positano, then the following day do the same visiting Salerno. Sorrento was a lovely small town with a very small, manmade beach. We wondered around the top of the cliff where there were little tourist shops, restaurants and coffee bars where we had our lunch and other refreshments, enjoying the view across the bay and the Isle of Capri. The next day, driving to Salerno it was totally different. The countryside was very dry and parched and consisted mainly of small farms. We saw a lot of very small, primitive houses with women and many children who looked extremely poor. We also saw quite a few priests wandering the farms and when we returned to the hotel we asked our waiter why there were so many priests around the area. He explained that they were very disliked and resented, but the people in the area were very religious and superstitious, so the priests could go around the farms demanding the best produce for the church, for which they never pay, and the farmers would give them what they wanted as they did not want any bad fortune.

Our next trip was to Capri. There was a ferry from Positano leaving four times a day, so we took the early one to be able to have plenty of time to explore the island. The ferry boat was very small and I was relieved that the sea was very calm as I am a terrible sailor and easily get seasick. The island was not very large but very beautiful with colourful flowers beds everywhere. We had information and maps of the island so we knew where the places were that we wanted to visit, of which there were very few. Our first visit was to be the blue lagoon. On the quayside there were several boatmen who had rowing boats and we hired one to take us there. Although the place was not a great distance away it was a slow journey with only one man rowing, but it was well worth it being rowed gently on this beautiful blue sea.

When we got off, the boatman pointed to a cave, telling us that was the blue lagoon. From a distance it looked very small, but when we arrived we saw there was a large entrance to the cave. The boatman rowed us straight into it and then we realized why everyone tells you to see the blue lagoon. The cave had a very large ceiling, being dark makes the water look a deep purple colour. And the sun shining onto the water through the large entrance make it shimmer on to the walls making the whole place magical. We spent a little time there taking photos of the lagoon before being rowed back to the quayside.

When we started exploring the island we found that there were a lot more people on the island that we thought, most of them were British all queuing to take pictures of Gracie Fields' house, a very popular pre-war English singer and film actress. One of the men gave us some advice not to eat, drink or buy anything near the house as everything there was twice the price as elsewhere on the island. We found out afterwards that he was right. After we had our lunch, we wandered around the island which was very beautiful with seats at different points for us to admire the opposing coastline. We visited the tourist shops, which we found very annoying as practically any object in every shop that you lifted to inspect played Graces Fields' hit song (*Isle of Capri*).

We caught the early ferry to have our tea in the hotel and discussed our trip, all of us saying that although the place was very beautiful we wouldn't be able to stand listening to the Gracie Fields song again. The following day we decided to visit Naples. We allowed ourselves plenty of time as it was a large town to explore, but we were very disappointed. Although it is a major town in the area, we found most places were very poor, very dirty and tired looking, although we visited a couple of very good museums with fantastic collections of ancient artefacts. Also there were very elegant shopping areas near the rest of the town which we found of very little interest; maybe we should have hired a guide.

The last two days that we spent with our American friends was first to visit Herculaneum and the following day Pompeii. Both places were in a sense very similar, having both been excavated from the volcanic ash, Pompeii being the most interesting. It was much larger with many more buildings. Thereafter we parked the car by the entrance and, after buying our tickets, entered. There were guides available taking small groups of people around the town. In those days there were no restrictions as to where you could walk or how close you could inspect inside the houses; the only place the ladies were not allowed was the brothel where they had ancient pictures of couples having sex in different positions. After our tour finished we wandered around the town for a while before collecting our car. While walking back, I started felling a queasy. At first I thought it was the heat, as it was very hot, but it couldn't have been as I always had my hat and drunk a lot of water, remembering my days in the desert. I stopped, leaning on a wall as I felt a bit dizzy while Aileen and our friends walked on, not realizing that I had stopped and the next thing I remember lying on the grassy verge with three worried faces looking down on me, Bob washing my face with a damp handkerchief. With help I managed to get up and walk the rest of the way to the entrance where there was also a bar/restaurant. My stomach was rumbling and I only just made it to the toilet, having to pay few liras for a sheet of toilet paper to a woman responsible for the toilets. I then realized that I had food poisoning from a salad that I had eaten the day before. When I rejoined our party, who were ordering their lunch, I ordered nothing to eat accept a large bottle of soda water. I drunk several glasses of soda water which helped a bit, but I was still going to the toilet every ten minutes, having to pay for toilet paper each time. I was so fed up having to pay each time that the next time I went I picked up one of the rolls of toilet paper, gave the woman a 500 lira note and told her "no more charge". After sitting in the bar for a couple of hours and me having drunk 2 litres of soda water, which seemed to settled my stomach, we decided that we could return to our hotel where I always carried medication for stomach upset.

Twenty-five years later, while on a cruise, our ship stopped at Naples and we decided to visit Pompeii again. It was a great disappointment; there were large numbers of tourists from different nationalities with their own guides, especially Japanese and German, all eager to go through the entrance. Once we were through the gate we found the place packed with many more people that made it very difficult to walk in the narrow streets without bumping into other people. The houses were barred with warning signs telling us not to enter for safety reasons and, although they had a much larger museum with many more artefacts on display than before, there was none of the fun of exploring the town and it all felt very clinical.

Pompeii was the last trip we did with our friends as they were leaving early Sunday morning for home and they had to pack and do some last minutes shopping. We decided that as we were going to Rome, where would have to do a lot of walking, we would spend the rest of our time wandering around Positano and lazing around on the beach, which we did.

Early on Saturday morning we left for Rome, the town which we had already read several books on, so we were eager to see all the ancient sites. The journey would take about six to seven hours with a break of two hours at Mount Casino for the driver to have a rest and for our group to visit the monastery there, which had been totally destroyed during the war, as well as the Polish war cemetery where the Polish battalions suffered some of their biggest casualties when they tried to break through the German defences. We arrived at Mount Casino at midday. The monastery was situated on top of the mountain. We had to drive up the mountain on a reasonably good road and when we reached the coach park, there were quite a few coaches there, some Italian but most from other European countries. We were told by our guide that a lot of the people there were pilgrims as it seemed that when the monastery was flattened by bombing during the war the only thing that survived damage was a statue of Christ that was situated in front the monastery, which was considered a miracle and started a flood of pilgrims.

The guide gave us a small lecture about the monastery, telling us that after the war they found the original building plans and the structure that we were looking at had been completely rebuilt exactly as it was before being destroyed. Inside was still a long way from being finished and it was also being restored to the original plans. Then the guide took us inside and although the place was huge, with the scaffolding and the amount of pilgrims and tourists being there it was most difficult to wander around. One side was practically finished with its frescos decorated and the columns and ceiling glittering. The guide explained that they were gilded with real gold which was extremely expensive. We wandered around a bit longer, but being so crowded, hot and stuffy we decided to leave, look at the fantastic view from the top and wait for the rest of our group so we could all visit the Polish cemetery which was not far away in a valley at the foot of the monastery.

When the rest of our party joined us we drove down to the cemetery, which was quite large; I believe there were some 3,000 graves all beautifully kept. It was sad place but I was interested as there were a few graves with a Star of David. I visited them all, wondering if there was anyone buried there that I knew from my home town. After a while we joined our coach and drove to have some lunch and then on to Rome, where we arrived at 5p.m. in time to have some tea. Our hotel in Rome was situated just out of the centre of the town, with easy access to the places we wished to visit. Our tour representative welcomed us, introduced our tour guide that would be guiding us for the next five days to the major sites and told us the times of our meeting in the morning. She also gave us a map of Rome marked out with the important archaeological sites and how to get there, general information of meal times and what facilities the hotel had to offers.

The room that was allocated to us was comfortable but a bit noisy as it overlooked a main road, which we didn't mind as we enjoyed watching the locals going about their business. The following morning we all assembled outside the hotel where our coach was parked and our guide Marco was waiting for us. Our first tour was to be around the Vatican. The first place we visited was St Peter's Church which was very impressive; after we entered, Marco took us around explaining all the aspects of the church. Then we left for the Pope's residence and after a short tour we departed for the Sistine Chapel, which was to be the highlight of our tour, and the library through which you had to walk to reach the chapel. The library was very long with magnificent painted ceiling, all the walls lined with bookcases holding thousands of beautiful leather bound manuscripts. From there we entered the chapel, which took your breath away with the wonderful painted ceiling and the walls, one which had the famous fresco of the last supper. I took many photos of the ceilings as at that time there were no restrictions on taking pictures. In 2012, I was in Rome and I wanted to visit the same places again but when I arrived at the chapel you could hardly walk around as there were so many tours and people queuing, many souvenir stalls and individual sellers. I was informed by one of the guides that it would take two to three hours to enter, so we gave up.

We did several other tours with Marco to the Colosseum, where we were able to wander all over the place, the site of old Rome to see the ruins of the senate house and the site of Circus Maximus. The last couple days we wandered about, looking at some other places of interest that were mentioned in the guide book, did some shopping and on Friday we prepared for our long journey back to London. We were back home Saturday at noon.

1962

This was the second best and most eventful year of my life. Just after Easter we went out for dinner with our neighbours and great friends René and George to our favourite Turkish restaurant. During the meal we were discussing holidays. We had been on holiday with them several times before and the holidays had always been very successful. George was telling me that he had just bought a low mileage Hummer Super Snipe car and he and René were thinking of touring southern Europe, and if we were interested we should join them. I asked him what sort of tour he intended to do. He told me that they were intending to drive all the way to Athens.

Greece was one of the places that we always wanted to visit and we accepted the invitation, subject to what dates would be suitable to all of us. I suggested that for us the best time would be the beginning of June, also it would be the best time to travel before the weather in that part of Europe gets unbearably hot. George said that time of year would be alright for them for they were thinking of similar dates and we decided to leave London on the first Saturday in June.

After we had our meal we returned to our friend's flat for coffee to discuss further our holidays. We decided, like on our previous holidays, we would split all our expenses in half by keeping a little book where everyone noted their spending and at the end of the holiday we worked out who owed whom money. George produced some maps that he had picked up at the travel agents of the places we would travel through and we started to discuss the best way to travel and which route to take. George suggested that that we send the car and our luggage by train and ferry to Cologne which we could load the night before arriving there next day at 3.30p.m. and we could catch early morning ferry to Cologne arriving there at 12.45p.m. saving us time loading and unloading the car and giving us a chance to have lunch before picking up the car. From Cologne we would pick up the Autobahn to Munich where we would spend the night and then to Salzburg in Austria. The next day we would cross the border of Austria at Villach into Yugoslavia to Zagreb and stay the night there, then the following day Belgrade where we would stay two days to have a rest and have a chance to explore the area. The last town that we would stay the night in Yugoslavia would be Skopje from where we would cross into Greece and then drive on to Athens.

When we returned to our flat we were both excited at the prospect of driving to Greece. When the time came near our departure, of course, Aileen and René – who were great friends who people often took for mother and daughter, both being redheads – got busy with what clothes and shoes to take while George and I concentrated on making sure that we had bottles of water, a spare bottle of oil and a Jerry can of petrol as we had been advised to take these things as in Yugoslavia sometimes it was difficult to acquire petrol and oil.

On Friday night we drove the car to I think it was Victoria Station to load it with our luggage on to the train, which was a lengthy business, before getting home for an early night to be ready in the morning for our journey to Cologne. In the morning, we caught the boat train; it was a pleasant journey, especially crossing the Channel, which was very calm. Having some time to wait before we could pick up our car and being hungry we made our way to a nearby restaurant for our lunch. George, René and Aileen have never been to Germany before so from my previous experience I advised them not to order too much food. While having our drinks we studied the menu and we ordered pork escallops with potatoes and sauerkraut. After short while the waiter appeared with a covered dish and when he took the cover off there were four escallops and substantial amount of sauerkraut and potatoes. They started to help themselves to the food but I told them to wait a minute as the waiter came bearing three more identical dishes. They looked at them at amusements and I explained that the portions they serve in Germany are far larger that we get in England. We were only able to eat half of our meal and, after coffee, we departed to the railway station pick up our car which was waiting for us in a huge car park.

After presenting our documentation and receiving information where to pick up the autobahn we were off to Munich. George and I would share the driving and we had a strict rule from previous holidays that no matter where we were we changed over. The distance to Munich was about 270 miles and, although it is quite a long journey, travelling on the Autobahn which has no speed limit, we managed to do it in less than six hours. Having been in Munich before when visiting my uncle, we drove to the hotel where I used to stay and acquired four rooms and dinner for us in the hotel.

The next morning, after breakfast, we paid our bill and filled up with petrol at the nearest garage and proceeded on our journey to Austrian border on to Salzburg and then Villach where we would cross into Yugoslavia and on to Zagreb. The journey was very enjoyable as we were travelling through mountains so the view was magnificent, and the traffic was light going to the border. Once we arrived there we quickly were passed through the Austrian border but on the Yugoslav side we had a bit of a hold up as the border officials insisted on inspecting all documents and vehicles thoroughly. After about forty minutes we were through on the way to Zagreb.

The change in driving in Yugoslavia was drastically different. Although the road was good and at first there was some traffic, it soon thinned out and after about 25 miles you were lucky to see four or six vehicles an hour. As we proceeded further we were lucky to see one or two an hour, and if the vehicle coming towards us had a British number plate we all waved to each other and stopped to exchange information. Driving through by each small town or village there mounds of watermelons and children trying to sell you wooden carved objects. The prices were ridiculously cheap; Aileen and I bought four large wooden sets of salt and pepper grinders as presents for our families and a very large watermelon for which I paid the princely sum of fifty pence. As we were traveling we found out that everything was extremely cheap compared to prices in England.

On our way we stopped for lunch at a fish restaurant. Inside they had a huge tank with live fish in it, where you could choose your fish and it would be cooked and served to you with vegetables, bread, mineral water or wine. For sweet they had several types of cake with thick cream and finished the meal with coffee. We were a bit surprised that the table setting had only a quarter of a paper serviette for each person, and we soon discovered that specified what class of restaurant it was: quarter was third class, half was second, and a whole one was first. Being a communist country, it seemed that certain goods were extremely short and were rationed. The whole bill for the four of us with the tip came to just over £4. We proceeded on our journey but now every time we saw a petrol station we stopped to top up with petrol, as the last couple stops they either didn't have petrol or the pumps were not working due to a power cut, which was not an unusual occurrence.

The temperature was getting very hot and without an air conditioner in the car it was becoming uncomfortable. By the time we reached Zagreb at 5p.m. it was about 90 degrees. We stopped at the tourist office to enquire about hotels and we were informed that there were no decent hotel rooms available as the Communist party was having a big conference in town and all the first and second class hotels were booked, but he suggested that on the outskirts of the town there was a huge privately-owned villa which had been converted into a hotel. After phoning to see if there were two double rooms available, he told us to go there straight away before the rooms went, gave us directions on how to get there and we arrived at the villa early evening. The villa was very large and looked very luxurious; it had thirty-five rooms with a huge garden and small woods nearby. We found out later that before the war it belonged to an extremely wealthy family and after the war it was bought by another family who turned it into a hotel. We booked in for two nights on a half-board basis and then we were shown our rooms which were on the first floor, very large and furnished in semi-antique furniture, but very comfortable.

As we were unpacking, René came into our room and said: "Tim, our central heating is on and the radiators are boiling. Do you know how to turn them off?" I went into their room and tried to turn their valves off, but to no avail. I thought that this was ridiculous, so I went down to the reception to complain. The manager was most apologetic, explaining that they had been waiting two years for a new pump for the central heating, which had to be ordered from the ministry in Belgrade and they were still waiting for it to arrive, but he would get their maintenance man to fix it. True to his word, after little banging the radiators were cold.

After unpacking having had a shower and a rest, we went to the open air restaurant which was situated on one side of the villa. It had a huge barbeque range and all the meat dishes were cooked on it. The meal was fantastic and with the gypsy band playing it made for a wonderful evening. We returned to our rooms after dinner as we were very tired and went quickly to sleep; we had separate single beds as they didn't have any double beds available. At about three o'clock I suddenly woke up gasping, completely dehydrated, feeling as if I was being boiled. Being half asleep, I didn't know what had happened then I realized that my bed was against the central heating radiator which had suddenly come on and was baking hot. On the nearby table there was a jug of water and some bottles of water, I grabbed and opened one of the bottles and started drinking and in my other hand I held the jug, pouring the water over my head. Aileen woke up to see this apparition sitting on the edge of the bed pouring water over its head and asked what was wrong. When I told her about the radiator she went into hysterical laughter, but after she had got it out of her system she did go into the bathroom, got a towel and began to wipe me down.

At that time of night there was nothing I could do about the radiator, but in the room we had a very large open window under which Aileen's bed was situated, so I moved my bed next to hers. When we had gotten married, Aileen and I had discussed having a family; we both wanted children, but not straight away, so we decided that when Aileen felt that she was ready for children we would try. As we couldn't get to sleep we were lying there chatting about the holiday, but it soon became one of the momentous nights to remember when suddenly, out of the blue, Aileen turned around to me kissed me and said: "darling you know when we discussed having children that we wouldn't try until I was ready, well I think I am ready now." I was startled and overjoyed and that was the night my daughter, Mila, was conceived.

In the morning, after having some breakfast, I went to see the manager to complain about the heating. He was most apologetic and told me that he will make sure that all the central will be switched off and as a gesture of good will he would reduce the price of our room. After breakfast we decided to visit the town to have a look around and have our lunch there. There were very few things to buy, mainly local produce of very little interest to us. The whole place was very rundown and the locals seemed to be very poor, but the restaurant where we had our lunch was excellent. We returned to our hotel to spend our afternoon in the hotel's beautiful garden, and before dinner we made ready for our journey the following day.

The following morning we settled up with the hotel and with the reduction it came to £22, which was ridiculously cheap, and then we were off to Belgrade. The journey to Belgrade was a pleasure to drive as it was very quick with no traffic on the road and we arrived there just before lunch. We drove to the best hotel in town, a very modern-built post-war construction, but the reception told us there were no rooms available as the Communist party, again, had a big party conference, but they advised us to try another one nearby, a five star hotel built before the war which had a very good reputation.

When we entered this other hotel, the reception entrance was amazing; it was all in an art deco style with huge armchairs everywhere. The reception told us they had two rooms available with a bath and shower, so we booked in and when they took us with our luggage to our rooms and opened the door it was a lounge furnished with settees, easy chairs and coffee tables all in red Moroccan leather, but no bed. I asked the porter where the bed was, and he opened another door to another very large room, beautifully furnished with a huge double bed and he pointed to another door and informed us that in there was the bathroom. After he left we started to unpack and taking my wash things into the bathroom I couldn't believe what I was seeing: it was very large with the largest bath I've ever seen, 3' tall and 6' long. The shower was also big, with the shower head about 6" across. I climbed into the bath laid in it and called Aileen and when she entered, she couldn't see me and asked where I was. I sat up and she jumped, startled. We had a good laugh and I said: "Darling, we have been given a suite that god knows how much it is going to cost, but we are going to enjoy it for this is real luxury."

When we had showered we went to reception to join René and George, who informed us that they had similar rooms, so I went to the reception desk to inquire the price of our rooms. I had a big surprise; the price was £5 per person per night including breakfast, which could be served if we wished in our rooms. I asked the concierge if he could recommend a good restaurant where we could have our evening meal; he told me there are several nearby, but if you want a good meal and a pleasant evening, they had a very good restaurant on the roof garden with entertainment. If we were interested we could book a table with him, but should do it as soon as possible as it gets booked up very quickly. We had a little conference with George and René and they thought we should book it, which we did.

When the time came for our evening meal, we took the lift to the roof garden and when we entered it was stunning like the rest of the hotel. The garden was handsomely arranged with banks of flowers and young palm trees all around the roof, the tables were set up as good as any five star hotel in London with linen table cloths, napkins and silver-plated cutlery. On one side there was a stage where there was an orchestra already playing gypsy melodies, the other side was laid out for where the food would be prepared before being served and in the middle a small dance floor. We were shown to our table which was in a prominent position to be able to see the cabaret and then the waiter produced the wine and food menu, which was quite impressive. We gave our order for our food and wine, a bottle of white and red, and asked the waiter to serve the wine first so that we could have a drink while waiting for our food. Shortly our food arrived and, although we had different dishes, we all commented that they were some of the best we ever had.

During the meal the cabaret started, which consisted of a girl singing popular songs in the country and then came a dancing group who did very fast and exciting dances to Gypsy music. All in all it was a most enjoyable evening. When I received the bill I was in for another surprise, as the whole bill for the four of us including wine, other drinks and a tip came to £11.50. When we returned to our rooms we went straight to bed as we had all had slightly too much to drink. In the morning during breakfast we discussed whether to book same table for our evening dinner that night, but decided that as we were leaving very early the following morning we will have a leisurely day walking around Belgrade, which wasn't all that interesting and in places pretty drab. We had a reasonable lunch, visited a museum which was very interesting. We soon returned to our hotel, did our packing and prepared for our journey to Skopje.

When we left Belgrade the roads were still clear of traffic but the countryside was changing; whereas in the north most of the population was catholic, so we saw many churches and the architecture of the houses was very westernised, as we travelled further south we started seeing mosques and some of the buildings in a more eastern style, many Muslim women covered up carrying their babies bundled in thick blankets and the men wearing Muslim head coverings. We also came across many small bands of Gypsies traveling in their caravans. When we were fifteen miles from Skopje, we realised why we had seen so many gypsy bands, as about three miles behind hedges there were thousands of gypsies in different clan groups in their colourful cultural costumes. We parked behind some other cars, most with foreign registration plates, and asked one gentleman what was the occasion of this gathering. He explained that this was the place where once a year all gypsies from central and eastern Europe have a festival where they exchange news of their travels, news of relatives that couldn't come and where on their travels were the best places to stage their caravans, and in the evening they have big parties with entertainment of music and dancing, to which many locals come to watch.

We stayed for a while watching them practicing their music and dancing and then carried on with our journey to Skopje. The town seemed to be split by the river into two halves, one half Christian with several churches the other side Muslim with their mosques, all connected by the six-hundred-year-old bridge. Large part of the town seemed to be very old, with many parts dating back to the Middle Ages, but another sizeable part of the town had been destroyed during the civil war, which was after WWII, but of course the houses couldn't be replaced and I've been told that the replacements built since are in an ugly modern style and the town has lost its charm. Originally, we were only going to spend a short time there but we found the place so very interesting, especially when we found out that we had arrived on their main once-a-week market day and all of us wanted to go to it, so we found a sort of B&B which was not the most luxurious.

In the morning we left for Athens. As we neared the border the traffic increased mainly from Greece and we found out that there was a bit of smuggling going on, as certain goods couldn't be obtained in Yugoslavia were driven over the border from Greece. Just before we crossed the border in the small town I found heaven: it had one of the largest pastry and Baklava coffee houses and I told our party we must take a Coffee break for I must try the pastries. Luckily the others were all in agreement; we entered the place and were hit with the smell of freshly baked pastries. We ordered our coffees, of which they had several varieties and then the pastries. Aileen, René and George were not keen on very sweet pastries, but I ordered my Baklava and when it was served it was 4 ½" by 4 ½", the largest I'd ever eaten and was a fantastic flavour and texture. While eating it they asked me, "How can you eat such sweet cake in the morning?" My answer was "with greatest of pleasure."

We proceeded on with our journey into Greece, travelling through Salonika to the sea coast where we would stop for lunch before carrying on to Athens. Once we crossed the border the contrast between the two countries was immense: there was much more traffic, with congestion at some points, people were much better dressed, and the shops were full of goods to buy; no wonder there was so much smuggling going on. We travelled through some beautiful Greek countryside with large olive groves, some cherry orchards and hazelnut bushes. When we reached the coast we found a good fish restaurant near the beach to have lunch. We all ordered freshly grilled trout with vegetables, fizzy water and delicious bread. While waiting for our meal, Aileen borrowed George's car keys, rushed to the car, got her travelling case out, went inside the car and changed into her swimming costume, before running to the beach and jumped into the sea and had a ten minutes swim, dried herself off and came back to our table just as our lunch was being served. George asked why she had gone for a swim. She explained that she was very hot she hadn't swum in the Adriatic Sea before and didn't know if she would get the chance when we were in Athens. I remembered that Aileen had a thing about swimming in different seas or lakes to see what they were like.

We all enjoyed our meal and for sweet I had another Baklava and when came to paying the bill the price was similar to what we paid in Yugoslavia. After lunch, we continued our journey to Athens, arriving there late in the afternoon. We drove to the tourist office for hotel information and local maps of the area. We didn't want to stay in a five star hotel so they recommended a four star hotel which was situated in the centre of Athens next to the liberty, which had been built in the ancient classical style. They kindly found out if the hotel had rooms available for us and for a small fee they booked them. When we arrived at the hotel the porter took our luggage and another told George that, for a minimal sum, the car could be parked overnight in the hotel's secure garage and in the morning it would parked for us outside the hotel with the keys with the front desk clerk. George accepted the offer. We went to our rooms which were well appointed and, after showering, resting and changing, we had a snack in the hotel bar and then went to bed.

The next morning, as promised, our car was parked outside the hotel. During breakfast we decided that the next couple days we would spend relaxing on the Athens beach as we'd had a long journey and were still very tired. After breakfast we collected our swimwear and drove to the beach. In Athens, no matter where you drove, you could see the Acropolis and Aileen and I were itching to explore it. It was very hot, the temperature was around 85-87°F and it was a pleasure to get to the beach where there was a cool breeze blowing from the sea. The beach was not very large, with part of it having a brush roof under which you could lay on mats which were supplied, as well as changing lockers for which you had to pay a small sum for the use of. We spent a very enjoyable day there with swimming, ice-cream and snacks, before returning to our hotel. As usual, I asked the concierge where the best place to have a good meal and entertainment and he suggested the roof restaurant at the George V Hotel, at which they kindly booked a table for the four of us.

In the evening, we took a taxi to the hotel for our meal; I didn't want us to take the car as we would probably have a few drinks with our meal and the drivers in Athens were not the safest ones, as they seemed to race each other to the traffic lights and if the lights turned were red they jammed their brakes to stop. We could hear their brakes screeching all night as there were traffic light outside our hotel. When we arrived at restaurant, the layout was similar to the one in Belgrade, the only difference being the cuisine was Greek, which used a lot of Feta cheese and flavoured everything with mint. But the great disappointment was the wine: everyone suggested that we should try the Greek wine Retsina so we ordered a bottle. When the waiter filled our glasses we and took a sip of it we all spat it out for it was one of the worst tasting wines we had ever drunk; it must be an acquired taste as how anyone can enjoy a wine tasting of strong resin I don't know, but the Greeks seemed to like it. One thing which made the evening was the view. The hotel where we were dinning was situated not far away and just below the Acropolis which was lit up with many spotlights, giving it a brilliant white colour. While eating we could gaze in wonder on this magnificent, perfect structure, and we all decided that next morning instead of going to the beach we must go and see it!

In the morning, before going for our breakfast, we inquired with the Concierge as to whether it was not too late to book a tour to see the Acropolis and the different sites around Athens. His reply was no, as the firm that runs the tours phones the hotels every morning. He could book us in with the firm and the coach would pick us up from the hotel at 10 o'clock, the tour lasting about 5 hours. We had a small discussion and decided to book. After breakfast we got ourselves ready for our tour and waited in the foyer with several other hotel guests for the coach, which arrived on time. It seemed that we were the last party to be picked up and before continuing on our tour, our guide proceeded to outline how we were going to spend our time. First, we would be visiting the Acropolis where he would give us a little lecture and a little booklet about the Acropolis and the temple nearby, then, being a large area, we will have an hour and a half to wander around the place. We then drove to the Acropolis, which was only a short distance away and when we disembarked the coach, the guide gave us our little booklet and told us if we had any questions he would be sitting on a large block of stone at the foot of the Acropolis, but we must be back at coach by 12.30p.m. to drive to Piraeus for lunch and then to Corinth to see the canal.

We then left him and started exploring the place; the area the Acropolis occupies is much larger than it looks and when one walks up the steps the interior is huge. You can only admire the people that built it so many years before with its huge columns and the enormous roof. It lets your mind imagine what sort of effect it would have had on the population when they looked at it when it was first built. The temple just across from the Acropolis is just as impressive with its six statues of gowned women holding up the roof. Unfortunately at that time we couldn't enter the interior as the roof was being repaired and was unsafe for the public to enter. Aileen and I visited Athens about twenty years later and it was horrible. It was impossible to wander around with the hordes of people from different tourist parties all jostling to take photographs, most of the parts of the Acropolis were roped off and there were only certain parts inside that you could walk with tapes tied around the columns marking a path.

33 - Aileen in front of the Acropolis.

After we had all met up at the coach we were taken on a short journey to Piraeus, which is Greece's major port, where the driver drove us to the seafront for our lunch, with the courier pointing out some fish restaurants that we ought to try for their specialities. We tried one of the fish restaurants where they served us a marvellous fish meal, but we never discovered what was the fish we ate, as neither the waiter nor anyone else in the restaurant knew the English name for it. We had some time spare so we had a little wander along the seafront watching the small fishing boats coming in and departing, most of them painted blue with the evil eye painted on their bows; it made a lovely sight, especially with a beautiful blue sky shining above us.

The last part of our tour was to visit Corinth. Aileen and I had read the history story about the canal but had never seen even a picture of it so when we arrived there the driver stopped a short distance from the bridge and when we disembarked the guide told us to walk across the bridge and when we get halfway across look down and we would see the canal beneath it. We all started to walk across and when we looked down it took our breath away. The canal is perfectly straight, the sides which were 700' high were sloping down to the water at a very sharp angle and were also perfectly straight. At that time there was a small freighter going through the canal and looking down at it looked like the boat that I played with in my bath when I was a boy. I marvelled at the craftsmanship that had built such a perfect canal with the tools and instruments that were available to them at that time. On the way back the guide took us on a short tour of Athens showing us several places that we ought to visit which we did on our own in our car.

The last two days we visited two of the nearby islands by taking the ferry from Piraeus and then our holiday was over. We left Athens on the Friday after lunch to travel to the Yugoslav border where on the Yugoslavian side there was a motel where we were going to spend the night. It was a recently built place all in wood. We asked the manager if they served meals and if they had either shower or bath facilities in the rooms. He told us that they served evening meals and there were washing facilities in the rooms, but the two showers for us to use were in a communal room next to our rooms. As we were staying one night we decided to book in and order our evening meal. We went into our rooms which were plainly furnished but comfortable with a beautiful view of nearby mountains in the distance. When Aileen and Renée came back from having their shower, she told me that the water in the shower was not to warm but sufficiently pleasant so George and I went to have our shower. We had just lathered ourselves with soap when the water stopped. We waited under the shower for about ten minutes when it came back absolutely freezing. I quickly washed of the soap, dried myself went into our room and told Aileen what had happened and she laughed, thinking that it was extremely funny. I dressed quickly as I wanted to have a word with the manager to find out what happened to the shower. When I went into the foyer the was no one at the desk so I went outside to sit and have a smoke and warm myself in the sum when I noticed that there was a well at side of the motel with a queue of people from young children to elderly folks all holding some sort of container to carry water from the well to the back of the motel.

Eventually, when the manager was back at the reception I told him about my cold shower and I also asked him about the people that carrying the containers of water. He was most apologetic about it all and explained that all the water used in the motel came from the well. Until a year ago it was pumped directly to their storage tanks but then the pump broke and ever since they have been waiting for a new pump, so when they have guests, they have to get anyone that is available to fill the tanks and it takes an hour to warm the water. We left the motel very early the following morning as we had only allowed ourselves two days to catch the early evening car ferry at Calais to Dover from our departure from the Greek border. We worked out that, as there was so little traffic in Yugoslavia and on the autobahn in Germany, and with two of us driving, if we stopped for the night in Heidelberg we could easily do it, which we did and arrived home Sunday evening around 8 o'clock.

Six weeks later, Aileen informed me that she had seen the doctor for a check-up, where she had been told that she was pregnant. We informed our families, who were delighted. As soon as I could I made an appointment at the council housing department to see if I could acquire a bigger flat. The housing manager was the same one that I had dealt with before, who was most helpful, who told me that there were always tenants moving out and as soon as one of the flats became available he would send me the details and viewing times. Aileen and I discussed that before the baby arrived she ought to learn to drive as she would need a car to get about with the baby; I would book for her some driving lessons to which she agreed. At that time I didn't possessed a car as I found having one unnecessary, living next to a tube station, so we discussed what sort of car would suit her and eventually, after looking at several cars, decided on a Mini.

Aileen was still working for her firm as a model. She worked there until she was seven months pregnant and only managed one driving lesson a week, so I thought I would give her a surprise. I spoke to my brother-in-law, Peter, who knew the manager of a garage in Poland Street and he was sure we could get a good deal from him. On Saturday morning, Peter and I went to see him, and he informed us that he had only one red Mini Morris left in stock and, after checking it over and taking it for a test drive, I thought it was a marvellous little car. I asked him what the price was as I wanted to purchase it. He looked at Peter and said: "As you are his brother-in-law, I can give you a 10% discount, so the price is £465. We will do all the paper work, temporary insurance and tax disc, for which there will be an extra charge and you can pick the car up in two hours' time." Peter and I went for a wander around the market and when we returned to the garage, the car was ready. I drove Peter home and then to our flat where I parked it right outside the building.

When I entered our flat, Aileen was already waiting for me for as usual on Saturday; we used to go to my parents for lunch and as we exited our flat I said to Aileen: "Look, there is a red Mini parked here, let's have a look at it." She looked all around and I asked her whether she thought it would a suitable car for her. She told me she loved it so I took the car keys from my pocket gave them to her, "Have a look inside; I bought the car as a surprise for you this morning." She gave a big shout of joy, with people turning around wondering what the noise was all about and then we drove to mum's for lunch and to show off her new car. Aileen started having her driving lessons in her own car, but when she was three months pregnant her doctor advised her after she had some more tests that it would be advisable for her to stop driving. After Mila was born, she decided that she wasn't comfortable driving and never drove again.

I received some correspondence from the housing department informing me that in two months' time there would be a two bedroom flat available and we would be told when we could inspect it. We were also given the details of our new rent and the new deposit. I started thinking that perhaps we ought to think about buying a house. I asked Aileen what she thought of the idea, explaining that I had enough money from my job at the time, plus the money I had made from the sale of the house that I owned with my father, to put a deposit on a house and with what we would be paying in the new rent it would cover the mortgage. She asked me where I was thinking of buying. I said that we couldn't afford to buy one in St. John's Wood, but somewhere nearby that was less expensive. I told her that, with a house, if anything happened to me, she would have some sort of security. After having a little thought Aileen agreed that perhaps it was a good idea and acquired brochures from several local estate agents and used our weekends to inspect different properties.

After looking at around eighteen properties, all of which we rejected for one reason or another, we were in despair and were thinking of giving up the idea of owning a house. I couldn't afford a four bedroom house and with most three bedroom houses, the rooms were too small, the place was too far away from local facilities and in an area that we didn't wish to live. Then one morning, in the post there was brochure from a local estate agent and inside it there was on offer a property in West Hampstead in our price range, which after looking on the map would be in an ideal place for us; it was right in the middle of my sister's and dad's houses. I told Aileen that I would go and have a look at it and if it was any good we can inspect together it later. I phoned the estate agent and he agreed for me to borrow the keys allowing me to inspect the property.

When I arrived at the address, I found a four storey building at the end of a Victorian terrace, with a driveway space large enough to park a car. It was a quiet street but dilapidated as none of the houses looked like they had been decorated since before the war. Before I entered I was lucky to meet the lady who owned the house next door and gave me some information about the area and the property. In the street most of the houses were bedsits there were only five or six families that occupied one house completely. The one that I was inspecting hadn't been lived in for the past year, as the previous winter the boiler on the first floor had burst, flooding the two floors and as that time there wasn't any one living on these floors, the water had poured in for a whole day until someone notice it was flooding the basement.

Since then, it had been left to dry out and to get rid of the smell caused by the damp.

I entered the house through the front door; it smelt a musty as it hadn't had any heating for a year, but it wasn't too bad. I went upstairs and although structurally it was quite sound, the floors and the decoration were in very bad condition and I didn't think that it had been decorated since before the war. I inspected the ground floor and the basement, which was in similar condition; the back room, which must have been the worst flooded and last to dry out, was covered in green dry algae. In the basement there was a back door that lead to a small patio and steps to a small garden. Altogether the house had eleven rooms and two bathrooms. The main rooms were 16'x 16'and the small ones 12'x15'. When I returned home, I told Aileen all about the house, saying that I knew it was not quite the house what we were thinking of, but I wanted her to see it before we decided as it has a lot of possibilities.

When we drove back to the house and before we entered, I warned Aileen that she must be careful walking up the stairs and entering the rooms as a lot of the floorboards were loose and uneven and I didn't want her having an accident with our baby. After the inspection I asked her what she thought of the house. Her reply was that she liked it and she liked the small garden and the size of the rooms with the high ceilings, but was worried that it was very large and was wondering if we could afford it. I responded that when I was looking over the house I thought that it would be ideal for us, as if we were going to buy a house so Aileen had some security, this would be even better. We could split the house in two, with us having the five rooms downstairs, the large bathroom and the garden. The upstairs four rooms we could turn for the time being into bedsits so Aileen would also have income. As we would like another child we would have room to expand.

We discussed some more what sort of improvements and which walls we could take out to make more of an open plan and eventually, after thinking about it, she said: "If we can afford it lets go for it." The following day I went to the estate agent,

Bennett's, in Cricklewood, to inform them that we were interested in buying the advertised property in his brochure. He looked in his ledger and said that unfortunately since the brochure had been printed the owners had upped the price by another £2,000 to £7,500. I told them I would have to discuss this with my wife and I would phone them if we were still interested in the property. When I returned home I told Aileen the bad news which made her very disappointed her, telling me that she had been really looking forward to living in that house and area. I suggested that before we decide anything, I would ask dad, who had been in the property business all his life, to have a look at the property and tell us what he thought of the house. Over the Sunday, dad and I inspected the house thoroughly, and after inspecting the house from top to bottom, including the loft, his verdict was that the house was sound – but there would be a lot of superficial repairs that would need to be done. Also, he said, I ought to install central heating in our part of the house. He advised me, although the house cost is a little more than I had expected to pay, remember that what is expensive today is cheap tomorrow; it was advice that I never forgot. I told Aileen dad's verdict and we decided to go for it. It would mean that it would take all the money I had, including the money I was holding back for doing up the house, to put down the deposit and I would have to borrow money from the bank for the repairs. I phoned the estate agent informing him that we would buy the house by putting the deposit down with our solicitors, subject to us getting a mortgage. Shortly, we had a reply that the arrangement was agreeable to the vendor, and they gave us the name and address of their solicitor.

We started applying to different building societies and we came across the same trouble we had encountered when buying the previous house; none of them were lending money for a four storey house, classing it as a commercial building. We nearly gave up the idea of buying a house again, as we had put in so much time inspecting houses and this was the first one that we both liked, then Peter suggested that I speak to a manager of small building society in Brighton that he had been dealing with, as he may be able to help. A week later Peter informed me that the following week the manager would be in London, having explained to him my problem he arranged for all three of us to have lunch to see if he could sort out the mortgage. When we met, during lunch we discussed my finances and my problem and, having made some notes, he explained to me that their building society is very small one, they take slightly higher risks and they charge a slightly higher interest rate. I would have to take out an endowment insurance policy through their society, and he gave me the details of the cost. The interest rate at that time in main building societies was 16% and theirs was 17.75%. I quickly worked out the figures of what my weekly cost would be and it seemed that I could afford it. We agreed that the loan would be for 20 years at the end the loan would be paid off by the endowment insurance policy. I accepted all he said and, after him taking some more notes and asking for the name and address of my solicitor, he told me that the paperwork would take about week and would be sent to my solicitor for me to sign. When they received the documents back, I would have a mortgage. The money would be transferred to my bank in a fortnight's time. I couldn't believe how easily it all went after the weeks I spent trying to get mortgage from other companies.

I was completely elated and couldn't wait to get home to tell Aileen the good news. I told her that now that I had the money, I was going to try to get a reduction on the price of the house. I phoned my solicitor instructing him to get in touch with the vendor's solicitor and tell him that I was having trouble acquiring a mortgage and the maximum I could pay for the house was £7,000. Three days later the reply came back that they had accepted the offer. I transferred the money to our solicitor to complete the sale and they transferred the deeds for the house to us. We became the proud owners of the house in Gladys Rd. at the end of January, 1963.

1963

As soon we had the deeds, Aileen and I went to the house we started to go over it properly and discuss how we would organise the house for our needs. All the money that I had at the time had gone into buying the house and I would need a loan from the bank. I went to see my old bank manager Bill Hatchard and explained my situation to him. He suggested that before he lends me the money I should get a builder to give me an estimate of how much it will cost to do the work. During our discussion he mentioned that the bank had a customer who was a builder who had done jobs for several of his customers and it seemed that his work had been satisfactory. Hatchard was willing to give me his phone number to see if he would like to do the job and if he could give me an estimate, which I accepted.

I phoned the builder, explaining what I needed and asking if he would be interested in doing the job. He was and we made arrangement to meet at the house. He arrived at the house in his van, where Aileen and I were waiting for him. He introduced himself as Mr. McIntyre. He was about forty years old and about 5'2" tall; we discovered later that he used to be a boxer in the welterweight class. We explained to him what work we wanted done. The house would be split into two halves, with the semi basement to have everything repaired and central heating fitted. The four upper rooms needed the walls repaired and waterproofed, papered and all wood surfaces painted, with a wash basin to be fitted in each room and an Ascot water heater fitted above the basins, the water being supplied to them from the bathroom water supply. He was taking notes and measurements of everything I said, saying that he would do the costing at home and send me the estimate.

We received the estimate two days later, which stated that should everything be agreeable he could start the following week and the cost for the whole work would be £1,450, with a third of it paid at the start of the job for materials, second payment half way through the job and the rest of the balance on completion. The job would take about five weeks if there were no complications. I straight away phoned him to accept. The house had to be rewired so we employed an electrician that my dad used who worked for British Telecom. He came to the house and estimated the cost rewiring and fitting the points and switches as £150. He would also arrange with the electricity board to supply and fit coin meters and work with the builders so that that they could fix the walls after making holes to put the wires through. Next I had to get an estimate for furnishing the rooms we were going to let.

We had very good friends Alan and Pam Finkel with whom we used to socialise and they were coming to see us that Saturday for dinner. He had quite a big business refurbishing palaces in Saudi Arabia and I thought that what we required would be too small a job for his company but maybe he knew someone that could supply our need. Over dinner, when I explained to him our need, he right away said his company could do the job at the right price, explaining that originally when he started his company his main business was small buildings. If I had the time tomorrow he would come over and we could go over to the house to see what was required and give me a quote of the cost. The next day when we met at the house he brought some brochures for us to look through and advised us about what we would need. We then went over each room with him making notes and when we finished he read out a list of all the things that we would need for each room: it would consist of all furniture, cutlery, cooking utensils, bedding, china, a small Belling cooker, table lights and linoleum for the floor. The cost for the whole lot would be £400 and he could deliver all the goods as soon the rooms were ready. I realised that after seeing the prices in the broachers that he was charging me at wholesale price, which was very kind of him, and of course I accepted the offer.

Now that I had all the estimates I went to my bank manager to ask him for a loan £1,500. After looking at the estimates he said he can give me the loan and suggested that I take a loan of £2,000 in case there were additional expenses that often cropped up in such a big building job. I took his advice, accepted the loan and as soon as I arrived home I phoned the builder and the electrician to tell them they could start working on the house the following Monday. I met them there at 8.00a.m. to let them in.

On Monday, when I arrived at the house the builder and his plasterer, central heating man and the electrician were waiting for me. I explained to them that I wanted them to start on the two lower floors with central heating to be completed first, as we want to move into our part of the house as soon as possible, as our baby was due in beginning of April and I had to do some fitting and decorating before we moved in. For the next two weeks the work proceeded smoothly, with the basement wall taken out and all the water pipes laid for the central heating with all the radiators connected and fitted to the walls, waiting for the boiler to be installed.

The following Monday morning, at work I had a frantic call from the builder that a council inspector had come around and stopped all the work in the house because I had not submitted a working plan of the work that was being done in the house. I asked to speak to him and told him that I was informed that, as there was no main structural alteration to the house, I didn't need one. He then told me as the house is being partitioned there would have to be some fire safety precautions. I made an appointment with him to meet me and my builder at the house the following day and explain to us what was needed to which he agreed. The following day when we met the council inspector he explained that by partitioning the house in two we would need a building plan drawn by an architect specifying what exactly what was going to be done in the house and what fire precautions were to be taken to contain any fires. I asked him if he could do the drawings, but he said no as he wasn't allowed as he worked for the council but his friend in the adjacent council might do it. I asked him if would be so kind to phone his friend who agreed to come over right away to see what was required.

Within twenty minutes he was at the house, the two inspectors my builder and I went over the house room by room, they explaining to me what extra work would have to be carried out for fire precautions and when we were finished with the inspection the inspector said if I was agreeable he can have the plans ready for me the following afternoon and the cost will be £10. As promised, the inspector who was doing the plans and lived only a short distance from me came over the following day with the drawings, for which I paid him £10. He then suggested that he would phone my council inspector informing him that I had the drawings and whether we could proceed with our work; his reply was that we could proceed but he would come in few days' time to check on what was being done.

After he left I phoned my builder to tell him that he could start working in the morning and I would meet him there to discuss the plans and what extra costs there would be for the additional work. When he arrived we went very carefully over the plans and the only extra work that would have to be done on the ground floor would be for an extra little hall that had to be built between the two rooms and all the doors upstairs to be fitted with rising-butt hinges and the inside of the doors to be lined inside with asbestos sheeting. The extra cost of the work and materials came to £150. The work restarted the following day and in two weeks most of the work on the two lower floors was nearly completed except for the central heating boiler, enabling me to start planning the decorating and building of wardrobes in the part of the house that we would be occupying.

The following week was when my trouble with the builder started. After one day of work he phoned me to tell me that he was ill with the flu and that his doctor had advised him to stay in bed for at least a week. When he started again the first thing he did was to ask me for extra money to buy the boiler. I told him that was not in our agreement but to speed up the work I gave him the money. Then he started missing working days by working two days one week, three days on another, with excuses such as his plumber or his carpenter being ill and hadn't arrived or he was waiting for materials. Aileen and I were getting quite worried as our baby's due date was getting ever closer and we were hoping that that the house would be ready before it was born, but we soon realised that it would not be possible with the amount of time that had been lost by the builder.

It was now seven weeks since he had started work and he was only halfway through the project. I had one incident with the builder which made me weary of him. When our part of the house was completed but not decorated, I decided to decorate the baby's room so at least one room would be clean and free of dirt and dust so it could become the nursery. While I was preparing the radiator for painting by undoing the nuts with a very large shifting spanner, the builder came up to me asking me if I could advance him some more money. As he was speaking to me he took a cut throat razor out his top pocket and started trimming his nails thinking that it would intimidate me. I raised my big spanner and told him: "If you don't put it away this spanner is going right across your head." He quickly put it away and started sniffling telling me that he was short of money to buy materials for the house. I asked him to order the materials and give me the bill so that I could pay it and then deduct it from his bill and when he had done some more work I would give him some more money.

The materials arrived and the work started but again he started missing days and I was getting angrier and angrier with him. Aileen went in to labour early in the morning on Saturday 5th of April. I drove her to St Mary's Hospital where she was taken to a maternity ward. After she was consulted by the doctor I asked him if I should wait. He told me that nothing was going to happen for a while, so I should go home and they will phone when the birth was due. I returned home to wait and phoned mum and dad with the news, both of whom were absolutely delighted and then in the afternoon I phoned my close friends Peter and John with the news, who insisted to come over to keep me company while I waited. They arrived after lunch with a bottle of wine which calmed me down a bit, but still there was no news from the hospital. Early in the evening I phoned the hospital and they informed me that Aileen still hadn't gone in to into full labour.

Peter went to get some fish and chips for our supper and while eating John suggested that we phone some of our other friends to come over and we could have a game of poker while I was waiting to stop me worrying. Two managed to come over and we could start playing. While we were playing I kept phoning the hospital, but by 1a.m. there still wasn't any news. We stopped the game and the boys left for home and I lay down on the bed waiting for the phone call from the hospital. I dozed off and at 3a.m. the hospital phoned, telling me that I was a father of a baby girl. I asked them why they didn't phone me as I wanted to be there at birth of my child. The nurse told me that when Aileen had started giving birth there was another patient giving birth at the same time and they didn't any one spare to phone me. I asked if I could come over to see Aileen and the baby but they said 'no' as Aileen had endured quite a hard time giving birth and she and the baby were sleeping. They suggested I come about 7a.m. I couldn't sleep anymore and at 6.30a.m. I drove to the hospital where the nurse took me to a smaller ward where there was Aileen and another patient with a cot beside each bed with a baby in it. Aileen was awake and looked worn out but radiant, and the baby was still asleep. I gave her kiss and a big hug asking her if she was all right and if the baby all right. She told me that they were both all right, the birth had been quite painful as our baby was quite large weighing 8lbs 6oz. Then the nurse took the baby out of the cot and placed it in my arms and when I look down though it was one of the most wonderful things that had happened in my life; she looked so beautiful.

Before the birth we discussed names and decided if we had a girl her name would be called Mila Tanya, her first name being after my aunt's father's sister who died in the holocaust. Mila was born 6th April 1963. While talking to the nurse she asked me why Aileen kept on asking her if it was possible to put Mila's birth date as midnight on the 5th when she was filling in the birth certificate. I explained to her that if Mila had been born on the 5th, I would have gained £60 in child tax rebate. I was informed by the doctor that if everything went well I could take them home in four days' time, which I did. As soon as I arrived back home I phoned mum, dad, my sister and Aileen's mother – unfortunately her father had died just before Aileen became pregnant – to tell the news of the birth, but I asked them not to visit at the hospital until the afternoon visiting time as Aileen was very tired.

Before Aileen had gone into hospital we spoke to one of our neighbours who we were friendly with and was a large manufacturer of luxury prams, asking him if he could supply us with one of his prams. He produced some brochures for us to choose one which we did and he told us that it would be delivered as soon the baby was born, so when I brought Aileen and Mila home the pram was waiting with the porter and I made sure that everything was ready for them including food so that Aileen wouldn't have to go out. I was so happy with all of us together, the only disappointment being that we were not together in our own house.

The work at the house was progressing very slowly through the builder missing so many days; it had been twelve weeks since he had started and in the two upper floors only one third of the work had been done. Aileen and I discussed the situation, as it was costing a lot of money having to also pay the flat's rent, the interest on my mortgage and payments on endowment insurance. I spoke to the builder to tell him that I was absolutely fed up with him and gave him three weeks to finish the all the work. If job wasn't completed by that time I would be deducting £25 a day to cover the cost of our flat and lost rent for the upper rooms. He didn't like it and he argued but I told him that three weeks was ample time to finish the job.

We decided that as our part of the house was completed we would move in whilst work on the upper half continued and, as the house was partitioned, the builder could work without having to come into our part. I phoned the housing manager to ask if it was alright if we vacated the flat in two weeks' time and he said that would be fine as there was a tenant waiting to move in. He would come and inspect it to see if anything had been repainted, redecorated or needed cleaning, as everything had to be left in the same condition as when we took over our flat, otherwise we lost the deposit that was left with the council when I had moved in. My sister knew a painter and decorator who had done several jobs for her and his work was excellent. He had degree from City & Guilds, but he couldn't make enough money decorating so he worked as a porter in Smithfield Market but took on odd jobs; his name was Pete. I got in touch with him to see whether he could decorate our flat and he agreed to come to decorate our flat so it would be ready for inspection before we moved.

As promised, Pete came on the Wednesday before we moved the following Saturday, did the painting and decorating and finished by Saturday morning. Pete also agreed that the Thursday before we moved he would start to paper and paint our new kitchen so that Aileen had a clean kitchen, which was good as two weeks' previously I had bought a new gas cooker and I had arranged with the Gas Company to connect it on the Saturday while Pete was there. I phoned the housing manager to come the following week and inspect the flat, which he did and everything was to his satisfaction. The removal van came on Saturday morning but the man had underestimated the amount of furniture we had and so had some difficulty loading the van, but we arrived at our house just before lunch.

The builder was finishing the last room on his last day in the house and I went to check if everything was satisfactory and I noticed that there was a damp patch above one of the fireplaces which should have been waterproofed. I told him that it would have to be done before I paid him. He grumbled and argued and as I was walking down the stairs and entered our part of the house. He came rushing down the stairs and attacked me, jumping on my back and punching me. He wasn't a large man and I managed to swing him around, grabbed him by his neck and banged his head against the wall, shouting at him to pack it in. Pete, who was working in the kitchen, came running and when he saw what was happening shouted at the builder that if he didn't stop he would be badly hurt and parted us.

I told the builder to finish the waterproofing and get out of our house and I didn't ever want to see him at our house again. I would come to his house the following day and settle our bill in full, which I did. I told Aileen what had happened, that I was stopping the builder doing any more work and that I was going to pay him the full amount as otherwise I would be worried all the time about him coming around when I wasn't home asking Aileen for more money; I didn't trust him at all and wanted to be rid of him. I arranged with Pete to paint and paper our part of our house when we sorted out our furniture and to install any wardrobes that needed to be built-in. At long last we were in our own house.

Now that we were in our house we discussed what carpets and furniture we would have to buy, as moving from a small flat the amount of furniture we had made the our new place a bit sparse. We made a list and phoned Alan Finkel to tell him that he rooms upstairs were ready for him to furnish, and at the same time asked if he could give me an estimate for the furniture and furnishing that we would require for our own place downstairs. A few days later Alan came with a large van bringing all the stuff we had ordered and a Lino fitter to measure out how many square yds of Lino were required. He also brought samples for us to choose a pattern, colour and quality. After calculating everything he told us that it would take two days for the Lino to arrive and two to three days to lay it. So, a week later, our letting rooms were ready to let to tenants. We decided that we wouldn't start letting until we were a bit more sorted in our own place, deciding what carpets to buy, where to build our wardrobes and cupboards etc.

We were nearly finished sorting everything we had bad news. I received a letter from Bill Hatchard, my bank manager, stating that the Bank of England had asked all the banks to call in all unsecured bank loans, which was called the Credit Squeeze, and that as my loan was unsecure, as the deeds of the house were held by the building society, he had to call in the debt. I straight away went to see him to see if there was any way that he could help me. He explained that these instructions came from the head office and he would help me if he could, but in this case there was nothing that he could do for me. When I returned home, I told Aileen what had transpired with Bill Hatchard and that at present I really didn't know what we were going to do.

That night I lay in bed, not being able to sleep, worrying. It was the first time since I was a young boy that I cried, as I felt such a failure. If there was no one that I could borrow money from I would have to sell the house and all our plans for our future would be gone. Aileen woke up, wondering what was wrong with me. After telling her how I felt and how worried I was she made a suggestion that I speak to Dad, as he had been dealing in property most of his life and he might have some suggestions, but in the meantime that we should get some sleep and in the morning we could discuss our situation and phone Dad to see if he had any ideas.

In the morning, I was still very agitated and worried so I decided to take Aileen's advice and phoned Dad, who suggested we all come to dinner and see if we can find a solution to my predicament, to which we agreed. After dinner, Dad asked me to show him the letter that I received from the bank. After reading it he said the only problem that he could see was that my loan was unsecured, so if I made another appointment with my bank manager, he would come with and see if we can sort it out. I made the appointment with Bill for the following Monday. When we arrived at the bank, Bill saw us straight away and when we were seated Dad asked him if there was some way that my problem could be resolved. Bill explained to us that as I didn't have any collateral to back up my loan I would need a guarantor to pay off the loan if I couldn't. Dad asked him if he could be the guarantor as, although he hadn't much cash money, he owned two houses in St John's Wood which had been converted into flats, one still with a mortgage, the other free of any debits. Bill's reply was that the houses would be a sufficient guarantee and if Dad would fill in and sign some forms, the loan would be approved, with condition that I pay off the loan over two years.

On the way home, Dad asked me if our upstairs room were ready for letting. I told him that as soon as Aileen had finish making the curtains we would start letting the rooms which would give us a little help to pay off the loan. When I arrived back home I explained to Aileen what had transpired and, although our loan was secured and I still had a few pounds in the bank to pay Pete, after that I would be completely broke. Then Aileen surprised me. She informed me that she had a couple hundred pounds in her post office account that she had saved from the money I gave her for housekeeping and, if it would help, I could have it. I thanked her for this wonderful offer, but told her to keep it for her and Mila for any emergencies that might arise. Then we discussed what we were going to do. "As soon as you have made the curtains for the rooms upstairs," I said, "we will start renting them which will help with paying off the loan, as I am broke and have to pay it off at over £100 a month. We will also have to budget for council rates, electricity, gas, water rates and the car, which will be essential for us. Even with the rent from the rooms, it will only leave us with just enough money to live on. It will not be possible for me to hire any workmen to do work in our part of the house, so I will have to do it using all my spare time." There would be no poker games, no parties or going out until we were solvent again, and I couldn't see any other options. Aileen said: "The only thing that is worrying me is that are you sure it won't be too much for you?" I told her not to worry as I was healthy and pretty tough and with a bit of help from her, we would manage.

We decided that what was to eventually be our dining room would be my workroom. My biggest problem was procuring wood, which was expensive and I needed quite a lot for building cupboards and wardrobes and replacing some of the floor boards, so I put a roof rack on the Mini and started going around the skips. There used to be a lot of new wood chucked out into skips and anything that was useful I tied onto the roof rack and brought it home. At one time I had so much wood on the roof of my Mini that when going around one of the corner it nearly tipped over. Once we had sorted out what we were going to do we realised that before we did any work we would have to start letting the rooms as we needed the income. Aileen was recommended a letting agent with whom she arranged a meeting where they would explain commission, rent books and what sort of rent we could expect to charge in our area. His advice was £2-£3 a week with two weeks' deposit. We decided that we would charge £2 for the smaller rooms and £2.50 for the larger rooms, which would give us £9 a week which would be great help to our finances.

Aileen was going to run the lettings and our finances as she was very good at book keeping and I didn't have the time to do it. Our first tenant was Ghanaian who worked for the B.B.C. World Service, translating Shakespeare into Swahili and who spoke beautiful English. Within a fortnight we had all our rooms occupied with an Indian boy who was an accountant and two English girls, one a teacher the other a secretary. They all mentioned that our rooms were some off the best they had ever rented and some of them stayed with us several years. Soon after we let our rooms we realised that some of our neighbours were avoiding us. We couldn't understand why as we hadn't had any quarrels with anyone until I spoke to a Polish neighbour's son, who asked me if we let any rooms to any coloured tenants. When I told him that we have two, he explained that all the landlords in the area were English and when letting rooms have signs in their front windows: "No dogs, Irish or Blacks." I told Aileen about it and we were disgusted as we had several Indian and African friends that we had made at the Overseas League. Eventually, as more and more immigrants arrived from the Commonwealth the whole thing died down.

After we sorted out our letting we started working on our rooms. Normally, I would usually come home from work about 7 o'clock, have my supper and a little rest then start working on the walls until two in the morning, leaving the sanding and preparation of the woodwork for Aileen when she had some time in the day. Luckily, I never sleep more 5 ½ hours, so it was no problem for me. The first room I did was the bathroom. When I started stripping the old paper I found that there were four or five layers of papers, which made it very difficult to strip. Not only that, when I peeled of the wallpaper, large parts of the plaster fell out which I had to re-plaster. I found out later that all the other rooms were in the same condition. Along with building a hot air cupboard, it took me 10 weeks to finish the bathroom. The bedrooms – which were much larger and there was a lot more work to do, such as making built-in wardrobes in ours and Mila's room – took me until the end of the year. At Christmas, Aileen insisted that I have rest from work in the house until the New Year.

1964

Aileen and I discussed several times that it would a good idea if we had some sort of pet for Mila to grow up with and we decided on a dog. My sister Rozia heard about it and told us that she had friends that bred beagles as well as several other breeds and we could go to her friend's farm and see what dogs they had on offer. If we would like one she and Peter would buy it as a present for Mila's birthday. We thought about it and as we both liked the breed, we accepted the offer. We went to the farm the first available Sunday. I can't remember where it was, but it took 1 ½ hours to get there and when we arrived the noise of dogs barking was deafening. Rozia's friends invited us into their farm house, gave us tea and we discussed what sort of dog we required. We explained that, as we only had a small garden, it would have to be a reasonable size dog that was good with children. After discussing different breeds, they suggested that a beagle bitch would be our best bet as they are very placid and they don't bite, but only hold being hunting dogs. They had a two-week-old litter of puppies that we could see, bred from two champions dogs and they had already been named and registered with the kennel club, so if we wanted we could train the dog to enter competitions.

When we were shown the pups, we didn't bother to see any others as they were so beautiful. Aileen and I decided on one that we both liked and Mila seemed to take to. We went back to the farms house to discuss the price, which was £80. Rozia paid, and we were then asked to name the puppy; we named her Lindy. We were also told that that we she wouldn't be delivered to us for another eight weeks as she had to be vaccinated before delivery and that would not be done until she was ten weeks' old, which was fine as it would be in time for Mila's birthday.

Lindy was delivered the day before Mila's birthday and we hardly recognized her having grown so much. She started running around the house; luckily we had everything ready for her, basket, collar, lead and plastic sheeting. While we were talking she jumped on the settee and in minutes she had managed to damage both ends. We put her in the hall and shut all the doors. When I went to get our coats I found she had pulled down my coat, chewed up my wallet, my Parker fountain pen and my slippers. We forgave her as she was the most loving dog; she was very wary of cats and hated being bathed. She was marvellous with Mila; they played together all the time. She became part of our family, everybody loved her and brought treats, especially mum who used to supply her with big bone marrow. During summer, when Mila was old enough to run, she and Lindy used to wait outside the house and as soon they saw me come around the corner from work they used to run to meet me.

Once, when Lindy was old enough to mate, we found her a pedigree Beagle owned by a family that lived not far from us. We put the two dogs in the garden to get acquainted but for five hours they did nothing but sit and look at each other, so we gave up and never tried again. Twice she escaped from the house and we spent hours looking for her and then in each case three days later she came home sitting by the door waiting for us to let her in. It was a complete mystery where she was for the three days. She was much loved and she gave us all a lot of pleasure. When she was just over fourteen she started crying and limping. At first we thought it was arthritis, so we took her to the vet who gave her some medication for her pain but then she started crying more and more. We took her again to the vet to X-Ray her and find out what was wrong. As the surgery was very busy, Aileen left her with the nurse to pick her up later. When Aileen went to pick up Lindy she was told that she had been put down. Aileen was furious and vented her outrage in the surgery, arguing that we should have been notified before that sort of decision was taken and after she calmed down, it was explained that after the X-Ray Lindy was diagnosed with the late stages of cancer, so the vet put her down, which he said was the only humane thing to do. When we heard the news we were all terribly upset, especially Mila, as for her it was like losing a sibling and for us it was like losing a close member of family and we still miss her very much.

During the year I still carried on working the long hours, as the downstairs rooms and the halls were a much bigger job than I had first anticipated; the painting and decorating wasn't finished until the beginning of 1965. Although our financial situation had slightly improved through my salary increase, Christmas bonus and rent from our lettings, we still owed money to the bank and didn't have money for essential furniture, so I decided to make it myself. I made built-in cabinets, free standing ones, a coffee table, a drinks cabinet and fireplace. I couldn't afford to buy power tools except for an electric drill and a few clamps, so everything had to be cut by hand. By Easter, the long hours seemed to have caught up with me and everyone was telling me how tired I looked and Aileen and the family started nagging me that I must have a holiday before I became ill. I kept on telling Aileen that until we paid off the bank I couldn't afford it. Aileen mentioned that we still had a small Post Office account where she had been saving small amounts of money and was supposed to be going towards buying our carpets. We could wait a little longer for our carpets, my health being more important. Also, she could do with a holiday.

We looked at some brochures and decided on what was within our price range. We settled on Italy, a small place called Dana Marina, which was a short distance from the French border. We always liked Italy and we knew that they would be child-friendly. When we told mum and dad about it they were delighted and few days later told us that they would like to join us as they could look after Mila in the evenings so that we could have some time to ourselves. As new parents, the idea appealed to us so we agreed. We booked our holiday for the second Saturday in July, when the weather still wouldn't be too hot, and made a list of things to take, especially for Mila being only 2 ¼ years old. We had been told by friends that some things that were required for small children may not be available in a small town like Dana

Marina. We would be flying, but mum and dad would be travelling by train as dad was scared of flying and refused to fly, so we would arrive at the hotel early afternoon and they in the evening.

At the end of May I had a most wonderful letter from my bank manager in my morning post informing me that my loan was fully paid up and my bank account was now in credit. It felt as if a huge weight had been lifted off our shoulders. I told Aileen the good news, who right away arranged one of our friends to babysit so that we could go out and have a celebratory dinner, the first one in two years. During our dinner I promised Aileen that this was the last time that we would ever be in debt and if we wanted to buy something and could not pay for it upfront, we wouldn't get it. From then on, for all the fifty years we were together we never had money problems or any arguments about money again.

Now that we were solvent I was able to take sufficient funds for us to spend on our holiday without having to count every penny. On the Saturday of the start of our holiday, we left for the airport in the late morning to catch our plane. Everything went like clockwork; you only had to wait only half an hour to board the plane in those days as you didn't have the security procedures that you have today and the plane only carried 60 passengers. It was propeller driven and at customs, if you had a British passport, you were just waved through. The flight was very pleasant, being a sunny day, and took about 3 ½ hours, landing at Genoa where we boarded a coach to Dana Marina, arriving at the hotel around teatime. We found that it was a family owned hotel, which was good as we found they always take good care of their clientele.

The courier from the tour company met us, gave us a registration card to fill in and hand in at the reception desk with our passport where we would be given the key to our rooms. She also told us that our luggage would be brought to our room and after we had freshened up that we should come down to the dining room for tea where she would give us information about the hotel, our table places, meal times and places of interest in the town. Our room was on the first floor and was very large, beautifully appointed with a large double bed, a small bed for Mila and a large bathroom. It also had French windows opening onto a balcony overlooking the sea.

When we all met up in the dining room we found that there were several other families with children Mila's age, which was good as small kids usually make friends quickly with other kids when playing on the beach. First, we were allocated our table in the dining room, which was for us, mum and dad and a high chair for Mila. Then the guide gave us all the information of meal times, hiring equipment on the beach and where to shop. One interesting piece of information was that there was special small sandy beach next to the main beach only for children, the water being about 18" deep, with deck chairs, loungers and tables for the grownups to watch the children.

After tea we relaxed in the garden, waiting for mum and dad, who arrived shortly before supper. The food was good with a fairly decent menu with variety of dishes to choose from, and after supper we decided to have an early night as we were all extremely tired. This was the first time in two and a half years that I felt completely relaxed, not having to think about the long hours and what work I had to do in the house. The next day we all went to the children's beach, which, as promised, had water just over a foot deep, and so we could leave Mila with the other children to play in the water and watch her sitting in our deckchairs. Being the first day, we only spent only two hours on the beach as it was very hot and we took care not to get sunburn.

After lunch and a short rest we went for a walk around the town to do a bit of window shopping. There were quite a few shops and we found the prices very reasonable, especially the clothing, so we bought a few things: for the ladies some silk scarves, dad and I some ties. While walking around I found just the shops I'd been looking for. Since the birth of Mila I had wanted to buy Aileen a piece of gold jewellery as she loved gold, in celebration of Mila's birth, and for all the hard work helping me in the house, which I hadn't been able to afford before. While we were window shopping in one of the shops there was a beautiful gold bracelet watch which we both admired. A couple days' later after lunch, while Aileen was resting with a mild migraine, I went back to the shop to see the watch and the price. When the salesman told me the price, I said that it was a bit out of my reach and I told him how much I was prepared to spend. He told he could take a little off the price, but not down to what I was willing to pay. I told him I would have to think about it and would come back the following day to discuss the price.

I visited the shop for the next three days, and each day he reduced the price slightly. On the third day I bought it, the price being only 5% more that I wanted to pay originally. On the last day of our holiday at breakfast I presented the watch to Aileen as a belated birthday present. She was so surprised and delighted and couldn't believe that I had managed to buy it and that no one noticed me going to the jewellers so often.

Returning home, at the airport there was the usual rush to buy duty free tobacco goods, spirits and wines, meaning everybody boarding the plane came on with extra big plastic bags beside your hand luggage. Our journey home was uneventful in good weather, arriving home on Saturday afternoon. In the evening, after putting Mila to bed, we discussed our holiday and decided that we will try to go abroad at least once a year and as my finances improved. We travelled further afield and throughout our life we travelled to 32 countries, visiting some of them several times; altogether we travelled abroad 81 times, the last being three months before Aileen died.

A few days after we came back from our holidays, my Uncle Joe phoned me to see if I would like to go to the Frankfurt fur fair for two days as he had a spare ticket since one member from his firm's party that was going was ill. I was rather surprised as since I had left his firm his attitude towards me had been rather cool and he hadn't spoken to me for the past three years. After asking him what dates, I told him that I would have to see what work I had in my diary and that I would phone him the following day. I discussed it with Aileen, as I was a bit worried as she was pregnant for the third time having had two miscarriages previously. I explained that the trip would be over the weekend, with me coming home Monday night and I would have to be very careful that my chairman doesn't find out, as he disliked my uncle, although I'd mentioned to him a little while back that that soon I would have to go to Germany on family business for my father to see my Uncle Gustav and this would be a good time for him to meet me in Frankfurt. Aileen thought it was a good idea as it would save me an extra journey to Munich.

I phoned Uncle Gustav to see if he could drive up to Frankfurt on the Saturday and that I would be there, giving him the date and the name of the hotel, which was the Frankfurter Hof. He was quite agreeable to the idea, he knew the hotel having stayed there several times and would be there in the afternoon. He told me to book him a room for one night. I then told my chairman that I would be away on the Monday, giving him the date. I told him that should anything urgent occur, I was sure my senior cutter would be able to deal with it. I then phoned my Uncle Joe to accept his offer, who asked me to come by his firm so that he could give me tickets for the trip. He also informed me who was going with me, who turned out to be three friends that I had worked with when I was working for my Uncle.

Uncle Joe had arranged transport to take us all to the airport. We went in a taxi where there were several other furriers that knew me and knew my chairman traveling on the same plane. I told them that it was a coincidence that I was on the same plane as my Uncle Joe, explaining that I was travelling to meet another uncle on family business, making sure that they all knew that I was travelling separately to my uncle. The flight was only an hour but pleasant as I was able to catch up on all the news of my friends that I had worked with, had a few drinks and the usual bag of peanuts. When we arrived in Frankfurt, Uncle arranged a car to take us to our hotel, which was huge – it had been built after the war and consisted of two tower blocks with an underground tunnel connecting the two buildings, which was useful as our party was split between the two buildings. Uncle Gustav arrived in the afternoon and he joined our party for dinner where we discussed our program for next day.

After dinner I spent some time with Gustav settling my father's business with him as I wouldn't be seeing him before returning to Munich very early in the morning the following day. In the morning we left for the fair at 8.30a.m. I'd never been to the fur fair in Frankfurt before, so I was amazed how huge it was; it was the largest in the world, consisting of five huge pavilions with traders from all over the world. I'd never seen so many furs or equipment for furrier and the two days that I was there left me completely exhausted. On my final night before leaving for London, after dinner Uncle Joe asked me to join him in the lounge, saying that he wanted to discuss something with me. When we were seated he said that he had a proposition for me: he would like me to come back to his firm and take over the main workroom. Of course, it would come with an increase in salary and in time you would be in charge of all the workrooms. I thought for a minute before replying: "Since I left your firm I have become quite successful. When I left your firm after you let me down twice, I was offered the opportunity to start a new workroom by my new firm who had lost all but three of their staff through bad management, giving me free reign over who to employ and how to run it. I have now four cutters, six machinists, two apprentices, a liner, two finishers and a tea lady. All my craftsman work to a system that I devised, so that if one is ill another can take over his job if necessary. My staff have been with me since I employed them when I first started the workroom, I am my own boss and anything that is necessary for the workroom is paid for without any question. My pay is twice as much than what I was paid when I was working for you plus 20% bonus at Christmas. Since I've taken over the workroom the firm has won the top prize in the international fur competition for design and workmanship every year, which they have never done before. Our turnover has grown by a considerable margin, having customers in many countries, one being King Hussein of Jordon, for whom I've made coats for his wives and family. I have a wife, a daughter, a mortgage on our house and I have just finished paying off all my debts: I cannot take the chance if things go wrong. I am very happy in my job, contented and proud of what I have achieved, that's why I won't be joining your firm."

Returning back from Frankfurt, the atmosphere between and my uncle and myself was very strained and he hardly spoke a word to me. When we arrived back in London I thanked him for the trip and apologised that I couldn't accept his offer; he never said a word. When I returned home I told Aileen all about my trip and the offer that my uncle proposed to me, which I turned down, and I told her that I believed the whole idea of the trip was to make me the offer. She agreed with me and was glad that I didn't take it after all the trouble I had before.

Three weeks after I had returned from Frankfurt tragedy struck. On Friday, coming home from work, I found Aileen in the bathroom lying on the floor in a pool of blood. She had miscarried again and she couldn't phone as she was scared that if she went down the stairs she might have fallen down. I immediately phoned the doctor, who arrived very shortly to check her over and told me that as far as he could see she was alright, but he called an ambulance to take her to the hospital for a proper check-up, where they kept overnight. When I came to the hospital to pick her up the doctor told me that she was alright, but for the next few days she must rest which was fine as being the weekend I would be home, but to be on the safe side I phoned my boss explaining what had happened and to say that I might not be in on the Monday.

When we returned home, I discussed with Aileen what had happened and told her that I didn't think should try for another baby anymore. She had had three miscarriages, this one was the worst, and it was lucky that I had come home in time to get a doctor. Next time we might not be so lucky and it could endanger her life. Mila needs a mother and I need a wife more than we need another child. After she thought about it she agreed and we never again tried for another child.

Two months later, coming back from lunch, the secretary told me that I had an urgent call from my mother. I called her right away thinking that there might be something wrong with dad, when I spoke to her she told me that Uncle Joe collapsed at work, having a heart attack. He was very poorly and wanted to see me. I told her that that I would visit him in the next two days. I went to visit him at a private clinic on Harley St. and when I saw him he really looked very ill. When I spoke to the doctor he informed me that uncle had a serious heart attack. He was very weak and when he leaves he must have a lot of rest and do as little work as possible, and no flying for some time. He was very civil to me and we had a chat about the family. I told him about our tragedy and how disappointed we were with our loss. I made several more visits to see him, as although we didn't see eye to eye he was my favourite uncle. On my last visit he asked me when he was back in his flat if I would come and visit him as he wants some to discuss some matter other to what we discussed before, to which I agreed.

When he left the clinic and was back in his flat, I went to visit him. He still looked very ill but I was curious what he wanted to discuss this time. We had a drink and a chat and then he started telling me what he wanted. He started by telling me that he will only be able to do only three or four hours' work in any given day and he needs someone he can trust. He wanted me to be deputy managing director, to run all the workrooms including purchasing pelts and anything else that is required, either with the staff that already worked in the firm or if I wished, to hire my own. The firm had started a new company, Miss Deanfield, which needed to be developed, which produced fun furs for the younger generation, which was being sold in stores mainly in Scotland – the Macdonald stores. I would also have own my office and a secretary, expense account which I would draw from Uncle Zygmunt, who was responsible for company finances, and of course a raise in my salary.

This was a real surprise. I told him he would have to give me a couple of days to think about it and discuss it with Aileen. I owed Uncle Joe a lot, as if it weren't for him and his connections my family would not have made it to England and we would have perished with the rest of the family in the holocaust. When I returned home I discussed the proposition with Aileen, she agreed that I must help Joe as she knew the family history but she told me that I must have a contract with the firm so that if anything goes wrong I was protected. We made a list of what I would have to ask for in the agreement. Over the weekend I visited Joe again, explaining to him on what conditions I would be willing work for him. First, he must spend every working day for at least five hours for the next two months guiding me on who is important to the firm, who are the most important fur suppliers and what agreements he has with them and introduce me to them. He must introduce me to the buyers from the stores that deal in our goods so that I can discuss with them what style of garments that would sell in their establishment. Lastly, I want an official contract from the firm that says that if he doesn't keep to any part of this agreement and I decide to leave because he hasn't kept to our agreement, I get two years' salary as compensation.

He looked at me and said: "You don't trust me." I told him it's not a question of trust; it's a question of being sensible and protecting my family, also so that I could prevent arguments if things go wrong. He looked again at what I proposed and said: "Maybe you are right. I'll get our solicitors to draw up a contract and I and Zygmunt will sign it." I would not be able to start straight away as I have to give my firm four weeks' notice and finish all the jobs that I was working on. The following week we signed the contract, but I still had this uncomfortable feeling that something was missing and then I realized that that Uncle Joe wasn't the same uncle as when I worked for him before; he seemed to have lost his drive for new ideas and running the business. Perhaps it was because of his heart attack.

There was another brother working in the firm who was in charge of the cold storage, Uncle Izydor, with whom I grew up with in Poland as his family lived in one of my father's flats and who taught me to make my own toys. I asked him what was wrong with his brother. He told me that he hadn't been right since his wife Odette died and had trouble with her cousin. I told him I knew that Odette had died but not in what circumstances, and asked him if he could elaborate. He explained to me that about three years ago Joe owned a property in Paris, which he sold for about £350,000 and gave Odette nearly half to ease the tax liability should he die. Shortly after he discovered that for some time she and her cousin had been lovers and had also become drug addicts. He beat up her cousin and left Odette, starting divorce proceedings. About couple months later, while in Paris the police contacted him informing him that she and her cousin had been brought to the hospital unconscious having consumed a large quantity of drugs and, although they had undergone emergency treatment, they were still unconscious.

When he arrived at the hospital he was taken straight to the ward and spoke to the doctor in charge of them who informed him that they were extremely ill, still unconscious and in present condition he was very doubtful if they would survive and told him the was no point of him waiting; should there be any change they would phone him at his flat. Late that night he received a call from the hospital that Odette has died but her cousin survived. A couple of days after they had her funeral, which uncle arranged. He went with a friend to her flat to sort out her things he came across her will and found out that she left everything to her cousin. He was furious and straight away went to his solicitor to put a stop to it, claiming that being her husband he was entitled to her goods. Of course, the cousin counter-claimed and the whole thing went to court and eventually was settled out of court to save lawyers' fees, which were huge, and Uncle inherited three quarters of her estate.

Since then, Uncle Izydor explained, he'd never got over it and was still grieving. After hearing the story I wondered if I had made a mistake to work with him but I was determined to help him and make a go of the job. On Friday, before we had our usual meeting to discuss the week's progress, I managed to speak to the chairman privately, telling him that I will be leaving the firm in a month's time. He was quite shocked, asking me if someone upset me or someone had offered me more money. I told him it was none of these things and explained to him I owe my uncle a great debt by saving our family and now that he is seriously ill and asking for my help I must repay the debt. I also told him that working with the firm for the last ten years have been some of the best and happiest years in my life. I also told him that I will be staying for another month to finish all the outstanding jobs and should he need my expertise on any specialized jobs like Sable or Chinchilla he can get in touch with me and I will come over to help out.

He thought for a minute and said: "You know that this news is a great shock to me as it will be to the rest of the staff which have been with you from the time you started rebuilding the workroom; we now have the reputation of producing some of the best garments in many of the countries that we export to and I do understand that you must help your uncle in his hour of need, but we will be keeping your job open for the next two months after you leave and see how you get on in your new job then we will see about advertising for your replacement." When the rest of the management and staff found out that I was leaving the firm they were also shocked but also understood why I was leaving and on the last day with the firm they gave a party for me, presents and good luck wishes in my new job.

On the Monday when I started my new job at Deanfield Fur Models, I was surprised that Uncle was already in his office (I forgot that he always liked to be in the firm before the staff). There was no need to introduce me to the staff as I worked with most of them previously; the people I didn't know were the secretary that was allocated to me and one or two of the staff that had joined in the last couple years. As promised, he introduced me to some of the people that I needed to know like the buyers in Harrods, Fortnum & Mason and one buyer from Scotland who was in London at that time, some skin merchants from whom they occasionally bought raw furs. He asked me to go through each department to see how they were working and see if any improvements could be made, which we would discuss at the end of the week.

That Friday after we had lunch at the Brown's hotel which was just across the road from the firm. Afterwards, the two of us returned to his office to discuss what I found out on my tour of the firm. I told him that I thought that the firm is one of the worst I had ever come across. I told him bluntly: "You have too many general managers each looking after their own patch. They tried to hide certain things from me, but I found out that in each workroom there were cutters working on their own private jobs using the firm's machinists, equipment and goods. Each time I asked them who gave them permission to do the work I was told that Uncle Zygmunt knew all about it; that is something you will have to sort out as he is your brother. I am almost certain that some other members of your staff are involved. Your stockroom is a mess, you have hundred-odd mink and other skins hanging in the stockroom which could be sorted into bundles and in slack season made up into jackets and other garments which would be ideal for sales in stores. There a lot of old garments in stock, some that were made in 1940, one of which I made when I was apprentice in Leeds; we have to put them in an auction to make space and get some money for them. You buy your skins piecemeal from skin merchants instead of buying in the auctions twice a year, which costs the firm at least 20% more and I am almost sure that your stockroom manager gets a cut when he buys from them from merchants. All in all, from of what I've seen, a certain proportion of the staff is running their own little business on the firm's money. Next week on Monday you must go through the stock books with the firm's accountant as I am certain there will be some discrepancies in some of the departments. Also, speak to Zygmunt to sort out the workrooms as if there isn't sufficient work for all the staff there will have to be some reductions in how many we have to employ."

He took my advice and the second week I was there he started going through the books, but on the Wednesday when I came to work he was missing. I asked the secretary if there was a message from my uncle, but she told me: "Didn't you know that that he was going to Paris and will not be back until Sunday?" I was really annoyed, as I knew that the firm's branch in Paris closed down after Odette's death, so the trip couldn't be business-related and without him I couldn't implement any changes, so for next two days I was filling my time by checking what work was being done in the workrooms. On the third Monday, when I arrived at work he was in his office, no apologies or anything so I said that our agreement was that he spend two months with me to show me all the aspects of the firm; without him here I could not do my job. If he is going to start going abroad again leaving me here it's not going to work. He promised me that that he wouldn't do it again until the two months were up. The third week started well: we made one or two changes, and he gave me advice on certain things I wanted to do, but on Thursday, again, he didn't turn up for work. I asked his secretary where he was, and she told me that after I went home he had a call from Paris from some of his German business friends to ask if he could come over to discuss a business proposition. As he isn't allowed to fly, he went to Victoria Station and took an overnight sleeper to Paris.

This time I was really furious. I went for a walk to cool down, and while walking and thinking what to do I decided to visit my old firm as there were still one or two things to check on with the jobs that I left for them to finish. When I walked into the office and Sidney saw me he grabbed me and took me straight away to the governor's office where I was asked to sit down and have a drink. While having a chat they asked how I was getting on. I told them that it was difficult thing to answer, as I was having some difficulty with the staff and an annoyance with my uncle and up to now it's difficult to say how it will go. After having another drink, governor said to me: "You know, Tim, how we valued your time with us and appreciate all you have done for the firm and we should have done this long time ago: if things don't work out, you know we want you back, but should you decide to come back we have a proposition for you. If you decide to return you will become director, with a certain amount of shares in one of our companies, you will have an expense account and car allowance and every two years you will accompany me to the Frankfurt fur fair. Your salary will be the same as you are receiving at your uncle's firm, with increases that are revised every year." I thanked him for the offer and agreed to give him my answer the following week.

Walking back to the firm I mulled over the offer from my old governor and how I felt about continuing to work for Uncle

Joe. I decided to give him one more chance to keep his promise but that would have to be the last one time. I felt that he had lost his interest in his business and I felt that I couldn't jeopardize my future and the wellbeing of Aileen and Mila if he didn't keep his word, as he had let me down several times before. I explained to Aileen what had transpired and the offer I had from the governor and what I've decided to do. As always, she was most supportive and told me to do what would be the best for us. His secretary informed me that Joe would be back in London Saturday morning, so in the afternoon I phoned him and when he answered there was no apology or excuse for what he had done. I kept myself very calm and told him straight that that this has to be the last time that he lets me down by going away; I expect him to be in the office on Monday and for next six weeks and if he disappears again in that time I will leave the firm. He promised me again that he will stick to our agreement and we parted on good terms.

On Monday morning, when I arrived at my office he didn't appear. I waited the whole morning for him to get in touch which he didn't. This time I had enough, and so after lunch, with the help of my secretary I wrote out a long report for Joe of what was wrong in the firm and my recommendations for what should be done, sealed it in an envelope, gave his secretary the envelope with strict instructions not to show it to anyone and give it only to Joe on his return. After tea, I went to see Uncle Zygmunt enplaning to him that I was leaving the firm and why. His face lit up with pleasure and I knew he had never wanted me in the firm in the first place as I was finding out many things that were going on in the firm behind Joe's back and all the faults that were in the firm. I also informed him that I would be claiming on my contract that Joe didn't fulfil his part of the deal and that I should be paid, never expecting to get the money (it was paid 24 years later, but that's another story).

When I arrived home I told Aileen what I'd done. She was delighted and told me she was seeing the trouble I was having with Joe but she didn't want to influence me as it had to be my own decision. Over the weekend I dug out my tools, and phoned the Governor to tell him that I had accepted his kind offer and asked when I should start again. He said "Monday if you can, but come about 9.30a.m. as I want to give the staff a surprise." On the Monday, when I arrived at the firm, governor was already in his office. He told me how delighted everyone was that I was coming back, we discussed his offer and he told me that sometimes during the week his solicitor will come up to the firm to draw up a contract with all the details that I was promised. Then he took to me to the workroom and when the staff saw me they all got up to greet me; it was like a homecoming. My work bench was just as I had left it, there was a brand new white overall for me so I laid out my tools. I then discussed with the governor what job he wanted me to start on. He told me there were two bundles of skins with patterns hanging in the stockroom waiting for me marked which one to do first and gave me a list of all the jobs that were in hand to check if there was need of any changes and then he left me to get on with my job. I went around to all my cutters to see what they were doing and gave some of them advice, then I picked up my bundle of skins and started working in the job that that I loved, where I stayed for the next 26 years until my retirement.

The last two years at work were not too happy as the work dried up completely and we literally had no orders through the success of the animal rights movement. We are the only country in the world that lost its fur trade, which was the best in the world with the best craftsmen and it cost 30,000 jobs and millions of pounds of revenue to the country in exports. Our managing director and friend Sidney, who was one of the best salesmen I have ever met, retired a year before me and was never replaced and I think that was part of our trouble. I lost some of my younger staff who saw no future in the fur trade and at one of our board meetings just before I retired I suggested that, as it was costing the firm around £250,000 a year to keep open it would make sense to close the firm, sell the stock, pay generous redundancies to the staff, some of them having worked at the firm between fifteen and thirty years. The governor was dead against it and after I retired he kept the firm open another two years before he closed it with a loss of £500,000.

Now that I'd settled back into my job and being a director I had a few more extra responsibilities. I started coming home a bit later than before and a bit tense. Aileen was a little worried that I was doing too much and suggested that I should take up some sort of hobby to relax me. I told her that I would think about it. Our secretary mentioned to me several times that she belonged to the polytechnic rifle and pistol club in Regent St, just a short distance from the firm and were looking for more members and I asked her if she would take me with her when she went next time for me to see what it was like. When we arrived at the club she introduced me to the president and other members that were there, who asked me if I'd done any shooting before. I told them I'd been shooting rifle since I was twelve and a pistol in the army, but that I hadn't done any shooting for the past ten years. The president asked me if I would like to go on the range and shoot a target to see what I was like.

I was supplied with a club rifle and ten rounds of ammunition and the president came on the range with me to see how safe I was with a firearm. After I shot he went down the range to get my card and after totalling my score, which came to 87/100, he said: "You will do and we would be pleased to have you as a member." He then told me all about the club how much the club fees were, the competitions they do and that there were three teams: A, B, and C. With my score I could qualify for the C team. I told him that I must discuss it with my wife and that I would come down to the club the following week. When I arrived home I told Aileen all about the club and asked her if she would mind as I would have to attend the club twice a week to do competitions. Aileen was delighted that I had found something to relax me. The following week I joined the club and I was informed that I'd been selected for the C team. After a short while, when I was tested and received my rifle class A shot badge, I was moved up to the B team with an average 98.6/100 and when I started shooting pistol I also was in the B team with an average 97.3/100. I was reserved member on both A teams but never a permanent member as the members on the A teams used to shoot every day and had much better quality weapons and regularly scored maximum. Some shot for the county of Middlesex and two represented England in the Olympic games.

I managed to win some medals, silver spoons and some trophies. I shot several times at Bisley when our teams reached the finals and Aileen and Mila accompanied me several times. At the beginning of the eighties the students at the polytechnic started having strikes and sit-ins which prevented us from shooting on the range and which lost us several competitions. The captain called all the committee members to a meeting to discuss the situation. He explained that we couldn't continue like this and told us that he has had discussions with another club captain that was in charge of another range near Blackfriars Station, who was much better equipped than us but had financial difficulties and were looking for a partnership with another club. We, on the other hand, were quite wealthy, having several years ago £40,000 left by one of our members who passed away. He asked if we should go and meet them, inspect the range and their facilities and see if it would suitable for us to join them. Everybody agreed to the suggestion so he chose five members to go with him to discuss the situation. We arranged a meeting and when we met them they took us to inspect the range I was one of them.

34 - Shooting at Bisley.

We found out that the range was situated by the Blackfriars Bridge under the Thames, very secure with several steel doors. The only disadvantage we found was the amount of steps we had to climb down, but their range was superb with four firing points, which was two more that we had on our range. There was a separate office which acted as members' club room where we could make tea or coffee and their firearms and equipment were much better than ours. We also found out that during the day the range was used for training the armed police and several other civil service clubs. After the inspection we told the other club's president that we liked what we had seen and we will present our findings to our members for their approval, which we did and they all agreed to the merger. We informed the other club of our decision and had several meetings with the other club to formulate a new charter of rules and a new name for the club. The five members that negotiated the merger became founder members; I was one of them and became part of the new club committee. We named the club City of London Rifle and Pistol Club and we managed to persuade an ex-Lord Mayor of London to be our first president; with him as our president we were the only club that was allowed to use the City of London seal. I was active member of the club until I was 83. When Labour came to power on a promise that they would ban all hand weapons – which was the silliest things they ever did – they had to buy all of them off all the clubs and gunsmiths at the original price, which cost them nearly £31m. Also, in doing so, they lost all track of all the weapons, as before if there was a gun crime the police used visit all the gun clubs to check our guns to see if any of them had been used by the criminals as all our guns were registered. When we handed in our weapons they paid us the full price as new and most of us bought our weapons second-hand, so we all made a profit; I made nearly £460. I lost all interest in the club after Aileen died, and most of my old friends in the club had either moved away or died by then.

My father-in-law died just before Mila was born and we used to visit Aileen's mother Elsie as often as we could. I was very fond of her; she was a lovely lady and used to tell Aileen how lucky she was having a husband like me and I used to tell her how lucky I was to have a wife like Aileen and we were worried about her living on her own. In 1970, she told us that her landlady who owned her house had died and she had stipulated in her will that her long term tenants, if they wished, could buy the houses for £750 each. I knew that she had very little money and only her widow's pension, so I suggested to her that I would buy the house for her. She told me that she didn't want to be owner of the house but that I should buy it. I bought the house and told her that I don't want any rent and I would pay all the rates and any repairs that were needed. We were much happier that she wouldn't have any money problems, but although she had relations living nearby we still worried about her being on her own.

35 - Family in the 1970s. From left to right is my sister, my father and me.

A few weeks later we had a phone call from her niece Gay to tell us that Elsie had had a fall but she was alright, just a couple of bruises. But then a few weeks later she had another fall. Aileen and I became very worried; we discussed the situation and decided that, as we had a tenant moving out from the largest room in the house, we could refit it with all the mod-cons and move Elsie upstairs. We phoned Elsie and invited her to come and spend the week with us and, if she was agreeable, I would pick her up the following Saturday. She was delighted to accept the offer as it had been a long time since she came to London.

On Saturday, early in the morning, I drove to Alverstoke where Elsie was already waiting for me, so I just put her case in the back of my Mini and drove straight back to London arriving home just before lunch. After lunch we discussed the whole situation about her living alone, her falls and how worried we were about her and suggested to her to come and live with us. We explained to her that the room that she would occupy is the largest in the house, its fully fitted with a bed, table and chairs, an easy chair, electric cooker, fridge, television, electric fire and a large wardrobe, and fitted with a wash basin and hot water Ascot. The bathroom is also on the same floor and we would fit a new carpet on the floor. There was a church up the road, she would be completely independent and we won't be in each other's pocket. We told her not to decide right away, but as she is staying with us for the week she could occupy the room to see how she liked it, to which she thought was a good idea.

After three days she told Aileen that she would like to come and live with us, but insisted to Aileen that that she must pay us rent. When Aileen told me about it I was dead against it and after talking it over we decided that as Elsie is so adamant on paying rent that with the money Aileen would open a post office account so that every so often she could buy herself clothes, extra food that she enjoyed and feed the electricity meter. Just before Elsie moved to live with us we had an offer for her house that I bought of £5,000. I discussed it with Aileen about whether we wanted to keep it as a holiday home or sell it. we decided to sell it as if we wanted to keep as a holiday home or rent it we would have to spend money putting in an indoor bathroom and a toilet and did not want to go the whole process of dealing with the builders, but we would give Elsie half of the proceeds. However, when we suggested it to Elsie she absolutely refused to take the money saying "I don't need the money, and I never been so well off as I am since I came to live with the family, to have an indoor bathroom where I don't need to take a zinc tub and boil water for it and an indoor toilet where I don't have to go outside in the garden in all weathers; living with you it's my height of luxury."

We used to take Mila abroad since she was two and half and when she was seven she came home one day from school and asked me why we couldn't go on a proper holiday like her friends. I asked her what she meant. "Well," she said, "all my friends go on holidays to Butlin's or Pontins and have great times." I told Aileen about it and we had a good laugh but then we thought about it we thought it was perhaps a good idea as we could take Elsie with us. When we asked Elsie if she would like to come with us on holiday to Butlin's she was delighted and told us that she couldn't remember last time she had a holiday. I booked the holiday for us with Butlin's on Bury Island in Wales and when we arrived there it was raining and it rained for the next fourteen days. Aileen and I were a bit miserable having been used to having sunshine on our holiday, but Elsie and Mila had a ball. There were two shows each day and there were so many activity groups that Mila could join. That was the last time we went on a fortnight holiday in England.

Elsie loved living with us, loved babysitting Mila and looking after her if we wished to go out. Elsie lived with us for twenty years until 1990 when she died at the age of ninety-two. When she reached ninety, living on the first floor she no longer could manage the stairs or go shopping and every morning Aileen used to shout up to her if she needed any shopping. Then one morning when Aileen shouted to her there was no reply. Aileen knew that she should be awake as she always heard mum moving about. She rushed upstairs she found her mum sitting on a stool by the washbasin with a flannel in her hand dead. She must have died only a few minutes before Aileen shouted to her. She was and still is greatly missed.

When Mila was four we enrolled her in Hampstead in a kindergarten called House on the Hill. We were a bit disappointed with it as she didn't seem to learn much there. When she was five she had to change to a proper school in which we were very lucky. Mila was born in St. John's Wood and when we lived there Aileen had the foresight to register her at Robinsfield School, which was in the next street behind our flat. Aileen went to see the headmistress to see if Mila was still on the list and was told that she was. Mila was accepted to start in autumn, which was good. The girls that went Robinsfield were automatically accepted to Barrow Hill School, also in St. John's Wood. At that time we also put her name down for Queen's College in Harley St. when Mila was due to change school again. Aileen mentioned this to Mila's headmistress, and she told Aileen that as Mila is very artistic, and Queens had a very small art department, she heard that the pupils there are very badly behaved and a better school for her would be Haverstock School in Chalk Farm which has a has a much larger art department and would be a better school for her to attend.

Aileen and I talked over the suggestion and decided to arrange to go and look over the school. When we arrived there we were met by the master of the first year class who took us around the school. We were most impressed and we decided there and then that that it would the right school for Mila. The teacher introduced us to the headmaster and, after giving him all the information about Mila, he told us there was no problem with her joining the school and she could join in September when she leaves Barrow Hill. After she joined Haverstock she seemed to be very quiet, but after a while when asking her what she was learning her answer was "nothing." At first we thought that she was going through a period of settling in but after a while we got a bit worried about her for she always gave the same answer, so Aileen went to see the headmaster on this matter who told her that she had some difficulties and was slow understanding some of the subjects. Aileen asked him if he knew that she was dyslexic. He said no and he said that he would give the information to her teachers to help her when she finds some of the lessons difficult.

When she was fourteen she informed us that she wished to go to college or university when she left her school. We were very pleased with her decision and from then on she started studying as soon she came home from school. After she had her tea she would go to her room study until dinnertime, have her meal and then go back again to her room and study until ten o'clock. By the time she took her final exams she came one of the top girls in her class. She applied to the Middlesex College to study furniture design but she was told that this course was fully booked up and would have to reapply again next year. She tried several other colleges to no avail. Then one of her teachers suggested that if she were to apply to do a course that wasn't full, when she was accepted she could change to another course. The following year she applied and was accepted by Middlesex college to do a course in furniture design. I helped her on several scale models projects that she designed but she wasn't all that interested in woodworking and switched to glass making, experimenting in glass and metal. She was told that it wasn't possible but she did manage to make several pieces. She acquired a book on glass, written I believe by Professor Watkins who was a professor at the Royal College of Arts and when she tried some of the projects in the book and they didn't work she used to phone him to find out why they didn't work.

Then she became interested in metal and silverwork which she did for the rest of her time until her graduation. She graduated with BA 2.1. When she graduated she told me that she would like to apply to Royal College of Arts to study for an MA and asked if could I afford it. I told her to apply and not worry about the cost, just go for it. She applied to Royal College of Art and was granted an interview. When she came home I asked her how the interview was. She told me that it was alright, but she didn't think she would get in as there were something like five hundred applicants but only five places. A week later she received a letter asking her to come for another interview and bring her models of her projects. Mila asked me to take her and her models to the college where we were met by the tutors, who took her and her models to their office. The interview seemed to last ages and they told her that they would like her to leave the models with them for a week. When we left I said to Mila that they seemed to be interested in your models so there may be a chance that you might receive a place after all, but Mila didn't think so.

A week later she received a letter of acceptance to the college. Shortly before the students graduated they had a graduation exhibition of their work where they could sell some items. The college had the privilege of taking from each student one piece of work for their collection. Mila, who didn't get on with one of her tutors as he didn't think much of her work told her: "I don't think we will have one of your pieces for our collection." On the day of the exhibition, which was always well attended, Mila had among her exhibits three silver jugs. One visitor who was walking with his friends was a friend of Princess Diana. When he came to Mila's stand and inspected her jugs, he turned to his friend saying that they should add her jugs to their silver collection and bought them for £5,000. This was the largest price that had ever been taken at a graduation exhibition. Her tutor heard about it and came to Mila saying "I think we better add one of your pieces to our collection."

The graduation day was a very grand affair. It was held in Albert Hall. When Aileen and I arrived it was already half full and by the time the president started it was packed. The stage was all set for the ceremony which started at 11a.m. Suddenly, dead on time, trumpeters from one of the guards regiments marched onto to the podium and blew a fanfare. Then the procession started with the president, the deans, masters and the rest of teaching staff in their regalia. After them came all the students in their gowns who were to receive their certificates of their walking on the podium. When they were all seated the speeches started, beginning with the president then some of the senior masters and when the speeches finished there came the presentation of the certificates. Each student name was called out, who then walked up to be congratulated and given his or her certificate, which took ages as all of them had to be presented and then it was over. Mila had her MA which she succeeded in doing all on her own.

Before leaving the college she and three of her friends decided that after they had their degree they would start a workshop together, which they did in the Holborn area. One of her first successes was when she made some serviette rings which were seen at one of the shows by a *Daily Telegraph* reporter and the picture was published in their weekly magazine. Orders poured in and she must have sold about sixty of them and she was still getting the odd order for several years after. Sometime later, Goldsmith's Hall had an exhibition of serviette rings and after the show they acquired hers for their collection and invited her to join their Guild. She also was one of the first women to become a Freeman of the City of London.

Her next big order was to make Rimmonim for the Liberal Jewish Synagogue in St. John's Wood. She gradually became known for her Judaica silverware. She exhibited in U.S.A. and are three Jewish museums across the globe have some of her work in their collection, as well as numerous other museums, collections and synagogues. In London, the Jewish Museum, which never buys new silver, had an exhibition of Etrog boxes in which she exhibited her design, and they bought hers for their collection. One recent highlight was when won an international Judaica competition in Paris, the piece being bought Berlin Jewish Museum.

Sometime before Mila qualified, Aileen and I discussed what to do about our house. When we bought it was with the intention that if anything happens to me Aileen would have income from the part we rented, also it was always our intention that that eventually when we didn't need the income Mila could have her own place. Now, with us being financially secure we knew that when she graduated Mila would like a place of her own. We discussed it with Mila and we told her that I would transfer upper half of the house to her and, although there was need for some building work and central heating to be installed, of which she insisted to pay for, by then I would be retired I would be able to decorate, fit out the kitchen and build the cupboards in the bedroom. Of course, she was delighted: she would have a place of her own, but it took nearly a year before it was finished, having the usual trouble with the builders and, being an old house, it had very high ceilings and a healthy amount of quirks that we weren't expecting.

36 - Photo of my daughter, Mila, when she was younger.

I never spoke or heard from my Uncle Joe again. Eight months after I left his firm to go back to Witte's in 1967 mum phoned me at work to inform me that he had died in Cologne, Germany, at the house of his friends Mr. and Mrs. Lehman. Uncle Zygmunt wanted me to go with him and fetch his body back to England. I told governor the news and informed him that I would have to take a few days off to go to Germany; he was very good about it and told me that being early summer we weren't all that busy, so I should take whatever time I needed. In the evening I met up with uncle at my parent's home to discuss how we were going to travel to Germany. It was decided that mum, my sister Rozia, her husband Peter, Zygmunt and myself would be flying to Cologne to pick up Joe's body and all his belongings, his post mortem report and death certificate. We would also have to hire a lawyer to acquire the necessary documents for us for taking a body back to England.

We flew to Cologne and when we arrived there we went straight to our hotel and phoned the Lehmans to make an appointment to see them later on in the afternoon after we had had a meal. When we arrived at the Lehmans' apartment we discovered that Joe had a permanent room at as it seemed that since Odette died he had been spending a lot of his time in Germany with them. They showed us his rooms where there were nine suitcases packed including a hunting rifle and a 22. Calibre pistol; it seemed that they all used to go to Austria during the hunting season. Unfortunately we had to leave the firearms behind as although I belonged to a rifle and pistol club and had a firearms certificate, I didn't want the hassle with customs when coming back to England. The Lehmans were most helpful by explaining what we had to do taking the body back to England. They spoke to their lawyer who agreed to see us straightaway and when we arrived at his office he explained that he can do all the paperwork but we would have to speak with the management of the synagogue where Joe's body is being held so they can make arrangement to acquire a lead-lined coffin to seal his body in, which is necessary before his body can be shipped back to England. The bill for the synagogue had to be settled before we departed and our solicitor's bill with several other small bills that Joe still owed would be sent to the London office.

The whole thing took two days to arrange. The third day we had to visit several departments to sign documents for the release of the coffin. The next morning we had to hire three taxis to take us and all Joe's cases to the airport. When we arrived at the airport and checked in the luggage we were informed that we would have to pay for the excess weight; the cost came to nearly £100. When we arrived in London we took the taxis to Uncle Joe's flat where we left his entire luggage and sat down to discuss what to do next. We were told by Zygmunt that Joe didn't leave a will of which I was a bit suspicious and it was decided that Zygmunt, Peter and I would be executers of Joe's estate. There were five beneficiaries: my Mother, Uncle Izydor, Zygmunt, Uncle Albert in U.S.A. and Uncle John's daughter Susi, who also lived in the U.S.A. Over the weekend we had a meeting where we discussed how to proceed. First we would have the accountant to make a list of all his assets and debts in England, and then Zygmunt, Mum, Rozia, Aileen and I would travel to Paris. We knew that there were assets in Paris consisting of money and furs, as when the Paris branch of the firm was closed down the stock was stored in cold storage in Paris. Most of the furs belonged either to his late wife Odette or to the firm in London. The firm would help to bring the furs back to England.

The assets in Austria were very small and stored in a hotel, so Zygmunt and I would go and fetch them, and in Switzerland there was a small bank account and a few personal items which we would also fetch by going there when we were next in Paris. We left for Paris early Monday morning. When we arrived in Paris and after producing the correct documents we were able to remove the furs and returned with them to London. While in Paris we acquired solicitors to search and make a list of Joe's assets in France. Several weeks later, we received a list of his assets from both solicitors, which was a big disappointment and a shock to all of us. First, in England, he owed £87,000 to Inland Revenue in unpaid taxes which he hadn't paid for eleven years and some smaller loans which would have to be repaid. Luckily, some had a statute bar as they were more than seven years old. His main assets were the shares in his firm, of which he held a controlling interest of 74%, and after we had the accounts we found that, except for the stock, there was very little capital as he used to take amounts of cash out of the firm's accounts and spend it in France.

The accounts from the French accountant were not good either, as they showed that there was only £20,000 in his bank account and a deed to a piece of land about twenty miles from Paris. We knew that after Odette died and her estate was settled he had in the region of £250,000 and we thought that there must be money in some other account. It was decided that Zygmunt and I would go to Paris and try and find out what happened to the rest of Joe's money. We flew to Paris and the first thing we did was to go to several different banks to check if Joe had any accounts in them, but to no avail. We than decided to speak to Lehman's son who was working for Joe as his private secretary in France and Germany, to see if he might shed some light on our problem. We phoned him and the news that he gave us was not good. He explained to us that after Odette died and he found out about her cheating on him he went a bit crazy. He lost all interest in his fur business and started an investment business with the money he had in Paris.

Unfortunately, he mixed with the wrong people. One man put a proposition to him to buy shares in a paper mill in Spain which supposed to produce a new kind of paper. He went to Spain to see the mill where he was shown an empty factory and was told that the factory was waiting for machinery that was on order. He was so impressed that he bought £80,000 worth of shares. The man kept on sending him reports on how the factory was progressing and then they stopped. He tried to get in touch with the man but no one knew where he was, so Joe went to Spain. When he arrived there he found the factory completely empty with a 'for sale' sign. He went to the estate agent who informed him that the factory had been on the market for nearly a year and there had been no interest in anyone wanting to rent it. He then realised that he'd been conned, went to the police but nothing came of it and the man was never found.

Then he decided to invest in old masters. He met a so-called art dealer at a dinner party and while chatting he told Joe that there had been a surge in people buying old masters for investment which have been gradually going up in price. Joe told him that he might be interested of investing in one. The man told him he is a private dealer and when he hears that someone wishes to sell a picture he goes to value it and he knows someone who would be interested in buying such picture and he acts as a go between, earning a commission from the buyer and the seller. A few weeks' later he phoned Joe to tell him that if he was still interested in buying a picture, he has been offered an old master by a woman whose husband died and she needed to sell some of his pictures to help her to pay for her death duties and if he would like he would make arrangements to go and see the picture. Joe was interested and went to see the woman. The picture was by a well-known artist – I don't remember the name – and was shown the picture of it in an art book among the artist's other pictures. The man also told him that the picture was very sought after and he could acquire it at a very good price, but before he decided to buy it they would have to have it seen by a specialist in this artist's pictures. Joe was keen to buy the picture and they went to see the specialist to authenticate the picture. The specialist that they saw looked at the picture and told them that the picture looks genuine but he would do some tests and send them the results in few days' time. The results came a couple days later with the verdict that the picture was genuine. Joe decided to buy the picture and so he went to the woman to negotiate the price. The women wanted £90,000 but settled eventually at £72,000. Joe liked the picture and had it hanging in his flat. A year later he noticed that the pictures of that artist had gone up and would give him a nice profit if he decided to sell it in an auction. He put it in an auction in one of the auction houses in Paris but a few days later he received a letter from them telling him that they couldn't sell it as the picture was a fake and would have to be destroyed.

On the two deals he did he lost nearly £160,000. He couldn't believe that he had been so naïve to be conned twice. He started spending money like there was no tomorrow. He twice organised shooting parties in Austria to hunt boars for which he picked up the bill, then several times when he was in Switzerland during the time when the watch fair was on. He would attend and go around the different displays and buy not one or two but maybe a dozen or more of some of the expensive gold watches, spending anything between £10,000 and £15,000 and then arrange a dinner party and give them as presents to both men and women. Two years' ago he had a heart attack and was strongly advised not to fly as it could kill him but he took no notice of the advice and it seemed he had a sort of death wish and, of course, that was what killed him.

His private secretary also gave us information of two small bank accounts, one in Germany and one in France. All in all we manage to recover just over £30,000. While in Paris we went to see the lawyer that Joe used to discover more about it and if it would be possible for us to sell his land there. When we met him he seemed to know all about it. He told us we could sell it but there was a problem: when Joe was offered the land it was owned by a farmer and was situated at a crossroads just outside the green belt area and would suitable for a garage site. Being friendly with half of the French government ministers, Joe checked with one of them who was responsible for the green belt area and was told by him that there would be no problem with building a garage there, so he bought the land for £10,000. Just after he bought the land the French government introduced a law that all land sales have to pay V.A.T. and that's when the dispute started, with both Joe and the farmer wanting the other to pay the tax, the dispute going on now for three years. There was also an annual tax of £320 on the land that hadn't been paid since he had bought the land. He suggested that we pay the V.A.T or find a buyer that would buy the land at a reduced price and pay the V.A.T.

We flew back to London and had an administrator's meeting to discuss the latest information. Peter and I wanted to sell the land at a reduced price but Zygmunt suggested that his son in law, who owned a huge property company and had properties in France, would probably be able to find a buyer for the land, so we decided to let him try. The saga with the land went on for nearly eighteen years with Zygmunt insisting that we would find a buyer. In the eighties the French government extended the green belt so our piece of land became useless. We tried to give it to the local town to make it into a park but they weren't interested with the V.A.T. outstanding. We were still paying the yearly tax and Peter and I suggested that we stop paying the tax and the government would claim the land in payment of taxes. That's what we did and we never heard anything more about the land. We decided to change our solicitors as we found the ones Zygmunt recommended to be absolutely useless dealing with the revenue and we settled with a firm in lower Regent Street. Within a short time they made a deal with the inland revenue that we would pay a percentage of the debit and the rest yearly from the interest from Joe's shares in the business, otherwise we would have to put the estate into administration to show that it would be bankrupt and they would get nothing, to which they accepted. After twelve years we had enough money to give £10,000 to each beneficiary. Unfortunately, my mother died 1976 so the money went to my father. We carried on with the estate another ten years, settling several debts that were still outstanding and searching for any assets that might belong to the estate. My dad died 1987 so my sister and I became beneficiaries. I retired in 1990 and we all agreed it was time to settle the estate. The biggest asset in the estate was the Deanfields Fur Models company which Zygmunt was running and making profit that enabled us to pay Inland Revenue, but as with Witte's business was hit by the prevalence of the animal rights campaign in the mid-eighties, so by 1990 and we all agreed that the firm should be sold. We had several offers but most of them were for the name not the stock. There was one man who we knew who had done business with the firm before and was interested in making an offer, and he asked if he could work with Zygmunt in the firm for a few weeks to get the feel of the place, to which we agreed to. After several weeks he put in an offer for the business. We let Zygmunt to do the negotiations as, except for the yearly balance report, Peter and I knew very little what the business was worth.

Then, early in July 1990, just as Aileen and I were loading our luggage into my new car for a tour of Scotland I had a call from Zygmunt that he needed me to come to his house to sign transfer papers for the business. I explained to him that we were just off to Scotland and it would have to wait until we came back. Anyhow, I was not willing to sign anything unless the firm paid me the £5,000 it owed me from when Joe broke our contract. He thought for a minute and told me that if I stop by the house and sign the contract he would have the cheque waiting for me. When we arrived at the house I left Aileen in the car with the language and went inside where they were all waiting. Zygmunt gave me my cheque which I scrutinised very carefully, signed the document, excused myself and said my goodbyes. When I joined Aileen, I told her that first I was driving back to my bank to put the cheque into my account to make sure it had not been cancelled; that's how I got my £5,000 after so many years. After the sale of the business in 1990 the work on the estate was finished. It has taken twenty two years and after paying all the debts we had £75,000 in the kitty. The share to each beneficiary was £25,000, but it was not worth the amount of time and work it had taken to do it all.

In 1995, Mila told us that she had met a man that she wished to spend the rest of her life with and would like us to meet him. Until then we were a bit worried as she didn't seemed to have any interest in settling down. His name was Simon and when we met him I liked straight away and over the years came to love as if he was my son. We discovered that he was younger than her and Aileen was a bit apprehensive about it, but I told her not to worry; we had always taught her to think for herself and anyhow, Aileen was years younger than me and that had worked out alright. Two years later, Mila was pregnant and gave birth to a son Aleksander, our grandson, which was a great delight to us as we never thought that we would ever have grandchildren. As Mila was still working she asked us if it would be possible for us to look after Aleksander during the day, which we did until Aileen died so tragically in 2006.

Aleksander was a delightful baby and it was joy to us watching him growing up. Mila was pregnant again just after Aileen died and gave birth to a daughter Sofia, who is growing up to be a beautiful, intelligent girl. I am very lucky to be able to see my grandchildren most days, and when Aileen died Mila wanted me to eat with the family every day, but I declined telling her that she has enough to do bringing up her family and I have to live my life the way I've always been used to, but I do have dinner with them twice a week. I am proud of my family and the way they progressed and achieved.

**37 - My grandson
Aleksander, matriculating
into Emmanuel College,
Cambridge.**

Simon, who when we first meet was just finishing studying for his finals in Film and Television went on to be part of the senior management in several international companies. Mila, with her silver designs are admired in many parts of the world.

**38 - My granddaughter,
Sofia, in one of her
tapdancing outfits.**

Aleksander, who is studying for a degree in Philosophy at Emmanuel College, Cambridge has, among other interests, learnt to play multiple instruments and decided to look after my garden as I can no longer do it. Sofia, who is also talented in writing short stories, is also learning gymnastics, tap dancing, drama and learning to play the piano. They all look out after me, especially Mila. I wouldn't wish for a better family of whom I think is the best and I love dearly.

My story is finished and in the winter of my life, looking back, I see how lucky I've been through my life. I was lucky in having Uncle Joe in England and managed to persuade his brothers Zygmunt and John to help the family to come to England before the outbreak of war. Except for after buying our house and us having such a hard time before becoming solvent, we were never in debt ever again and we managed to lead a comfortable life. I had a job which I enjoyed doing; in forty-five years of my working life I've never been unemployed. My main worry has always been that I would not be able to provide for Aileen and Mila if I should die. In this respect I was very lucky to have some very good friends who were investment brokers who advised me where to invest. I always discussed with Aileen any deals that I made, seeking her opinion. Although every year we went on holidays abroad in Europe our wish was always to travel farther afield and now we could fulfil our objective to travel far and wide all over the world and go on many trips and cruises. I also think how lucky I was to survive the blitz, when I saw some terrible sights of people that were killed just a short distance from where I was. I am also very lucky having my daughter, Mila, and her family, who are looking out for me and watching my two grandchildren growing up with great pleasure. Also my sister, who always fusses over me. But most of all I was so lucky meeting Aileen with whom I fell in love the moment I saw her; from the moment we met we never parted and were together for the next fifty years.

Now, at the aged of 93, I still live with my daughter, son-in-law and grandchildren in our house on Gladys Rd. As my family knows all too well, there are far too many stories from my life to fit into this book, like when I and Aileen met the Queen, or when we all drove across through America (and Death Valley) in a Cadillac, or any of the many great things that happened to me from 1964 to now, that they have heard from me as I sit there on the sofa on a Friday evening.

I was never an academic person, so writing a book always seemed out of the question to me. As a child I had just about got a handle on Polish before I had to learn a whole new language. My English has never been the best, and I have never been able to write a lot, so being able to write my memoirs is one more achievement that I can be proud of. However, it wouldn't have been possible without the help and support of everyone at the University of the Third Age (U3A) and their Writing Your Memoirs course.

Joining the U3A class was a great help to deaden some of the pain of Aileen's death after her passing by being able to listen to the members of the class and their adventures and troubles; we have all become good friends and meet up regularly. Yet, the sadness of her death is with me all the time and probably will be until I die.

31675533R00262

Printed in Poland
by Amazon Fulfillment
Poland Sp. z o.o., Wrocław